MY OLD KENTUCKY HOME

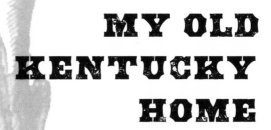

MY OLD KENTUCKY HOME

THE ASTONISHING LIFE AND RECKONING
OF AN ICONIC AMERICAN SONG

EMILY BINGHAM

ALFRED A. KNOPF   NEW YORK   2022

Library of Congress Cataloging-in-Publication Data
Name: Bingham, Emily, author.
Title: My old Kentucky home : the astonishing life and reckoning of an
iconic American song / Emily Bingham.
Description: First edition. | New York : Alfred A. Knopf, 2022. | "A Borzoi book"—
Title page verso | Includes bibliographical references and index.
Identifiers: LCCN 2021042232 (print) | LCCN 2021042233 (ebook) |
ISBN 9780525520795 (hardcover) | ISBN 9780525520801 (ebook)
Subjects: LCSH: Foster, Stephen Collins, 1826–1864. My old Kentucky home. |
Slavery—Kentucky—Songs and music—History and criticism. | Popular music—
United States—To 1901—History and criticism. | African Americans in popular
culture. | Kentucky—Social life and customs—20th century.
Classification: LCC ML410.F78 B55 2022 (print) | LCC ML410.F78 (ebook) |
DDC 782.421640973—dc23
LC record available at https://lccn.loc.gov/2021042232
LC ebook record available at https://lccn.loc.gov/2021042233

Jacket illustrations from a theatre program of
"The Stephen Foster Story" by Paul Green, 1960. Artist unknown.
Jacket design by Jenny Carrow

Manufactured in the United States of America
FIRST EDITION

To Stephen, who brought me home to Kentucky

Their griefs are transient.
Those numberless afflictions . . . are less felt,
and sooner forgotten with them.
—THOMAS JEFFERSON, *Notes on the State of Virginia* (1787)

*The sentimentalist is he who would enjoy
without incurring the immense debtorship for a thing done.*
—JAMES JOYCE, *Ulysses* (1922)

It wasn't sweet and it sure wasn't home.
—TONI MORRISON, *Beloved* (1987)

CONTENTS

MY OLD KENTUCKY HOME, GOOD NIGHT!
Stephen Foster, 1853

The sun shines bright in the old Kentucky home,
'Tis summer, the darkies are gay;
The corn-top's ripe and the meadow's in the bloom,
While the birds make music all the day.
The young folks roll on the little cabin floor,
All merry, all happy and bright;
By'n by Hard Times comes a knocking at the door,
Then my old Kentucky Home, good night!

Chorus

Weep no more, my lady,
Oh! weep no more today!
We will sing one song
For the old Kentucky Home,
For the old Kentucky Home, far away.

They hunt no more for the possum and the coon,
On meadow, the hill and the shore,
They sing no more by the glimmer of the moon,
On the bench by the old cabin door.
The day goes by like a shadow o'er the heart,
With sorrow, where all was delight:
The time has come when the darkies have to part,
Then my old Kentucky home, good night!

Chorus

The head must bow and the back will have to bend,
Wherever the darky may go:
A few more days, and the trouble all will end,
In the field where the sugar-canes grow.
A few more days for to tote the weary load,
No matter 'twill never be light;
A few more days till we totter on the road,
Then my old Kentucky home, good night!

Chorus

PREFACE

The Forgetting

There was a time when it was just a song.

I grew up in Kentucky a few miles from Louisville's Churchill Downs racecourse. Though "My Old Kentucky Home" was our state anthem, it got little notice in my household except when it materialized, grandiose and opaque, each Derby season. Sick at home one day in the 1970s, I stampeded through Margaret Mitchell's *Gone with the Wind*, the 1936 best-selling, Pulitzer Prize–winning romance of the Civil War. Well into the tale, Union forces are advancing on Confederate Atlanta. Inside Aunt Pittypat's town house parlor, Scarlett O'Hara and Rhett Butler try to dispel a cascading sense of doom with a duet of "My Old Kentucky Home." The novel reproduced lines from the song that I had never heard. I sang them quietly to the melody I knew:

> *Just a few more days for to tote the weary load!*
> *No matter, 'twill never be light!*
> *Just a few more days, till we totter in the road!*
> *Then, my old Kentucky home, good night!*

With the adults of the house off watching the horse race, I hummed the misunderstanding that "My Old Kentucky Home" was a wartime ballad about defeated Confederates straggling back to families and homesteads, a forerunner of scenes Mitchell lingered over in later chapters.

I now understand the truth that the famous American songwriter Stephen Foster's "My Old Kentucky Home" was first and always a song about slavery. At the same time, for me and so many, it has conjured "tear-compelling" pangs of homesickness, visions of loved ones, innocent times when life was "all merry, all happy and bright." Tapping into a universal emotion and layering it on top of a pretty tune helped make a temporal hit into one for the ages, dear to millions of white people, their children, and their children's children's children and beyond. In the case of "My Old Kentucky Home," that process traveled a uniquely American journey as this song about slavery became a treasured anthem, repeated, taught, and passed down, bridging a nation's disconnect between history and fantasy.

See, for instance, my father in 1956.

As a marine, he led a mortar platoon posted to the Japanese island of Okinawa. World War II had been the core international event of his childhood—his father served almost the whole conflict in the navy—and my dad spent two years in military service after college. On his days off, he rode around on a Yamaha, taking in the East China Sea breezes and indulging in his photography hobby. One morning, as he admired a side street in Nago bursting with hibiscus blossoms, a faint sound reached him. "I must be really sick," he thought. Maybe he needed a psychiatrist. Rounding a corner, he found a group of children—offspring of a native population that the bloody 1945 Battle of Okinawa between the United States and Japan had sliced by half—"doing calisthenics and singing" "My Old Kentucky Home." He felt catapulted out of time and space. It was one of the most "unbelievable experiences" of his life. Most islanders reviled Americans; how could a melody about home in Kentucky be on the lips of their children?

My father had no idea that a century earlier, in 1853, Stephen Foster's music sailed into Tokyo Bay with Commodore Matthew Perry's warships. Wearing blackface, members of Perry's crew entertained representatives of a shogunate that had barricaded Japan from the outside world. Shared laughter across cultures over minstrel show portrayals of blackness eased what was otherwise an unsubtle case of gunboat diplomacy and helped open Japan to U.S. trade in advance of other countries.

It was never just a song, and its full history needs to be told. Its full powers need to be understood.

Each year on a Saturday in May, as the front legs of the first Kentucky Derby horse touch the dirt track on the way to the starting gate, hundreds of thousands of eyes—many watching the nationwide television broadcast—fill with tears. The gleaming brasses of the marching band exhale the sedate opening notes of "My Old Kentucky Home," and spectators at Churchill Downs rise to their feet in a mint julep mist, roar in anticipation, crane their necks for a view of the entries in the nation's oldest continuously held sporting event, and sing the well-worn words on the jumbotron. By the time the horns hit the high notes of "Weep no more, my lady," keen for the "Kentucky home," then dip longingly on "far away," many succumb to an emotional moment unmatched in American sport. It is almost irresistible. The beloved *Sports Illustrated* writer Frank Deford declared, "Any good man will cloud up when they play 'My Old Kentucky Home' and cry outright when he realizes he is standing in one of those rare places where beauty and history bisect for an instant." In this setting, "Weep no more" means something like the opposite: "Go ahead and cry."

But whose beauty? Whose history? There's reason to weep, but not

"No other song on earth has the power to move a Kentuckian as 'My Old Kentucky Home,'" said the humorist Irvin Cobb. In his 1924 book *Kentucky*, a family and its hounds gather around the Victrola for a lachrymose moment.

the reason the vast majority of people watching the Kentucky Derby imagine. As the poet and critic Claudia Rankine has written, "Fantasies cost lives."

The hit from 1853 sits on a short list of melodies that have endured from bygone centuries, and an even shorter list of songs performed en masse in public. Where "The Star-Spangled Banner" is remote and formal, "My Old Kentucky Home" is simple and companionable, calling up longing, pride, sorrow, joy. It conveys the unity of "Take Me Out to the Ballgame" with none of the goofiness.

Before Foster even penned the lyrics and set down the tune, the song was a misrepresentation. This is how it worked: composed by a white man from Pittsburgh in the voice of an enslaved Black man from Kentucky, "My Old Kentucky Home" was sung for white audiences by white men, their faces smeared in burnt cork, pretending to be Black. It resounded in blackface minstrel performances on Broadway in New York and circled the globe, entertaining everyone from Australian outbackers to European royals.

Yet Foster's ode to my state describes one of the cruelest tableaux in the panorama of American experience: human beings bought and shipped downriver to die in the place Black people knew as "nigger hell." Almost no one knows this, and those who do rarely speak of it.

The singing goes on.

Stephen Foster's admirers have celebrated his uncanny ability to translate emotion into music. Textbooks honor his works as the "national heritage, part of our shared experience as a people," an expression of "the American spirit," as "genuine folk" music and "perhaps the most typical native product." The claims of authenticity for the deeply inauthentic are legion and of great consequence. As an export to the world, "My Old Kentucky Home" presented the plantation as a cherished American home. It indulged key myths white Americans still tell themselves about slavery and race, and in this sense the pioneering composer from Pittsburgh is perhaps rightly seen as America's quintessential troubadour. "My Old Kentucky Home" is a spy hole into one of America's deftest and most destructive creations: the "singing slave" whose song assured hearers that the plantation was happy and a place where Black people belonged. Its beginning lines establish a toxic illusion of contented bondage. Later verses take as settled fact that "the head must bow and the back will have to bend, / Wherever the darky may go." Its comforting chorus enacts the lie that people forced into slavery were unresisting, unmanned, perversely grateful.

The real Kentucky home of the enslaved was shot through with violence—rape, assault, deprivations of all sorts, the disregard for family ties—and the constant threat of all these. Sophia Word recalled that when her owner decided "to sale one of us he would go out and talk to the old slave trader like he wuz g'wine to sale a cow." This was how her aunt and cousins vanished from her life forever. In another instance, not long before the Civil War began, some of Christian County's leading citizens decided that a Black minister enslaved by an elderly woman was too intelligent to be trusted. On an appointed day, Henry Cox's wife, five children, and a crowd of onlookers watched armed men load him onto a wagon bound for the Cumberland River and the boat that carried him down the Mississippi to a New Orleans auction block.

In the 1850s, the loss of a parent or a child to the domestic trade in enslaved people likely afflicted half the Kentuckians trapped in bondage. "An honest assessment of America's relationship to the black family," Ta-Nehisi Coates has written, "reveals the country to be not its nurturer but its destroyer."

Music is among the deepest means of human connection; it can also be a form of mind control. Generation upon generation, "My Old Kentucky Home" has inhabited hearts and memories. In perpetual reprise, it seems to stand outside time. But this music has a past informed by thousands of performances, enactments, critiques, and defenses that, over time, encapsulate the United States' contradictory and contorted relationship to slavery and white supremacy. We do not deny its reality, and the terror is plain to see. Nonetheless, Stephen Foster gave its victim a voice that sings that pain into nostalgia. Millions upon millions have sung along.

This book is my effort to scrub it of its decades of nostalgia and burnt cork and confront what is underneath.

The "father of American music," the progenitor of pop, was born in 1826 on the Fourth of July and grew up alongside his young nation's foremost cultural creation, the blackface minstrel show. The English novelist

William Makepeace Thackeray marveled after attending a blackface act on a visit to the United States that a "minstrel with wool on his head" and "corked face" playing a banjo could set his "whole heart thrilling with happy pity." Stephen Foster's minstrel compositions—some rollicking like "Oh! Susanna," others nostalgic "plantation melodies" like "My Old Kentucky Home"—still endure.

Frederick Douglass, the great abolitionist leader, despised blackface minstrels, calling them "the filthy scum of white society who" denigrated his race for profit even as they stole "from us a complexion denied them by nature." As a fugitive from bondage, Douglass knew its horrors firsthand, and he fought to enable millions to escape its grip. When he noticed that the tune brought white folks to tears, he tried to put those tears to good use. Perhaps some of them were for the man sold off to die, and perhaps white men and women could be encouraged to think on that fact and act. Perhaps, in spite of its blackface roots, this song might "awaken antislavery principles."

Nothing of the sort happened. Chattel slavery disturbed relatively few white minds, and white action was rarer still. "My Old Kentucky Home" never became an abolitionist rallying cry.

By the 1930s, "My Old Kentucky Home" was, as the historian Thomas D. Clark wrote, "a living symbol of a happy past." As it reached its centennial, however, those who sang, promoted, and held it dear faced a dilemma: it was known to offend Black Americans. A source of pride and sentiment for many whites tormented many Blacks. What to do about a single song that showcases an American paradox, a culture's persistent need to explain away what cannot be excused? The question isn't exactly new. It was raised almost with the birth of blackface, most often by the proud but often powerless and unprivileged. Their history, too, must be told if we are to know how to answer the question in the twenty-first century.

Memory and forgetting are ignited by desire, need, and fear. They don't just happen. This song's story tracks both what has divided Americans, white and Black—the realities of slavery and racial prejudice—and what has often brought them together: culture and music. Commerce and its interests supply a steady backbeat. Stephen Foster and the many who performed and advocated for his music met a nation's need to divert responsibility; they were also, significantly, bit players in making profit off that need. When, during my research and writing of this book,

I have heard others exclaim, "But we always sang it! It's just a song! Must we be so serious?" I know the answer. We must.

On a spring day around the turn of the twenty-first century with out-of-town guests flying in for Derby weekend, I suddenly recollected the "understanding" of "My Old Kentucky Home" that *Gone with the Wind* suggested to me as a child. I typed the song title into a search engine on my computer, and in a moment I was reading the original 1853 lyrics. I flushed. Simple chronology made clear that Stephen Foster had not written a Civil War ballad; the first shots were fired at Fort Sumter eight years *after* "My Old Kentucky Home" was published. Though I had scarcely given the question of what the song was about a conscious thought in decades, during all that time I had substituted a Confederate veteran for a human being sold to certain death in a sugarcane field. With a nudge from Margaret Mitchell's pen, defenders of the "Lost Cause" of chattel slavery had become the victimized subjects of my state anthem. Year after year, no matter where in the world I happened to be, I tuned in to watch the parade to the post and felt my heart yearning. Sometimes I sang along. Over and over, I accepted the invitation to cry. What in heaven's name, I wondered, could my tears mean?

Faced with this question, I went digging for clues in overlooked lives and events, forgotten theatrical scripts, newspaper articles, old letters, memoirs, souvenir trinkets, scratchy sound recordings, crumbling photographs. I told myself I was uncovering the biography of a song. As I began piecing together its life span, it started looking like something else, something more confounding, more damning. My *Gone with the Wind* misapprehension was no mere childish matter. Foster's song was always more than just a song.

I am a historian by training and profession; I am also a privileged white Kentuckian descended on both sides from people who owned people. Because fencing off these identities felt untenable, I have included occasional passages about personal and family experiences in connection with "My Old Kentucky Home," slavery, and race alongside the remarkable historical characters and events that make up the tale of this very American song. My and my family's stories are not special. They are sewn in the fabric of a nation lurching toward a reckoning with the illusion that "we" as Americans were ever singing "one song for the old Kentucky home far away."

I was brought up in a family of newspaper publishers, and my last name was, for many, a synonym for "liberal." Racial slurs were never tolerated in our home. Around our 1970s dinner table, I picked up the notion that while some prejudiced (other) people might make things unpleasant for minorities, barriers to equality were fast tumbling down. And yet. When rumor had it that my family's new neighbor might be the world-famous Muhammad Ali, the chilled response of the adults reminded me that he was instead the world-famous Black Muhammad Ali. History is not a very comfortable place. Nor a very distant one. It is in us, like a song.

The question of what ought to be done about an icon as all-American as "My Old Kentucky Home" sparked the research that became this book. The contradictory story of how a single piece of music can be so seductive and also so destructive, how a melody can be so memorable but also so formed by forgetting, is a story for a country yearning for healing.

MY OLD KENTUCKY HOME

1

'TIS SUMMER, THE DARKIES ARE GAY

Stephen Foster, Ethiopian Songwriter

We begin 387 miles northwest of Louisville, Kentucky, in Pittsburgh, which is 186 miles mostly west and a little north of the gentle sloped battlefield outside Gettysburg, Pennsylvania. Chronologically, we are nearly a decade from the Confederate general Pickett's failed charge up that slope, a failure that tipped the balance of the Civil War for the Union.

We begin in 1852. Stephen Foster's brother owned a side-wheeler steamboat. Twenty-five-year-old Stephen, his wife, Jane, and a group of friends booked a discounted passage down the Ohio from Pittsburgh to the junction with the Mississippi and all the way to New Orleans. For more than five hundred miles each way, the passengers gazed at Kentucky's muddy shore. The boat would have docked briefly at Louisville, and the party would have had the chance to disembark to stretch their river legs. But not much more than that.

In early 1852, Americans everywhere were thinking about Kentucky. Harriet Beecher Stowe's just-published novel, *Uncle Tom's Cabin; or, Life Among the Lowly,* the most talked-about piece of fiction in the young nation's history, opened on a Kentucky "farm." Foster doubtless heard and possibly read about the saintly Tom, sold to cover his enslaver's speculations, who dies under the lash on a Louisiana sugar plantation just as his Kentucky master's son arrives to buy him back and bring him "home." Stowe was protesting the Fugitive Slave Act, which implicated the whole of the nation in upholding chattel slavery. With archetypal characters embodying pathos and ethos, and limned in Christian ethics, Stowe hoped to motivate an insufficiently incensed white electorate. She supplied her readers with white villains to blame and white heroes to claim. Consciously or not, Stowe also drew key character traits, such as Uncle Tom's fondness for white folks and the Black child Topsy's thickheaded haplessness, straight from the American blackface minstrel show.

In its first six weeks, the novel sold twenty thousand copies in Pittsburgh alone.

The Fosters were die-hard Democrats. They aligned politically with the slaveholding region that supplied the raw material that made the national economy hum, while Stowe stoked a controversy that threatened American peace and prosperity. But Americans had long been entertained by Black bodies and their afflictions, and in Uncle Tom, Stephen could detect echoes of his earlier minstrel works that referenced loyal Black men fond of loved ones, "masters," and plantation homes.

Stephen Foster, undated, ca. 1850s

Uncle Tom's Cabin undoubtedly fanned the flames of the slavery debate; it was also bound up with the economy of chattel slavery that it purported to oppose and touched off a bonanza of spin-offs—dolls, teaspoons, wallpaper. Songs, too.

Some time after the riverboat journey, Stephen composed a yearning melody in a somber adagio tempo with a lump-in-the-throat chorus. The opening lines of "Poor Uncle Tom, Good Night"—revised and published in 1853 as "My Old Kentucky Home, Good Night!"—reproduced *Uncle Tom's Cabin*'s peaceful opening scene on a Kentucky plantation. While in the novel greed and foolish speculations lead Tom's owner into debt, Foster used shorthand with "Hard Times." The sale of an enslaved man was in this account nobody's fault. "De time has come when de darkeys hab to part," Foster wrote. In the chorus, moreover, Tom's faith in a worthier world provided relief from earthly trials:

> *Oh good night, good night, good night*
> *Poor uncle Tom*
> *Grieve not for your old Kentucky home*
> *You'r bound for a better land*
> *Old Uncle Tom.*

"Poor Uncle Tom, Good Night" resolved the burden of Tom and all Black people like him in death. Its final verse was the end of Tom. It called no one to task and signaled the perpetual subjugation of one race of people to another:

> *De head must bow and de back will hab to bend,*
> *Whereber de darkey may go;*
> *A few more days, and de troubles all will end,*
> *In de field wha de cotton had grow;*
> *A few more days for to tote de weary load,*
> *No matter, it soon will be light;*
> *A few more days for to totter on de road,*
> *Den poor uncle Tom good night.*

Stowe was driven by outrage at a man-made system that brutalized human beings. Whereas her praying protagonist is in the prime of manhood and dies by vicious lashings, the minstrel songwriter's version does not call on God or perform good works. Foster's Uncle Tom is "old" and undisturbing and succumbs, as if naturally, without drama. Foster's musical translation of Stowe's tale captured a measure of the slave trade's pathos, but it also presented tragedy as fate.

Stowe's book was Stephen Foster's catalyst, but to make sense of this song and Foster's musical portrayal of a Black man, we must step back further, almost two decades to 1835. For several weeks running, a small audience settled at the appointed hour onto benches in a musty carriage house in a Pittsburgh alley. A gaggle of neighborhood boys began playing a tune and dancing round while nine-year-old Stevie Foster, his face sooted dark, sang his little heart out on "Long Tail Blue." "Jim Crow is courting a brown gal, / The white folks called her Sue; / But I guess she let the nigger drop / When she see my long tail blue." The diminutive "star performer" regaled the spectators with the ballad of a free Black dandy competing with "Jim Crow" for a woman's sexual favors—his double-entendre secret weapon being an outrageously long tailcoat/phallus.

> *Jim Crow got mad and swore he'd fight,*
> *With sword and pistol too;*
> *But I guess I back'd the nigger out,*
> *When he saw my long tail blue.*

. . . .

> *Now all you chaps that wants a wife,*
> *And don't know what to do;*
> *Just look at me and I'll show you how*
> *To swing your long tail blue.*

The crowd grinned and hooted, for that was the point, and entertaining is how minstrel shows coaxed coin from white Americans.

The prepubescent impresario moved from "Long Tail Blue" to "Coal Black Rose" who is courted with a banjo and promises of "possum fat and hominy." The tunes were naughty and irresistibly catchy. According to his older brother, Stephen's performance of popular "Ethi-

The prime innovator of early blackface minstrelsy was Thomas Dartmouth "Daddy" Rice, pictured here as the character Jim Crow. His 1832 portrayal of a ragged enslaved man dancing and singing nonsensical lyrics ("Weel about an' turn about, and do jis' so / Ebery time I weel about, I jump Jim Crow") catapulted him to fame. Rice toured his shows in London, Paris, and Dublin.

opian" melodies was judged so "true to nature" that he won "uproarious applause." Of course the opposite was true. Inauthenticity—silly and absurd, lampooning and derisive inauthenticity—was what drew forth the applause.

The shows went on three nights a week with the front man earning a guaranteed sum from ticket sales and the other boys dividing what was left. Feeling rich, they walked their coins downtown to the Pittsburgh Theater and bought cheap seats in the pit, where they heard (but couldn't see) famous actors like Junius Brutus Booth hold forth. A dismissive contemporary critic tarred blackface songs as spawn of "the very lowest puddles of society." But little Stephen Foster was hardly the spawn of society's bottom rung. It is more accurate to say that the songs he performed were just one of the many spillways for the entertainment of white America. It is not at all surprising that a path went directly from a makeshift back-alley theater to Junius Booth performing Shakespeare on the city's main stage to his son John Wilkes Booth murdering Abraham Lincoln at Ford's Theatre decades later in hopes of preserving the Confederacy and slavery. This is not coincidence but ubiquity, a culture steeped in race.

Foster's biographer Ken Emerson has suggested that Stephen and his pals sang and played in blackface "because it was popular, because

For a neighborhood minstrel act, nine-year-old Foster is said to have performed "Coal Black Rose," an 1830s hit song that mockingly describes a battle between two men over the same woman. The printed sheet music exaggerated the subjects' physical characteristics and lampooned their attempts to appear respectable.

it was 'cool,' and because it offered a freedom that white middle-class culture couldn't furnish." "Freedom" doesn't seem at all apt. "License" seems more apt, in the sense that blackface afforded white performers and audiences license to express openly what white middle-class culture expressed constantly yet obliquely: the mix of superior power and fear and awe that came with thoughts of blackness. Perhaps this helps answer just *why* this type of entertainment, born in the 1830s, took the nation and world by storm in the 1840s and became the most significant American cultural creation up to the advent of Hollywood. The fraud of miming blackness served whites, then and ever since. The critic Saidiya Hartman has written of the way minstrelsy forged American conceptions of "blackness [that] aroused pity and fear, desire and revulsion, and terror and pleasure." Stephen Foster soaked daily in this blackface way of seeing and acting and laughing and feeling, which denigrated Black people while it proved how fascinating, and useful, they were.

Foster's promising 1835 debut represented his lone turn on the boards. He was too shy and his mild tenor too weak to reproduce that early theatrical success. Yet his life story, the history of popular music, and American culture itself are all inseparable from the framework set by the blackface minstrel show he imitated as a child.

Stephen was the next to last of ten children in a middle-class family whose fortunes had been sliding downward since his birth in 1826. His father, William B. Foster, invested in real estate, scrambled for political offices and appointments, and started businesses including a stagecoach company and a general store, failing more often than not. William also battled a drinking problem. At a high point in his career, Foster senior acquired land for a bucolic "White Cottage" in a suburb, now Pittsburgh's Lawrenceville district. When Stephen was three, the house was sold to pay creditors.

Financial strain hung about the Fosters like the window curtains they carried from home to home. At the time of Stephen's brief theatri-

The "father of American music" was born at the White Cottage on the outskirts of 1820s Pittsburgh, a fast-industrializing city at the junction of the Ohio, Allegheny, and Monongahela Rivers. Burdened by debt, Foster's father sold the property when Stephen was three years old.

cal stint, they were renters. They clung to bourgeois comforts, such as domestic servants that they could ill afford. About the time Stephen was jumping Jim Crow, the grateful family received an "excellent coloured girl" as a "present" from a friend. This indentured servant with three years remaining on her contract required no pay. (Pennsylvania's Gradual Abolition Act permitted binding the minor children of enslaved people to indentures until they were twenty-eight years old.) She labored in an often-unhappy home.

The eldest Foster daughter, Charlotte, had a flair for music. When Stephen was three, the family learned of her untimely death during a visit to distant kin in Louisville, Kentucky, and seven months later a baby brother Jim followed Charlotte to the grave. Stephen's mother, Eliza, suffered a breakdown, and her careworn face was forever engraved in her children's minds. "All my gone by hopes are nothing but a dream," Eliza wrote mournfully to another son. Before folding her letter, she added that Stephen was marching around the room with a drum and a feather in his hat "whistling old lang syne." He was trying to cheer her up. Early on, Stephen found in music both an escape and a means of channeling loss into joyful distraction.

To support aging and dependent parents, the Foster sons needed to secure gainful careers and the children of both sexes needed to make good marriages. One of Stephen's brothers courted the daughter of a Maryland planter with 250 human chattel, but the flirtation fizzled out. His elder brother William Foster Jr. became a railroad engineer and began supporting the household when Stephen was still learning to talk. The duty of the youngest son was to work hard at his lessons. But "Stephen was not," his brother Morrison observed drily, "a methodical student." Instead, he adored music. At seven, he picked up a recorder-like flageolet and taught himself to play "Hail, Columbia," a patriotic march composed for George Washington's inauguration. Stephen's earliest surviving letter begs his father to bring home a "commic [sic] songster," a book of blackface tunes. Patriotism and white supremacy floated through the rented rooms.

Fooling around with music was a distraction if not an impediment to Stephen's future. Sent off to a boys' academy in northern Pennsylvania at fourteen, he wheedled the brother who paid the tuition his parents could not afford. If "Brother William" would send money, he promised to go at his books six hours a day and give "attention to my music" only before bed. Ultimately, Stephen revolted, ran away home to Pittsburgh, studied mathematics with a tutor, and succeeded in begging for enough lessons to learn the piano and how to write musical notation. Social life interested him no more than prospecting for a career; he devoted every free hour "to musick, for which," the father conceded, "he possesses a strange talent."

While Stephen avoided grown-up responsibilities, his older brothers were making their way in industrializing America as striving apprentices and "practical business men." Morrison Foster, who was three years older, worked for Hope Cotton Factory, making long buying trips to the South. Indeed, cotton was Pittsburgh's leading industry, and he managed to get Stephen a job inspecting bales on their way from the Pittsburgh wharf, but the young man struggled to keep it.

Music offered no conceivable path forward. At the time, respectable society regarded "a young man addicted to music" as "a worthless fellow whose fate was the poor-house." Music teachers and dancing masters were ubiquitous, usually foreign, often scapegrace drifters. If some musicians were seen as predatory, others were deemed "a sort of third or harmless sex . . . to be relieved of responsibility for thus wasting their lives, because they knew no better."

Foster turned twenty in 1846. Finally, he agreed to keep the books for his brother Dunning at his Cincinnati wholesale mercantile brokerage. The office near the river city's wharves negotiated purchases and arranged shipments at another swollen node of the nation's cotton-driven economy. The labor of more than a million enslaved workers boosted cotton to more than 60 percent of U.S. exports. The historian Edward Baptist estimated that more than half of the national economy "derived directly or indirectly from cotton." Slavery was the goose that laid the "golden egg" of prosperity.

The brothers who supported Stephen's education, paid his wages, and later enabled him to focus on composing music were up to their armpits in the cotton trade and its derivative commerce. He grew up amid a surging economy—"slavery's capitalism," the economic historians Sven Beckert and Seth Rockman called it. In Pittsburgh and Cincinnati, Foster confronted a diurnal "blur of commodities and capital that flowed between" and crumbled distinctions between the regions.

A few outspoken and committed abolitionists petitioned Congress and led boycotts, but they failed to dent the global demand for the durable, comfortable fabric, and the Fosters denounced them.

Stephen composed songs in his spare time to share with family and a few friends who gathered for amateur evening harmonies at home. In Cincinnati, Foster gravitated to the nearby music shop of W. C. Peters, who previously plied his trade in Pittsburgh and sold Stephen his first flute. Foster played on the shop's piano, browsed the stock of sheet music, and spent his clerk's wages. Peters was his first publisher, printing "Old Uncle Ned" in 1848 with a cover featuring a blackface minstrel troupe called the Sable Harmonists. The ode to an "ideal slave" mourned by the "massa" began in a moderate tempo:

> Dere was an old Nigga, dey call'd him Uncle Ned
> He's dead long ago, long ago!
> He had no wool on de top ob his head
> De place whar de wool ought to grow.

Copyrighting the work had not crossed his mind; Foster hesitated even to put his name on something so coarse and simple. Peters and various pirate publishers made a mint, and Foster earned not a penny from "Old Uncle Ned," which sold tens of thousands of copies in dozens of editions.

Stephen was prouder of "What Must a Fairy's Dream Be?" and entered the ballad in a song competition sponsored by a Pittsburgh ice cream saloon. Miss Clara Bruce gave it her best effort, but the ice cream crowd much preferred blackface-style "Ethiopian Refranes." Stephen was in Cincinnati, so for the next song "battle" his brother Morrison submitted "Oh! Susanna." Arguably, on that warm fall night in 1847 pop music was born. The melody took the bounce from the rowdy, peasant polka and married it to the unlikely tale of a Black man with a banjo traveling *north* from Alabama, his "true love for to see."

The cotton current was sweeping thousands of Black men in the opposite direction. Verisimilitude not only wasn't the point; it impeded emotions that set white feet to tapping, which was the point. Foster packed "Oh! Susanna" full of absurd contradictions like "The sun so hot I froze to death." He cited an industrial disaster that claimed five hundred Black lives, but jauntily, the banjo still on knee. The sheet music introduced "Oh! Susanna" "as sung by Mr. Tichnor of the Sable Harmonists" and written and composed by S. C. Foster, perhaps to distinguish him from the radical New England abolitionist and friend of Frederick Douglass's Stephen S. Foster. Peters reportedly paid $100—likely one-third of Stephen's bookkeeper's salary. "Oh! Susanna" represents the first known instance of "real money" landing in a song-writer's pocket. Until this point, the early nineteenth-century composer and singer Henry Russell explained, writing songs professionally "would have meant simple starvation."

But the sheet music business exploded in the 1840s. New canals, turnpikes, and steam-driven riverboats and trains cut distribution costs. Playing piano became a touchstone of middle-class identity, and popular songs, not classical pieces, were the hot sellers. Blackface troupes embarked on national tours, like "songbirds," one observer noted. A *New-York Tribune* correspondent heard "Don't you cry for me!" peal from gambling saloons and tents in California gold rush settlements. The tune "was always encouraging," the journalist Bayard Taylor explained, because "even its most doleful passages had a grotesque touch of cheerfulness."

People everywhere knew "Oh! Susanna," though almost no one knew its author. Eventually, Foster, or perhaps a savvier brother, recognized the financial rewards that might be reaped. Still, it was a risky business, morally as much as financially. When the Massachusetts-born George Frederick Root published minstrel or popular songs, he concealed his identity. "Any line of music, as a business," was unsavory, he wrote. The minstrel line smelled the worst.

Foster plunged in anyway. One day in 1849, the twenty-three-year-old applied the formula he used to calculate commissions on cotton shipments to the first known music royalty contracts. For every copy of future songs sold, Firth, Pond & Company of New York and F. D. Benteen of Baltimore guaranteed the author two cents, about 8 percent of the retail price. His belly full of fire, Foster steamed back up the Ohio to Pittsburgh to move in with his parents and make music full-time. His brother Morrison floated his rent and living expenses. Stephen set to work, shutting himself up for hours. He had never felt so free.

Six months later, in July 1850, he stood, pale and frightened, before a minister and pledged himself to nineteen-year-old Jane McDowell, whose striking auburn tresses featured in the later song "Jeanie with the

Foster appears confident in this possible self-portrait on the back of the sheet music for "Old Folks at Home." The 1851 hit is estimated to have sold more than eighty-two thousand copies.

Light Brown Hair." Their courtship had begun as Stephen steered into his unorthodox career and she recovered from her father's death and a broken engagement. Stephen was an odd and likely a rushed choice. Despite his prolific songwriting, sales were slow and Jane and Stephen made their home with his parents and brother.

Had American copyright law covered live performances, the couple might have bought themselves a mansion based on "Oh! Susanna" proceeds alone. But another half a century passed before the American Society of Composers, Authors, and Publishers (ASCAP) collected licensing fees on behalf of composers. Foster's only income came from sheet music sales; seeking a boost, his New York publishers struck a deal with the leading blackface impresario E. P. Christy. Appropriate Foster sheets would be presented "as sung by" Christy's Minstrels.

Minstrel showmen advertised blackface music and dance, birthed by and among working- and middle-class people in northern urban centers, as the most original "species of National Amusement," and relentlessly promoted it as authentically Black. Wearing burnt-cork makeup to create exaggerated "Negroid" features, they sang about an exotic region "down south," a land of happy, ungainly, singing people who never worried about their next meal. These depictions and their wide acceptance by audiences did incalculable social and human damage.

Minstrel shows encompassed contradictory white supremacist notions of Black musical virtuosity *and* Black primitiveness. Some scholars have posited that by denigrating blackness, blackface performances eased tensions between urban immigrants and native-born Americans. People were uprooting from the Old World, and those born on these shores abandoned farms for mills and land to the south and west. No wonder music about bygone homes became so popular: think how the 1823 song "Home! Sweet Home!" ("there's no place like home") has endured, even as its melody slipped into obscurity.

A more peaceful, rural home became a common nostalgic reference, but in her 1861 memoir, *Incidents in the Life of a Slave Girl,* Harriet Jacobs struggled to explain to white readers that there was no comparison between what she had known in the South and what migrants left behind. "I would ten thousand times rather my children should be the half-starved paupers of Ireland," Jacobs vowed, "than the most pampered slaves of America."

Poking fun defused social tension, and the mask of blackness was useful in mocking everything from politicians to foreigners, Shakespeare to Shakers—the powerful and the marginal. The acts cast a potent spell. "A minstrel show came to town," recalled one Rhode Islander, "and I thought of nothing else for weeks." The craze reached into the White House, where showmen performed for the "Especial Amusement of the President of the United States, His Family and Friends."

The "millionaire negro singer" Edwin Pearce Christy (a white man) topped the crowded field of America's signature entertainment. Stephen Foster's elder by a decade, Christy first assembled his ensemble in a Buffalo brothel frequented by Erie Canal barge workers. He transferred the troupe to Manhattan, and from 1847 through 1854 they played nightly at lower Broadway's twenty-five-hundred-seat Mechanics' Hall. Foster songs furthered Christy's project of making blackface safe for the ballooning bourgeoisie while retaining its working-class base. Whereas blackface performances were initially brief comic entr'actes within larger circuses or plays, Christy mounted full-length stand-alone entertainments and charged accordingly.

Every famous minstrel impresario had a self-promoting pedigree as an expert in Black speech, "superstitions," songs, and dances. Christy professed to come from a "highly respectable" Philadelphia family, yet he joined a circus as a youth, then oversaw a New Orleans ropewalk

Christy's Minstrels promoted songbooks of melodies, as performed "at their concerts with distinguished success." The designs suggest the elaborate production values of 1840s and 1850s minstrel shows. From on high, Edwin Pearce Christy oversees the musical lineup—banjos, fiddle, tambourine, and bones—and the staged frolicking and cross-dressing.

where enslaved workers hand-twisted hemp into cord. From them Christy claimed to have (for free) "acquired" valuable "knowledge of the negro's peculiar characteristics."

But blackface minstrels invented most of their content and then copied and embellished what other whites created. The ruse worked not just because few who paid for seats had ever visited a plantation. It worked because the mark of race was everywhere, and everywhere white Americans viewed the stigma of skin color through a glass darkly.

Minstrel songs much more closely resemble Irish and English melodies than anything African, though the performances included germs of African dance and culture. The banjo—a key minstrel show instrument—came to the Americas with captives sold into bondage. The chorus so central to minstrel songs and to American pop music may stem from the call-and-response of plantation work songs and spirituals. Through assertion more than in fact, blackface minstrels established "Black" culture (really, white ideas of blackness as uncivilized, inane, emotional, crude, overly sexual, but also "naturally" musical and athletic) at the foundation of performing arts in the United States.

It is significant that those supposed qualities and capacities remain racially stereotyped to this day and are an enduring burden to Black Americans. The blackface minstrel form, moreover, existed under white control and for whites' amusement. So-called Ethiopian delineators sketched scenes that presented slavery and white superiority as natural law. In the hands of inventive white "imitators," the "curious" shards of Black self-expression formed into sharp-edged and dehumanizing caricatures named Jim Crow, Zip Coon, Aunt Chloe, and Delilah. A patron attending a minstrel show was being taught what Black people were.

Like P. T. Barnum, who made a fortune turning sideshow acts into a must-see New York City "museum," Christy adapted and regularized blackface to better attract "ladies and gentlemen." He banned whistling and disruptive outbursts and disallowed encores—typical features of rowdy, working-class theaters. His minstrels always concluded with a "playlet" or skit typically set on a "happy" plantation, with the whole corked troupe joining in the song and dance. Christy merged sentimental four-part harmony with the slapstick routines, wild dances, and banjo-and-bones fare. Raunchier segments remained: no show was complete without "Miss Lucy Long." If Lucy became a "scolding wife," her suitor vowed to "tote her down to Georgia / And trade her off for corn." Ha-ha. In the 1850s, Christy's Minstrels became a required stop for visitors to New York City, the place to go for "genuine negro fun." For twenty-five cents, a person could laugh, then weep, then laugh some more until their "sides fairly ached."

Since courting Jane McDowell, Stephen Foster had labored to make good on his career gamble without what he called "the Ethiopian business," the musical trade in blackness. Jane was pregnant in 1851, and he sent tune after tune into print. These all-but-forgotten works—

including "Mother, Thou'rt Faithful to Me" (a "beautiful and expressive ballad," according to his publisher)—were parlor songs, genteel, wispy, and lachrymose. In part out of preference and in part for the sake of his new family, he ensured that no blackface acts besmirched the sheet music. Did Jane press him to do this? Foster had committed himself to a musical straight and narrow, but debts were mounting. He owed his brother Morrison almost $400—about $14,000 in 2021. A certain hubris propels all artists, and Foster believed his parlor songs would find a large audience. But respectable melodies like "I Would Not Die in Springtime" scarcely sold at all.

Jane Foster delivered a baby girl, Marion, on April 18, 1851. The outwardly joyous event threw Foster into gloom. Stephen bent over his worktable and tabulated the days, 271, from his wedding to Marion's birth. The husband doubted his wife. At a time when only children were rare, Marion Foster never got a sibling. After the baby arrived— perhaps even earlier—Stephen and Jane likely suspended sexual contact. Trapped in a souring marriage in a crowded house with a new baby and little income, Stephen reverted to blackface. "Ring, Ring de Banjo" came first, followed by "Oh, Boys, Carry Me 'Long," reiterating his 1848 hit, "Old Uncle Ned." Christy used both songs in his show, but Foster, needing immediate cash, made the impresario an offer.

For $10 (about $340 in 2021), Christy's Minstrels could perform "Oh, Boys, Carry Me 'Long" "before any other band gets it." In the upbeat ditty, a dying man bids farewell to merry comrades who "sings a song / De whole day long." Before "guine . . . Where all de niggas am free," the narrator leaps from his deathbed to console his owner: "Massa, don't you cry." Christy paid the $10, and Stephen paid his brother William two months' rent. Foster sweetened the deal for "Old Folks at Home" (1851), his only work to outsell "My Old Kentucky Home." For $15, Christy got songwriting credit in addition to advance rights. The crowds at Mechanics' Hall went wild for the lilting tune—"Way down upon de Swanee Ribber / Far, far, away"—about an aging Black man "longing for de old plantation / And for de old folks at home." The melody supplied Christy's zany blackface act with an emotional crescendo that hit the market as the Fugitive Slave Act was implemented, subjecting any Black person to capture and return if an "owner" swore an affidavit. Officials who failed to assist could be fined $1,000 (some $34,000 in 2021). Free Black people, like Solomon Northup, author of *Twelve Years a Slave*, could be snatched and sold into bondage. Thousands fled to Canada for protection, and abolitionists pressed northern states to nullify the law, while "Old Folks" imagined Black people fondly remembering—rather than running from—the site of bondage.

As "Old Folks at Home" royalties rolled in, Foster's professional leap seemed to be paying off, but his struggle to reconcile his reputation with his need to pay the rent continued. The boy who had imitated white men imitating Black men pledged to stick to blackface songs free from "trashy and offensive words" and violent or sexual references, and in doing so "build up a taste for the Ethiopian songs among refined people." In making racism softer, less offensive, Foster ironically cemented his complicity in promoting the "singing slave" and the idealization of slavery the trope carried with it. Foster had now decided to compose minstrel songs "without fear or shame," but "a little matter of pride" ate at him. Foster requested that Christy take his name off future printings of "Old Folks at Home." "I cannot write at all," Stephen explained, "unless I write for the public approbation and get credit for what I write." He offered to repay the $15. The minstrel king dismissed him as a "Vascillating Skunk & Plagiarist."

Foster's output went into free fall; he published only four songs in 1852. "I Cannot Sing Tonight" expressed his blocked, muted misery. Back from his steamboat journey to New Orleans, unhappily married, boarding with his parents in his brother's house, he worried over his latest effort, "Poor Uncle Tom, Good Night."

At some point, Foster thought better of what he'd done and went back over the lyrics. Being "the best Ethiopian songwriter" meant creating touching melodies for refined people, the same audience he aspired to reach with his parlor music. Line by line, he stripped out the "Negro" dialect from "Poor Uncle Tom, Good Night." "De" and "dey" became "the" and "they," and "cotton had grow" became "sugar-canes grow," a grammatical fix that kept the rhythm without losing its southern setting. It was one thing for Christy in bug-eyed blackface to croon and ham about "de troubles" on Broadway, but for ladies and gentlemen who could afford sheet music, singing that way in their own homes could be awkward. Perhaps they would rather not *sound quite like* blackface minstrels. The chorus, with its soaring melody and lyrics, was completely new. It ingeniously evoked the ladies Stephen hoped would buy and sing his music:

Weep no more, my lady,
Oh! weep no more today!
We will sing one song
For the old Kentucky Home,
For the old Kentucky Home, far away.

Leaping from "Uncle Tom" to "Kentucky Home" made aural sense; the phrases are like fraternal twins, and by losing "Tom," Foster concentrated on "home." The song still tells a pitiful tale: a nameless "darky" looks fondly on a once carefree life in slavery, submits to "Hard Times," and exits this world, head bowed, back bent, in song, but the new refrain took a turn. It distanced the singer from the mourning individual to a collective "we" mourning *and* celebrating a *shared* home.

Given the "troubles" as well as the immense profits slavery generated, ending the problem with death supplied a resolution absent political answers. Emancipating and integrating ex-slaves into society was inconceivable to most white Americans. Many white supporters of "free soil and free labor" regarded slavery with dismay not for staining the nation's founding principles but because its "efficiencies" undercut their access to land and jobs. Adding free states to the Union might shift Senate control against slaveholders and their right to hold human property. Hence the hot debates—and pitched battles—in western territories then organizing into political units. All this was well known to Stephen Foster when he composed a pastoral scene where either "de birds make music all de day" or "the birds make music all the day." He introduced Uncle Tom, and then ripped a family apart.

"Poor Uncle Tom, Good Night" had become "My Old Kentucky Home, Good Night!"

American attics, basements, garage sales, and no small number of parlors and living room shelves are awash in centuries of racist objects. Stowe's book and Foster's song sit at different points on that spectrum, but unquestionably join a tide of material things that reflect back the thoughts and feelings of a nation. All one needs to do is look.

While helping a close friend sort through her mother's condominium after she died, I was given a two-inch, time-darkened alligator snatching a Black toddler's backside. Between forays to Staples for heavy-duty garbage bags, boxes, and packing materials, we talked about my recent research trip (Harvard University's Houghton Library holds an extensive archive called the American Minstrel Show Collection). She guessed the alligator was a souvenir from a Florida vacation her mother took with her family in the 1940s. "It's so horrible," my friend said. "I obviously don't want it." I took the thing.

We could fill a hundred museums with items long considered amusing or "cute" even as they demeaned people, including children, to justify their subordination. I know only one, the Jim Crow Museum of Racist Memorabilia at Michigan's Ferris State University. One day, I swaddled the figurine in bubble wrap and mailed it to Michigan.

The movement to end chattel slavery had its own songs and singers. They were vastly outnumbered by generations of Americans who sang songs and enjoyed souvenirs that aligned with racist sensibilities. Foster for one loathed conflict, sought comfort, craved and required public and family approval. The alterations he made before publishing "My

As it was in Foster's song, the old Kentucky home is imagined as a slave cabin in an undated early twentieth-century postcard. It expresses the era's white supremacy, which saturated souvenirs, household objects, and marketing campaigns for consumer products like Maxwell House coffee.

Old Kentucky Home" depoliticized the lament, setting Stowe and her battles at arm's length. The verses followed the plot of *Uncle Tom's Cabin* while plausibly denying any direct relation to it.

Deleting "Uncle Tom" evaded the acrimonious debate engulfing America. The new refrain introduced a lady, floating above and apart, releasing the emotion the song's sad circumstances provoke. Told to "weep no more," she is really being urged to cry it out. The invitation to sing "one song" together offers a lifeline. The person-owning wife in *Uncle Tom's Cabin* begs her husband not to sell Tom and then vows to somehow buy him in atonement. Stowe also shows Tom's wife, Aunt Chloe the cook, shattered by the separation. Before the trader in human flesh drives Tom away, the two women share a moment of far-fetched female solidarity.

In the blackface world of Stephen Foster and E. P. Christy, indeed, even the term "Black lady" was a supreme joke. Black female characters (played by cross-dressing white men in cork) were never ladies but rather highly sexualized "wenches" or simpleton "mammies." Foster's new chorus could be played as minstrel humor. Or it could be sung straight, unmarred by inelegant "Black" dialect. It worked particularly well for the white women who chiefly bought and played sheet music. A tale of woe perhaps aroused sympathy, but the performance was one where white tears, not slavery, assumed center stage.

THE CORN TOP'S RIPE

White Men's Music

Blackface minstrelsy, forever linked to its barroom beginnings, was a shadow Stephen Foster yearned to escape. In attempting an escape, he wrote enduring songs that helped genteel whites remain genteel. His songs worked the muscle of whiteness, the certainty of superiority so robust that it could morph into a violent fist, a sneering guffaw, or even, as Foster proved, a sentimental tear. "My Old Kentucky Home" was "white" or genteel enough to let into the (middle-class) house and just "authentically Black" enough to be not of that same house. Given his songs' popularity, it is safe to say that a significant percent of white America, across all classes and geography, knew Foster's tunes well enough to hum them, even sing their lyrics, and knowing the songs allowed the genteel to declare them beyond the pale. Not for the first time and decidedly not for the last, white presumptions about Black behavior and bodies put money in white men's (it was almost always white men's) pockets even as they denigrated one race to help elevate another. Think Elvis's hips and the Rolling Stones' "Brown Sugar" and white people in their living rooms tuning in to *Soul Train*. Each wave of fascinated white disapproval reestablished the racial tones of popular low culture and genteel higher culture.

It is a lesser irony of the story of "My Old Kentucky Home" that the class Foster wished to associate with refused him because of how catchy they found his blackface songs. He covered Americans' racist tracks with sanitized, less "trashy" material, and thus built "a taste for the Ethiopian songs among refined people." It was work he excelled at. The white public responded with enthusiasm, but it couldn't save Foster, not during his lifetime, anyway. The cork that defined his success had penetrated too deeply. The counterfeit he and other "Ethiopian delineators" cast upon the market stuck and became a powerful means by which Americans learned to feel all right about racism.

Christy's Minstrels slotted "My Old Kentucky Home" into their show, and those who heard it, whether clerks or bank presidents, newly arrived immigrants or ministers with wives and children, could buy their own copy "arranged for pianoforte" at the Music Depot next to the box office. "My Old Kentucky Home" was "No. 20 of Foster's Plantation Melodies as Sung by Christy's Minstrels"; Christy's name dwarfed Foster's. Meantime, a pirated "My Old Kentucky Home" song sheet printed by H. De Marsan dispensed with gentility, offering instead a crudely caricatured banjo player singing to his "lady." This mocking approach to a song about the slave trade might have matched what many people saw on minstrel stages and in their minds, but it wasn't what middle-class women wanted to prop on their pianos.

By cleaning up the lyrics, killing off the controversial enslaved figure, and finally both affirming and drying sentimental tears, "My Old Kentucky Home" aimed at the exact spot where minstrelsy and the parlor merged. If enough people bought and treasured "My Old Kentucky Home," they might also buy the "higher form of music" Foster wrote but could not sell. If only they would cross over with him, he could earn his keep and the respect he pined for.

The lower Manhattan office of Firth, Pond & Company, the country's largest music publisher, occupied a mansion that had once been George Washington's headquarters, and Foster must have been warmly welcomed when the hitmaker appeared there in person in 1853. He came on business—a rare effort at professional self-promotion. "My Old Kentucky Home" was selling fast, and Foster also called at the *New York Musical World,* whose editors printed a small notice about the visit. Blackface music was a genre the *Musical World* detested, and the weekly journal was free with advice for the talented Pittsburgher. He should "turn his attention" to more elevating "white men's music." Foster assured them that this was his plan. But "Mary Loves the Flowers" (1850) earned him a few dollars, whereas "My Old Kentucky Home" brought $1,576 in royalties. If Stephen Foster had written only plantation and blackface material on the level of his latest works, he could perhaps have stayed afloat. It was becoming clear, however, that his desire to appease the gatekeepers of refinement was in a contest not only with good business but also with his fondness for alcohol. Foster's addiction to drink deepened more decidedly each year even as his most popular songs demarcated racial difference for a dividing nation.

For the *Musical World*'s condescending critics missed a deeper irony. Whether they approved or not, blackface minstrelsy *was* white men's music. Authored by whites, performed by whites, and consumed by whites, it helped whites line their understandings of race. Foster's gentrification of the minstrel terrain made the genre more respectable. Layering a song about an enslaved man sold south to die with respectability to ease its public consumption by whites was part of the work of "My Old Kentucky Home" from the start.

Apart from the would-be tastemakers at the *Musical World,* it became more common to claim that popular songs resounding with "blackness" were the true *American* music. The ability to display "native" creative forms mattered to a nation anxious to distinguish itself from the "Old World." Thus, the virtuosic New Orleans–born classical pianist Louis Moreau Gottschalk (1829–1869) worked "My Old Kentucky Home" into his "Columbia, caprice américain," opus 34. On tour in Europe in 1853, he delighted audiences with a "boisterous romp" that drained every ounce of pathos from Foster's tune. By cutting the yearning chorus and revving the tempo, Gottschalk produced a joyous, left-hand-leaping marvel filled with "coruscating runs on the treble." There was nothing sad about Gottschalk's interpretation of a Black Kentuckian's lament, and audiences responded enthusiastically. The sound was proud, patriotic, playful, all-around American.

Foster's "plantation melodies" supplied a denigrated genre with a respectable veneer, and while Gottschalk made a bid for an inauthentic but Black-tinged music as essentially American, a pair of nineteenth-century teenagers reveal how the white middle class domesticated blackface minstrelsy. Emily McKissick, born in 1836 in Albany, New York, followed the latest popular music as Americans her age still do today. The McKissick household of 1853 encompassed father (president of Albany's board of trade), stepmother, and several younger half siblings. Sixteen-year-old Emily attended an esteemed female academy and studied piano. That instrument was the McKissick parlor's centerpiece, a sonic accompaniment to idealized domesticity. Emily used her spending money to buy sheet music and left a book of her favorite songs to posterity. Bound and protected between leather covers, it was a Victorian girl's mixtape or Spotify playlist, and "My Old Kentucky Home" came third in the folio. Further back in the book was Foster's "Farewell, My Lilly Dear"; Emily had "crossed over" from his popular minstrel work to the parlor genre he preferred, just as the Pittsburgh songwriter hoped. But "My Old Kentucky Home" was the one that touched the young New Yorker's heart. McKissick carefully penciled its second and third verses (which were printed separately on the sheet music's final page) beneath the notation in order to see them as she sang and played. When she married one of the young men who gathered at her house for musical evenings, she carried the volume into her new life, and Emily's children grew up with "sing one song for the old Kentucky Home" sounding through their comfortable domicile. Later in her long life, she introduced the song about slavery to a new generation of piano students. Emily died in 1919; for half a century she linked her transit to the beyond with the one an enslaved man endured. Across the song's title page in her volume was inscribed, "A long, sad 'Good Night' to our / 'Old Kentucky Home' till we / reach the shore of the / Heavenly Home!"

When Mabel Osgood was growing up in 1860s and 1870s Manhattan, "My Old Kentucky Home" was already old. The progressive-minded Osgoods (the father was a Unitarian minister) revered Abraham Lincoln and enjoyed going to minstrel shows. When "Father Abraham" was assassinated, six-year-old Mabel feared that the "little colored children would be sold again" into bondage. In the realm of music, she pointedly rejected the lessons that in her view produced a generation of "thin-voiced, bleating singers" of " 'music in the home.' " Her mother, gifted with a beautiful voice, had her own bound volume of favorite songs from her youth and would take them out to entertain the family in their house on West Eleventh Street. Osgood particularly recalled the cozy feeling of her mother's singing "My Old Kentucky Home" on winter evenings. "Father was resting," Osgood remembered, "and the

Foster's popularity within American minstrel shows had a counterpart in bourgeois households. Music publishers targeted young white women, while magazines such as *Godey's Lady's Book* offered aspirational images of middle-class domestic leisure.

room was dark except for the firelight, and the closed shutters kept out the jingling bells of the Sixth Avenue street cars." She judged the minstrel song superior to the "serious and conventionally pathetic" tunes that dominated her mother's repertoire. "This was the real home music," evoking safety, family intimacy. "Even the saddest darky melodies" set in a faraway South were, she wrote, "refreshing."

For young Emily and Mabel, home was a center of stability in an undependable, grimy, industrializing world that exploited poor and Black people even as it made life comfortable for families like their own. As white women of privilege, they wielded a measure of cultural and moral power. Emily was a teacher. Mabel knew to worry about "little colored children." The terrible tale contained in "My Old Kentucky Home" became homey, familiar. It was useful as a way to think about the life beyond this one or establish one's musical taste as superior to the "conventionally pathetic." Foster's song of "virtuous suffering and familial disintegration," as the historian Eric Lott has written, anchored "'blackness' as a fundamental source" of generalized white American middle-class sentiment, sentiment that almost wholly bypassed both the politics of slavery and actual "black feeling."

As a song of a family torn apart gained traction in middle-class parlors, a chasm opened in the Foster household. Jane's "tempestuous outbursts," as noted by Foster family members, were likely exacerbated by the drinking. Jane took Marion and moved in with her mother. But few details about the breakup or Stephen's life survived the bonfire his brother made two years later with packets of old family letters. Stephen's despair over his marriage tipped into depression, and he drank even more. The alcohol intake was unfortunate, and the way the first professional pop songwriter leaned on family for financial support was a matter of regret, but by the standards of the era marital separation was unspeakable. Divorce just wasn't in the vocabulary of mid-century middle-class Americans.

Stephen responded to Jane's desertion by selling their furniture and decamping to Manhattan, perhaps for encouragement from people who understood his work, or at least relief from private guilt and public shame. He was trying to complete an extended arrangement for strings, flute, and piano (suited for performing at home) of eighty-three classical and opera airs, polkas, and his own parlor ballads—the kind of work the *Musical World* would approve. Royalties for his plantation songs were coming in but were not enough to dig him out of debt. He also now faced the expense of separately supporting his wife and child or the humiliation of not being able to do so.

Even as Foster's capacity to benefit from the fact faded, *Uncle Tom's Cabin,* the novel that first inspired "Poor Uncle Tom, Good Night," became the most produced play in the nation. The best seller inspired countless adaptations, many including performances of "My Old Kentucky Home." The novelist Henry James remembered the way the drama "flutter[ed] down on every stage, literally without exception, in America and Europe," and if millions read the book, fifty times that many saw it as a play. The first stagings were by blackface minstrel troupes. (In fact, mid-nineteenth-century American theater and blackface "overlapped

and nearly coalesced" and remained entangled well into the movie era.)
In a telling bit of difference, whereas the abolitionist Harriet Beecher
Stowe publicly objected to staged versions of her work, Foster had no
qualms about his music being embraced by any and all. The variety of
Uncle Tom's Cabin productions and the fungibility of "My Old Kentucky Home" attest to the song's potency across audiences and the
generations who heard and sang it. Entertainment value, not political
change and rarely if ever abolition activism, motivated the producers of
these plays; Foster's music worked nimbly into dramas that ranged from
mildly antislavery to overtly white supremacist.

Sam S. Sanford, "rated as one of the best comedians of his time,"
pioneered blackface cross-dressing, creating the "wench" character that
became a minstrel show staple. In 1853, he was also the owner of the new
six-hundred-seat blackface Opera House in Philadelphia. In the spirit
of filling seats, Sanford invited students from local colleges to a free
preview of his own *Uncle Tom's Cabin! or Real Life in Old Kentuck!* Many
were from the South and these sons of Dixie fumed when they learned
that Stowe's dangerous book was getting a public staging.

But Sanford's Uncle Tom (played by the minstrel master himself)
was a rebuke to abolitionism. *Real Life in Old Kentuck!* depicted not
sorrow and cruelty but "the merriment and pastimes of the glories"
of actual "slave life" as he "knew it" from professed personal experience. Sanford's comic Tom comes home to his wife, Chloe, "happy . . .
with plenty of money." They would "radder be on de Old Plantation,"
according to the playbill, than live free in Cincinnati. A scene titled
"MAKING LOVE BY MOONLIGHT" rested on gags about Black
people's innate promiscuity. Eliza (who in the book crosses the frozen
Ohio barefoot to save her child from being sold) and her fellow runaway, George, "jump the broom"—a crack about the absurdity of Black
wedlock. George then serenades her with "My Old Kentucky Home," a
place where Tom is never sold and they have no reason to flee. Together
they sang,

> *Den hand de Banjo down to play*
> *We'll make it ring both night and day*
> *And we care not what de white folks say,*
> *Dey can't get us to run away.*

Sanford enacted racist minstrel tropes to defend the institution Stowe's book decried and turn the plantation into a carefree site of liberty. In appreciation, the satisfied southern youths lofted the minstrel onto their shoulders and carried him triumphantly all the way to his home. Saturday matinees were added for "ladies and children," and Sanford said he pocketed $11,000 for a nine-week run, putting his new establishment on a firm footing. Dozens of minstrel companies adopted or imitated the show, known as "Sanford's Southern Version of *Uncle Tom's Cabin*" or simply "Happy Uncle Tom."

That same year, 1853, as Foster fled Pittsburgh for the metropolis, the ten-year-old future novelist Henry James attended a more enduring theatrical version of Stowe's novel at New York's National Theatre. P. T. Barnum and others were mounting comic burlesques of *Uncle Tom's Cabin,* but Henry James Sr. advocated abolition (along with utopian socialism and other radical ideas), and the family ventured "deep down on the East side," where educated people such as they rarely went, to see what the child understood to be a "rude" performance. George Aiken's show was a "family" affair, mounted with the thespian Howard clan, and five-year-old Cordelia played Little Eva, whose grateful father buys Tom after he saves the child from drowning. Aiken's play ran more than eight hundred performances. With seven acts and thirty-four scenes, the play was the first piece of American theater to dispense with unconnected comic or acrobatic entr'actes, though it was packed with blackface minstrel songs for dramatic or comic effect. Uncle Tom sang "My Old Kentucky Home" in mournful fashion, gathering audience sympathy—and faint hope in despair. His terrible whipping near the play's conclusion made clear that not all plantation scenes were pleasant, and a hostile *New-York Tribune* called the play an "Abolitionist part[y]." Critics have noted how slippery a quality empathy can be, particularly with respect to representations of racial brutality. The "facile intimacy" of identification works by arousing a sensitive and sentimental witness—effectively displacing or repressing the original subject or victim and his or her pain.

For the knowing Jameses, the lowbrow melodrama ensured that terror remained at a comfortable remove. Recalling the experience, James described his family's response to the overacted *Uncle Tom's Cabin:* "the point exactly was that we attended this spectacle just in order *not* to be beguiled, just in order to enjoy with ironic detachment and, at the very

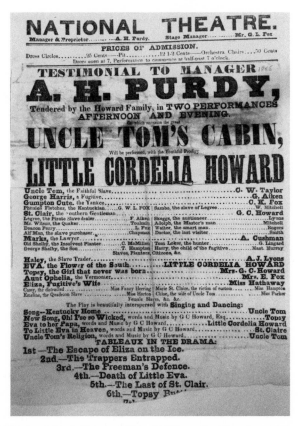

The "faithful slave" Uncle Tom sang "My Old Kentucky Home" in this long-running New York production of Harriet Beecher Stowe's sensational 1852 novel.

most, to be amused ourselves at our sensibility should it prove to have been" activated.

Just as Stowe's story was put to use eliciting different emotions from different white audiences, so, too, was Foster's song.

Following the Civil War and into the twentieth century, traveling extravaganzas known as (Uncle) "Tom Shows" "plied the backroads and railway spurs of small-town America." Live bloodhounds and "picka-ninny" dancers and other bells and whistles were added along the way. Stephen Foster songs provided the soundtrack, helping them achieve what his biographer Ken Emerson called "total market penetration—indeed *saturation*—long before radio."

"My Old Kentucky Home" (whether in blackface shows, sheet music in proper parlors, or stage versions of *Uncle Tom's Cabin*) turned slavery into profitable entertainment that gave white people an emotional release. Through the 1850s, people held in bondage risked their lives to ride an Underground Railroad engineered by an interracial band of conscientious lawbreakers; at the same time the most popular songs showed Black people content within slavery—singing, reminiscing, yearning for old times. Foster's cleaned-up minstrelsy wrapped cruelty in sentiment.

What did Black Americans of the 1850s think? Few of their responses to Foster's music were recorded by white people. Moreover, when millions endured bondage every day and even free Black Americans experienced severe economic and social exclusion, a sentimental song ranked relatively low on the list of matters demanding attention. The worn-out, dying, harmless, and "sympathetic" figures Foster used in songs like "My Old Kentucky Home" and "Old Uncle Ned" were wounding and emasculating, though not, immediately, lethal. They brutalized the spirit of real Black Americans while bending white minds about what blackness meant.

Martin Delany was Foster's fellow Pittsburgher, a journalist, abolitionist, and early Black nationalist. Sentimental plantation songs incensed Delany, and in a scene from his 1861–1862 novel, *Blake; or, The Huts of America,* he flipped Foster's "Old Uncle Ned" from a paean to a life of loyal servitude ending in heaven, "whar da good niggas go," to an enslaved man's "summons to insurrection." With "old master's dead," Black men should prepare for battle. Riffing on the lyrics and rhythm of "Old Uncle Ned," Delany had one character rouse his compatriots with a promise that the condemned sinner who claimed to own their bodies would

> *no more tramp on the neck of the slave,*
> *For he's gone where slaveholders go!*
> . . . .
> *He's gone where they all ought to go!*

Frederick Douglass tried to find a glimmer of hope in "My Old Kentucky Home." "I am not well," he told his audience in early 1855 during a lecture sponsored by the Rochester Ladies' Anti-slavery Society to benefit his newspaper and aid Black fugitives on their passage to liberty. Years of lecture tours had exhausted him, as had bitter divisions within the abolition movement. He feared that the rigidity of his mentor William Lloyd Garrison might lead northern states to secede from the Union—to preserve their own moral purity. This would not set Douglass's people free. Garrison circulated scandalous rumors that Douglass was an adulterer, threatening his ability to lead.

In this dark hour, Douglass looked to "the poets" for comfort and strength to carry onward. Henry Wadsworth Longfellow "whisper[ed], in every hour of trial and disappointment, 'labor and wait.' " A pragmatist, Douglass was ready to "unite with anybody to do right," possibly even promulgators of blackface music. For all their "ugly stereotypes," minstrel songs were "our national music," Douglass told his audience, and some, like " 'Old Kentucky Home,' and 'Uncle Ned,' . . . can call forth a tear as well as a smile." If such music could "awaken the sympathies for the slave, in which anti-slavery principles can take root, grow, and flourish," there was perhaps some hope in that. Having experienced bondage himself, Douglass articulated a version of Foster's music that might start serious conversations in parlors, over pianos, possibly expanding the movement.

Douglass was reaching; there were whole books of antislavery ballads, and "My Old Kentucky Home" did not appear in them. The Black abolitionist and poet Joshua McCarter Simpson, hoping to "kill the degrading influence of those comic Negro Songs . . . and change the flow of those sweet melodies into more appropriate and useful channels," took the melody of "My Old Kentucky Home" and set it to new, liberationist lyrics. Simpson called it "The Fugitive's Dream," but it was a nightmare. An escapee who has reached Canada finds himself back in Kentucky. When the "old master" asks him for "a walk,"

> *the first thing I know I'll be standing on the [auction] block,*
> *Or be writhing 'neath a sweet "ninety nine" [whip].*
> . . . .

> *Weep no more, old master—*
> *Weep no more, I pray;*
> *I will sing one song at my old Kentucky home,*
> *And return again to old Canada.*

As for Stephen Foster, he never lifted his pen to aid Douglass's, Delany's, or Simpson's cause. As will be seen, a single speech by Frederick Douglass has recently been seized upon to claim that Foster was either an abolitionist or a sympathetic fellow traveler bearing Douglass's stamp of approval. This is flatly not true.

White people in the 1850s used the phrase the "Old Kentucky Home," sometimes ironically, to ridicule fugitives and defend chattel slavery. Soon after Douglass delivered his Rochester address, a far-fetched account in *The Louisville Daily Courier* described two Kentucky runaways in Canada who asked their enslaver for money to "return to the 'old Kentucky home.'" He went to retrieve them himself and claimed that a mob of white abolitionists forced the pair to remain out

The abolitionist and poet Joshua McCarter Simpson set his song "The Fugitive's Dream" to the melody of "My Old Kentucky Home." In Simpson's nightmare, an escapee living in "old Canada" imagines himself back in Kentucky, threatened with whipping or being sold downriver by his "master." The song appeared in Simpson's *Emancipation Car: Being an Original Composition of Anti-slavery Ballads, Composed Exclusively for the Under Ground Rail Road* (1854).

of fear that they would reveal "the abject conditions of the Free Negro in the North." In another newspaper account, an escapee declared that he was "perfectly satisfied that Canada is no place for a darkie. He longed to get back to his 'Old Kentucky Home.'" These unbelievable accounts, reassuring to white readers in a slaveholding society, ran counter to the constant flow of fugitives, and one Tom Bishop was having none of it. In 1860, he escaped from Louisville by hiring himself out as a riverboat deckhand. When the boat docked again in the city a few weeks later, Bishop was discovered and turned over to authorities, reportedly "very much exasperated at the idea of being taken back to the old Kentucky home." Perhaps Tom Bishop joined the twenty-four thousand Black Kentuckians who took up arms against the Confederacy four years later, when Abraham Lincoln permitted them to enlist.

For one young American who did take up arms for the Union, "My Old Kentucky Home" *was* an antislavery song. When the underage Chauncey Cooke signed up for military service, his father instructed him never to forget the "four million slaves whose liberty is at stake in this war." Private Cooke of Wisconsin's Twenty-Fifth Volunteer Infantry was ready to shoot any man who snared a fugitive back into bondage. Writing home in May 1863 from his encampment in western Kentucky, Chauncey reported a puzzling discovery. He had asked every Black person he met, but "the darkies don't know anything about the song of Old Kentucky Home, except as they have picked it up from hearing the whites sing it." It gave the boy a "curious feeling" to have been so misguided. "I guess I must have thought it came out of some negro's heart." Foster's inauthenticity was momentarily exposed. Cooke felt uncomfortable, confused, a little foolish for being taken in. Yet for a time "My Old Kentucky Home" rallied a private in his principled struggle for the soul of the nation, just as Frederick Douglass wished.

What would Foster have wished? Stephen Foster, as we have seen, lived as well as he did in large part due to the tentacles of the antebellum slavery economy that extracted life and labor from one group of human beings and spread its value to another. In this he was hardly alone; so, too, did much of America. It was a fact many preferred to ignore or gloss. He wished to make a career off melodies like "Annie My Own Love," but instead concocted "plantation airs" as improvements on a genre he would have preferred to leave behind. Foster's position on slavery likely mirrored both the ambivalence and the white supremacy of his fellow countrymen and -women. The "singing slave" content in Kentucky could resolve this tension for those who felt uneasy about slavery and preferred free labor but rejected emancipation and recoiled at racial equality—really just about everybody white. "My Old Kentucky Home" transmuted that ambivalence beautifully into song. The "trouble all will end," Foster had written, "in the field where the sugar-canes grow." Even Abraham Lincoln supported keeping slavery only where it already existed—if that could have saved the Union.

Within the bitter politics of the era, Foster was capable of cruel mockery. During the presidential campaign of 1856, he was back in Pittsburgh, where the Foster men were busily supporting the Democrat James Buchanan, politically "a Northern man with Southern sympathies." Buchanan was also family; Stephen's sister was married to the candidate's brother.

The Fosters would have voted for him anyway. Doing his political part, Stephen composed a campaign ballad for the local Buchanan Glee Club, which he led at rallies in and around Pittsburgh in the months before the election. "The Abolition Show" (also called "The Great Baby Show") lampooned his opponent's supporters as "genmen ob color" and "women and boys." While Republican John C. Frémont blubbered about "Bleeding Kansas," where pro-slavery and antislavery settlers were battling for dominance, Democrats with "Old Buck in command" would put things right. For Foster men, the biographer Emerson tartly observed, preserving the Union clearly meant "tolerating if not toadying" to the "slavocracy."

Buchanan won, but there were no White House festivities for Stephen. His New York publisher refused to advance any more funds, and he took the drastic step of selling the rights to future royalties on his most popular songs. Firth & Pond would retain all proceeds from "My Old Kentucky Home." Melancholy and alcohol, the "Devouring Enemy," overcame him. Jane escaped for months-long visits to distant relations. Stephen spent the Civil War years alone in New York City, where, his wife lamented, "wine flowed freely—like water." His brother Morrison sent packets of decent clothes, and still the songwriter suffered "from sheer want." One night at his lodging on the Bowery, so the story goes, he stumbled in his room and struck his head. Stephen arrived bloodied at Bellevue Hospital with thirty-eight cents in his pocket and perished a few days later, aged thirty-seven. "He suffered much," Jane said, "and died for his fault," but his family concealed the mortifying particulars, and his passing was scarcely noticed. For all his hits, Stephen Foster was no celebrity.

Stephen Foster's intention for one song (much less his opinion on slavery and race) is ultimately vastly less important than the way the public experienced and absorbed his work over generations. In the aftermath of the Civil War, a profile of the songwriter appeared in *The Atlantic Monthly*. Robert Nevin, a Pittsburgh native and friend of the composer's, presented Foster as a racial progressive, lifting minstrelsy from its "vulgar" origins and presenting the "negro" as more than "a thing of tricks and antics." Plantation melodies like "My Old Kentucky Home," Nevin

In the years after his death, Foster's family tried to conceal the composer's alcoholism and near destitution. A 1916 music magazine put the situation gently: "During his last days in New York, Foster's means were greatly reduced, and it is reported that his workshop was the back room of a friendly grocer who provided him with the paper needed for his compositions."

believed, "taught us all to feel with the colored man the lowly joys and sorrows." That, of course, had been the point. Not to encourage a reckoning with the exclusions and injustices Black people suffered, but to allow whites, especially genteel whites, to feel a cathartic pity for the joys and sorrows of a lowly Black race. Yes, Foster granted his imagined bondsman the capacity for nostalgia, "the most popular emotion of the day," but his inauthentically authentic song did more to extend than to reform minstrelsy's problematic archetypes.

Nevin's optimistic assessment of whites' ability or desire "to feel with the slave" appeared as President Andrew Johnson signed stacks of pardons for Confederate officers. Post–Civil War manifestations of multiracial democracy were pounded with repressive, violent waves of white resistance. Frederick Douglass fought up to his death in 1895 to gain fair treatment and fulfill the constitutional promise of enfranchisement for Black Americans. A war to end slavery had been fought and won; the war to make possible racial equality, or even anything remotely close to it, had not. If Robert Nevin thought Foster's sentiments capable of "teaching us" (whites) to truly embrace a shared humanity, he was wrong. The opposite proved true. The sorrowing singer in "My Old Kentucky Home" had only a life of bondage to look fondly on. Not a life of uplift to anticipate, or a socially redemptive path to follow, and there was no hint of a desire for justified repair or vengeance. To a nation wedded to an ideal of itself as progressive, the truths of gross racial disparities and the tolerance for inhuman treatment were damning. Better to substitute the emotional resonance of "darkies" crooning about the lost plantation home.

Had Stephen Collins Foster been less inclined to depression and addiction and more fortunate in his marriage, he might have lived to witness his rehabilitation as the "father of American music." Even if that reputation rested on his blackface minstrel works and not the songs he preferred but that white Americans had far less use for, Foster would have welcomed his elevation at the turn of the twentieth century as a benevolent transmuter of authentic Black feeling. All along, the white-manufactured authenticity about blackness was a means for people who looked like him to both police their gentility and defend their innocence.

· · ·

"DE OLE KENTUCKY HOME - FAR AWAY."

In their lithograph *De Ole Kentucky Home—Far Away* (1885), Currier and Ives restored the "dialect" that whites assigned to Black American speech but that Foster had stripped from his 1853 melody.

I arrived at the University of North Carolina in Chapel Hill in 1989 as a graduate student expecting to study southern history and make some kind of profession of it. I came for training in how to use facts, documents, and more, things you can hold and cite, to explain the past and open it for others to see for themselves. But history always does work beyond marrying fact to chronology. It works to tell stories, in ways similar to Stowe's novel and Foster's songs. It encourages some considerations and discourages others. I already knew that no small number of historians since the end of the Civil War had behaved as Foster did, telling our national story in ways those in power could make comfortable sense of, and I wanted to do something different. By writing new histories, I wanted to contribute in some way to the understanding of our collective past. All that old history, particularly when it came to race, exerted a gravitational pull that as a student I was only dimly aware of, even though it stared me almost daily in the face.

"BINGHAM" was etched into stone above the door of a three-story brick classroom building that anchored a high-traffic corner of UNC's quadrangle. I was aware of my North Carolina forebears, who for multiple generations ran a school that served as a feeder for the state university. But I wasn't prepared to see the name enshrined on campus, and it made me more anxious than proud. Bingham Hall threatened to out me before my peers. I worried about being viewed as a legacy and less qualified than they were for my slot in the program. Like so many privileged white women before me, I feared losing status (and the illusion that my status was all of my own making). I might have worried about quite different things had I understood whom the building honored and the legacy of white supremacy contained in it.

It was many years later (long after I left Chapel Hill with my degree) that I learned any details about the life of Robert Hall Bingham (1838–1927). My grandfather's grandfather operated a classical academy not far from Chapel Hill, and held fourteen people in bondage. Robert graduated from the state university in 1860, enlisted in the Confederate army, and was captured, imprisoned nine months, and freed in time to witness General Robert E. Lee surrender at Appomattox. Back home, he became an instructor at the Bingham School, which during wartime had adopted a military curriculum complete with barracks and a drill field.

Teaching school by day, Robert Hall Bingham was also riding out at night, assaulting and intimidating freedmen and white Americans who sympathized with them. Only in my forties, and only because I was researching a biography of another forebear, did I learn the story *his* son proudly told hundreds of times. His "earliest memory" was "of clutching my mother's skirts in terror at a hooded apparition, and having my father raise his mask to relieve me." State authorities accused the ex-Confederate Bingham of Ku Klux Klan vigilantism in the 1860s, but before he was held to justice, anti-Reconstruction, white "redeemer" Democrats took power in the state capital. Year in, year out, he educated young men in Latin and white supremacy, teaching them to honor the Lost Cause and uphold the racial order his violence helped establish. He loved his alma mater, too, returning to campus often for reunions, and later helped secure for the university its largest endowment gift. This was the man Bingham Hall honored. Robert Nevin wrote in *The Atlantic Monthly* promoting Foster's power of sentiment for interracial understanding, while Robert Bingham marshaled white vigilante power. The truth was, these were different means to the same end.

. . .

A handful of early minstrel songs such as "Oh! Susanna" and later "plantation melodies" like "My Old Kentucky Home" form the core of Stephen Foster's legacy, working to define what it meant to be American and white. A parody of "blackness" lay at the heart of the young nation's most original and exportable national entertainment and persisted long past emancipation. In Paul Beatty's 2015 novel, *The Sellout,* a washed-up Hollywood actor living off his glory days illustrates white receptiveness to blackface stereotypes. "That's the beauty of minstrelsy," Beatty's narrator darkly observes, "its timelessness . . . [t]he soothing foreverness." Stephen Foster's audacious career as a songwriter ended unhappily, but half a century after he wrote "My Old Kentucky Home," he was on the cusp of becoming a national icon.

THE LITTLE CABIN FLOOR

"Negro" Minstrelsy

During a visit to New Orleans in 2008, my husband and I took our three children on an excursion up the River Road to visit Evergreen Plantation. A historical landmark, it is privately owned and boasts of being "the most intact plantation complex in the South." All these centuries later, it still produces sugar on its acreage. The topmost banner on its website informs you that it actively maintains a slavery database and aims to reconstruct and remember the lives of the more than four hundred enslaved men, women, and children who once harvested its sugarcane fields. In 2011, Quentin Tarantino would film portions of *Django Unchained* (a revenge fantasy in which a once-enslaved man guns down some of his tormentors) at Evergreen. My children were twelve, nine, and three years old and the visit was anchored by a picnic on the lawn outside the white house Evergreen's owners first built in 1790 and embellished in 1832 in the Greek Revival style. The history of Evergreen was and remains malleable, waiting to do new and different work.

At the time of our visit, a 1947 photograph by Clarence John Laughlin called *Receding Rectangles* hung on my wall. Laughlin's print captured in delicate gray scale Evergreen Plantation's row of emptied but intact slave dwellings, which stretch behind the white house away from the Mississippi. Viewed from the side, their framed porches create a telescopic effect. Laughlin was drawn to death, decay, and the surreal, and *Receding Rectangles* evokes all three, but its beguiling geometry struck me most of all. The structures had survived slavery, and in the hands of the photographer somehow transcended their past. Like any artwork one sees daily, the cabins became familiar. Their sinister purpose receded behind the symmetry.

Like art, the histories we tell ourselves become familiar, customary, but we put them to purposes far beyond aesthetics.

In the waning days of Reconstruction, a popular songwriter with a day job as Louisville's librarian envisioned a tribute to the fiftieth anniversary of Stephen Foster's birth. Will S. Hays also managed a troupe, Crème de la Crème of Minstrelsy, and blacked up on special occasions, but his wife would not allow him to take the group on the road. Hays authored hundreds of songs, sentimental ones like "You've Been a Friend to Me" (1879), which the Carter Family adapted in the twentieth century, and racist minstrel tunes like "The Unhappy Contraband" (1865) about a Civil War–era fugitive who wishes himself back in a cotton field. Hays's tunes represented the formerly enslaved as patently "ill-equipped for freedom." Hays appreciated, and probably envied, Stephen Foster's talents. Foster would have turned fifty in 1876, and though his songs endured in popular memory, he had faded to obscurity. Promising to publish "nothing to put a blush upon the cheek of [Foster's] kindred and friends," Hays wrote to Morrison Foster, proposing a newspaper feature on his brother's life. Morrison declined. The origin of "My Old Kentucky Home" grew foggier.

But not the song itself; never the song itself.

When the Civil War ended with slavery abolished amid jubilation for freed people, relief for the victors, and defeat for the Confederacy, Foster's melody sounded in surprising new settings. Black Americans starting without resources made herculean efforts to stabilize families, gain literacy, and establish an economic foothold. Great strides were made, yet, in a betrayal whose effects remain in sharp disparities in wealth, health, education, and housing, systems formed to contain the freedom, opportunities, and citizenship of Black Americans. A war fought to end slavery was over, but white America had little appetite to ensure that the imposed peace produce racial equality. The possibility of a multiracial republic was gradually snuffed out as southern white leaders—with the acquiescence of the larger nation—deployed mob violence and codified a system of racial control nicknamed Jim Crow. Jim Crow segregation was not by accident named for the simpleminded dancing minstrel show character Thomas D. "Daddy" Rice created in the 1830s, when Stephen Foster was a child, setting off the blackface craze that defined the songwriter's career. Jim Crow was a nation's shorthand for blackness.

"My Old Kentucky Home" adapted to a postwar nation where white controls over Black lives were simultaneously contested by a minority *and* enforced by a majority. In such a context, the melody had a settling effect. The Bromo-Seltzer company included it in its "Collection of Popular Songs," sold in drugstores as advertising for its hangover and pain remedy. At times, it assumed a bleached-white veneer. The Franco-Italian soprano Adelina Patti enchanted the audience at Paris's Grand Opera House with a surprise rendition of Foster's plantation melody. Gilded Age Americans cried encore when she gave them "this sweet, simple ballad." "Strong men were weeping," according to one attendee, "and women were hysterically giving vent to emotions they did not try to control." Flowers rained onto the stage and a bankroll of bills thudded at Patti's dainty feet. In a high chamber of classical musical performance, the great Patti recalled a time before the bloodshed. When she told them to weep no more, they couldn't stop.

A touring "mulatto" minstrel called Blind d'Arnault materializes in the fictional 1890s Nebraska hamlet of Willa Cather's novel *My Ántonia* (1918). D'Arnault bent with "docile subservience" over the hotel piano, delighting his listeners, including Cather's Virginia-born narrator, Jim Burden. The musician had "the happiest face" he had seen in years. Hearing him play and sing "My Old Kentucky Home" transported the western settlers to pastoral places with stable hierarchies. "To hear him, to watch him," the narrator thought, "was to see a Negro enjoying himself as only a Negro can." Whatever troubled Burden and the white people of Black Hawk, blind, unthreatening d'Arnault cheered them by appearing to be happy. Happy despite Jim Crow, happy despite his blindness. The "singing slave" survived emancipation as the "ideal Negro" for a white man like Jim Burden.

White people who heard "My Old Kentucky Home" in the decades after the Civil War generally thought of it as an old "negro" song, full of "simple pathos." Foster's parlor-blackface hybrid found an important new venue a few years after Appomattox when the touring "Colored Students" of Virginia's Hampton Normal and Agricultural Institute performed it after the spiritual "Go Down, Moses." "Tell old Pharaoh / To let my people go" rubbed up against "We will sing one song / For the old Kentucky Home, / For the old Kentucky Home, far away."

The Old Testament–inspired plea for liberation shared one thing only with Foster's hit—an association (in Foster's case a deeply inauthentic one) in the minds of whites with plantation slavery. The first song yearned for freedom, the second for "home"—in slavery. In an evening of jubilee songs, billed as "genuine soul music of the slave cabins" and "wild" emanations of "children of nature," the familiar, European-sounding strains of "My Old Kentucky Home" offered white audiences an "elevated" interlude that to them remained "Black."

THE HAMPTON COLORED STUDENTS.

When the Hampton Colored Students and similar groups included Foster's plantation melodies in fundraising concerts, they provided a familiar sound to audiences more accustomed to minstrelsy than to Black spirituals. This stamped a minstrel song as more authentically "Black" than it was.

Hampton's neatly dressed students and other "Jubilee Singers" personified Black aspirations and respectability as they appealed to sympathetic whites for charity. The Fisk Free Colored School in Nashville assembled the most famous group, which toured for years to raise enough money to erect a campus building. Crucially, the collegiate singers also unlocked an American entertainment business that had previously been almost entirely sealed against their race.

For Black musicians and performers new opportunities came with costs. More and more nonwhite singers, dancers, and actors made it onstage in the 1870s, 1880s, and 1890s, but whites still produced the shows, owned the venues, and controlled the content. Blackface minstrelsy was a known commercial quantity, and Foster's plantation melodies supplied reliable inauthentically authentic "Black" material. When formerly enslaved Americans and their children took the stage in the post–Civil War decades, Foster's music became more convincingly "true" to white listeners. It was not just a song about Black people but a song perceived to be by and of them. The white men of blackface minstrelsy posed as race scholars, skilled in showing the ways of Black folk. White people liked to believe that such performances required no skill for those with African blood endowed with native-born musical and dancing ability. No significant production involving Black talent during this era escaped the dark shadow of the "minstrel mask." The genre and its racist tropes were sealed into American show business.

A pair of spectacularly gifted sisters from Sacramento, California, worked Foster's "My Old Kentucky Home" into their signature 1870s act. Anna Madah Hyers (ca. 1855–1929) and Emma Louise Hyers (ca. 1857–1901) grew up middle class in Sacramento during California's gold rush years. Even as small children, their lives revolved around music. Their father owned a barbershop and hired piano and vocal instructors for the girls even as white state legislators banned Black children like them from public schools and men like their father from voting or testifying in legal cases involving whites. At their formal debut in 1867, the sisters were twelve and ten years old. As teenagers, Anna Madah and Emma Louise performed operatic arias in Italian. Their "mature and perfect" voices invited comparisons to white artists like the "Swedish nightingale," Jenny Lind, and critics referred to them as "young ladies." At such moments, the future seemed to promise respect and equal treatment across the color line. By the time they reached New England in the 1870s, Anna Madah (soprano) and Emma Louise (contralto) formed the first all-Black classical music stage act. Their very presence in these spaces defied conventional notions about Black women, a group represented up to this point by black-faced white men in skirts. Instead, the Hyers Sisters' versatile work as singers and actors broke racial and gender stereotypes (Emma Louise often adjusted her voice to tenor and performed in drag as her sister's love interest in operatic duets) while demanding respect as professional artists.

But the classical act didn't sustain the sisters for long. Over time they added popular music to their repertoire, including "My Old Kentucky Home." In 1876, the Hyers Sisters' manager commissioned Joseph Bradford to write a "Great Moral Musical Drama" tracing an arc from slavery to freedom to thriving Black citizenship in a renewed nation. Born outside Nashville into the slaveholding elite, Bradford was studying at the U.S. Naval Academy at Annapolis when hostilities erupted in 1861. The youth enlisted in the Union fleet and spent the war maintaining the blockade that shut off cotton exports to Europe—the Confederacy's economic lifeline. Bradford's father disowned him for this act of disloyalty. After the war, Joseph took his mother's name and embarked on a stage career that eventually brought him to Boston, where his progressive views on race were more acceptable.

Most northerners supported emancipation, but in the decade since that achievement questions about the peaceful absorption of formerly enslaved southerners into the nation remained unresolved, largely because it remained implicitly and explicitly resisted. This was violently true in the former slave states. In 1875, in Clinton, Mississippi, where Black men had taken part in elections, an altercation between white Democrats and predominantly Black Republicans erupted at a large Republican Party rally. Days of white attacks on Black citizens followed, leaving some fifty dead. The governor's pleas for aid from Washington went ignored. Similar atrocities went unpunished in South Carolina. Northern white support for Reconstruction had weakened while southern white Democrats reclaimed political control, state by state. As the Hyers Sisters took Joseph Bradford's *Out of Bondage* on the road, the new president, Rutherford B. Hayes, ordered the last federal troops out of the South and shut down the remaining Freedmen's Bureau offices.

Ex-slaves were on their own. The play's "slight" plot, woven through with classical, popular, and original music, aimed at rallying support for civil rights and demonstrating that formerly enslaved people could thrive in a just nation.

To make this simple but increasingly contested message palatable for white audiences, Joseph Bradford included familiar minstrel humor and sentiment. *Out of Bondage* opens in a cabin, with characters bearing stereotyped names, speaking largely in "dialect," and singing a great deal. But Bradford also created something new in American theater by focusing entirely on a loving Black family and leaving out white people altogether. As Union forces approach, the parents (Uncle Eph and Aunt Naomi) and their offspring confront a dilemma. Their enslavers have fled, but Eph decides that "it's too late for us to make any changes, old woman." Hearing "de shout of freedom," the young people, includ-

The 1876 play *Out of Bondage* featured the sisters Anna Madah and Emma Louise Hyers with the "Negro minstrel" Sam Lucas in "The Only Colored Dramatic Company in the World." The plot follows a family from enslavement to freedom in the North, where they support themselves by performing a repertoire that spans "My Old Kentucky Home" and Verdi.

ing Emma Louise and Anna Madah, bid farewell and head north with "hope and joy the heart can never tell."

Years have passed when the second act begins. After much searching, the children and parents reunite in the North, where they live in "elegant" surroundings and dress for work in fine clothes. Back on the plantation the children had sounded "like twenty-seben mockin' birds singin' in a magnolia tree in full bloom," a talent the four young people have turned into paying work. At a musical recital the parents are seated "among the white folks" because "here there is no distinction of color, all are free and equal." The concert included the tower scene duet from Verdi's *Il trovatore* alongside "My Old Kentucky Home."

With the *Out of Bondage* tour of 1876–1877, the Hyers Sisters marked a path out of the wilderness of the slaveholding era: a path in which hope, faith, and demonstrated talent and respectability would enable Black Americans to overcome white prejudice. Mark Twain beat his own trail to their shows, vowing he would journey "a mile and a half in the most furious tempest of wind and snow . . . to see the plantation sketches of the Hyers Troupe and hear their exquisite music." New York's *Evening Telegram* declared that their "refinement, culture, and attractiveness" merited "first-class audiences and first-class appreciation." Still, the playwright and his stars threw their white audiences plenty of minstrel bones to gnaw on. It is unclear whom the joke lands on when Uncle Eph declares, "Yankees is a heap bigger fools than I took 'em for" to "pay to hear cullud folks sing."

While the Hyers Sisters played the New England–New York circuit, a "retired negro trader" in Kentucky used Foster's melody to exonerate himself, mock abolitionists, and defend slavery as a benevolent institution. Tarleton Arterburn and his brothers had formerly trafficked in human beings, penning them in "iron-barred coops." In 1876, his office building was slated for demolition, and Arterburn was cleaning the place out. A reporter from *The Courier-Journal* called on the merchant, who flourished an old "bill of sale of a woman who is still with me . . . the best cook in Louisville." The year "My Old Kentucky Home" was published, it showed that Arterburn had paid $675 for nineteen-year-old Cindy. Around the same time, none other than Harriet Beecher Stowe came to his establishment intent on liberating one of his chattels.

Arterburn shouted for the "bright mulatto girl." When Cindy arrived, Arterburn explained, "This lady wishes to take you to New York, where you will be free and have a good time. Show that pretty foot of yours and tell her whether you wish to go or not." This command he concluded with "the wink." Understanding the white trader's intent, she answered, "I sorter 'spects Cindy 'drather stay in Kentuck." He then told her to entertain Stowe and her escorts with "My Old Kentucky Home." They applauded and then left empty-handed.

It was a fact that by the 1850s the Arterburn brothers' slave pens were a regular stop for tourists visiting Louisville, giving Tarleton repeat opportunities to tell his tale. But that is where facts end. Harriet Beecher Stowe never came to Kentucky after Foster's song was published. Tarleton Arterburn used the melody in a manufactured memory that "proved" slavery in Kentucky was preferable not just to bondage in the cane and cotton fields of the Deep South but to freedom in the North. The slaver delighted in the idea of Cindy telling Mrs. Stowe to "weep no more." Arterburn's apocryphal tale was believable to *Courier-Journal* readers and to a nation that left Black people throughout the South undefended.

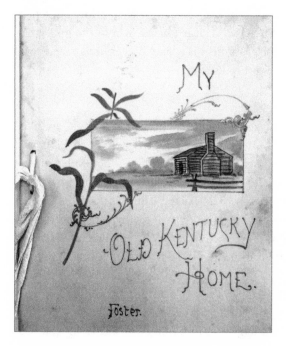

The cover of this undated volume aimed at the gift book market featured a ripe corn top. Such books introduced Foster's song to a new generation of readers.

Popular illustrated "gift books" of the 1880s and 1890s used "My Old Kentucky Home" in less overtly political ways. The gracious but lost plantation lifestyle they depicted was largely the life of white enslavers. One publisher called the story "touching to eyes and ears." Marketed to northern, middle-class readers, especially women and girls, one "My Old Kentucky Home" volume came tied with a ribbon, its pale, vellum cover embellished with a cabin. The Boston publisher Ticknor and Company produced a more successful "Old Kentucky Home" in 1888. Its gilded pink-and-green floral cover resembled the parlor walls where such books (inscribed to sweethearts, mothers, sisters, or children) frequently landed. Each pair of Foster's lyrics got its own picturesque scene.

Foster's "My Old Kentucky Home" mentioned only a cabin, but the Ticknor and Company gift book opens with a pillared "big house." Fine horses stand tied to a post near the door. An enslaved couple strolls in the foreground. Three pages later, "Hard Times" have come to stay. The house is abandoned; its gate hangs akimbo, and the roof is caving in. A well-dressed white woman of the 1880s crying into her handkerchief in an elaborate dining room illustrates the chorus "Weep no more, my lady." A Black butler bearing a silver tray is poised to serve her, yet the "lady" bows her head in sorrow for *her* lost Kentucky home "far away." White women readers found someone to identify with.

A parallel story picks up in the second verse and tears are here as well. "The darkies have to part" showed a Black woman on a cabin porch, her back to the viewer, holding an apron to her eyes. Far in the distance, a tiny man on horseback drives a male figure down the road. The show of emotion from the white "lady" paves the way for a reality the white reader could never know. The tearful scenes exist side by side, as if the losses (one of a beloved home, the other of a beloved human) carry equal weight. The song's final verse reverts to the Gilded Age present. To illustrate "The head must bow and the back will have to bend / Wherever the darky may go," a gray-headed man in ragged trousers, eyes downcast, presents himself at a genteel doorway, hat in hand. A frowning white gentleman points off to the side, and the final pages reveal the man's fate. Twenty years after slavery has ended, he is in a cane field. A mounted overseer holds a whip. Blackness is passivity, labor, hardship, degradation. Tears change nothing.

Along with the work it did mediating whites' relationships with the

The Boston publisher Ticknor and Company issued a series of richly illustrated "song" books in the 1880s. In engraving for the chorus "Weep no more, my lady" and lines from the third verse, "The head must bow and the back will have to bend / Wherever the darky may go," the illustrator Charles Copeland provided contemporary scenes of racialized social, economic, and emotional hierarchy.

history of their fellow Black Americans, "My Old Kentucky Home" kept adapting to novel creative forms. Lantern slides offered a late nineteenth-century theatrical View-Master experience. Between the 1890s and the second decade of the twentieth century, audiences viewed lantern slide shows in darkened, communal spaces, between vaudeville theater acts, during reel changes in nickelodeon theaters, community halls, lodges, and schools. Six vibrant, hand-painted glass slides told the tale of Foster's song, but others illustrated Bible stories, the life of George Washington, and famous works of literature.

Joseph Boggs Beale is considered "America's first great screen artist" for his understanding of continuity, visual storytelling, and the use of

shadow and light, and he produced more than two thousand lantern slide drawings for the manufacturer C. W. Briggs Company. Growing up in Philadelphia, he attended the pro-slavery *Uncle Tom's Cabin* at Sanford's Opera House. He also cheered the new president when Lincoln passed through the city in 1861. When the Confederacy invaded Pennsylvania in 1863, Beale joined the reserves as a regimental artist. Beale's "My Old Kentucky Home" replicated blackface motifs— exaggerated facial features and stereotypes including a propensity for unfettered dancing, eating watermelon, and hunting possum. But the artist was unflinchingly direct about slavery, far more direct than Foster himself or Ticknor and Company's gift book. Beale swept his viewers into a Black family's tidy cabin brightened with decorative touches. There is no looking away when a white man's actions land a husband and father of five on an auction block. The same distinct characters who dance and play the banjo by the cornfield in the first slide gather around a collapsed and weeping mother in the next. The lyrics say to "weep no more," but the tears continue to the next frame, in which a man with a whip pulls the father away as his littlest child reaches up to him in vain.

No other illustrator of "My Old Kentucky Home" took such a direct approach to Foster's oblique reference to "Hard Times." Beale's illustrations relate Black pain and white iniquity with Stowe-like emotion and sensation. His slides did not tap into abstract or universal experiences of separation or homesickness. For theatergoers to sing along to a piano plying the old song in the dim glow of the magic lantern would have been incredibly morbid. Beale's illuminated "My Old Kentucky Home" stood at odds with minstrelsy's white myth, which transmogrified the anguish of slavery into white nostalgia. Predictably, sales were weak for the "My Old Kentucky Home" series.

Prior to moving pictures, projected lantern slide shows related songs, historical events, poems, and Bible stories, often accompanied by live music. For his rendition of Foster's "My Old Kentucky Home" (1896–1897), the artist Joseph Boggs Beale used colorfully painted glass slides to create a tense image of a man being parted from his family.

. . .

The most revolutionary change to come to "My Old Kentucky Home" and to minstrelsy in the decades after the Civil War involved not the medium or technology that transmitted it but who did the singing. By 1900, the celebrated purveyors of blackface (their exploits are collected in a richly illustrated 1911 volume, *Monarchs of Minstrelsy*) had nearly vanished from venues like Sam Sanford's Opera House. Some men of Sanford's generation found easier lives writing handbooks for do-it-yourself minstrel shows, which flourished in community groups all over the country. The reigning stars of the post–Civil War blackface stage were known as "Negro minstrels," literally "Blacks in blackface." Hearing "My Old Kentucky Home" performed by Black people rather than by whites pretending to be Black enhanced the authenticity of Foster's song for white audiences and possibly made its soothing notes and destructive stereotypes even more convincing.

The "Negro minstrel" Tom Fletcher (1873–1954) grew up in Portsmouth, Ohio, with a view across the river to Kentucky. His father shoveled coal for steam-powered boats, and his mother cooked for the family of a local judge. As a treat, his mother's employers took young Fletcher with them to see a touring "Tom Show." A few performers with bit parts looked like him, and Fletcher decided then that he too would be "a showman." He learned to sing "My Old Kentucky Home" and "Oh! Susanna," practiced dance steps, and volunteered to hand out flyers whenever a minstrel show came through town. His father idolized Sam Lucas, a Black singer, composer, and actor who toured with the Hyers Sisters in *Out of Bondage* and became the first person of his race to play Uncle Tom onstage. At fifteen Tom joined Howard's Novelty Colored Minstrels as a drummer, blacking up for nightly shows with ten or twelve fellow players in small Ohio, Kentucky, and Indiana towns. He recalled suffering from cold and the shadow of threat. The local people were "very tough on us." Black residents of these areas "knew their place," and the troupe regularly passed road signs directed at people of his complexion warning, "Read and Run." The entertainers were permitted entry, but audiences, who paid to see the shows (Foster songs were staples), taunted them with slurs. It was the price to pay to send his mother $5 a week.

Tom Fletcher wanted safer, better-paying work and more creative license, but with the exception of the considerably more respectable Hyers Sisters, the traveling minstrel acts of the 1880s demanded the same degrading role—ten or twelve poorly paid Black men under a white manager. The range of artistic expression was so narrow, Fletcher later remembered, it could come down to the size and shape of a minstrel's exaggerated makeup mouth. It therefore seemed like a step forward when the Hyers Sisters' Black stage manager, Billy McClain, envisioned a big entertainment that would permit dozens of singers, dancers, and musicians to showcase their abilities.

Billy McClain's landmark musical productions, *The South Before the War* (1892) and *Black America* (1895), advertised themselves as grander reflections of Black people than any entertainment in the United States to date. Born in Indianapolis in 1866, Billy performed in bands and minstrel acts as a teen. With a "fertile brain and boundless energy," McClain spread his talents across minstrel comedy, acting, dancing, boxing, songwriting, and playwriting. He had gall, too. In 1880s or 1890s Kansas City, police took him into custody "for having too much jewelry for a colored man," until he proved that the $7,000 worth of diamonds, "37 trunks, 13 hat boxes, 24 rugs, 14 brass instruments, 3 typewriters, 9 bird cages, 7 dogs" were rightfully his. McClain and his singer-actress wife, Cordelia, were Black theater royalty.

In 1892, McClain pitched an idea for a traveling show to a Louisville political boss who operated a string of burlesque and vaudeville venues across the Ohio Valley. Why pay other shows to fill his theaters when, with Billy's help, John Whallen could produce the entertainment and pay himself? Lavish sets would provide a backdrop for life in antebellum times, a "picturesque spectacle" mixing plantation minstrel fare with the latest songs and dances. "Boss Whallen" ran Louisville's Democratic Party out of his Buckingham Theater, where scantily clad women amused male audiences. The Whallen machine unashamedly suppressed Black Republican votes, but McClain would have to overlook politics to access Whallen's capital. Whallen knew the fantasy of "old plantation life is always enjoyable" to white people, and nostalgia made "My Old Kentucky Home" a reliable favorite. The Buckingham Theater had entered a "realistic" slave cabin covered in picturesque vines in the Louisville Commercial Club's 1888 parade of industry and commerce. The float contained a living, smiling Black man, waving from the window and met with cheers. Those who knew Reverend Drake, once enslaved

The Buckingham Theater's float for Louisville's 1888 parade of commerce drew applause with a waving "uncle" inside his "Old Kentucky Home." The cabin was likely repurposed from the set of a "Tom" play—a perennial entertainment loosely based on *Uncle Tom's Cabin.*

but now a temperance preacher, might have laughed to see him on the payroll of a man whose burlesque business depended on free-flowing alcohol.

With *The South Before the War,* Whallen gave McClain a unique opportunity. Black people had almost no access to leadership roles in show business. Billy hired nearly a hundred Black performers. The call went out from the Buckingham: "Clever Colored Talent Wanted Quick." "Ladies and Gents of experience, refinement, and culture in Cake Walking, Shouting, Singing, Plantation Melodies, Quadrilles, Wing, Reel and Buck Dancing" were invited to apply. "Also all Sports of the Ancient and Modern Africans, Colored Orchestra, etc. Telegraph at once." The ad did not mention that to cater to whites' fascination with slavery days, these experienced dancers and singers would be required to pick *real cotton* in the ersatz field that served as the show's visual anchor. Indeed, the scripted elements of *The South Before the War* was as racially demeaning as any minstrel show, indicating how painfully limited McClain's influence was over the content. One scene that passed for slapstick called for a steamboat named the *Robert E. Lee* to dock at a levee where resting stevedores were pricked in the feet with needles or prodded with hot irons. "Can you smell him cooking?" one character asked.

Such was the context for the "pickaninny chorus" performance of "My Old Kentucky Home" in "Under a Southern Sky," a skit within the 1892 show. Many years after escaping bondage in Kentucky, Uncle Eph returns to his wife and children, frozen in place on the plantation where he left them before the Civil War. Eph collapses after the son of his enslaver attacks him for abandoning "old master" on his deathbed. The Black children sing him out of this world and into the next with "My Old Kentucky Home." The star roles—Eph and his wife, Chloe—went to a pair of white blackface veterans. But the national entertainment paper, the *New York Clipper,* confirmed that "genuine colored men and women" filled all other parts and excelled in the musical and dance numbers.

The South Before the War toured as far south as New Orleans and as far west as Chicago, giving steady work to the McClains and the "2 Pickaninny Bands, Grand Colored Chorus of 50 Voices, 40 Buck Dancers, 4 Quartettes, 30 Jubilee Shouters" that rounded out the company. In Washington, D.C., *The South Before the War* was sold out, and one newspaper noted the audience was "equally divided between whites and blacks." The white press praised the show for its superior "antics of niggerdom." Objectionable as the plot points and white commentaries were, Black theatergoers came to witness the artistry onstage, expressions of resistance (or at least survival) in a society where Black opportunities were so frequently crushed. McClain's success was a triumph. As lynching spread unchecked, he treated the troupe with dignity and embodied the possibility of promotion in the business. Though he answered to white men, Billy had proved he could make a hit, and Boss Whallen awarded him a medal "for successful stage management."

McClain's next project aimed for a more uplifting effect. In 1895, McClain persuaded Nate Salsbury, producer of *Buffalo Bill's Wild West* show, to let him use its Brooklyn location and repurpose its log cabins as slave dwellings for a new extravaganza. Billed as the music director, McClain probably created, wrote, and managed *Black America,* by far the largest all-Black show to date, with a cast of five hundred. That summer, it ran twice a day in Ambrose Park, capacity seven thousand. It went on tour with a leaner troupe, occupying large outdoor and indoor

The *South Before the War* company posed with the group's private Pullman car, "Hattie," in Merrill, Wisconsin, in the 1890s. Bunking on the train was a necessity when hotels would not accept Black guests. This show—which launched Billy McClain to the highest position held by a Black man in American theater management—toured widely.

venues in the Northeast, and closed at Madison Square Garden. Summer was the slow season for regular minstrel and vaudeville shows, so McClain had his pick of Black talent. He selected his wife, Cordelia, as the featured soloist for "My Old Kentucky Home."

In the 1890s, respected social scientists theorized that Black Americans, having failed to adapt to freedom, were likely to die out. The "Black disappearance hypothesis" put the onus on the race for allegedly innate pathologies; W. E. B. Du Bois and a generation of Black leaders ran themselves ragged refuting white supremacist ideologies based on biased data. *Black America,* an Epcot-like edutainment plugged as an "EXHIBITION OF NEGRO LIFE AND CHARACTER," was McClain's effort to assert that Black America and Black Americans were not going away. The show's finale aimed to clinch the argument that Blacks' evolution to full citizenship was real: an all-Black detachment from the U.S. Ninth Cavalry executed precise drills to an all-Black marching band. This was the age of Darwin, so the show presented the musical race rising to such orderliness from the primitive Congolese jungle to the cotton field, showcasing the "phenomenal melody of his voice." Prior to curtain time, twenty-five-cent ticket holders wandered the grounds, also the performers' living quarters. They could see an acre

"My Old Kentucky Home" was sung in operatic fashion in *Black America,* an 1895 traveling show involving hundreds of performers who danced, executed military formations, and picked and pressed cotton. The show might have introduced "The Laughing Song" (*pictured top left*), which the first Black recording artist, George W. Johnson, made into a record three years later.

of real cotton and watch it ginned and pressed into bales. They peeked in on supposedly natural scenes of Black people at leisure, playing cards or courting. "These are not actors," declared one newspaper notice.

Before opening day, the cast paraded down Fifth Avenue. Most went on foot, but Cordelia McClain, as a prima donna, processed by "open carriage." Twice a day during the run, she appeared in formal dress singing "My Old Kentucky Home" in European concert style, backed by a "Monster Chorus." The song was presented as refined—like "Madame Cordelia" herself. Just a handful of Black women had appeared on American stages, and Foster's melody, an ornament in so many parlors, was a means to illustrate a Black woman's respectability. Cordelia sang the song straight, but how she handled the lyrics is not known. Did Madame McClain stick to the first verse with its vaguely interrupted plantation myth, "'Tis summer, the darkies are gay," followed by "Hard Times"? Or did Cordelia McClain sing it through—with its indictment of the trade in human flesh? Did the audience cry? Whatever dignity she brought to the atmosphere did not last; in the next number, "Watermelon Smiling on the Vine," a burro led by an aged "uncle" rolled up with a cartload of melons. A "mad scramble" ensued, with dozens of performers cracking open and "uninhibitedly" devouring the bright red fruit.

Ricocheting from racist burlesque to liberation, *Black America* concluded by dropping twenty-foot-high banners of John Brown, Abraham Lincoln, Harriet Beecher Stowe, and Frederick Douglass from above. McClain insisted on including the leading "lion" of his race, who had died early that year, while spectators got the message that Black progress had come chiefly from the actions of white people. *Black Americans* were, at any rate, on American soil to stay. White producers got to see "colored talent" by the hundreds, and many participants' show business careers leaped forward as a result. Still, they were forced to live in "slave cabins" on a reconstructed "plantation," pick fake cotton, and remain "in character" as ticket holders wandered through their quarters. The McClains were native northerners, professionals like many of their fellow cast members in *Black America,* though Salsbury's promotional materials (with an eye to authenticity) pretended that "all these negroes came from the South" and were not "show people" but "genuine." In exchange for the hope of progress, the performers validated plantation fantasies that whitewashed Black Americans' histori-

Abolitionist heroes marked the finale of the 1895 extravaganza, *Black America*. John Brown is pictured above.

cal nightmare. White America has demanded similar compromises ever since.

The cumulative effect could be souring. *Black America* drew good crowds, but supporting what amounted to an entire town proved too costly, and the planned European tour never materialized. McClain grew bitter as white producers and venue owners siphoned profits off Black backs. In a dispatch from California, where an 1899 revival of *The South Before the War* was doing good business, he reported that "My Old Kentucky Home" never failed to make "the most stupid person exert themselves by way of applause." It is as authentic an opinion as McClain ever committed to paper.

During a period historians characterize as "the nadir of American race relations," perhaps 200,000 people saw *Black America*. Whole professions and institutions stood closed to Black people. Lynching reached gruesome heights. While Billy and Cordelia found a measure of success in the 1890s, white mobs killed thirteen hundred Black people with impunity, and hundreds, perhaps thousands, more were executed after rushed trials with all-white juries and no constitutional protections. By the turn of the century, the McClains had decamped for Australia. They lived and performed overseas for much of the next two decades. McClain wrote to Indianapolis's Black newspaper, *The Freeman,* that he would return from self-imposed exile in France only when his people could somehow stand up to the theatrical establishment that humiliated and shut them out. With white-owned theaters refusing to book Black-produced shows, it was impossible to sing their own songs and tell their own stories. The "Negro must wake up and march on," he urged. Just how one did this in the face of violence-backed systemic racism was unclear.

The first generation of professional Black musicians and actors who rose through Negro minstrelsy and Billy McClain's "cavalcades" regularly performed "My Old Kentucky Home." Some joined segregated guilds like the Musicians' Mutual Protective Union and made it into the middle class. Top stars (McClain with his trunks full of fashionable outfits or a bejeweled Sam Lucas) flaunted their wealth, proving success was possible, but only by perpetuating to some degree disparaging racial caricatures. Cordelia McClain's operatic presentation of "My Old Kentucky Home" tried to wrap the minstrel classic in dignified Black femininity, but overall, sung by "genuine" Black performers, the message remained one of Old South nostalgia. Black artists were told to be grateful for work where they could get it. All the same, they were committed to delivering transcendent music and dancing. With only a sliver of Black Americans permitted to work outside sharecropping, domestic service, and the lowest-paid manual labor, the price of the minstrel mask was worth paying for a shot at fame and the opportunity to practice one's art.

From plays like the Hyers Sisters' *Out of Bondage* to dark theaters where Joseph Beale's magic lantern shows cast their spell, from Louisville's Commercial Club parade to the simulated working plantation of McClain's over-the-top *Black America,* a cabin represented "My Old Kentucky Home." It made sense. A cabin is the only dwelling "My Old Kentucky Home" mentions. White people readily pictured Black people in cabins, and many wished they would stay in these poor, rural homes rather than crowd into cities. The iconic cabin was also (sometimes mythically) celebrated as the birthplace of presidents. The log structures sheltered Appalachian families and western "pioneers," too, potentially connecting the melody to a shared national heritage.

During my family's visit to Evergreen Plantation—where the cabins Clarence John Laughlin photographed still stand—my young children raced up and down double spiral staircases to the loggia of the grand house facing the river that carried the cane sugar that made Evergreen's white family rich. We also explored the double row of twenty-two cabins behind the house, set precisely along a live oak alley. It made me dizzy with déjà vu. I had looked so many times at Laughlin's photograph before the day I stepped onto their rectilinear thresholds, portals into so many lives. Whereas the "big house" was full of furniture and objects, these broom swept spaces, though fully three-dimensional, were absolutely vacant.

Evergreen Plantation's "slave dwellings" are exceptional for being so well preserved. Since the Civil War, thousands of burial and housing sites have collapsed or were demolished, sometimes plowed under by tractors, erasing them from the landscape. A movement has begun to reclaim and restore them to the national story. It is an effort that faces headwinds. Our culture teaches us that good tourists admire and often aestheticize the past through its architecture. We are not taught to question either the past or the architecture. The long list of enslaved people's names posted on one of the cabin porches by those in charge of Evergreen Plantation failed to animate the structures. It did not then occur to me to connect them to my state anthem about the Kentuckian who perishes in "the field where the sugar-canes grow."

4

THE SUN SHINES BRIGHT

White Reunification

In the first decades of the new century, "My Old Kentucky Home" became a newly beloved hymn, sounding forth in officially sanctioned public settings. It smoothed the path to a cross-sectional American reunion defined exclusively to meet white needs, feelings, and desires, a unity that self-consciously discriminated against its Black citizens. The "home" of Foster's 1853 melody was clearly a cabin housing enslaved people, but in the early twentieth century the "Kentucky Home" appeared more and more often as a spacious plantation house. Beginning with elite heritage groups, some of which overtly memorialized Confederates and the Confederacy, fascination with the planter class and its homes surged. A growing stream of tourists set out to explore their country, including below the Mason-Dixon Line. It dawned on Kentucky's white leaders that they could lure visitors *and* enhance their state's image with a song that felt inviting ("My"), nostalgic and reassuring ("Old"), exotic ("Kentucky"), and universal ("Home"). Amid mass immigration, industrial strife, women's suffrage, world war, and racial unrest, the classic tune, a white tonic spoken through a supposedly Black tongue, evoked rural safety, gentility, and a lost world where Black people knew their place. In the lexicon of white remembrance few words were rendered as useful as "lost," especially in the sense of the Lost Cause, which was used to lend the defeated Confederacy a nobility that required a historical oxymoron white America was willing to accept: benign, even benevolent slavery.

Black leaders and performers remembered the past quite differently. One newspaper cried impatiently in 1900, "We have long thought there has been a little too much bragging about the joys of the old Kentucky home."

White America formed a consensus around racial segregation and severely limited nonwhites' civil and human rights. The U.S. Supreme Court upheld excluding Black people from public facilities in *Plessy v. Ferguson,* branding them with "a badge of servitude," as one dissenter wrote. Facing this onslaught, Tuskegee College's president, Booker T. Washington, offered white America a conciliation that many leaders and philanthropists gladly accepted. In all things social he proposed that "Negro" and white "can be as separate as the fingers" of a hand. In 1895, Washington promised (with the help of white donors) to train members of his race to pursue and be content with agricultural work and modest skilled trades. Genteel, moderate whites viewed Washington's approach as an acceptable compromise. For some Black southerners, it brought needed resources, but it was at best an infuriating feint imposed by a racially hostile America. And it was at this moment in our history that the Foster family, sensing an opportunity, broke decades of silence. In 1896, the songwriter's brother Morrison published *Biography, Songs, and Musical Compositions of Stephen C. Foster.*

Following the publication of the Foster biography, Pittsburgh mobilized on behalf of its native son. Nearly fifty thousand gathered in Highland Park in 1900 to witness the unveiling of a life-size memorial. Foster's only child, Marion Foster Welch (who had been suing for access to royalties from his music), pulled a rope, and a sheet dropped to reveal a pensive bronze figure dressed in a cravat and tailcoat, absorbed in penning a song. At his feet a ragged, balding Black "uncle" with a wide minstrel grin plucked a banjo, his face tilted upward to the great songwriter. In the Italian sculptor Giuseppe Moretti's arrangement, Foster's inspiration came directly from "lowly" Black folks. The master converted it to music people around the world sang and loved. Three thousand schoolchildren entertained the throng with Stephen Foster's romping minstrel numbers, plantation melodies, and a few parlor favorites. *The Pittsburgh Press* pronounced that "so long as people have hearts to respond to mel-

The St. Louis society photographer and Union veteran Fitz W. Guerin staged this tableau during the Spanish-American War. The Confederate gray and Union blue united to liberate "Little Cuba" (represented by a girl) from her European shackles. "My Old Kentucky Home" became a point of shared nostalgic pleasure for whites in the North and South in the 1890s as they colonized new territories and consolidated racial segregation at home.

odies which perfectly and fully express the best sentiments of domestic life," the name of Foster would rest secure in their "affections." "My Old Kentucky Home" was hailed in the press as a simple, universal tune about family, home, and longing for better days gone by.

At the turn of the twentieth century, a "romance of reunion" soaked American culture, symbolized by handshakes between old men who had battled each other in the 1860s. An urban, industrial, and increasingly foreign-born society stoked fears among the native-born that their nation was weakening, dangerously diluted. True Anglo-Saxon manhood was thought to be under threat. If not defended, another loss. The ideal white southern gentleman "permanently cast in a military mold" offered an insurance policy, ready to protect abstractions like honor, nation, and womanhood with a kind of manliness that office jobs and acquisitiveness were supposedly bleeding out of northerners. When the United States declared war on Spain in 1898, the first military conflict since the Civil War, members of the House of Representatives sang both "Dixie" and "The Battle Hymn of the Republic." As they readied to fight an external enemy, they acknowledged past divisions and mutual respect. Some believed the "splendid little war" that released Cuba from Spanish rule and made American colonies of the Philippines, Guam, and Puerto Rico would accomplish "the permanent obliteration of all sectional distrusts."

"My Old Kentucky Home" was not a popular Civil War melody, but it worked a nostalgic magic when the mood was retrospective. In 1896, an Italian street performer sang it in front of a Philadelphia hotel. An onlooker described a "soldierly-looking man with flashing dark eyes" as a "former Kentuckian ruined by the ravages of war," who wept as he tipped the singer. The northerner who observed the scene was equally touched.

This spirit of whites eagerly overcoming "the late unpleasantness" brought Union veterans to Louisville, Kentucky, in 1895 for their annual reunion—the first time the encampment took place in a former slave state. Local leaders, including prominent Confederates, welcomed them, and the economic boon 150,000 visitors brought with them, with parades and fireworks. Five years later, another mammoth crowd descended on the city for the United Confederate Veterans (UCV) annual pilgrimage. The Grand Army of the Republic organized early after the war, while the UCV began only in 1889. But it grew quickly. And not alone. By the time the southern veterans gathered in Louisville, the United Daughters of the Confederacy (UDC) had 412 local chapters whose work spread Lost Cause culture through the former rebel states and beyond.

It was an age in love with "heritage." Sociability under the cope of Anglo-Saxon superiority drew elite (or aspiring elite) white native-born Americans to heritage societies that granted them an elevated position in the "family of man." Members of the Sons of the American Revolution (founded in 1889) and its sister organization, the Daughters of the American Revolution (1890), had to prove descent from a veteran of the war. The Colonial Dames (1891) were more lenient; no military service was needed, only a colonial-era forebear. No one needed to say that descendants of colonial-era Native Americans and Africans enslaved during that period were not welcome. With foreign-born residents composing up to 40 percent of U.S. cities, these affinity groups granted important "old immigrant" credentials. At Louisville's 1900 encampment, the various Sons and Daughters intertwined: "Confederate women who are also Colonial Dames" organized a special reception.

The city of Louisville had been overwhelmingly pro-Union in the 1860s, but in 1900 the visiting "grays" were told, "Make yourself at home, boys. The old Kentucky home is yours." "My Old Kentucky Home" was one of two songs the Confederate Glee Club performed for the reunion's opening ceremonies. On the final night, at a concert for ten thousand in Reunion Hall, a local minstrel bandleader drilled sixty singers and musicians, guaranteed to be "typical Southern darkies." "My Old Kentucky Home" closed out the program's first half, and between songs the audience was treated to "plantation scenes" and madcap "buck and wing dancing." "Darkies Sing" ran the next day's headline.

The Foster family had correctly spied the opportunity. These mass performances helped turn "My Old Kentucky Home" into the celebratory ritual it remains today. They were hardly uniquely astute. The opportunities for reconciliatory nostalgia were everywhere in evidence.

The Daughters of the Confederacy proved to be fabulously effective fundraisers, organizers, and lobbyists. Up went a phalanx of monuments to Confederate soldiers and heroes across the region—some even outside the South. Members promoted a comprehensive pro-Confederate version of history by supporting scholarship, stocking library shelves with approved books, and inserting their interpretation into statewide school texts. Correcting "wicked falsehoods" (including the idea that the system of bondage was cruel) became a guiding aim for the Daughters of the Confederacy. Their publications asserted that slavery had no part in causing the conflict, which they insisted was a battle over the principle of states' rights. Their slaveholding parents and grandparents were not "rebels." A catechism for Confederate-descended children asked, "How were the slaves treated?" The answer: "With great kindness and care in nearly all cases."

Most people who heard "My Old Kentucky Home" picked up only the first verse and chorus, but attentive Daughters of the Confederacy like Nannie Ringo Mitchell in Paris, Kentucky, detected dangerous similarities between Foster's popular tune and the antislavery tale of

Uncle Tom's Cabin. Mitchell, a member of the UDC's local chapter, was compiling a book of approved Lost Cause songs and decided to bring "My Old Kentucky Home" in line with the group's racial and historical dogma. "My Old Kentucky Home" is sandwiched between "The Conquered Banner" and "God Save the South" in the 1901 volume, *Songs of the Confederacy and Plantation Melodies.* (It was not the first nor last rewrite the song underwent.) The old minstrel melody appeared as Foster wrote it up to the last verse, after which Mitchell inserted her own ending. Nobody had been sold away. "Hard Times" didn't blast a man from his family to the sugarcane field, but instead sent him gently to his heavenly reward for a life of (involuntary) service.

> *At last he sleeps in the meadow near the shore,*
> *Of virtues no tombstone does tell,*
> *Secure he rests and of trouble knows no more,*
> *For to slav'ry he has bidden farewell;*
> *The weary load he has borne beyond the dome,*
> *Where ever shines glory's own light,*
> *His task is done and he's in his heav'nly home,*
> *So My Old Kentucky Home, good-night!*

The songbook went through multiple editions, which the Daughters of the Confederacy advertised for years in the magazines *Confederate Veteran* and *The Lost Cause.* Mitchell packaged and mailed orders out of her bluegrass Kentucky home.

A 1906 "playlet" called *My Old Kentucky Home* that made the rounds of northern vaudeville theaters reveals the focus shifting from the home of a slave to the planter class. The plot centers on a romance across the Mason-Dixon Line, and the only thing standing in the way of the geographically challenged lovers is a cartoonlike unreconstructed ex-Confederate—"Colonel Calhoun Is My Name, Sir. Doggone Them Northerners." The stage was set with a mansion covered in picturesque vines. As the curtain lifts, Calhoun's daughter, Jasmine, plays "My Old Kentucky Home" on the piano. Grant Adair, a northern tourist driving through Dixie, zooms up to the house in a late-model automobile whistling "Yankee Doodle." Jasmine swoons for the car and the man who shares a name with the Union commander; her father recoils at both. But, with filial fealty, she sympathizes with Daddy's travails.

JASMINE: And they took our negroes away from us didn't they?

COL: Most of 'em and ah wish to the Lord dey would come back and take de rest of 'em! . . .

JASMINE: Are they any better up north daddie?

COL: Yars 'um they is! and the futher no'th they get 'um, the better they is. Ef they could put um all up at the no'th pole they would be perfec! Jas perfec!

The concept of removing free Black people from American soil altogether originated in the founding era, when Thomas Jefferson and other members of the American Colonization Society proposed to ship former slaves back to Africa. The Great Migration of many Black southerners would eventually remove the source of Colonel Calhoun's complaint, but Jasmine forces a reckoning with his (and the South's) weakened state. Grant proposes, and with the old man's reluctant blessing the couple drives off to live at his home, promising to return each summer. The old Confederate remains behind in every way, but his Kentucky home is dignified and beautiful, with "Weep no more, my lady" drifting from its windows. The marriage has reunited the sections, and the North has won, yet even in defeat the South retains a faded charm. Who wouldn't want to visit?

Guests assembled in an actual vine-covered antebellum Kentucky mansion to celebrate the union of Margaret "Madge" Rowan, forty, to a St. Louis widower named Jack M. Frost. The year was 1895, the place Bardstown. The groom's knack for public relations showed in the newspaper announcement, which had a musical theme: Madge's mother was cousin to Francis Scott Key, author of "The Star-Spangled Banner," and Stephen Foster "was visiting" his Rowan cousins when he wrote "My Old Kentucky Home." Known today as the "Bourbon capital of the world," the small city of Bardstown boasts nine distilleries, and the brown spirit "flows everywhere but the kitchen faucet." Surely it flowed as Jack, Madge in her white lace, and their guests celebrated at Federal Hill, as the Rowan home was known. Even the pink silk menus for the reception were printed with a picture of Madge's cherished homeplace.

Stephen Foster's growing profile and the vogue for heritage—old lineages, old homes, colonial and revolutionary times, and the

Confederacy—helped the Frosts as they promoted Federal Hill's historical importance. A *Ladies' Home Journal* feature titled "Romances of Some Southern Homes" paired the fad for colonial and early American architecture with the excitement of wartime and other violent episodes. Federal Hill appeared alongside the house where the Confederate cabinet held its last meeting before the surrender. Madge's grandfather the U.S. senator John Rowan had no military record, but he and Madge's father shared a propensity for "settling polite questions on the field of honor." They were said to be "dead shot" duelists. Such flourishes of virile white manhood appealed to readers fretting over the effects of an enervating capitalistic society. A touch of culture rounded out the story of Federal Hill as told in the magazine article. The great composer of "Southern songs" was John Rowan Sr.'s "protégé," and as such Stephen Foster made "his home there most of the time."

It was bunk. Useful, protean, workable bunk. Far less useful were facts, among which are these:

No clear evidence shows that Stephen Foster ever darkened the Rowan door. Charlotte Foster, his "songbird" sister who died in Louisville when Stephen was a toddler, did in fact visit Federal Hill. In 1828,

Beginning in the 1890s, the owners of a Bardstown, Kentucky, house known as Federal Hill circulated the myth that Stephen Foster composed the song there. The tale clung to the mansion like the vines in this 1904 postcard.

eighteen-year-old Charlotte found an escort to bring her to Cincinnati and then Louisville on an extended visit to relatives—not uncommon for a young woman on the marriage market. Through her hosts, the Barclays, the vivacious Charlotte met *their* Rowan cousins, who invited her to Federal Hill. The kinship tie was remote, but "they claim me as a relative and treat me as such," Charlotte told her parents back home. The senator was at the height of his career, an enslaver with a portfolio of commercial real estate along Louisville's wharves. Charlotte, whose father had aspired to such success but fallen short, was mesmerized. She listened with rapt attention to the "great man" hold forth, holding her breath "lest I should loose [*sic*] a word." Meanwhile, his son Atkinson began to court her. Atkinson Hill Rowan was "very clever and generally considered handsome," but Charlotte did not respond to his overtures.

On a second extended visit to Louisville, Charlotte Foster fell ill with fever. Her former suitor kept watch at her deathbed. Four years later he perished, unmarried, in the 1833 cholera epidemic. The outbreak claimed eight white members of the Rowan family and eight people they enslaved. After 1833, the bitter memory of these losses kept the Rowans almost entirely in their Louisville home. Growing up long after Charlotte and her uncle had died, Madge (the Rowan who got married at the home in 1895) must have heard something about Stephen Foster, but the link to Charlotte only came to light in the 1930s when scholars accessed Foster family letters. A brief flirtation between two young people was the seed of truth for elaborate fictions the Frosts erected around their Bardstown home.

By the time he moved there in the 1840s, Madge's father, John junior, had no interest in the thirteen-hundred-acre plantation. A trained lawyer who never practiced, the younger Rowan had taken his Maryland-born wife, Rebecca, to Mississippi in 1835 to catch the cotton boom. When that failed, they returned to Kentucky, and John was recruited for political office. The elder Rowan nixed that idea; the younger man was in debt. He should take responsibility for his growing family and manage Federal Hill to productivity. When "Judge" Rowan died in 1843, he left an estate so entangled with creditors that it took half a century to settle. From its brief 1820s heyday, the Rowan fortunes (and Federal Hill) spiraled downward.

John junior obtained a diplomatic appointment as special envoy to the Kingdom of the Two Sicilies, and for two years the large family exchanged Kentucky for Naples. No further appointments came Rowan's way. With his finances in disarray, they returned to Bardstown, where three more children were born. In 1855, baby Madge contracted diphtheria. According to family lore, her father was keeping watch over her in an upstairs bedroom when he tumbled from a window and tore open his throat on a tree branch as he fell. It was quite the story. Perhaps depression had overtaken Rowan and he took his life, which could explain his unmarked grave.

Madge grew up with nine siblings in a house the family did not even own and could not afford to maintain, scraping by on small remissions from the senior Rowan's estate. Without money for tuition, her brothers worked the land with an elderly enslaved couple. Her mother eventually leased the tillable acreage to Felix G. Murphy, a Rowan neighbor and slave trader. After decades of hard times, Madge's marriage to Frost— society pages referred to him as the "scion of a wealthy and aristocratic St. Louis family"—seemed likely to release those still living at Federal Hill from financial strain and permit them to better care for the old home.

Jack Frost had no apparent profession, but his grandfather was St. Louis's first millionaire, and Jack's father, a pro-slavery Democrat, commanded a secessionist paramilitary organization. In coordination with the Confederate president, Jefferson Davis, he plotted to seize St. Louis for the rebels. The couple regarded Federal Hill as an emblem of lost glories neither of them had ever known, indeed glories that had never existed. Nobody could refute the tall tales they planted in newspapers. More important, nobody wished to. These published sketches gave a glow to the slave-built "House Still Standing Where the Famous Song Was Written."

Turn-of-the-century Kentucky needed a new glow. Nobody understood this better than the journalist Robert Elkin Hughes. The assassination in broad daylight of Governor William Goebel on the capitol grounds in 1900 cemented a picture of lawlessness and disorder; Hughes turned his reporting into *That Kentucky Campaign,* a book about the election that ended in bloodshed. The state's largest paper, *The Courier-Journal,* made Hughes its "Main Street Man" covering business, and as secretary of the Commercial Club, Hughes promoted Louisville's flagging economic development. With murderous Appalachian feuds a staple of American news, Hughes had a tough assignment. Lynchings and racial expulsions added to the sense of mayhem. Meanwhile, in southwestern Kentucky's Black Patch tobacco region, farmers warring over leaf prices torched warehouses and horsewhipped growers who undersold their product. An anonymous verse from 1901 lampooned "My Old Kentucky Home." Rather than birds, "the shotgun makes music all the day," and "the feud man hides in the corner of the fence / And waits for a shot at his foe."

Kentucky looked like a dangerous and unpleasant place to live, to do business, even to visit.

The 1904 world's fair (known as the Louisiana Purchase Exposition) in Jack Frost's hometown of St. Louis gave Kentucky a chance to hit restart, and Hughes took charge of the planning. Kentucky had under-invested in the 1893 Chicago world's fair, but this time the business-led "Exhibit Association" obtained a $75,000 allocation from the state legislature to build a showpiece "Kentucky Building." "My Old Kentucky Home" became the conceptual anchor of Kentucky's presence in St. Louis.

The state's souvenir fair button showed a white-pillared mansion and invited visitors to take a stake in the state with the line "Ky. Home, World's Fair—'It's Part Mine.'" Everybody who passed by the white wedding cake of the Kentucky Building heard Foster's tune floating through the doors that opened on all sides. A specially commissioned

The Louisiana Purchase Exposition (the St. Louis World's Fair) took place during seven months in 1904. The fair's Kentucky Building, known as the Kentucky Home, featured a player piano with fourteen arrangements of Foster's fifty-year-old melody sounding throughout the day.

player piano painted with scenes from the commonwealth resounded with the melody—in fourteen different arrangements—for a fair-long total of 8,275 times. Ten thousand copies of "My Old Kentucky Home" sheet music were handed out as door prizes to fairgoers entering the mansion.

Then there was the programming. To help drive visitors to the building, the First Kentucky Regiment massed for a rousing military parade on the fair's central plaza. Led by the commander of the Sons of Confederate Veterans, the troops marched in one direction to the strains of "My Old Kentucky Home" and to "Dixie" on the way back. Robert E. Lee's son complimented the exercises. The headline in Louisville read "Southern Airs Arouse Enthusiasm." The melody had become a symbol of southern patriotism. On the fair's "Louisville Day," members of the Igorot tribe gave "My Old Kentucky Home" a "surprising interpretation." The singers were from the hallmark attraction that promoted the alleged benefits of American rule in the Philippines, lately won by the United States in the Spanish-American War. Some twelve hundred tribespeople were in the display. Somebody from the Bluegrass State delegation trained a "quartet of brown savages" to sing "The sun shines bright in the Old Kentucky home" before a large crowd on the Kentucky Building steps. (In future decades the minstrel tune was regularly used to assimilate darker-skinned and foreign people.) Two months later some of the Filipino "boys" were still serenading a senator with the fair's favorite tune.

The larger purpose of the free-floating Foster tune, parades, performances, and giveaways in St. Louis was to shift the national impression of Kentucky and attract investment to the state. The Kentucky Building was styled as a "New Kentucky Home" where progress and nostalgia mingled like branch water and bourbon. Displays promoted mining, distilling, and agricultural industries, pitching Kentucky as a land of opportunity. Tradition and progress wove together. The commonwealth's "commercial self" unfolded in rooms of exhibits, while the hospitable porches and welcoming central hall promoted social networking. Kentucky offered "the opportunities of a new State with the home life of an old State." Nothing could be more removed from a lowly cabin than Robert Hughes's triumphant Kentucky Building; it was the second most visited after the host state Missouri's.

The visitors and potential investors Hughes and the commissioners welcomed to the New Kentucky Home were almost exclusively white. The Louisiana Purchase Exposition was not officially segregated, but Black visitors were barely tolerated, and the condition or progress of Black Kentuckians was not addressed. In 1893, the journalist and anti-lynching reformer Ida B. Wells had published a pamphlet in which she and Frederick Douglass explained to Chicago fairgoers why Black people were absent from the World's Columbian Exposition. "We earnestly desired to show some results of our thirty years of acknowledged manhood and womanhood," the abolitionist Douglass explained, but this had been rebuffed in favor of "Dahomians" brought from Benin "to exhibit the Negro as a repulsive savage." When Paris opened its Exposition Universelle in 1900, the young sociologist W. E. B. Du Bois, the first Black man permitted to earn a doctorate from Harvard University, helped design "the Exhibit of American Negroes." The prizewinning presentation of photographs, infographic charts and maps, legal codes, and literary work made visible "a small nation of people," one-tenth of the U.S. population, without caricature, "without apology or gloss, and above all made by themselves." There was nothing even remotely like that in St. Louis. The National Association of Colored Women meeting in the city that summer reversed their planned fair visit after realizing that they could not dine, enter souvenir shops, or even get a glass of water.

Jack and Madge Rowan Frost had wed in Bardstown but lived mainly in St. Louis and made the most of the chance to host Kentuckians who came to see the fair. Federal Hill was at last officially theirs (her grandfather John Rowan Sr.'s estate was settled in 1897 after more than fifty years of delay), and fairgoers heard a good deal about *the* Old Kentucky Home. A Bardstown native, charged with gathering historic "relics" to display in St. Louis, worked with the Frosts to create a "colonial" room in the Kentucky Building that connected the song, the state, the house, and Foster. A black-and-white photograph of the mansion hung on one wall, and Madge lent some pieces of "old furniture" from Federal Hill. These were laid out on an "old rag carpet" to evoke early Kentucky. Kentucky's governor, the Democrat J. C. W. Beckham, also a Bardstowner, was not satisfied. Something needed to tie the composer directly to the old house. Beckham ordered a fair commissioner to scare up a writing desk (later called a "secretaire") so thousands of visitors would picture the bard penning the song Kentucky stuck in nineteen

The "Foster Secretaire" was likely purchased in 1904 for the Old Kentucky Home exhibit within the Kentucky Building at the St. Louis world's fair. Years later, it was heralded at Federal Hill as the actual desk where the composer sat to write the famous melody.

million ears that summer. Federal Hill's first date with the tourist business was sealed with an awkward, inauthentic kiss.

How could it have been otherwise? In Gilded Age America, the authentic was routinely sought out so it could be put to work substantiating the inauthentic. History, so often written by the victors, can be made to serve that very purpose. Still, it was rattling to find in news reports about Louisville's 1900 reunion a familiar name among the candidates for "Commander in Chief" of the national Sons of Confederate Veterans: Robert Worth Bingham. My great-grandfather grew up at the Bingham School, my North Carolina family's southern-styled military academy where he and the cadets were taught to honor his father's bullet-ripped Confederate regimental flag. For years before the veterans of the Confederacy assembled in Louisville, Robert Hall Bingham, who had ridden with the Ku Klux Klan in the 1870s, attended the yearly pilgrimages. His son Robert Worth Bingham loyally accompanied him.

As a striving young attorney with an eye to public office, Bingham flourished his devotion to the Lost Cause, betting it would advance his ambitions. He had moved to Louisville and married into a prosperous manufacturing family that had sided with the Union. But ex-Confederates topped Kentucky's social and political ladder. When Robert Worth Bingham's bid to command the Sons of the Confederate Veterans ended in a rout, I doubt he was much disturbed. The Louisville insurance agent who won the vote for commander in chief had as *his* father the Confederacy's youngest general. By running for the post, Bingham got his name in the papers and an honorary role in the official ceremonies. At the "Lost Cause Ball," he whirled "pretty visitors" around the floor. The crowd roared when the band played "My Old Kentucky Home" and "Dixie."

For Kentucky, for the nation, for the reviving interest in Foster, and for the owners of an old house in Bardstown, the world's fair had proven that "My Old Kentucky Home" was an ideal touchstone, sounding past glories and lighting the path to a "sunny and bright" future. R. E. Hughes's two years of planning for a "New Kentucky Home" in St. Louis felt like the beginning of something great, and he hoped to keep the dividends flowing.

A winning concept arrived from Louise Lee Hardin, the editor of *Business Woman's Magazine*. The Louisville native proposed to invite "exiles" like herself back to their old Kentucky homes. In 1906, the Commercial Club took Hardin's idea and mounted a celebration that began in Louisville and radiated to every county in the commonwealth. "Home Coming Week" generated revenue in the short term. Even more, building on the hospitality that succeeded so well in St. Louis, the celebration promoted connections that could return the investment many times over. Kentucky suffered a steady drain of talent, and the statewide reunion relied on Foster to lure former residents and their capital.

As the state's Black population stagnated, Kentucky laid a bet to draw back straying whites, or at least some of their wealth.

Hughes and his team negotiated discounted train and steamship fares and placed ads in newspapers across the country. Stephen Foster and his old song were core to the marketing campaign. "Song Will Bring Wanderers Home," one promotion promised. Planners devoted a full day to Stephen Foster, and Hughes commissioned a statue to

Kentucky built on the success of the "New Kentucky Home" of the 1904 World's Fair in St. Louis with a Home Coming celebration in 1906 aimed at boosting economic development by bringing expatriates back to the state. The Louisville *Courier-Journal* portrayed an urbanized "refugee" embraced by the "old folks"— goateed "colonel" and long-skirted mistress—at their pillared antebellum-style mansion. The medallion at the bottom of the drawing reads "The Sun Shines Bright on the Old Kentucky Home."

be unveiled as a tribute to the man whose song "would live as long as the state he honored . . . has a surviving son or daughter." The sculptor Enid Yandell, another female professional living far from her native Kentucky, agreed to create the artwork, which was to be funded by collections from the state's schoolchildren.

The weeklong event kicked off with public registries for visitors to help locate friends and a "floral" parade in which Hardin rode in an open automobile to cheers. On Foster Day, more than a thousand children—the girls dressed all in white and holding white parasols, and the boys in white shirts—filed into the city armory. Full to the rafters, the space assumed a holy aura. Governors of at least three states were present, along with a former vice president and Stephen Foster's daughter, Marion. The program featured a lithograph of Federal Hill with the caption " 'The HOMESTEAD' that inspired Foster's gift to Kentucky" and printed all three of the song's verses. The text adapted Robert Nevin's optimistic line from an 1867 issue of *The Atlantic Monthly* that Foster had "taught us all to feel with the slaves the lowly joys and sorrows [his music] celebrated." No person of color was invited to speak of joys or sorrows or the work remaining to achieve "universal" sympathy. This gigantic whitewashing of America's racial realities reached its climax as a thousand white girls dressed in white performed the entirety of "My Old Kentucky Home."

According to a local reporter, the audience of twenty thousand, "heads bowed and eyes moist from the depth of the delicate sentiment, sat quiet" until "the suggested solace" of "Weep no more, my lady." Then they joined in, and "joyful grief" was followed by thunderous applause. One "Home Comer," his face streaked with tears, "raised his trembling arm" and cried, "My God! That song alone was worth coming all the way back."

The Home Coming concept was so successful that Virginia and Tennessee announced plans to hold their own reunions. In one respect, however, Foster Day was a bust. Less than $500 was collected from Kentucky schoolchildren, far short of Yandell's fee to produce a large sculpture. Whether because the fundraising was ill-managed or Kentuckians were too destitute or disinterested in Foster to contribute is not certain. Instead, a local artist produced a life-size plaster of the composer. The white form of Stephen Foster sat noble and erect in a Windsor chair. The money to cast it in bronze was never raised, and R. E. Hughes moved it to the entrance to Louisville's Commercial Club, where the melodist gazed blankly at the comings and goings of Louisville's leading men of business.

With the conclusion of the Louisville events, thousands of ex-Kentuckians boarded trains for their home counties. Members of the songwriter's family made a pilgrimage of their own to the "Old Kentucky Home" as honored guests of Madge and Jack Frost. Foster's granddaughter, Jessie Welch Rose, recalled that Federal Hill had no electricity and felt "just as it had been in slave days." Madge and Jack Frost pulled out all the stops, entertaining in their best version of pre–Civil War style. Half a dozen uniformed servants said to be direct descendants of

Though J. L. Roop's plaster model of the composer from 1906 was never cast in bronze, it was exhibited at Louisville's public library for decades. The artist moved to California in 1917 and created stop-motion animation for Hollywood productions and sculpted prehistoric animals for the La Brea Tar Pits in Los Angeles.

people earlier Rowans had owned waited on the visitors. The meals took days to prepare; horses waited in barns for pleasure rides. Foster's granddaughter returned to Pennsylvania convinced that the "chains of slavery were not always galling." Yes, there was plenty of fellow feeling across sectional lines, but Jessie considered herself and her forebears morally superior to her hosts and theirs. Her grandfather, she believed, stirred sympathy for "the colored man" and heard "the tears behind the laughter." Her fond appreciation for an inauthentic past served its purposes.

Cementing the connection with Stephen Foster's descendants was a dream come true for the Frosts. They began calling Foster "Cousin

Stephen." The publicity from Home Coming and Foster Day naturally drew people to the site itself. A housekeeper named Josie Montgomery remembered that after the 1906 jamboree "anybody would give five dollars to go through the house." Federal Hill was not open to tourists, but with the owners generally away servants led visitors into the unfinished cellar, where enslaved members of the household had lived, "just to have something to look at." (No separate housing for the people enslaved by the Rowans, no cabin as in the song, has been definitively located on the property.) Rowan employees welcomed the extra cash, and local shops started selling penny postcards depicting Federal Hill as the Old Kentucky Home.

Marion Foster's comments echoed travel writers from outside the region who described the South as a place out of time with a slower, more genteel pace and where old patterns of racial hierarchy lingered. Black people, in servile or quaint postures, appeared as relics, picturesque props untouched by modern problems like Jim Crow exclusions and the ongoing threat of violence. A faded southern aristocracy clinging to "history" and old houses fascinated white tourists from the North and West, people seeking relief from the strain of a competitive (and profitable) urban life. Such outsiders could taste the past but, like Foster's granddaughter, could also feel superior to southerners of both races. The whole package—old colonels, ladies, and belles along with "mammies," cooks and waiters, "pickaninnies," aged uncles, and lazy laborers—sold. No wonder Madison Avenue eventually picked up on the trend and built advertising campaigns for coffee (Maxwell House) and ready-made pancake mix (Aunt Jemima) using this same cast of characters to sell their products. This broadly American (*not* explicitly southern) craze for Old South atmosphere brought pilgrims to Federal Hill.

The curious increasingly came by car. Mass adoption of automobiles was years away, but in 1910 a New York scouting party for the sixth amateur endurance rally of the American Automobile Association (AAA) passed through Kentucky and pulled up at Federal Hill. The Glidden Tours were designed to show off the novel vehicles' usefulness and dependability and to promote better roads. They also mapped points of interest as stopping points. The Frosts were absent, but the AAA scouts talked with a "white-haired old negro" who asked, "How can I serve the young massas?" He pointed to the cemetery where the "distinguished" "old massa" Rowan rested. He indicated the "wood lot" where he and young "Massa" (Madge's father) had organized cockfights, since banned. "Now the fool law come and spoilt a genman's pleasure. Deed it does, Sah . . . times is done changed a heap since the wah." Such comments satisfied northerners' expectations about loyal Black folks and old-time pastoral pleasures and were aimed to yield a tip. When the Glidden scouts published their guide to the summer tour route in northern newspapers, they gave Federal Hill top billing.

The descendants of those who had fought a war to end slavery were now spending their vacation dollars and days to encounter slavery's fact-less artifice.

My great-grandfather Robert Worth Bingham, also a newcomer to Kentucky, applauded "My Old Kentucky Home" when the band played it at the "Lost Cause Ball" in 1900. During the peak of white anti-Black violence, he joined millions who celebrated the continued oppression that made the "New South" consistent with the "Old South" if you had dark skin. When his father died in 1927, he framed Robert Hall Bingham's North Carolina company's Confederate battle flag and hung it in his office. His progressive politics (anticorruption in the first decade of the twentieth century, women's suffrage in the second decade, fair prices for farmers in the 1920s, and opposing Nazi appeasement in the 1930s) never washed away the deep, dark well of white rage that persists even within the educated, the genteel, the liberal-minded.

Bingham poured that outrage along with his pride in his Confederate and Ku Klux Klan heritage into a 1937 fan letter to the author Margaret Mitchell. Reading *Gone with the Wind* brought back the riveting Civil War and Reconstruction stories that had filled his youth. Robert Worth Bingham was not born until 1871, but he knew how his father had been "at Appomattox, and came home, lousy, ragged, hungry and barefooted to the wrack left by Sherman. My Mammy had been my father's before me. I loved her next to my own Mother." Other characters slotted into Mitchell's script, validating its inauthentic "truth." "My mother was Melanie to the last emotion," he wrote, "but very beautiful. Melanie was beautiful too. Even you must not deny me that. They were saints, both of them, my mother and Melanie. They . . . glowed with inner fire, a spiritual fervor, which illuminated them all and all around them. My elder brother, my mother's first child, died in infancy, because no doctor could come, no medicine could be obtained."

"God damn the Yankees," he told Mitchell, "all of my blood who survived said [it] too." With *Gone with the Wind* she had given voice to a "voiceless people . . . tortured and robbed."

Something far more profound than irony made it possible to say this. Was it the certitude of racial superiority or the terror of confronting the truth that made victims out of enslavers yet said nothing of the millions robbed, tortured, raped, forcibly separated from loved ones, and denied medical care for hundreds of years? Their suffering did not matter next to what whites experienced. This was by design, by intent, with the intentions implicit and explicit spread across generations and millions of men, women, and children, spread as widely and ubiquitously as Foster's song, with its shifting, malleable lyrics, taking up occupancy in individual and collective memories.

Each generation has inherited a piece of this blindness and moral failure. Though nobody took me aside and explained slavery and Jim Crow and therefore the nature of my family legacy, I have, like so many, tried to do better and clung to the belief that I was doing better. As a young person, I believed that the road to the "level playing field" was being paved. With small adjustments and goodwill, things were, as the Beatles song said, "getting better all the time." It's a deeply American impulse, this faith in natural progress. Like so much, that impulse does work to deflect attention from certain facts, from other less progressive histories. It turns out that I was as ready to "sing one song for the old Kentucky home" as my great-grandfather a hundred years before me. During his day, white men used gruesome methods of extralegal violence to murder hundreds of Black citizens each year; during mine, police killed unarmed youths and our criminal justice system embraced the "new Jim Crow" of mass incarceration, which has ravaged whole communities. We both found ways to excuse or live with those facts.

5

TO TOTE THE WEARY LOAD

The Burden of Black Uplift

In 1911, the host of a private party in New York City upbraided the "Darkey Team" hired to entertain because they were playing "cheap" ragtime music instead of "Southern Songs." He was particularly irritated that the "stupid" singer knew just one verse of "Swanee Ribber" and hopelessly mixed up the lyrics to "My Old Kentucky Home." For professional Black musicians in New York, the Foster tunes were dated and demeaning, and the combo might have pretended ignorance to resist requests that insulted them artistically and politically. If so, they did this at some risk, even if only ensuring that they were not hired a second time by that particular patron. White Americans' need for Black people to authenticate the inauthentic required Black entertainers to demonstrate that "plantation songs" emanated from them naturally. They resisted this demand at different degrees of peril. Accepting it squelched creative genius and carried its own hazards.

State and local laws and community practices being enacted across the United States deprived Black Americans of political power, public spaces, education, home ownership, and professional training. Harassment from police and courts and extreme racial violence—not only in the former slave states—kept millions in terror and silence. Nongovernmental Progressive Era groups directed aid to immigrants and their families as they filled U.S. cities but ignored or minimized the needs of southern migrants. At the same time, immigrants, many from southern and eastern Europe (Italians, Poles, Czechs, and more), were given chances native-born descendants of slaves were not—hired for jobs, accepted into neighborhoods, placed in schools, and allowed bit by bit to pass into the fold of "whiteness." Rather than acknowledge these facts, leading social scientists calculated the prevalence of poverty and crime, disease and lack of education, and theorized that Black people were not suited to equal citizenship. An entire group was condemned for the depravity of a few and the (enforced) desperation of many more. Equally damning were the effects of these scholars' findings on Black psyches.

With white fingers forever pointing to deficits in education and morality, raising those standards became an obsessive preoccupation for some Black people. It shaped the programs put forward by leaders from Booker T. Washington and his humble manual training to W. E. B. Du Bois and his concept of a "talented tenth." Their shared project placed cruel and impossible burdens and operated with its own system of harsh internal judgments. Full dignity dangled always out of reach, never truly to be earned and only to be granted. But what to do when society ranks one's people at the bottom of the human pile? Demonstrating ability and achievement—in spite of impediments—was a way to sustain hope in a nation's promise of freedom, no matter how broken and incomplete.

A Black person who preferred the "new" ragtime sound irritated the white patron in 1911. His preference could also set him at odds with other members of his race. In was a catch-22: resist the stereotypes and prejudicial preferences of whites and risk a paycheck, an education, even a life. Accommodate those preferences and be co-opted into confirming them, at least to some extent. With white people sitting in judgment, "racial uplift" was not only farcical but also often the only game in town. All Black people living in the United States wanted to overcome white discrimination; in musical terms the project could mean spurning the artistically novel and seemingly "uncontrolled" (ragtime, early blues, or, worse, the exotic "coons" who fulfilled the part). Within a mainstream culture inflamed with Anglo-Saxon superiority, some decided that the way for Black performers to help Black people *and* win whites' respect was to sing songs like "My Old Kentucky Home."

Such a bid for Black dignity by making white Americans feel good about themselves required a measure of self-debasement. Black people at the turn of the century who voluntarily embraced "My Old Kentucky Home" telegraphed a safe but profoundly inauthentic message: that they too were nostalgic, not insulted, hurt, struggling, and furious with the forces thwarting racial uplift.

Classical musicians of color, members of Black social organizations, and "colored" children in segregated schools chose to sing Foster's tune to soothe fears *and* to stake a claim for mainstream (white) respectability. The song projected the unjust terms of interracial amity, the impossible corner Black Americans were forced into as post–Civil War hopes for full acceptance into the larger national polity cruelly receded. Black artists and the communities that created them might sing "My Old Kentucky Home" to applause. Some might even have believed that Foster's songs placed them and their forebears at the center of the nation's folk tradition. But any hope that they sang for a dignified acceptance was akin to singing for a supper they could smell but was never served. Whites had set terms, had arranged for an uneven and increasingly uneven playing field in every domain of life and citizenship, and rewarded behavior that confirmed their own biases. Black citizens in all walks of life set about proving themselves, and in so doing proving white biases wrong.

So it was that the strains of "My Old Kentucky Home" accompanied debates within the Black community about the means to achieving racial equity. Between 1900 and World War I, ragtime inspired Scott Joplin and scores of Black musicians, feeding the artistic revolution that left Foster behind and coalesced as jazz. But individual and communal uplift, measured broadly by increased financial stability, could involve abasements that cut against claims of equality. "Coon" songs poured forth from (white) Tin Pan Alley, and Black songwriters eager for market success contributed their own; the Kentucky-born entertainer Ernest Hogan's "All Coons Look Alike to Me" sold a million copies. The star comedic duo of Bert Williams and George Walker sang of watermelon eating, straight razor battles, and chicken stealing in "The Coon's Trade-Mark," making educated Black people wince in embarrassment. The talent of such performers was undeniable, and their monetary success impressive. Such work could contain stunning creative leaps. But "coon" stereotypes also reinforced the worst white biases and justified over-policing and harsh punishments. In comparison, Foster's old songs promised to de-escalate racist animus by implying that nostalgia for old days was shared across the color line. Viewed from this angle, "My Old Kentucky Home" was, to some, clearly preferable.

It was preferable in part because of the overwhelming falsehood Foster's minstrel songs' inauthentic authenticity set into motion. For decades, a white man's nostalgic plantation melodies had been folded into the repertoire of scholar-singers from esteemed Black institutions like Fisk and Hampton—at first to make jubilee songs and spirituals more digestible to white audiences whose ticket money built their class-rooms. Ultimately, many—white and Black—heard them all as genuine "Negro melodies." For those who saw Black respectability as the solu-tion to white supremacy, mastering Bach or Puccini—and throwing in a little Foster—was a means to challenge Jim Crow both honorably and safely.

The Black press worried that the more popular performers of their race jeopardized racial progress. One "uplifter" writing in the Topeka, Kansas, *Plaindealer* excoriated Bert Williams and George Walker for indecent "darky gibberish that is fancied . . . by those of depraved taste." It pained him that the "sweet refrains of [Stephen Foster's] weird, plain-tive plantation melodies have given place almost wholly to 'coon songs!' To think," he continued in despair, "that the pastoral beauty of 'My Old Kentucky Home' is sacrificed to the vulgarity of 'Crappy Dan' and 'Syn-copated Sandy,' " which featured Black men as professional dice players and wife beaters. Another Black newspaper urged freedmen to banish music that made them "look foolish." Had they forgotten that "colored men inspired exquisite stanzas of verse" by Stephen Foster? For those betting on Black respectability, these were the honorable alternatives.

Validation for this conservative approach, and for Black Americans claiming shared ownership of the nation's culture, came from on high. The Czech composer Antonín Dvořák, director for several years of New York's National Conservatory of Music and hailed for his Symphony No. 9, *From the New World,* pronounced, "The future of music in this country must be founded upon what are called the negro melodies." This ambiguous category he called the nation's "folk songs," wonder-fully able to serve "any mood or purpose." Dvořák most likely had in mind Negro spirituals but, perhaps inevitably given the durable claims of blackface minstrelsy to authentic blackness, he lumped Stephen Foster's popular plantation melodies into the same category. A Black editor gloated that Dvořák's dictum centering America's musical soul on the creative products of a people enslaved and oppressed would be a "bitter pill for prejudiced [white] musicians to swallow," and Dvořák's declaration sparked an impassioned debate over the nature of American national identity and the role of Black people and Black music in forming it. In 1894, the Czech composer arranged "Old Folks at Home" for soprano, baritone, choir, and orchestra, rewarding Foster's inauthentic authenticity. "What matters it to me," the composer quipped, "if the best negro melodies have been written by white men?" By riding the coattails of spirituals and being rearranged "as art songs" in classical form, Foster's music gained a measure of high culture respectability.

Meanwhile, the ragtime "Darkey Team" at the private party fumbled and "forgot" "My Old Kentucky Home." But the old blackface parlor tune cropped up at Black gatherings where the focus was on communal accomplishment. Raymond Augustus Lawson, the first Black classical pianist to accompany a symphony, returned to Shelbyville, Kentucky, in 1902 after graduating from the Hartford Conservatory. The Women's Improvement Club, of which his mother was a member in good standing, held a banquet to celebrate a prodigy who had left town as a youth and returned a credentialed professor. The evening began with "The sun shines bright," followed by Lawson's speech about his boyhood "in his Old Kentucky Home." A few years later, in the midst of Jim Crow and Lost Cause ascendancy, the Black-owned Indianapolis *Freeman* reported on "Frederick Douglass Day" exercises at a southern Indiana "colored" school. Students read Paul Laurence Dunbar's poem "Frederick Douglass" and sang "The Battle Hymn of the Republic," the signal song of the Union troops. Just a short distance from the river that once separated slavery from freedom, the school chorus also sang "My Old Kentucky Home."

Members of fraternal organizations and society elites relied on "My Old Kentucky Home" to convey respectability, national belonging, and positive communal feeling. Louisville's Black Knights of Pythias marched in a "monster parade" at a 1911 Indianapolis fraternal gathering, striking up "America," "My Old Kentucky Home," and even "Dixie." Foster's song wafted through a summer picnic attended by Washington, D.C.'s Black elite. Smithfield country ham, fried spring chicken, and cake were laid out for two young women making their social debut. After the meal, older guests sang along as Bismarck Pinchback, son of the first (and to this day only) Black governor of Louisiana, played the banjo and sang, "The sun shines bright." *Negro Minstrel Melodies* (1909), a volume of twenty-one classically arranged songs edited by Dvořák's collaborator, the baritone Harry T. Burleigh, included "My Old Kentucky Home" and eight other Foster songs and was for years advertised in the National Association for the Advancement of Colored People (NAACP) magazine, *The Crisis.* The bluesman W. C. Handy absorbed Foster's plantation music during his youth as a traveling "colored" minstrel in the 1880s. Musing about the "well of sorrow" that gave rise to "Negro music," Handy suspected "that Stephen Foster owed something to this well, this mystery, this sorrow. 'My Old Kentucky Home' makes you think so, at any rate." Thinking so was comforting.

"My Old Kentucky Home" floated up from sideshows and formal recitals. It followed "How to Spell Possum Pie" when the Great Van Amburg Show came to Cincinnati in 1905. Was the Black baritone who performed it mocking or serious? Or was it funny that he was serious? We cannot know. A few months later, it shared the same program with a cello solo and a Chopin piano sonata at a send-off concert for a Black Tennessee-born soprano. Foster's song helped elicit tears as Emma Azalia Hackley left to pursue her career in Europe. "My Old Kentucky Home" slid across boundaries watchfully patrolled by middle-class and elite Black Americans claiming a seat at a table where the deck was grimly stacked against them. For a despised minority, Foster's music was a tool that was rarely celebrated but broadly accepted for the work it could do.

In 1908, the segregated, mainly white audience at Louisville's Avenue Theater burst into applause as a radiant soprano known as Black Patti hit the last notes of her encore—"My Old Kentucky Home." The manager pressed a bouquet into her arms—the first time a performer of her race had been so honored in that city. Matilda Sissieretta Jones was nicknamed Black Patti after the white diva Adelina Patti, but she preferred to be called Madame Jones. Had one Louisville reviewer not seen her with his own eyes, he "would not have believed that the voice was that of a negress." Among the highest-earning Black artists in the

The soprano Matilda Sissieretta Jones was born in Portsmouth, Virginia, in 1869.
The first Black woman to sing at New York's Carnegie Hall, Jones entertained
President Benjamin Harrison at the White House. When racial discrimination
upended her operatic career, Jones toured with an all-Black minstrel troupe,
performing operatic works and, though she did not prefer them, at least occasional
Stephen Foster songs.

nation, Jones toured Europe at the head of a white company and entertained four consecutive presidents. Rossini, not Foster, was her usual
fare. It was, however, occasionally requisite.

And more so during the second act of a career that had begun with
immense promise and, for a white woman with her skills, would have
brought leading operatic roles. In the late 1890s, with doors closing to
her in American classical music, Jones signed on to an all-Black variety
show that boasted both "low" and "high," popular and classical elements. Unable to book hotel rooms, the troupe traveled and slept in
private train cars. Louisville was just another stop for the Black Patti
Troubadours, an act that promised plenty of "darky fun"—"coon comedy," cakewalks, and "jubilee shouts." Each evening climaxed with selec-
tions from her classical repertory. Madame Jones performed as soloist,
backed by a chorus whose members also provided the nightly "darky

fun." Negro minstrelsy was the revue's bread and butter; when Madame Jones rolled her peerless voice over "My Old Kentucky Home," though, she simultaneously satisfied white listeners and asserted her dignity as a Black woman. In the gallery seats, Black Louisvillians filled the segregated gallery because there were so few chances to witness Black stardom. Their pride in Jones was justifiable, but it required at least contemplating "My Old Kentucky Home" as a source of pride.

For all its vaunted usefulness as a means of racial "uplift," Foster's plantation tune was plain old white supremacist propaganda for a little girl in 1890s Charleston, South Carolina. For Mamie Garvin Fields, who would grow up to be a civil rights activist, "My Old Kentucky Home" represented the degrading atmosphere of racial oppression she and millions of other children struggled not to internalize every day. Almost all the teachers in Fields's segregated public school were white and the education was poor, but the "rebel tradition" got top billing. Each week the children recited "The Blue and the Gray," an 1867 poem that called on them to celebrate the sacrifices of both Confederate and Union soldiers and to "banish our anger forever." They sang "Dixie," "in dialect," and then "My Old Kentucky Home" or "Massa's in de Cold Ground." In 1909, at twenty-one, she became Charleston's first Black public school teacher in part to upend a system that had forced her to vocalize a white view of the past that honored Confederates and sentimentalized slavery in "the land of cotton."

Black parents in Boston likewise rose up against Foster's "plantation melodies." The first documented public debate over the songs' racist symbolism and stereotypes sparked a white counterattack that resounds a century later. Boston schools were integrated in 1914, and the district's brand-new textbook, *Forty Best Old Songs,* was state of the art for American music education. But it included seven tunes with racial slurs— "coon, nigger, and darkey." Parents, ministers, and community leaders, backed by the fledgling chapter of the NAACP, demanded protection for their children. At a crowded meeting, school board members were told that since the book came into use, some pupils tormented their nonwhite classmates with the ugly words. One boy came home "heartbroken." A teacher asked a student (the only Black child in the room) to demonstrate how to sing the lyrics in dialect. "We are endeavoring to forget the sins of the white man," one protester told the board. To have children subjected to such music spun the world backward, erased the damage of slavery, and reinforced the kind of denigration that they were trying so hard to overcome. Whites could say no harm was intended, but the objectionable terms were never kind, "always used in the sense of epithets." Following the testimony, the Boston school board chair, George E. Brock, announced to the assembly, "The term 'darkey' is one of reproach. Personally I never thought of it before." The members of the board voted unanimously to reject the book.

The white Boston school board's willingness to hear "My Old Kentucky Home" as harmful in 1914 was exceedingly rare if not unique among white officials at any level. (It still is, to this day.) Over the next decades, countless blackface tunes, pitched as "folk" songs and therefore innocent, were absorbed into songbooks aimed at young people, a little-noticed whitewashing of minstrelsy through infantilization. Federal policymakers routinely ignored objections from Black citizens. The previous year, President Woodrow Wilson issued an executive order formally segregating the racially integrated federal workforce. When Black leaders objected, Wilson lied that both races were happier under the new rule. The Black-owned *Washington Bee* hailed Boston's board of education for caring about the views of a racial minority; in contrast, southerners like Wilson liked to call themselves the "Negro's . . . true friend" but actually demanded subordination, "flunkeyism and bootlicking."

The white response to Boston's removal of *Forty Best Old Songs* from its classrooms is a reminder that music has always been an American battleground. One scathing reaction from Hartford, Connecticut's Southern Society ridiculed the Black parents as oversensitive "snowflakes" and accused the school board of caving in to dangerous nonsense. These melodies were "part of the most precious musical heritage of our people as a whole," the society declared, and vowed to protect them from assault. *The Indianapolis News* editorialized that Boston's "absurd" decision took Stephen Foster out of context. If anything, the songwriter had been too generous in his depictions of Black people and bestowed on "the Negro . . . virtues he did not possess." A Georgia editor welcomed any music that reminded "the black man" of "the happy and carefree days when his 'white folks' took every responsibility from him." It was alarming to another white respondent "that the descendants of Uncle Isham and Mammy Jinsey should be ashamed of the tuneful ditties that were dear to their ancestors. For these old songs preserve memories that should not be allowed to perish of the primitive virtues—fidelity, affectionate disposition, and cheerful contentment within a narrow dispensation—of a race which under more benign conditions is in danger of losing its best endowments."

Whether as cultural treasures, stereotyped keys to understanding the nature of Black people, or warnings to certain present-day citizens against aspiring beyond their lowly lot in life, "My Old Kentucky Home" had fiercely loyal defenders. No district appears to have followed Boston's lead. The city was beyond the pale of reason; as one paper concluded, "Pass the beans."

Music generally and "My Old Kentucky Home" specifically cut across debates within Black America about what was appropriate in "Negro song." At least one Black leader publicly joined the criticism leveled at the "radical" school board. Emma Azalia Hackley, a concert soprano born in Reconstruction-era Tennessee, had faced total exclusion from "legitimate" classical stage work. Rather than compromise her standards of propriety by sharing a vaudeville stage, Hackley pivoted to music education. She gave private instruction (young Marian Anderson was among her protégées) and developed mass singing programs to promote Black dignity. Hackley aimed to instill the quality she affectingly called "somebody valuation"; joining in a chorus helped her singers experience themselves as "somebodies." Dubbed "the vocal teacher of ten thousand," Hackley was also an unapologetic snob with no use for popular Black music. By the second decade of the twentieth century that meant ragtime and the razors and chickens of transparently demeaning "coon" songs. It did not, however, mean "My Old Kentucky Home."

The month *Forty Best Old Songs* was dropped, Hackley's chorus performed for a large audience at Boston's Symphony Hall. The concert, misleadingly advertised as featuring only "Negro composers," would "preserve precious folk" traditions. Hackley slipped Foster in among the spirituals, as expressions of the "soul of a toiling, hopeful people."

Another "race woman" of the Jim Crow era deployed "My Old Kentucky Home" in a vastly more confrontational way. The elocutionist and actress Henrietta Vinton Davis put Foster's nostalgic plantation song to the work of crediting Black heroism, and Black female heroism in particular. Davis's play, *Our Old Kentucky Home* (ca. 1898), appropriated Foster's familiar tune in the interest not of mere uplift but of something more like Black Power. Davis (1860–1941) was an experienced performer when she wrote and produced *Our Old Kentucky Home*. Born to free parents, Henrietta became a teacher at fifteen, first in her native Maryland, then in a Louisiana freedmen's school, where she witnessed the desperate hunger to "rise up" through education. Returning home to care for her ailing mother, Davis won a coveted civil service position as the first Black employee at the District of Columbia's Recorder of Deeds. Three years later, in 1881, Frederick Douglass was appointed to head the office after campaigning for the Republican James Garfield for president. (He had hoped for a more exalted diplomatic post as a reward.) Working alongside the great Black statesman was an honor; however, Henrietta dreamed of a broader canvas for her talents. Elocution would be that canvas.

Victorian Americans prized oratory. Professional elocutionists like Henrietta Vinton Davis delivered literary classics in staged recitals that were the polar opposite of vaudeville and minstrelsy. She pursued elocution at a time when acting in plays onstage cast a woman's morality into question. By contrast, reciting offered an acceptable way to demonstrate her talent and advance her race. In all her days, Davis never ceased carrying the load of this responsibility.

Douglass personally launched Davis at her 1883 debut. The Black press rhapsodized over the "beautiful quadroon" and "our first American lady reader" after hearing her deliver famous speeches from *Romeo and Juliet* and *The Merchant of Venice*. She signed with a prominent Black agent, and Harriet Beecher Stowe's husband introduced her in Hartford, Connecticut. When Douglass attended the 1883 National Convention of Colored Men in Louisville, Kentucky, Davis performed on the program. "The color line meets [the Black man] everywhere and in a measure shuts him out from all respectable and profitable trades and callings," the gray-haired Douglass declared in a keynote address, though the local editorial page raged at him for "merely preaching the gospel of discontent." Not white prejudice but only the "negro himself," spoiled by "idle habits," was responsible for his condition, was the firm judgment of the men who wrote the news. It drained and infuriated twenty-

Henrietta Vinton Davis, pictured in 1893, wrote and performed the lead role in the radical play *Our Old Kentucky Home*. After decades battling bias in her profession, Davis joined Marcus Garvey's United Negro Improvement Association. "Lady Davis" became the highest-ranking woman in the organization.

three-year-old Henrietta to see the way white people dismissed her and her people.

For fifteen years, Davis mounted elocution performances, "striving to uplift the standard of her race's excellence." She married and left a baritone who abused her. She toured the West Indies and crisscrossed the nation, sounding her "rich, flexible and expressive voice," as far south as Vicksburg, Mississippi, in recitals for mixed audiences where possible but, as the iron curtain of Jim Crow fell, in all-Black churches and halls. The "color line" imposed on the "legitimate" stage kept Davis, like Sissieretta Jones, professionally marginalized. Had she sought personal success alone, Davis, described as "no darker than a Spanish or Italian lady in hue," could have found it by passing for white. But that would have meant selling out her people, and that Davis was unwilling to do.

Henrietta Vinton Davis's play, *Our Old Kentucky Home,* represents her fury at injustice, her determination to represent race onstage realistically, and her blunt faith in Black female power. A woman (Davis herself) headlines this tale of survival and heroism that reconstituted the Black family in the old Kentucky home. Davis reworked the trope of the Kentucky plantation, and a song that meant one thing at the play's beginning means something very different at its end.

Our Old Kentucky Home opens the way countless vaudeville plays and blackface minstrel shows ended: a quartet of "slaves" under a shade tree serenade a white family gathered on a veranda. Then the scene shifts to a New Orleans auction, where the white Kentucky colonel Knott purchases the "creole" Clothilde, played by Davis. Some of her fellow "merchandise" is shown beaten and prodded; Clothilde, rather than shudder under the "leer" of the all-male crowd, gazes back defiantly. That meeting of the eyes (forbidden in the everyday practice of slavery and Jim Crow) signals the risks Clothilde will take. The story moves upriver to Kentucky rather than downriver, as in *Uncle Tom's Cabin,* a clue to its upside-down plot.

The enslaved people of *Our Old Kentucky Home* resist their condition in varied and coordinated ways—the opposite of the minstrel stage's carefree or loafing or comical figures. When Colonel Knott's son, Courtney, a college student home for recess, attempts a sexual assault, Clothilde insists in her French accent, "Aldo I am a slave, M'sieur, I am a leddy." A Black woman's "honor" is an absurdity to Courtney, and he vows to "show" her "what we do to leddies of your kind in Kentucky." The white "belle" Courtney has been courting interrupts the violent encounter, and when Basil (the enslaved son of Colonel Knott and therefore Courtney's half brother) hears of it, he vows to guard Clothilde. (Basil and Clothilde also begin a courtship.) The enslaved cook helps by tainting Courtney's food, sending him to his own rather than Clothilde's bed. Showing white men sexually victimizing Black women violated all rules of propriety in the 1890s; to this day whites struggle to acknowledge the rape, sexual exploitation, and forced breeding embedded in the Black experience. Clothilde's superhero ability to escape such abuse asserted a personal and communal integrity that slavery and Jim Crow systematically denied.

The second act begins amid the Civil War. Union soldiers are camped on the plantation, and the house has become a general's headquarters. Basil has joined the fight for freedom, and his enslaver, Colonel Knott, is being held prisoner and awaits execution for smuggling Union military secrets to the Confederacy. The "bottom rail on top" reversal continues to the battlefield, where Basil meets and captures his white half brother, "young master" Courtney. Scenes showcasing Black valor in battle would not appear in mainstream American culture for generations; when they did, nearly a century later in the 1989 film *Glory,* the credits were unevenly divided with white allies. *Our Old Kentucky Home* underscored the force of Black freedom.

The superhero in this battle for freedom that is not granted but won is a Black woman. With Basil captured by Confederate forces, Clothilde sheds her Creole accent, dresses as a boy, and talks her way into the camp where he is imprisoned. Pretending to be the human property of the commander in charge, she frees Basil, who returns to the field of battle. Clothilde rescues Basil again during a skirmish, shooting dead two rebel soldiers. News finally arrives in the Union camp that the Confederacy's last arsenal has been destroyed, and Basil explains to his comrades that Clothilde was the one who laid the explosives. In a society that diminished women's contributions and dismissed Black women outright, Clothilde is collectively honored and thanked. "Credit" for ending the war, Basil says, "belongs to a black woman" who had killed white men.

Henrietta Vinton Davis lived out the enormous hopes Reconstruction-era Black Americans poured into education, work, and political struggles. While she was teaching in Louisiana, where the majority of inhabitants were Black, these aspirations were met with pitched battles and massacres. She witnessed federal forces abandon the fight for civil rights in the South and watched informal and legal discrimination throttle Black progress and her own career. The final act of her fantastical play ties up the romance between Clothilde and Basil and rights the hand of justice in the post-slavery era. The Union general who occupied the Knott plantation marries the white southern "lady" who witnessed Courtney assault Clothilde in the first act—symbolically subsuming the slave-owning South to Union power and love. The white couple, in turn, witnesses the legal union of Clothilde and Basil in a New York City church, a ceremony that poignantly echoes the thousands of freed people who registered their commitment to family with county clerks across the South.

White America, as we have seen, was obsessed with reunions and homecomings, and Davis fittingly wound up the play back in Kentucky. The heroes return to Colonel Knott's plantation, which they have purchased at auction. The reconstituted Black family includes the cook who guarded Clothilde from rape, and her husband, who deployed his comic antics as tools of resistance. Enslaved people survived brutal separations in part by expanding the concept of family, and although the older couple were not blood kin, Clothilde and Basil declare them the "only parents we have ever known." They will live out their days in peace on the old place—not as the loyal servants celebrated by white southerners after the war, but as respected elders. Basil welcomes all the people Knott enslaved as "tenants and neighbors." In a musical finale, the ensemble ritually cleanses the land with a rendition of "My Old Kentucky Home." This time, the song celebrates a spacious house of progress in freedom. Those who live there "weep no more." The leading lady, who had devoted most of her almost forty years to racial uplift, embodied female power and dignity on a grand scale. Her character gained a family and a home and slavery's wounds could begin to heal.

Few whites were ready to heal or even concede the need for healing.

In 1898 it was nearly impossible for a company led by a Black person to book a theater. Davis most likely managed it by passing. Pretending to be white could have also enabled her to rent rehearsal space and hire an integrated cast. But showcasing a white man (in the role of Courtney Knott) attacking Henrietta playing the innocent "Creole" Clothilde upended stringent taboos against cross-racial physical and sexual contact. Rehearsals began outside Washington, D.C., the same week heavily armed white supremacist citizens rampaged through Wilmington, North Carolina. In the only known coup in American history, the group ousted the Republican mayor and city council (consisting of Black and white officials), torched the Black newspaper and other businesses, and killed dozens of Black citizens. Thousands fled the "Wilmington Race Riot" in terror, and the perpetrators seized the reins of political power.

Meanwhile, Davis's troupe was printing up broadsides and playbills, assembling costumes, and building scenery. Just before the curtain rose for the first time on *Our Old Kentucky Home* in Fredericksburg, Virginia, a white actor who had read for the role of the lustful Courtney Knott reported Davis to authorities. *The Washington Star* published an item: a "comely, light-colored young women, with some dramatic ability," had amassed "several thousand dollars" to mount a shocking theatrical work that violated Jim Crow laws. Davis was chased from the city.

The tour struggled from the outset. Such a "startling" plot focused on "the sterner side of life"—slavery, rape, white male moral depravity—did not attract sizable audiences. The Hyers Sisters' *Out of Bondage* followed an enslaved family from the rustic log cabin to middle-class respectability in the North; *Our Old Kentucky Home* presented a vastly more disturbing picture of enslaved over enslaver, Black over white. The quality of the acting did not help. Davis was stellar, but she struggled to recruit talented thespians to join an integrated cast likely to be run out of any town. The play's final documented performance took place in Waterloo, Indiana's Opera House. The local press noted that the work was "taken from real life" and deserved the community's attention. Nevertheless, the company was forced to disband, and Henrietta spent several weeks with friends in Minnesota, where she gave an elocution performance at an African Methodist Episcopal church and a committee of Black citizens threw a reception in her honor.

Our Old Kentucky Home could never succeed in a world that insisted on perpetrating (or ignoring) the racial terror that Davis sought to upend. She left Minnesota the same day a white lynch mob in Newnan, Georgia, dragged Sam Hose from his jail cell. The Black laborer was accused of killing his employer (likely in self-defense) and raping the man's wife (she said it was not true). Hose was nonetheless burned alive in front of a crowd of thousands. The spectators came on specially scheduled trains to witness the well-publicized spectacle.

Henrietta Vinton Davis soldiered on. She nearly joined a "musical farce" headlining Ernest Hogan, the famous comedian known for his popular hit "All Coons Look Alike to Me," but could not ground her response to injustice in humor, even if her act formed the program's genteel, uplifting section.

Our Old Kentucky Home was a fairy tale, with a splash of revenge. Twenty years later, witnessing the ill treatment of Black soldiers and the rash of attacks on Black communities that followed World War I, Davis renounced the theater and entered politics, joining the United Negro Improvement Association (UNIA), Marcus Garvey's campaign for liberation through self-sufficiency. She quickly became the movement's highest-ranking female official, known as "Lady Davis." In the Garveyite fold, the standards of ladyship and Black respectability were no longer bounded by a sentimental minstrel song that inherently excluded her. Touching ground as Garvey's emissary in Liberia—where the UNIA planned a new African state, a refuge and home for Black Americans fleeing racial terror—she recalled lines from a poem by Sir Walter Scott:

Breathes there the man, with soul so dead,
Who never to himself hath said,
This is my own, my native land!
Whose heart hath ne'er within him burn'd,
As home his footsteps he hath turn'd
From wandering on a foreign strand!

She had found what felt like home, and it was five thousand miles from Kentucky.

Three brilliant women, Emma Azalia Hackley, Matilda Sissieretta Jones, and Henrietta Vinton Davis, toted the "weary load" of racial uplift through Jim Crow. They deployed "My Old Kentucky Home" to advance what they saw as their life's work. Though each fell in a different spot on the spectrum of challenge and accommodation, it was always a self-contradicting exercise: they challenged by, in some measure, accommodating the thing they meant to challenge.

By the end of World War I, "My Old Kentucky Home" was both an identifiably southern icon and an undisputed song of the nation in a country fast becoming a global power. White Americans traveling abroad were advised to know and be able to perform "My Old Kentucky Home" or "tell a plantation story or two" or else risk being judged lacking. Native American children forcibly assimilated in U.S. government-run boarding schools sang "My Old Kentucky Home" as part of their reeducation because the white majority deemed their nation's songs unworthy. Daughters of the Confederacy wept openly when it was performed after "Dixie" at their annual meeting and during morale-boosting sing-alongs. White southern troops in World War I insisted on "My Old Kentucky Home" as a counterweight to the Union-associated "Battle Hymn of the Republic." Debate within the Black community turned on what two steps back were necessary for three steps forward. In musical terms, Black performers and songwriters who embraced syncopated liberation upset members of the race who valued Foster's melody (even with its slurs) as a mark of "Negro influence" on American song and a channel to white sympathy. Jones, Hackley, and Davis and countless others performed Foster's sentimental plantation song. Some, like Davis, refused to take the second step back—as in singing "My Old Kentucky Home" to amuse and appease her oppressors or joining a "coon" show. Even the first step involved an impossible choice. To advance through the lesser abasement demanded the celebration of the horrid, the authentication of the inauthentic. The outlier that proves the possibility of white conscience, of Black life being nurtured rather than seen as disposable, is Boston's 1914 school board; Connecticut's mocking dismissal—"pass the beans"—was the norm. And the norm was policed by the lynch mob, whose actions were tolerated by the nation. "My Old Kentucky Home" as a "song of the nation" gradually grew in stature.

Henrietta Vinton Davis's protest play failed commercially, yet it captured an important shift—the same one that made the Rowan family's Federal Hill appealing as "the" Kentucky home—marking the song's new twentieth-century aspect. Once imagined as a crude, sometimes quaint slave dwelling, the song's locus had moved to the big house, the seat of power in a racialized landscape, a gracious, imposing marker of tradition. Davis intended to rewrite the terms of Foster's nostalgia to advance Black power, and Black women specifically. She did so at a time when nearly all of white America aligned against her.

Fascination with the Old South was becoming a mainstay of American consumer culture via advertising, radio, film, and tourism, but, as with nearly every facet of that culture, whites dictated the terms. The stage was set for a Kentucky home where visitors could enter a plantation house and imagine themselves living there. The verses about the slave trade that tore apart a family were right there, but dialed down to near inaudibility. Yet Henrietta Vinton Davis had, if only briefly, assembled a beloved Black community in *Our Old Kentucky Home.* In that imagined home, the broken ties and psychic wounds of centuries might heal. A very different fantasy unfolded as an official Kentucky Home assumed its place in the landscape.

6

WHERE ALL WAS DELIGHT

Creating *the* Old Kentucky Home

A hot breeze blew through Young E. Allison's almost-white hair as he swerved to avoid ruts on the road from Louisville to Bardstown in August 1917. The music lover, amateur historian, and longtime journalist helped organize the state's presence at the 1904 St. Louis World's Fair and witnessed the triumphant Foster Day at Louisville's 1906 Home Coming. The marketing potential of "My Old Kentucky Home" was patently clear to Young Allison, even if most people had no idea who wrote the song or who Stephen Foster was. He could change that. Tales of the song originating at the Rowan place had circulated for decades, but the specifics remained murky, and Allison, whose work had been published in national magazines, set out to establish the complete history of Foster's important time in Kentucky. Turning onto the rough drive that led to the house with its many-eyed brick walls, Allison parked his early-model automobile. He had an appointment with the mistress of Federal Hill and was prepared, he told a friend, to root out "the whole story of how ["My Old Kentucky Home"] was written."

That day, Allison did not imagine that he would lead an unprecedented public-private campaign to open Federal Hill as Kentucky's first historic home. And yet something along those lines had been percolating in his mind well before he approached Madge Rowan Frost for help with his Foster essay. At least as early as 1912, five years before he drove out to Federal Hill, Young Allison had envisioned Kentucky planting somewhere a "shrine" to Stephen Foster in some "central spot," a symbolic "home for all" that would welcome visitors from near and far. Allison was certain that tapping the song for tourists could boost the needy state's economy. Thousands, maybe hundreds of thousands, would come, wallets in their pockets, to honor the songwriter and soak up Kentucky heritage.

The My Old Kentucky Home crusade Young Allison would launch in the early 1920s harnessed the possibilities of expanding automotive tourism to white Americans' hunger for Old South heritage. One, perhaps unintended, result was that Kentucky was framed as explicitly southern. Unambiguously intended was attracting tourists and their dollars, and the state's malleable history had work to do in achieving that outcome. Allison stepped in to do that work. Tirelessly. *The* brick-and-mortar Old Kentucky Home in Bardstown depended on a narrative about the state, the South, the Civil War, and Stephen Foster that was riddled with contortions of fact—each of which bolstered representations of human bondage as mild and pleasant. Young E. Allison recognized the deficiencies almost from the start, yet countenanced them to achieve his goal and the social benefits he was sure it would bring. Nearly a hundred years later, Federal Hill remains a state park, host since 1959 to the outdoor summer musical *The Stephen Foster Story* and, according to its web page, "Kentucky's most famous and beloved historic site." Millions have visited.

Tourism in Kentucky had been rooted in the landscape wonders of Mammoth Cave (which had drawn visitors since the early nineteenth century) and the Bluegrass region's equine bloodstock farms. The new century witnessed a proliferation of "shrines" aimed at pilgrims. In 1905 the editor of *Collier's* magazine proposed a memorial to Abraham Lincoln at his birthplace in Hodgenville, twenty-five miles south of Bardstown. Six years later, President William Howard Taft dedicated the marble-and-granite temple that ensconced a log cabin purporting to be Lincoln's childhood home. In 1917, as Allison navigated the ruts on his way to his date with Madge Rowan Frost, a 351-foot obelisk honoring the "first" president of the Confederate States of America was under construction in Jefferson Davis's birthplace in tiny Fairview, Kentucky. Funded chiefly by the Daughters of the Confederacy, the me-

Born in 1853, the year "My Old Kentucky Home" was first published, the journalist and amateur historian Young E. Allison helped resuscitate Stephen Foster's reputation and in 1921 helped lead the effort to open a public "shrine" to the composer.

morial stands two-thirds the height of the Washington Monument. At the same time, the Kentucky Derby was gradually transitioning from a "pipsqueak Dixie picnic" to a premier national sporting event with a festival atmosphere that brought thousands of racegoers to Louisville, chiefly from the North and West.

Young E. Allison was born the year Foster published his tune about an American sold down the river to die in the sugarcane fields. His father was the county clerk in Henderson, Kentucky, a tobacco trading center on the big brown Ohio River. As a boy, Young understood what the song was about. The family was bookish and musical, too; they occasionally performed in public as a quartet. Allison recalled hearing songs from Stephen Foster's "starry pen" as a toddler leaning against his mother's leg, which transmitted the vibrations of the piano strings. As a child of twelve, he became Henderson's deputy clerk of court, running errands and copying deeds in his small, neat hand.

Young Allison's father might have cast the county's lone 1860 vote for Lincoln. When Union troops occupied the town, he became their local point person. At the age of nine or ten "little Yank" Allison became a camp mascot. He began editing the local newspaper when he was fifteen and moved on to Louisville's *Courier-Journal,* where he also reviewed plays and concerts. Allison published fiction and wrote the librettos for two original operas and an acclaimed poem inspired by Robert Louis Stevenson's beloved adventure tale *Treasure Island.* His career began as Jim Crow took root, and slavery and relations between races were themes in some of his essays. But these he published anonymously; in public, he muted those concerns. Active in the Republican Party that most freed people favored, Allison for a time edited and co-owned a paper affiliated with the party. By 1917, he had left daily journalism to edit an insurance industry publication. He pursued his literary activities on the side.

It rankled him that Foster had "lapsed into intangible and sentimental memory." Outside Morrison Foster's fragmentary 1896 memoir, little was known about the composer's life and career. A friend scoured the Library of Congress on Allison's behalf but came up with little beyond copies of sheet music. Allison sought input about the songwriter's time in Cincinnati from an amateur historian there. He followed *The Atlantic Monthly*'s lead and separated Foster personally from the blackface industry that paved his way to success. The composer "cared nothing for the minstrels, as such . . . only wrote *for* them," Allison concluded. In any case, he rightly argued, blackface, which demeaned the "negro character," was "not 'negro' at all." Instead, he called it "white excess" under burnt cork. Protecting Foster, Allison decried bigoted "white excess" without challenging a superstructure of theft, violence, denial of civil rights, and exclusion from opportunity that privileged and enriched white Americans. This position has been dear to polite progressives ever since.

Armed with an appealing tale, scant facts, and a conviction that elevating Foster would help elevate Kentucky, Allison wanted to pin down the story that had been circulating since the 1895 Rowan-Frost wedding of Foster's visit to Federal Hill. Madge Rowan Frost had been widowed and was spending less time in St. Louis and more time in Bardstown. She stayed aloof from her neighbors, however, depending for companionship on a parrot and several dogs. To have a man of Allison's stature take an interest in "those faraway beautiful days" was tonic to her heart.

Writing to Allison, Frost grumbled about the incompetent and "ineffi-cient darkies" working in her home. They made it impossible to extend, as she would have liked to do, "the hospitality of the olden times."

Judge Rowan's granddaughter had nothing to confirm that Foster visited Federal Hill, much less that he wrote "My Old Kentucky Home" there. Morrison Foster's memoir, which Frost lent her guest, made no mention of it. A scrapbook of clippings she had compiled over the years merely repeated the familiar claims. A few weeks after their meeting, Madge felt grateful that "in spite of the uncertainty" Allison had "not lost interest in the old house" and its owners. Allison did some spade-work of his own. He interviewed other Bardstowners, and one man in his nineties told of Foster's visiting John Rowan Jr. at his "chateau," its "fields and tobacco patches lively with the labors of many slaves," wan-dering among them with his flute and "trying out the plaintive strains he had heard." Allison knew sentimental fog when he saw it, but the tale fit his purpose. Back in Louisville, he drafted an essay about Federal Hill that framed the Rowans as members of a "half-feudal" aristocracy, "a race apart." Allison sent the essay to New York magazine editors, try-ing to get his "yarn" about Stephen Foster in Kentucky into print. None took it, and the manuscript went into a drawer.

Then, in 1919, Madge Rowan Frost declared that the "dear old Kentucky home" had "become too much." The house, which a local attorney called "a dilapidated pile," was going to ruin. In one of the more blatantly damning confabulations, which during Jim Crow elic-ited white sympathy, she blamed her trials on "good for nothing" Black people who worked for her, and yearned to "get out of their power." Perhaps Kentucky could borrow from a northern state's playbook. Frost had heard that New York was buying up "historic places." (Indeed the Women's Roosevelt Memorial Association had recently purchased Presi-dent Theodore Roosevelt's birthplace.) Madge turned to Young Allison for help with a sale that would open Federal Hill to visitors while pre-serving its "dignity and sentiment."

Allison was considering what, if anything, to do for the mistress of Federal Hill when Henry Watterson, the longtime and revered editor of Louisville's *Courier-Journal,* hung Stephen Foster out to a national audience as a "ne'er do well" and a plagiarist. *The Saturday Evening Post* published the seventy-nine-year-old Watterson's memoir as a serial, and Allison rose to defend the songwriter's honor and talent against the famous newsman. He reworked his essay about the Rowans and the composer's alleged Kentucky sojourn into a speech about Stephen Foster's superior craft. In 1920, it appeared as the pamphlet *Stephen C. Foster and American Songs*. Before Allison delivered his work to the state historical society, a poet read verses inspired by "My Old Kentucky Home": "When the darkey could his banjo play / At cabin door—at rest and free. / And sing: 'Weep no more.'" Possibly, Allison winced. He was trying to make a different point, one not about racial hierarchy but about a neglected "genius" of "universal" appeal whose best work went "straight to the heart." True, Foster suffered from a "weak and fatal love of drink," but like Italy's Giuseppe Verdi he had crafted a nation's music. The progressive Allison, the once-youthful "Little Yank" who wrote of discomfort with "white excess," hailed Stephen Foster for capturing his era's "emotional history."

The intimacy, harmony, and safety Allison experienced as a white child hearing Foster songs played in his home likely prompted his defense of the Pittsburgh composer six decades later. With Federal Hill now available, promoting Stephen Foster dovetailed with a fast-changing transportation economy, a growing market for American heritage, and a burgeoning fascination with plantations and the so-called Old South. It also appealed to a Republican governor eager to smooth Kentucky's reputation for backwardness, which telegraphed inhospitality to business development and tourism.

Only one American in every thousand owned an automobile in 1900; by 1913 that portion had climbed to one in thirty-five. Swaths of formerly inaccessible places opened to tourists when people could travel independently from rail lines and at their own pace. Between 1914 and 1917, automotive production quadrupled from under half a million vehicles a year to more than two million. The Good Roads movement rallied a coalition of drivers, civic boosters, farmers seeking easier ways to market crops, and politicians to extend and improve paved thoroughfares. One project, the Dixie Highway, would guide motorists all the way from Michigan via Kentucky to sun-filled Florida. The Bluegrass State was poised to take advantage of the traffic, because it boasted more than ten thousand miles of macadam pavement; Tennessee and Georgia combined had less than four hundred miles.

Automotive leisure travelers were generally well-off, native-born whites interested in the history of a nation that, with the end of World War I, had proven its influence on a global scale. "Washington slept here" claims cropped up like dandelions. Businesses counted the dollars pilgrims spent, and preservationists argued that entering such spaces had "mystical" effects: citizens would exit better educated and more patriotic. People flocked to George Washington's Mount Vernon and Andrew Jackson's Hermitage outside Nashville to see into the grand homes of great men. For all its pavement, Kentucky had no "house museum" to offer, and Lincoln's humble cabin with its dubious provenance did not quite fit the bill. Over the years, Bardstowners had witnessed plenty of disappointed curiosity seekers turned away by Madge Frost's sign: "Visitors Will Not Come in House."

Allison felt reasonably certain that Foster visited Federal Hill at some point even if he did not write the song there. His qualms focused more on the Rowans, whom he called in a private letter "a hard, selfish, and pretentious race." His language here is telling: the Rowans were a race, and a selfish one at that. Allison had originally referred to Madge's father as a heavy drinker, a "dilettante of art, politics, and literature" who never buckled to a profession and left his wife and children unprovided for. Such sentiments, however, were misaligned with most Americans' expectations. Indeed, one reason his first stab at writing about Stephen Foster in Kentucky might have failed to appeal to publishers was that it failed to offer up sufficiently idealized genteel antebellum enslavers.

The true north to Young Allison's compass that directed so much of his decision making was that no place in Kentucky had a *better* claim to the songwriter. Having declared Foster's significance in his duel with Henry Watterson, he rolled up his sleeves and determined to give the world a place to celebrate the author of "My Old Kentucky Home," which, as one supporter of the cause noted, brought a poor state "more publicity than any other one thing." A Republican attorney in Bardstown, Osso Stanley, signed on to help. Whereas private, female-run memorial associations had preserved presidential homes at Mount Vernon and the Hermitage, Allison and Stanley launched their crusade at the top, with the newly elected Republican governor, Edwin P. Morrow. The legislature agreed to a citizen commission charged with purchasing the place where "the immortal song" had been written. In 1920, legend slipped into the annals of Kentucky law.

Long before the state appointed the Old Kentucky Home Commission in 1920, picture postcards claimed it was the place "where Stephen Collins Foster wrote 'My Old Kentucky Home.'"

The Old Kentucky Home Commission balked at the $65,000 price tag Madge Rowan Frost hung on her homestead, especially because just a decade earlier the entire farm was valued at $10,000. Whatever its sentimental worth, the old house with "shattered windows and shutters akimbo, infested with snakes and wasps, furniture draped in shredded old bedspreads" was no shoo-in for a state legislature managing falling revenues. Morrow appointed three millionaires to the group, doubtless hoping that they would put up all or most of the needed funds. Instead, they bargained Frost down to $50,000 and obtained a $10,000 option on the mansion. The balance, they announced, would come from patriotic fellow Kentuckians. In a March 1921 meeting with the governor, Young Allison used the back of an envelope to sketch an Old Kentucky Home publicity campaign and statewide fundraising strategy. He charged himself with "general newspaper propaganda."

The "silver-tongued" governor Edwin P. Morrow called to his people, declaring that Foster's melody "has made us all better men, better women and better citizens. It has tugged at our heartstrings—let it now tug at our pursestrings." Some questioned the high price, but Allison reassured the public that the site would attract hundreds of thousands of yearly tourists on par with Philadelphia's Independence Hall. He also reminded them that the purchase included antiques, portraits, and other relics representing the "shared memory of Kentuckians." He tried to steer a narrative that was relatively factual, but a clear-eyed view of the past was at cross-purposes with the larger political and fundraising effort.

Locating Foster at Federal Hill was the problem, as it had been in 1904 when another governor ordered the purchase of a Foster desk for display at the St. Louis World's Fair Kentucky Building. "Meager Records Leave Doubt of Foster's Residence," announced one skeptical headline. The article repeated a tale about the bard lounging under the trees trying out the tune with help from his sister Charlotte, but she had died when Foster was three. Another story held that the composer visited Bardstown when he lived in Cincinnati in the late 1840s while he was tabulating cotton bales for his brother's shipping business—possible, but that contradicted a Frost family account of his handing the first draft of the song to Judge Rowan, who was buried years before the songwriter came to Cincinnati. Tales placed Stephen in Bardstown when the steamboat he rode to New Orleans in 1852 paused for a few hours in Louisville, but journeying forty miles each way to Bardstown and writing a song while he was there were out of the question. A favorite myth had the original manuscript of the tune (conveniently) destroyed in a blaze that damaged part of the house. But the fire occurred while the songwriter was a boy in Pittsburgh.

Allison concluded that the true origin of "My Old Kentucky Home" was "long since lost in the restorations" and the tendency to embellish was nothing more than the natural "desire for contact with the humanity of the past." If Foster had been there with the Rowans at some point, Allison felt that should suffice. A recent biography of the composer by a respectable music scholar did not help Allison's cause; the author dismissed the stories about Foster at Federal Hill as unverifiable.

For Governor Morrow and those asking for donations, it was essential that Foster be *definitely* placed, writing the song amid the waving cornfields and stately rooms of Madge Frost's house. The Old Kentucky Home Commission's "Let's Buy It" campaign otherwise appeared a transparent counterfeit—a boondoggle. Tasked with fudging the issue, Allison called the latest Foster biography "flimsy" and concluded illogically that no matter the stories ("some silly, some romantic") told about

"My Old Kentucky Home," "the only thing clearly true is that he wrote it at Federal Hill." It was a lie. No matter how passionately Allison believed in his cause, he also knew better. The slope only grew more slippery.

This compromise was but one—perhaps the least damaging—that Allison would make. He twisted himself into knots trying to honor Stephen Foster at Federal Hill without glamorizing enslavers or the "hopeless, tragic" institution of human bondage. When appealing for donations to purchase Federal Hill, Allison sometimes alluded to souls "lost . . . over the gaming tables" or sold as "punishment for their 'intractability.'" Nonetheless, at Bardstown he suggested (without a shred of evidence) that the songwriter witnessed slavery in its "highest" form. He knew in 1921 that for most traveling white tourists "My Old Kentucky Home" called forth "the glamor of the state's golden youth." Southerners saw in it "a romantic picture" of plantation days. Allison noted that "My Old Kentucky Home" "had a deeper and more significant meaning" in homes "where slavery was hated." (He had lived in such a home but didn't say that, and he knew only too well that the final verse, "now wholly ignored," told of a family broken.) To unravel the melody's layered meanings only complicated the work of fundraising and lobbying.

Potential contributors to the statewide fundraising effort to purchase Federal Hill for a "My Old Kentucky Home" tourist attraction were urged to let the song "tug at your purse strings." Those who gave could hang this small paper tag on their coat button.

The men running the "Old Kentucky Home—Let's Buy It" crusade filled its luffing sails with white plantation fantasies even as they promoted the song as a universal expression of "yearning of no race or color." The climax came in May 1921 with a statewide "My Old Kentucky Home Week." Church leaders wove Federal Hill into Sunday sermons. Schoolchildren earned certificates by selling postcards of Federal Hill, learned about Foster's life story, and presented costumed blackface "pantomimes," acting the part of (enslaved) "expatriates . . . endowed with gratitude and longing and resignation and the strange beauty that resides under the darkest skin—crooning the memories of this lost paradise." On Old Kentucky Home Day, volunteers in 171 towns sought donations; each location had a quota. Men solicited business owners and placed "Let's Buy It" placards in windows. Young women literally buttonholed citizens: donors received a small tag with an image of Federal Hill to hang on their coat buttons. The finale was an evening musical revue in Louisville's municipal auditorium aimed at the society set. Orchestral arrangements were interspersed with blackface minstrel acts. Lions Club members impersonated a Black trombone quintet, and sixty normal school students posed "as mammies and pickaninnies" in a lighthearted scene from "Federal Hill in 1850." Thanks to Allison, the local press covered every angle of the commission's efforts.

Contented and subordinate Black people were the order of the day, the week, the month, the entire Jim Crow era, and this white requirement for Black behavior has far outlasted bondage. No wonder the state's official pamphlet for the Old Kentucky Home campaign praised Foster for capturing the "kindly, childlike obedience and natural respect which emanated from the darkies" and hailed his prescience in foreseeing the "pathos and tragedy" that the Civil War would bring "the Kentucky people." Following this logic, enslaved Kentuckians were either excluded as "people" or assumed to have suffered from their emancipation—possibly both. With the feelings or experiences of Black people set thoroughly aside, whites convinced themselves that the tune "inspired a powerful sympathy and love of home between the races." Not surprisingly, the Let's Buy It campaign neither sought nor found any foothold with Black Kentuckians.

.   .   .

Two months after "My Old Kentucky Home" week, the Louisville educator and poet Joseph S. Cotter climbed the original limestone slab steps to Federal Hill's front door. He knocked. This was against protocol; people with darker skin and servants (usually the same thing) entered houses like Madge Frost's by the back door to underscore their lower status. But Cotter (1861–1949) laid special claim to the space Kentuckians were being asked to embrace as their patrimony. The Let's Buy It publicity struck a personal chord because his mother, Martha Vaughn, had lived there. Cotter's grandfather, a free Black man, hired out his seven children for long terms as indentured servants, and the year "My Old Kentucky Home" was published thirteen-year-old Martha was bound to the Rowans. Madge was not yet born, but Martha nursed her older twin sisters, milked the four cows, cleaned the house, and cooked the family meals. This was the era when Madge's mother, Rebecca, liked to show off the "costly garments" she had worn in Naples when her husband served as U.S. envoy to the Kingdom of the Two Sicilies. It was also the era when there were no tales being told at Federal Hill about Stephen Foster, whose song about a slave in Kentucky was spreading through the land on the tongues of minstrel troupes and printed sheets.

Cotter's mother was traded to another household and labored in what Joseph Cotter called a "half house of bondage," passed from one master to another until the Civil War. Before she was taken to Louisville in 1859, her father had "free papers" drawn up at Bardstown's courthouse to prove her non-enslaved status. Bounty hunters and thieves were snaring free Black people, and he feared Martha might be stolen and sold into bondage. The piece of paper offered modest protections. In 1860, a white manager of a Louisville tobacco warehouse and grandfather of the children she cared for impregnated Martha Vaughn. During Joseph's childhood, Martha worked as a laundress and managed to send him to school for a year or two. He picked rags, then found work at a brickyard, at a tobacco factory, and driving wagons. White Presbyterians opened a "colored night school," and in 1883 twenty-two-year-old Joseph Cotter earned his diploma.

The Old Kentucky Home Commission probably never pictured a pilgrim like Joseph Cotter, a man dedicated to racial uplift and a Black Kentuckian in search of his own heritage. Cotter, sixty, had located the ruined homestead of a great-grandfather who had purchased his own

The mother of the poet and school principal Joseph S. Cotter spent part of her childhood at Federal Hill in the 1850s as a bound servant. He visited the house in 1921 and was inspired to rewrite the lyrics to Stephen Foster's old melody, removing "darkies." The educator established a storytelling competition with a prize Cotter Cup for children at the "colored branch" of Louisville's library.

freedom in 1829, but Federal Hill was the only dwelling still standing that his mother had known in her youth. She died in 1906 soon after the Home Coming parade and celebrations, and Cotter had written to tell the Frosts about the long-ago connection between the families. Madge remembered, and that summer day in 1921 she invited the school principal and his local "little brown guide" into the wide hall. Frost toured them through the rooms, pointing out relics—the desk where Foster "wrote" his famous melody, a table where the Marquis de Lafayette had once sat, "vases, chairs, swords," and a book more than a hundred years old. Cotter watched the child gaze in wonder at "so much history" and thought to himself, "Could the inheritance of past ages be laid at the feet of the black child as it is at the feet of the white child, a new page would soon be written in the affairs of men." Slavery robbed Black people of wages, of freedom, of parents and children—of so much family history.

Cotter emerged from the "magic mansion" and turned down the "tree-gemmed" driveway. The out-of-time visit to the crumbling manor recalled an Edgar Allan Poe tale. Cotter thanked his mother's spirit, bound to that house as a child, for bringing him back. As he hummed "My Old Kentucky Home," parts of Foster's "wording and sentiment" grated on him. They didn't fit "the present-day Negro," Joseph suggested moderately. He advised that "unless there is a change, he will cease to sing . . . a beautiful melody." He set out to make that change, and his edits to the lyrics reversed the tide of sentiment from a past of bondage to a future of dignity and prosperity for his race. Cotter deleted the offensive "darkies" in favor of "Negroes" and amended two verses:

> *The day trips by with a solace for the heart*
> *To charm it and give it delight.*
> *The time has come when the Negro does his part*
> *To make My Old Kentucky Home alright.*

> *The time has come when the head will never bow*
> *Wherever the Negro may go.*
> *A few more years and he'll show the nation how*
> *He will thrive where the sugar canes grow.*
> *A few more years and he'll shift the weary load*
> *So that it will ever be light*
> *A few more years and he'll triumph on the road*
> *And sing, My Old Kentucky Home's alright.*

Two decades after Henrietta Vinton Davis created a fictive Black homeplace in *Our Old Kentucky Home,* Cotter's alterations reversed Foster's melody from a nostalgia-coated tragedy peopled by docile "darkies" to a celebration of Black progress. Both pressed back against the song's persistent whitewashing. To "triumph on the road" and make the Kentucky home "alright" required enormous effort and great faith. James Weldon Johnson and John Rosamond Johnson's turn-of-the-century "Lift Ev'ry Voice and Sing" (known today as the Black national anthem) struck a similar chord:

Sing a song full of the faith that the dark past has taught us,
Sing a song full of the hope that the present has brought us.
Facing the rising sun of our new day begun,
Let us march on 'til victory is won.

Cotter's alterations to "My Old Kentucky Home" were published in 1922 in *The Louisville Leader,* the city's Black-owned newspaper. But the proposal to update "My Old Kentucky Home" got little notice.

No wonder, when in that same issue *The Louisville Leader* was forced to address matters of life and limb, of violence that left "black bodies swinging in the southern breeze." Federal antilynching legislation languished in Congress year after year. It was a day of triumph for leaders like Cotter when Kentucky's governor, Edwin P. Morrow, signed a modest NAACP-backed bill aimed at curbing extralegal executions. Even then, mob brutality was too often replaced with state-sanctioned "legal lynchings," executions after convictions by all-white juries in trials where defendants lacked any semblance of competent counsel. Adapting a popular song that gave white people a warm feeling but made Black people queasy might have gone a little way toward humanizing Black people and their hopes, but Kentucky's population (89 percent were white) was not interested. For Kentuckians who were, as the *Leader*'s editors explained, "Jim crowed, lynched, the object of scorn and discrimination, always last and never first, the underdog day after day," the lyrics of Stephen Foster's "My Old Kentucky Home" were a relatively minor concern.

Allison and his fellow commissioners pressed ahead, lobbying the General Assembly to shore up the Old Kentucky Home's funding. For the organizers of Let's Buy It confronted an embarrassing truth. Young Allison had worked the press hard, and the commission paid to mail seventy thousand fundraising letters. Volunteers buttonholed passersby. Yet the campaign secretary conceded that the effort met "general apathy." Osso Stanley, the Bardstown attorney, failed to get local businesses to pony up their pledges and hit barely 25 percent of his quota. Neither did Kentucky children tasked with filling Rowan-home-shaped mite boxes close the gap. In addition to the purchase, the Old Kentucky Home needed extensive repairs before welcoming tourists. Kentuckians had not loosened their "pursestrings" very much, but their representatives in Frankfort granted the remaining $20,000 to buy the site and promised the same amount as an annual subsidy for operations.

With financing secured, the commissioners hired the honorary "Colonel" Benjamin LaBree to open Federal Hill to the public. LaBree was the only person without a southern war record to have a chapter of the Daughters of the Confederacy named in his honor. Lively and compact, he wore an impressive mustache. The Philadelphia native had arrived in Kentucky in 1886, and, though an outsider, LaBree struck Madge Rowan Frost as someone "born and destined" for the job. After failing in a trotting horse venture, LaBree rode ballooning Civil War nostalgia into a career—editing books and magazines such as *The Lost Cause,* marketed to UDC members. He built a strong network among well-to-do Kentuckians by performing the genealogical research they needed for their Sons and Daughters of the American Revolution applications. LaBree represented a professional vanguard of heritage work previously left to female volunteers and was bursting with ideas for the site. He proposed, for example, that Kentucky locate its central publicity office at Federal Hill and market tobacco, sorghum, and watermelons grown there under a My Old Kentucky Home label.

The July 4, 1923, opening date (Stephen Foster's birthday) maximized the patriotic aura Colonel LaBree wanted the house to exude. He confronted literal headwinds. Just weeks before the appointed day, a cyclone tore off a piece of the roof. Other members of the Rowan family regarded the "Old Kentucky Home" shrine as hokum, while Madge Frost argued with the state commission about which furniture the sale included, complained that taxes ate into her payment, and refused to vacate the house, insisting on helping LaBree with the preparations.

The tourist experience LaBree established at Federal Hill endured for half a century. Long-dead Rowan duelists were lionized as gilded Kentucky aristocrats. Unrestrained myths crusted over the house and its contents. Fantasies ran amok—about Foster, southern belles, and the requisite singing Black folks. The fiction of a thriving antebellum Old Kentucky Home defined the site when LaBree unbarred the door on July 4. According to a Louisville newspaper, the influx began early. "Those who would commune with the spirit of the past and enjoy first-hand the thrills of it, gathered at Federal Hill at 7:30 o'clock this morning. Horses . . . pulled buggies—there are many yet in Central

Kentucky's governor, Edwin P. Morrow, supported creating a tourist attraction around Foster's song. When the site opened, Morrow hailed Stephen Foster for making men's hearts thrill at the mention of home. Fundraising for the purchase and renovation of the property fell short, and Kentucky taxpayers have subsidized the Old Kentucky Home in Bardstown since 1923.

Kentucky." Then came the cars in "a stream of traffic that was a flood." Throngs entered the hundred-year-old great house on a hill "to learn," and "beautiful women" dressed in their grandmothers' hoopskirts guided them through the rooms, collectively embodying the weeping lady of the song's yearning refrain. LaBree pointed members of the crowd to Judge Rowan's grave, falsely claiming it had inspired Foster's song "Massa's in de Cold Ground."

Governor Morrow, who leaned on "The Old Kentucky Home" as a comforting and rhetorical rock of continuity while pushing for infrastructure and education expenditures, officially received the site from the Old Kentucky Home Commission on behalf of all citizens. All-white singers performed the song about "home—'the holy of holies.'"

Federal Hill became the core of Kentucky tourism. Visitors, most from the North, streamed through. A summer Sunday could attract 700, and LaBree's ledgers count more than 300,000 visitors from 1923 to 1931. The colonel personally conducted tours, dishing out a "taste of the hospitality" that made Kentucky famous. He discoursed on the "matchless old furniture and curios," which were claimed to be more numerous and significant than those displayed at Mount Vernon. Tourists could spend the night at a new motel across the road and "fall in the spirit of the witchery of the southern moon as it plays among the trees that canopy the avenues lined with stately residences." In Bardstown, visitors could live "again in the past."

The tourist site reshaped the song and Kentucky's image to the wider world. The song mentioned only a cabin home, but under Jim Crow the imagined Kentucky home of Foster's melody gradually morphed into a spacious plantation home that white Americans envisioned themselves inhabiting. Also expunged: the man whose forced removal gave the song its voice. Visitors absorbed the impression that if this was "the home," then the people far away who had to leave it were its owners. No other state had yet applied substantial taxpayer money to what the historian Fitzhugh Brundage has called the "commercialization of the southern past." By the end of the 1920s, with the Kentucky Home as a linchpin, the state's self-proclaimed heritage "progressed" steadily from Native American savagery to rustic pioneer settlement to refined plantation living that was all the more romantic because the Civil War snuffed it out.

The plantation narrative was heavy with political meaning when four times as many Kentuckians joined the Union army as fought for the southern cause. Kentucky also enlisted more men into the ranks of the U.S. Colored Troops than any state except Louisiana. Democratic state legislatures established pensions for veterans of the "Lost Cause," and, along with the Daughters of the Confederacy, opened retirement homes for the aged and infirm among them. The "Daughters" also erected a small forest of monuments across Kentucky. Union-affiliated monuments were (and remain) few. In the same period, mainly male, mainly Republican business leaders conceived and managed a crusade to spur economic growth by honoring a master songwriter born in Pennsylvania. That both their efforts ultimately presented Kentucky (to its own citizens as well as to tourists) as a fundamentally southern place where slavery (if unfortunate) was benevolent suggests how irresistible an idealized Old South was to America's white majority.

The success of My Old Kentucky Home in Bardstown spurred the

General Assembly to adopt as its official anthem the melody about slavery that "immortalized Kentucky throughout the civilized world and is known and sung in every state and nation." The old blackface minstrel tune became a sanctioned symbol as Kentucky itself was whitening. Between the 1904 world's fair with its New Kentucky Home theme and 1930, the Bluegrass State bled black. The number of white Kentuckians grew by more than 25 percent, but the Black population decreased by one-fifth as the Great Migration swept six million southerners beleaguered by Jim Crow into urban areas outside the South.

Kentucky's powerful had embraced "My Old Kentucky Home." But it was Martin J. "Matt" Winn, the "greatest and shrewdest showman since Barnum," who converted the work of earlier boosters, Old Kentucky Home commissioners, marketers, and politicians into a hat trick that lofted the Foster melody into the world of thoroughbred horse racing. It became and has remained a fixture—gluing anticipation to emotion for millions—on the first Saturday of May.

Winn was a merchant tailor with an eye for fast horses before he joined the management of Louisville's failing racetrack in 1902 to take charge of its amusement and catering departments. The story goes that thenceforth he lived and breathed the Kentucky Derby. He rose to track president, and when he was widowed, he outfitted a bachelor apartment overlooking the loop. Top owners with plenty of places to take prize three-year-olds succumbed to his unrelenting salesmanship. Kentucky's Derby (there were many derbies then) had been run each year since 1875, and Winn marketed the race as a vintage jewel with the paradoxically "fresh flavor of legend." The portly, bourbon-sipping (never before noon) raconteur swore by his public relations mantra: "Tell 'em about it, and tell 'em again. And again. And again." Winn took his show on the road, entertaining the horse world with assistance from a "long line of colored boys" who served Kentucky country ham and prize Prohibition bourbon. The track ran ads in midwestern and northern newspapers to attract spectators, and by the time of the Let's Buy It effort Winn had cemented himself and his Derby into legend, transforming a race that attracted a middling crowd of locals into the most glamorous equine competition of the year. Each spring, Louisville leaped to life as thousands, then tens of thousands of visitors arrived to be amused and catered to.

Innovations at Churchill Downs, such as the pari-mutuel wagering machines called totalizers that bloomed in the infield in 1908 so bettors could view odds and dollars wagered, unfolded in an atmosphere of tradition. But that tradition was not at first explicitly southern.

An upgraded 1912 clubhouse designed in a "colonial style" gave an anchoring aura for the "society" racegoers Winn wanted to attract. If the "ladies and gentlemen" came to the Derby and set the tone, "the ordinary people would beat the doors down to get in." During the 1930s, the Derby's and Louisville's tone shifted southward. A new entry gate from the early 1940s was "reminiscent of an Old South mansion." Genuflecting to an increasingly popular Lost Cause antebellum myth became a key tool for creating atmosphere and selling tickets.

Foster's sentimental minstrel song was right under Winn's nose, but it was not an official element of the Derby experience. However, right after the 1921 Let's Buy It campaign concluded, a Kentucky-bred

"My Old Kentucky Home" became a Kentucky Derby ritual in 1930, part of a strategy by the longtime track president, Martin J. "Matt" Winn, to anchor the race in an Old South aura.

colt triumphed at the big race. Spectators spontaneously "gave vent to their delight" by singing what *The Courier-Journal* called Stephen Foster's "joy-paean." In 1927, Chicago's WGN aired the first live Kentucky Derby broadcast, which opened with the Pullman Porters' Quartet "crooning 'My Old Kentucky Home.'" By Derby Day 1929, a year after the state of Kentucky adopted Foster's melody as its anthem, a brass band hired to roam the betting area and grandstands "exuded 'My Old Kentucky Home' at proper intervals." One Chicago racing aficionado rose to remove his hat whenever the song began, as if it were the national anthem. "He was plumb worn out from standing up and sitting down throughout the afternoon."

The song was one winner Matt Winn had overlooked. Finally, in 1930 "My Old Kentucky Home" assumed its sacred place at Churchill Downs. A crowd estimated at sixty thousand clutched their bets and hoped for a winner as the prancing three-year-olds entered the dirt track. At that "moment of moments," "My Old Kentucky Home" played "muted and slow." Winn had figured out that Foster's old melody was *better* than "The Star-Spangled Banner" to focus the crowd and capture the Derby aura. While Winn had been late to incorporate the song into his event, he did recognize its capacity to align local sentiment with a shifting regional identity. He swung late but hit the sweet spot, and the city followed his lead. In the early 1930s, a consortium of local businesses called Advertising Louisville switched the slogan that greeted drivers upon arrival on the river's Kentucky side of a new automobile bridge from "Louisville Center of American Markets" to "Gateway to the South."

"The sun shines bright" elevated the Derby's deepening Old South profile in ways "O say can you see" could not. Besides, it packed way more emotional power. For Winn and white racegoers entrenched in a Jim Crow culture and legal system that subordinated people with darker skin in countless ways, a onetime blackface minstrel song was more unifying, more satisfying, more memorable, and just as patriotic. In 1932, a "loud band" played "My Old Kentucky Home," and the crowd roared so deafeningly that the Derby horses spooked, forcing jockeys to wrestle them back into control. The University of Louisville marching band first performed the melody from the infield in 1936, by which time the sonic addition to the event aroused such hallowed reverence that out-of-towners assumed it had been in place since 1875. The song completed a sensory adventure into a benign South where visitors could touch down and be served by smiling Black waiters and soothed by Foster's ode to days on the old plantation. Winn built a ritual in which, "along toward sunset," racegoers would see the horses come onto the track. "Softly, came the strains of 'My Old Kentucky Home,' and, suddenly, a lump came to their throats," until "the cry, 'They're off.'" Back home, they could describe the elements. "And the next year," Winn wrote in his memoir, "they were back, perhaps bringing friends."

The developments at Churchill Downs elated Benjamin LaBree. Even more people would now visit the "antebellum mansion" where Foster "wrote the world's best loved ballad." But the curator's blushless showmanship had cost him Young Allison's confidence. As a founder of the campaign to create the site, Allison retained a proprietary interest in Federal Hill's success. Allison, too, had taken liberties with history, but he turned on LaBree, who seemed to know no bounds in this regard. LaBree claimed the Marquis de Lafayette had stayed there; in fact, Judge Rowan entertained the Revolutionary War hero in Louisville. Credulous visitors learned that eight presidents had darkened the Rowan door— "nonsense," said Allison. Postcards sold on-site explained that Federal Hill's bricks were imported from England and then brought on "sledges in winter along the Indian Trails, drawn by Oxen." In reality, enslaved people from the immediate area fashioned them one by one. Allison wrote blistering—albeit anonymous—letters to the editor, accusing the curator of trafficking in "tawdry myth and legend" that sullied the shrine. Such transparent falsehoods threw suspicion on the one essential myth: that Foster had come to Bardstown, written his song, "and left it sacred forever."

LaBree was the wiser marketer. He knew what visitors to My Old Kentucky Home wanted to see. They wanted Foster, yet Foster alone could not satisfy the appetite for plantation spectacle. So he hired "Old Joe" to play "My Old Kentucky Home" and pretend to be the son of the "Old Black Joe," subject of another Stephen Foster blackface melody. A 1930 photo spread in *Kentucky Progress Magazine* portrayed "the colored minstrel" playing the harmonica and claiming to be ninety-five. Federal Hill had always been his home, he told a reporter. But "I warn't no free nigger years ago when I come here." The wife of Bardstown's long-

Bemis Allen was a fixture at My Old Kentucky Home in Bardstown in the 1930s. Sometimes identified as the son of " 'Uncle Joe' Remus, one of the few Slaves of the Rowans'," and at other times as having himself been enslaved and living his whole life on the estate, Allen enhanced the plantation atmosphere by playing Foster songs on his harmonica.

time congressman laughed out loud when she saw the picture. "Joe" was Bemis Allen, "an old servant of my mother," Annie Johnson wrote. She doubted he had ever set foot on Federal Hill "until this money-making scheme was conceived." The work of this invented history had become, for Allen, work in fact.

My Old Kentucky Home's original curator might also have fabricated the "slave cemetery" in a field beyond the big house. Visitors often wondered where the Black people of Foster's song had sung "by the glimmer of the moon . . . by the old cabin door." Because the site lacked cabins, tourists were offered a burial ground. Crude creek rocks set at odd angles in contrast to the family's walled grave site clustered with clearly marked tombs. A singing Black man who never left his place of enslavement and a grand house full of grand people helped give Federal Hill its "atmosphere of tradition" that conveyed "the life pulse of Kentucky, historic, tragic, romantic." While even he believed in gilding the lily, Allison decided that LaBree had stretched the fragile cord of authenticity to the breaking point.

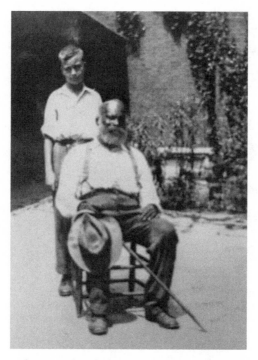

A newspaper story from 1931 described Allen as sitting "quietly in the shade" until asked to pose for pictures, at which point he "obligingly moves his chair into the sun." The family of this child sent the image to the home with thanks for a pleasant visit.

In 1931, LaBree lost his post. He fumed that his successor, a local Republican loyalist, knew nothing about Federal Hill nor the "publicity work" that had made it a success. Just what publicity work amounted to was widely understood. Even a friend of LaBree's conceded that the dapper "factotum" of Federal Hill had a propensity for twisting "the pug nose of truth." And with his departure, Young Allison was relieved, though what had been settled was a grievance that was increasingly more about personalities than facts.

In the years that followed, questioning the legend of Foster's presence was "like waving a red flag in front of a bull." More accurately, it was to no point. The collective investment in the legend vastly exceeded anyone's ability to dent it. A waggish Lexington scholar and antiquarian, John W. Townsend, joked that if he had just one question to ask when he died and went to heaven, he would pose it to Foster: "Stephie,

Visitors to My Old Kentucky Home for the 1936 Stephen Foster Festival were promised a welcome from what *Kentucky Progress Magazine* called "dancing and singing pickaninnies." In yet another reference to blackface minstrelsy, one of the children was posed eating a watermelon.

old boy, were you ever, just for a day, in Bardstown, Kentucky?" He anticipated that the answer was no.

Months before Young Allison died, Townsend ribbed him for the clever way he "ran around that Foster myth." The old journalist shot back with a new lie: "Mrs. Frost remembered as a girl his visit to Federal Hill." Madge wasn't alive when "My Old Kentucky Home" was published in 1853, and Stephen Foster came nowhere near Kentucky between 1852 and his death in New York in 1864. But getting the facts right wasn't the point, and near to his deathbed Allison knew it. He brushed Townsend off with a prediction: "Have it your way, but the other way will always be believed . . . which makes it Holy Writ and history."

At My Old Kentucky Home, Black human beings, when they appeared at all, remained a reassuring presence in an imaginary landscape of cornfields and songbirds. Actual Black people were less welcome, and knew it. Their proportion of the state population whittled down over generations. An estimated one in six of those enslaved in Kentucky was sold away to the lower South in the 1850s alone, shattering families. But that commerce at the center of Foster's lyrics remained obscure in the reimagined past. After emancipation and continuing well into the era of Allison's shrine building, Black Kentuckians fled to escape lynching, disenfranchisement, and cruelly limited opportunities under Jim Crow. Black populations in urban centers outside the South grew quickly in the 1920s and 1930s, and the influx aroused racist tropes of Black men in particular as hypersexual, diseased, innately criminal, unable to "adapt" to full citizenship. Joseph S. Cotter's vision of equity, of educated Black people accessing the resources to "triumph on the road / And sing, My Old Kentucky Home's alright," was, in this context, a threat.

While the redefined ballad no longer required a cabin to house its singer, the keepers of My Old Kentucky Home might have realized that their dishonest version of slavery required its own setting. To better portray contented slaves, Federal Hill in the mid-1930s opened a bogus new building, described as more-than-a-century-old "restored slave quarters," and used it as a gift shop. The Rowans' human property are known to have slept on the dirt floor in the mansion's cellar, but that image contradicted Foster's musical pastoral. This border state's Old Kentucky Home eased white anxieties and validated ongoing systems of white supremacy by enshrining a way of life that only antebellum one percenters had experienced while mounting and marketing an imagined geography of contented enslavement.

Between 1921 and 1930, Kentucky made a trifecta bet on "My Old Kentucky Home": tourist site; state anthem; Derby icon.

Without this lavish approval from officialdom, the song would not be with us still.

Even the Presbyterian missionary whose night school helped Joseph S. Cotter rise from poverty to be a poet and a school principal ridiculed his protégé's grievance about Foster's lyrics as mere "ultra-cultured Negro" thinking. If white citizens of the 1920s considered its impact on race relations or the feelings of Black people at all, they believed "My Old Kentucky Home" served the cause of "sympathy and love of home between the races." As a result, by 1930 the song was more beloved than ever—by whites. Kentucky politicians and business leaders—almost exclusively powerful white men—had distilled plain homesickness into pure nostalgia, one of modernity's most marketable emotions.

And yet. Young Allison knew another homeplace that could far more truly honor the melody's origins. As a young city editor back in 1881, he interviewed the Kentucky fugitive and later abolitionist whose 1845 *Narrative of the Sufferings of Lewis Clarke, During a Captivity of More Than Twenty-Five Years, Among the Algerines of Kentucky, One of the So Called Christian States of North America* informed the character of the runaway George Harris in Harriet Beecher Stowe's *Uncle Tom's Cabin.* Five decades later, the memory of the aged Clarke returning to the site of his bondage in Garrard County, south of Lexington, remained indelible. Allison was himself older than Clarke when he made a pilgrimage back to that Garrard County farm, where, miraculously, the cabin where he had lived in bondage was still standing. Allison's 1881 account of a Black man he plainly admired was reprinted anonymously, forty-seven years later, on the editorial page of the Sunday *Courier-Journal.* Allison also quietly began looking for funding to preserve and open Clarke's Kentucky home to visitors, where the experience of slavery would be centered on those it victimized. Though arguably more connected to Stephen Foster's song than Federal Hill, the cabin project fizzled before it even started. But for a generation or more, white people had been busily forgetting that enslaved people had resisted their bondage. Why would they? Allison himself had written of the "happy home" they had at Federal Hill.

By the time Allison died in 1932, Bardstown's Old Kentucky Home had become for all intents and purposes untouchable. Federal Hill could never have opened to the public without assurances that Foster wrote the famous tune there. Once the myth was in place, contrary evidence scarcely mattered. Allison was right about the holy writ. The shrine lived "on faith."

That faith continued with an occasional wink from those in the know, but I was not in the know before I fell under the spell of the celebratory hospitality and sporting thrill that Churchill Downs president Matt Winn erected around the race. "The first Saturday in May" was encrusted with tradition in my childhood, and being at least as subject to nostalgia as the next person, I later set out as an adult to recapture and make it my own. In my pleasure, I sang and taught others to sing.

The Derby of my early memory conjures the excitement of entertaining in grand style, with all the fluster and anxiety that precedes hosting and the satisfied exhaustion that follows it. Because my family owned print, radio, and television properties, the Kentucky Derby was a valuable tool to promote the companies and to foster relationships. My parents' out-of-town guests were publishers, editors, and broadcasters. I still have the sterling silver miniature horse that the *CBS Evening News* editorialist Eric Sevareid gave me in 1974. On Derby morning, 350 arrived at my house for brunch in hats and seersucker suits. I remember the roar of their voices and the melting mint juleps and half-eaten plates of turkey hash, grits, and "Derby pie" they left behind as the cars pulled out of the gravel driveway and pointed toward Churchill Downs. My sister and I were left to watch TV all afternoon. (We children were never ever invited to the Derby, though the adults promised to place our bets.) As they saddled the horses in the paddock for the big race, I prayed that my pick, guided by a jockey not much bigger than me, would finish in the money and dreamed of the candy bars I could buy if I won. That's when the song came on. I was breathless.

My first Derby as a host came amid a family crisis. My father and his siblings had clashed over management of the newspapers, and in 1986 my grandparents decided to liquidate their media holdings. *The New York Times* and CBS's *60 Minutes* gave the breakup prime coverage. Within two years, my grandfather had brain cancer and had fallen into a coma. Tubes fed and watered him. I was newly graduated from college and recalculating my career path now that the family business I'd been training for was kaput. I took a part-time job in adult education and tried to comfort my grandmother. Granny was in no mood to go to the Derby, and when she offered me her tickets, I jumped at the chance to break the gloom.

I met my date, a college friend with a proven track record for revelry, at the airport in the rusting green Ford pickup we had once used to haul ponies. On the Friday before the race my date and I attended a black-tie dinner and hooted over the one-liners of our tablemate the comedian Phyllis Diller. The next day, when the bugler called the Kentucky Derby horses to the post—to my eyes they are every year the most beautiful horses in the world—"The sun shines bright" arose from the marching band ranged in front of the tote board. I shushed our group. We stood at attention, programs in hand. We had not talked about the song, but I made clear this was important business.

I hardly could have said why. Somewhere in my bones, I knew the old d-word had been there in the lyrics. Had been but wasn't there now. If someone had said it, I would have recoiled. No one did and the melody rolled on. The music and the words washed over me, warm and frictionless. I wept on command, oblivious that some Black racegoers refused to stand for a sentimental song about slavery. This "moment of moments" was the final ingredient in the old white recipe I'd been following all weekend. I was playing the belle, welcoming my man from the North, flushed and bursting with what an editorialist writing for my family's newspaper (perhaps my grandfather himself) described as "the romance and the charm, the high bravura" of a "characterizing event."

Then "the fastest two minutes in sports" were over. A filly took the trophy for the third time in history. My grandfather had taught me to wager at the track as a child; he loved to play the ponies and even had his own bookie. That year, the race he adored could not rouse him, but another Derby fan had been born. My friend went home and repeated stories that neither he nor I knew had been planted by Matt Winn more than fifty years earlier.

"My Old Kentucky Home" inspired Kentucky to pioneer a concoction that dominated American plantation tourism for the rest of the twentieth century. Throughout the 1930s, more of these houses opened to the public, reinforcing white unity while suppressing the realities of slavery and white supremacy. More still opened in the 1950s as the civil rights era took hold. A white child of the Civil War, Young Allison perceived the song's cultural and commercial value as generative and regenerative, appealing across the Union and Confederate divides. "As a place of pilgrimage," Federal Hill invited "the Northerner, hand in hand with the Southerner," to honor Foster. As to the experiences of Black people, Federal Hill, and by extension Kentucky, was "the happy home of slavery." Kentucky officialdom defended the aesthetics of an institution the Daughters of the Confederacy praised for helping to civilize a race of people they considered primitive and inferior. In designating the mansion as *the* Kentucky home, the Let's Buy It campaign put a white family of enslavers at the center of the story and invited guests to come and admire them, gaze upon their priceless curios, and feel their sorrow and loss of status, property, and identity. My Old Kentucky Home always served as more than a shrine to Stephen Foster, and taxpaying citizens of all races supported its work, year over year.

WE WILL SING ONE SONG

Fostering an American Consensus

In late 1930, Josiah Kirby Lilly, a captain of the American pharmaceutical industry, sat surrounded by family, his eyes filling with tears. A new record of Stephen Foster songs by Nathaniel Shilkret and the Victor Salon Group played on the phonograph. "My Old Kentucky Home" in particular provoked a long-suppressed "flood of memories." His grown sons and their wives had gathered cozily on sofas in Melodeon Hall, a retreat outside Indianapolis that the patriarch of Eli Lilly and Company called his "little hut among the bushes," although it was much more than that. An architect designed the building for Lilly in the Tudor style, with seven gables and leaded windows. Melodeon was literal. This shrine to Lilly's love of music featured a full-size pipe organ and a state-of-the-art stereophonic loudspeaker system.

Lilly, known as J. K., was about to retire from day-to-day management of the business that had made his family multimillionaires, and he needed some new occupation to absorb his energies. The idea of collecting Benjamin Franklin papers and memorabilia was considered and discarded. Others had beaten him to it. As Shilkret and the Victor Salon Group played, Lilly turned to his son, a bibliophile whose collection included a Gutenberg Bible, and asked if there was a way to locate Foster's original compositions? Certainly, there was.

J. K. Lilly had guided his father's firm from a smallish producer of pills and elixirs to a major industry force that brought to market new drugs for venereal disease and insulin to treat diabetes. Portly and balding, with penetrating eyes in a smooth oval face, he could have stood in for the midwestern industrialist in a Hollywood casting call. In matters of business, he was cutthroat. While J. K. lived in luxury, he projected understated humility. The scars he bore from childhood—as an infant, an absent father; as a youth, a widowed father—were entangled with the South, and Foster's music opened a portal that helped him reckon with those wounds, eventually in the form of a crusade.

Over the course of the 1930s, J. K. Lilly and his associates seeded a national "Foster revival." The Pittsburgher who spent his last years selling his work for a pittance and spending the proceeds on Bowery beer could not have dreamed up a better patron. The drugmaker's effort and investment installed Foster in the pantheon of America's greatest artists; a decade after Lilly began collecting Foster's sheet music, the composer appeared on a U.S. Postal Service penny stamp. A new generation was learning Foster's songs. "There will never," predicted the author Alexander Woollcott, "be an America without them."

During the same time period, Hollywood fell for Stephen Foster and his music. Out of copyright and freely available for soundtracks, "My Old Kentucky Home" echoed through scores of films from Walt Disney's 1933 *Mickey's Mellerdrammer* to John Ford's *The Sun Shines Bright* (1953), with 1939's record-breaking *Gone with the Wind* in between. The 1930s saw two biopics released about the songwriter. By World War II, "My Old Kentucky Home" was as American as apple pie, and playing it was an act of cultural patriotism for a white majority. (It is no accident that the word "patriot" is used largely by white people embedded in expressions of white supremacy.) While rarely invoking it directly, the mid-century American entertainment industry preserved not just Foster's legacy but also the legacy and racial stereotypes of blackface minstrelsy.

Kentucky leaders had established a wide constituency for "My Old Kentucky Home" among tourists, Derby fans, and citizens who were repeatedly told it was *their* song that embodied the state's history as well as a universal longing for home. J. K. Lilly and Hollywood canonized it. Sanitized for white sensibilities, "My Old Kentucky Home" was institutionalized in public schools and the U.S. Army, embedded into celluloid, and spirited through radio frequencies, its notes reaching millions across America and beyond.

Josiah Kirby Lilly was born in November 1861 in Greencastle, Indiana. His father, Eli, had joined the "just and holy" cause of maintaining the Union and left his young family and apothecary shop behind. Eli Lilly's politics were conservative; almost no one else in his county backed the Kentucky Democrat John C. Breckinridge over the Republican Lincoln in 1860. He first met baby Josiah in 1862 on a visit home to raise his own unit, which fought to halt the Confederate advance in Kentucky. The company was captured in Tennessee in 1864, and Black soldiers serving with Lilly were seized and sold into bondage. Major Lilly was imprisoned in Mississippi.

On his release, Eli rejoined the Union army and spent much of 1865 posted in Mississippi. Surveying the disarray, he decided to plunge into the cotton business, where fortunes were being made. He leased a house and fourteen hundred acres between Vicksburg and Natchez from a man who, until emancipation, owned more than eight hundred human beings. The venture tapped into Lilly's own southern heritage. Eli was born on *his* grandfather's Maryland plantation. Eli's father, a stout Methodist opposed to chattel slavery, renounced his slaveholding patrimony and took the family to Kentucky. Still unsatisfied in a slave state, the father moved them to Indiana, where Eli and his brothers attended the Methodist Asbury College, later known as DePauw. But J. K.'s father, Eli, had no use for his parents' pious Methodism. Though he had fought to preserve the Union, Eli Lilly perhaps understood that his parents' principled stance on slavery had cost him a share of wealth, and in Mississippi he might reclaim it.

This is how Eli, his wife, Emily, five-year-old J. K., and a sister from Indiana moved into a white-columned house backing up to Bayou Pierre. J. K.'s first memories were of riding on a horse among "mountains of something white" (the animal was turning the cotton gin) and playing with a "pop gun" that "a big black man" had whittled for him. The boy showed off his marksmanship to his mother, seated on the house's wide gallery. But instead of wealth, the Mississippi venture yielded bushels of sorrow. The 1866 cotton crop failed. Eli's business partner absconded with their cash. Everyone suffered from malaria, which killed Emily, then eight months pregnant. In his final memory, J. K.'s mother was "yellow as gold, black hair, eyes closed." The boy journeyed northward with his grieving father and aunt by steamboat and train to Greencastle. Eli Lilly quickly departed again to recover his shattered finances, leaving J. K. for three years with his grandparents.

In his trundle bed, J. K. Lilly wept "softly from loneliness." Sounds of boys jeering out on the street, of hogs being slaughtered behind the house, and of drunken farmers shouting on Saturday nights all terrified him. Other sounds mesmerized the child. "Heavenly music" woke him one evening, and he called out, "Grandmother!! Is it angels?" She explained that he was hearing college students on the street below, serenading his aunts with Stephen Foster songs. "Oh, the comfort of it!" Lilly exclaimed. "I can never express what that singing and playing meant to me." As a pharmacy student in Philadelphia, J. K. enjoyed Foster and other blackface music in a livelier context, at minstrel shows. He remembered the "fusillade of Ethiopian talent" that included an end man with an "enormous mouth."

In 1930, aged sixty-eight, realizing that Stephen Foster's life story was misted by "traditions unbased on facts," J. K. Lilly vowed to repay the debt he felt he owed the man whose music had helped him as a child. There was a lot of work to do. No one could even say how many songs Foster had written, and Foster's own story had been lost to the melodies. Even a group of educated southerners who broke into "My Old Kentucky Home" during a 1934 visit to a Civil War battle site were flabbergasted when their Pennsylvania-born companion Malcolm Cowley pointed out that Foster hailed from Pittsburgh. The inauthentically authentic had struck again. Lilly would put "affairs right" by sharing Foster's works and clearing up the facts around "America's first composer of beautiful songs."

Within months, Lilly was the world's most significant collector of items he called "Fosteriana." Rather than cry foul when some of the sheet music proved counterfeit, he cheerfully set the record straight. The project became for him a "fascinating sport." Correspondence with dealers began flowing to and from Indianapolis, and Lilly's personal secretary, Dorothy Black, placed the most promising letters under an American flag paperweight on J. K.'s desk. Melodeon Hall was rechristened Foster Hall and housed eleven full-time employees. A recent Harvard gradu-

The pharmaceutical magnate J. K. Lilly Sr. began collecting Stephen Foster material in his retirement in the early 1930s and spent some $10 million to build his collection and enhance appreciation for the composer in the United States and beyond. Lilly (*far left*) is pictured at Foster's grave as part of services held each year on the anniversary of his death (January 13). Also pictured (*left to right*): Margaret Hodges (wife of Lilly's curator); H. Marie Dermitt; Burton Mustin; and Fletcher Hodges, the curator of Lilly's collection. Dermitt and Mustin were with the Allegheny County Civic Club.

ate, Fletcher Hodges, oversaw arranging and cataloging acquisitions and helped Lilly publish the *Foster Hall Bulletin*. For Christmas 1931, J. K.'s sons gave their father a 235-page bound volume containing the composer's handwritten drafts. They reportedly paid Stephen Foster's granddaughter as much as $25,000 (nearly $400,000 in 2021 dollars).

The family's liberality extended well beyond Foster's descendants and one another. Everything Foster Hall put out was free. Once Lilly owned every published Foster musical work, he had the facsimiles bound as the *Foster Hall Reproductions* and sent a thousand copies to U.S. and international libraries. He wrote to radio station managers suggesting that their in-house orchestras learn Foster's songs and slot them into broadcasts. To prevent his letters from being junked, he stamped the envelopes with "Nothing to Sell" or "A suggestion from Foster Hall."

Lilly then commissioned a songbook for use in schools. The booklet referred to Foster as "Stephen." The collector wanted the composer to seem approachable, a "lovable, child-like character" students could know "intimately." Foster Hall promoted the songbook in educational circulars, and more than 500,000 gratis copies landed in classrooms. Teachers, principals, and students wrote to thank Mr. Lilly and Foster Hall. One child with a physical disability told him the music made her want to dance, "which of course I cannot do." A Chicago settlement house teacher hoped she could convey Foster's greatness to the "little Mexican children" in her care, and Helen Sklar, an accomplished music student who won a print of Foster's portrait as a prize, commended the composer for expressing "so well the American plantation life." Lilly's efforts preserved Foster's language intact, with only a few exceptions. The "Oh! Susanna" verse containing the n-word was deleted. "Darkies" remained throughout. Of the forty-one Foster compositions reproduced in the simple, blue-covered paperback, "My Old Kentucky Home" was the first. Kentucky connections for both J. K. *and* his wife's family could have made "My Old Kentucky Home" a favorite. Lilly Ridgely Lilly grew up in Lexington, Kentucky, and died the year Foster Hall published the songbook. One of her last excursions was a drive through Kentucky, including a tour of the My Old Kentucky Home State Shrine.

Like Young Allison before him, J. K. wished earnestly to untangle the truth about Foster's presence in Bardstown. In 1933, "emissaries" from Indianapolis searched old issues of local newspapers for any mention of Foster. J. K. even advertised a "$100 REWARD" for evidence. The prize went unclaimed. To clear up the swirling myths, he concluded that Stephen Foster deserved a new, authoritative biography.

John Tasker Howard's one-volume history of American music placed Foster as "one of the greatest melodists we have yet produced," on par with the Austrian composer Franz Schubert. In 1932, he arrived in Indianapolis from New York to lecture at a local music club. Lilly invited Howard to survey his collection, which included treasures no scholar had ever seen—the manuscript notebook containing early song drafts ("Poor Uncle Tom, Good Night") and detailed accounts of income and advances on royalties. Howard held in his hand the purse

Foster was carrying at his death with its pitiful thirty-eight cents. Lilly then took Howard aside and "drew from his pocket a little check-book." The author returned to New York with money to cover two years of research and writing—plus a 20 percent tip.

Members of the Senate Avenue Colored YMCA Quartet anticipated a generous tip when they arrived at the Lilly home on Christmas morning in 1934. In a tradition dating to before World War I, the carolers "roamed" door to door, serenading some seventy homes belonging to Indianapolis's "most prominent" citizens. Lilly knew the singers well. It was the first Christmas since his wife's death, and he had asked the quartet to entertain the family on Christmas Eve. When he snored through their 7:30 a.m. Christmas Day rendition of "Silent Night," he joked to the quartet's leader, George Robinson, that next year they had better throw a brick at his bedroom window.

Robinson, Wallace Woolfolk, Charles Samuels, and Clarence Hicks had formed as the YMCA Quartet in 1913 to perform spirituals. But in 1932, they began providing the sound of Lilly's Foster Hall promotional program. To appreciate Stephen Foster fully, books and lectures were not enough. Lilly offered the men a rehearsal stipend of $50 a month, $10 for each evening performance, and $7.50 for matinees. Well after Black artists had moved beyond Foster and his blackface minstrel associations, the Indianapolis foursome changed its name and adopted an all-Foster repertoire.

In 1934, nearly fifty organizations—women's clubs, teachers' institutes, scout troops, Daughters of the American Revolution chapters, the Indianapolis Southern Club (a social organization for homesick southerners)—attended free Foster Hall Quartet performances, which included a presentation by Lilly or Fletcher Hodges on Foster and the collection. Concerts took place at Foster Hall, but the quartet also traveled to schools and performed for larger groups. The quartet originally sang a cappella, but J. K. preferred the more domesticated sound of vocals backed by piano, so Harry Campbell, who as a teenager accompanied silent movies on organ or piano and by the 1930s taught math at the "colored" public high school, joined the group. The quartet booked additional appearances at private events, club meetings, and professional conventions, which supplemented their income and further seeded the

Members of the former Senate Avenue Colored YMCA Quartet posed in J. K. Lilly's Foster Hall in Indianapolis. They performed as the Foster Hall Quartet in the 1930s for events J. K. Lilly organized and gigs they booked for themselves. *Standing left to right:* George Robinson (tenor), Wallace Woolfolk (tenor), Charles Samuels (baritone), Clarence Hicks (bass). Seated: Harry Campbell (accompanist).

sounds of Stephen Foster. "You fellows have walked into the hearts of thousands of people," Lilly wrote to the men early in 1935. "I envy you."

The "boys," as J. K. Lilly often called the musicians, were born in the 1880s and 1890s, the youngest one in 1902. They were raised amid mighty post-emancipation hopes for Black Americans as well as enormous hurdles. All shared Kentucky roots, and some had parents who had been enslaved. Like most of their neighbors in segregated Indianapolis, the singers' families had migrated from southern states. Working as stock drivers, mechanics, waiters, and boardinghouse keepers, their parents and guardians achieved stability and, for their children especially, education. The great labor of freed people to counteract within the home, school, and church the disregard for human decency and human rights they suffered under was largely invisible to their white fellow citizens. Even as they experienced exclusion and discrimination,

The Indianapolis musicians visited the composer's grave in Pittsburgh's Allegheny Cemetery. The quartet appeared publicly well into the 1940s, and "My Old Kentucky Home" was always a crowd favorite.

Black men and women recommitted to self-advancement. Had they worked at Eli Lilly and Company—they did not—the musicians J. K. Lilly envied would not have been offered any chance of moving beyond low-level custodial jobs.

And these were men of high achievement. The majority of Foster Hall Quartet members had attended college. The tenor vocalist, Wallace Woolfolk, the son of a day laborer, trained at the New England Conservatory. Clarence Hicks, who sang bass for the quartet, graduated from the all-Black Hampton Institute in Virginia and taught woodworking at Crispus Attucks High School, the city's first segregated secondary school. The baritone, Charles Samuels, grew up with an aunt and ten cousins after his mother brought him to Indianapolis from Kentucky and left him there. Samuels left school after eighth grade, served in the Spanish-American War, and worked as a public school custodian. The second tenor, George Robinson, was among a handful of Black students to attend the nearby Baptist-run Franklin College. He kept books for city, county, and state offices and directed church choirs and occasionally performed at private parties. The keyboardist, Harry Campbell, attended Butler University in Indianapolis, where, like Robinson, he was one of a small number of Black students. Campbell spent his twenties playing occasional classical programs and regular gigs at local nightclubs and hotels. When the Great Depression struck, Campbell fell back on his undergraduate degree and taught math and German at Crispus Attucks High School, where he came to know Hicks.

Hard times came knocking with the Great Depression. When Lilly added the quartet to his payroll in 1932, unemployment nationally was at nearly 25 percent. Black Americans, "last hired, first fired," lost their jobs at much higher rates, and 50 to 75 percent were thrown out of work. The county clerk's office let Robinson go in 1932, and by 1933 he told Lilly that all four singers were "on the bricks." The $50 a month, and $7.50 a matinee, J. K. offered was a godsend. Without the economic downturn, however, it is difficult to know whether a gifted instrumentalist such as Campbell and the spiritual singers of the YMCA Quartet would have been tempted by Lilly's Foster-only offer. The songs of Stephen Foster had no place in their churches, the Black YMCA, or the jazz and blues joints on Indiana Avenue. The old Kentucky homes their parents and grandparents knew in slavery times did not conjure warm nostalgia.

Nonetheless, for seven years, the Foster Hall Quartet sang of "darkies" in "My Old Kentucky Home" for audiences like the Women's Art Association of Tipton, Indiana, which heard the quartet perform at Foster Hall in 1934. One of J. K. Lilly's favorites, "My Brudder Gum," began with a racist trope: "White folks I'll sing for you / Nuffin else to do." On a recording of the song, however, the quartet used crisp, clear standard English, overriding the songwriter's "Negro dialect." At the same time, blackface antics were part of the act. Lilly asked the singers to reprise for a group of descendants of Civil War veterans "some of that very funny stuff." Robinson, Woolfolk, Samuels, and Hicks did not wear blackface, but by the simple facts of who was entertaining and who was being entertained, their work required them to repeat messages of white supremacy to almost entirely white audiences. A Foster fan from Louisville complimented the group's "interpretive genius native to the negro race." They became known to many as Lilly's Quartet.

Performing "My Old Kentucky Home" and the rest of the Stephen Foster repertoire kept the men, as Robinson reminded Lilly, out of the "SOUP LINE." Invoices from 1933 averaged to $33 a month for each member—not a living wage. Nonetheless, Lilly proposed dropping the monthly $50 rehearsal payment, which would reduce their income by one-third. Robinson said they "agreed you had been wonderful" in helping them "make a living" and would manage without the shared stipend. Thankfully, Lilly reversed course and kept up the much-needed retainer.

A single instance of conflict between the patron and the musicians survives in their correspondence. In 1937, Lilly donated his collection to the University of Pittsburgh, and dedication ceremonies were planned on campus for the new Foster Memorial Hall, where the archive would be housed. The bass singer and single father, Clarence Hicks, could not put on his white tie and tails to sing that day. He would be attending his daughter's college graduation. Lilly's response is not in the record, but the rest of the quartet made the trip.

The quartet's sponsored appearances dwindled after the collection left Indianapolis. But in the summer of 1939, with Jim Crow still entrenched in both American social mores and public spaces, Lilly and his children and grandchildren asked the men to his vacation house on Lake Wawasee near the Michigan border. After a weekend of entertaining, boating, and reminiscing, Robinson told Fletcher Hodges, curator of the Stephen Foster Memorial at the University of Pittsburgh, "We certainly had the happiest moments of our life with them." On Christmas morning in 1943, the group caroled at the Lilly home and stayed for breakfast, along with the secretary of the Black YMCA, F. E. DeFrantz. Lilly never changed his company's hiring or promotion practices, but within the bounds of 1930s and 1940s white supremacy there was warm cordiality.

J. K. Lilly had reshaped the course of the men's musical careers. Wartime patriotism revived interest in Foster and his music, and in 1945 the group—hailed as one of the city's oldest "colored organizations" and lauded for its renditions of the white composer's "folk songs and spirituals[!]"—landed a weekly spot on the local CBS radio station.

The strains of "My Old Kentucky Home" wafted through the golden years of radio in the 1930s and 1940s, activating nostalgia and sometimes drawing directly on white fantasies of plantation life. The first radio station began broadcasting in 1920; by the mid-1930s radio sets played multiple stations all day and into the evening, delivering national and local advertiser-sponsored programming into homes and workplaces. During

Piano students learned from books like *Treasure Chest of Stephen Foster Songs* (1940), absorbing minstrel imagery like this banjo player overlooking a cotton field and riverboat.

the Great Depression, more than half of households owned a radio, and the average American spent four hours a day listening. In 1941, a radio network strike over royalty fees paid to the American Society of Composers, Authors, and Publishers led to a boycott of all ASCAP-affiliated artists. For nine months, programmers played only non-ASCAP material or music for which the copyright had expired. Stephen Foster's work entered yet another revival.

John Tasker Howard's Lilly-funded biography, *Stephen Foster, America's Troubadour* (1934), inspired a great deal of Foster radio programming. And whatever impulse there had been to set the record straight when the book was funded had softened. By 1934, the wish to dispel myths had been mooted by their affectionate familiarity. The book dismissed the tales about Foster visiting Federal Hill, but Lilly and Foster Hall never pressed the point. (Foster Hall's *Songs of Stephen Foster* repeated for schoolchildren the story of the Pittsburgher writing the song in Bardstown with the caveat that it was "unverified.") The benefits of the site in keeping the songwriter's name alive were too great. WNYC in New York aired a fifteen-minute segment of "My Old Kentucky Home" and other Foster melodies featuring a mezzo-soprano. The announcer explained that "a shrine known as 'My Old Kentucky Home'" with a "slight connection" to the bard stood in Bardstown, but the song needed "no shrine to commemorate it, as long as its lovely strains are to be heard." A Stephen Foster radio drama for Columbus, Ohio's WBNS ignored the documented facts of Foster's life established by Howard. Actors impersonated the composer and his sister Charlotte standing "on the terrace of the Rowan estate, overlooking the cotton fields where the darkies were singing as they worked." Any close reader of the biography would know that Stephen would have been three at the time. According to the script, Charlotte exclaims, "No matter how hot it is they're always singing and happy. It's not like that up North, is it?" They were happy, Stephen explains, "because they love the Judge, sis." He feels a song coming on, upon which a soloist rendered "My Old Kentucky Home."

But the larger point of Lilly's Foster Hall endeavor, including Howard's *America's Troubadour,* was to solidly establish Foster as an *American* genius, not to be pigeonholed or over-associated with any one section of the country. In the broadest sense, this was both historically accurate (nothing was more "American" than the blackface minstrelsy of the 1840s and 1850s) and devastating evidence of the way the nation continued to countenance, celebrate, and whitewash a racist culture.

In 1939, the *New Yorker* writer and radio personality Alexander Woollcott waxed nostalgic about "My Old Kentucky Home." The Algonquin Round Table man of letters told the listeners of NBC's RCA-sponsored Saturday night variety show that the music flooded him with memories of his mother singing as she did household chores. The show's host, Nathaniel Shilkret, whose Foster recordings first inspired Lilly's collection, struck up the mournful tune. Until reading Howard's new biography, Woollcott had not known that "My Old Kentucky Home" and other favorites like "Old Black Joe" were "the work of one man." Even the urbane, sharp-tongued wit (who famously quipped that "all the things I really like to do are immoral, illegal or fattening") melted under Foster's influence. There would "never," Woollcott told his listeners across the country, "be an America without them." The Pittsburgh songwriter left a "legacy beyond price."

My grandparents hosted Woollcott in Louisville for a week in the 1930s. A heavy man famous for overstaying his welcome, he was the inspiration for the 1939 play and 1942 film *The Man Who Came to Dinner*. My grandmother Mary Bingham said he was the sort of houseguest "you had to be with every minute . . . forget all duties, children, everything." She must have blinked, for when Woollcott sat on and broke an antique chair, he held it up to my grandmother, shouting, "I'll sue you!" To smooth things over and keep him busy, she drove him to Bardstown. They toured the "lovely old house" made into a museum, as Woollcott explained to his radio audience, "on the bland pretense" that the Pittsburgher had it in mind when writing "My Old Kentucky Home."

Woollcott's wit captured more than he knew. The song, unmoored from its actual history, could do ever more disparate work.

On Louisville's WHAS radio in the 1920s and 1930s, every night before the 9:00 p.m. sign-off, a bell stroked the hour and the announcer hammered out "My Old Kentucky Home" on a xylophone affectionately known as the "Old Kentucky Home chimes." The station's signal reached most of the eastern half of the United States. In January 1937, after weeks of rain, the Ohio River breached its banks, submerging 70 percent of the city, overwhelming the water system. 175,000 residents (more than half the population) had to leave their homes. WHAS had become a round-the-clock nerve center for emergency communications, broadcasting weather updates, SOS calls, and locations where refugees could get food, water, and shelter. Ninety lives were lost, but the spirit of cooperation saved countless others. The receding waters left thousands of homes beyond repair.

At a "gloom-chasing" civic gathering, politicians stood beneath a banner that read "Louisville Marches On!" and promised the city would improve housing and services as it rebuilt. The audience of fifteen thousand sang the song about slavery in unison. "In a full-throated chorus, unquavering and sure," Louisvillians sounded "the strains of a song which flood . . . has given a new and richer significance." The melody WHAS signed off with each night became a hope and a prayer for better days, and to lure back national advertisers, *The Courier-Journal* placed full-page ads in big dailies proclaiming "The Sun Shines Bright on My Old Kentucky Home."

Radio sounded through millions of homes in the 1930s, but the decade's greatest entertainment came out of Hollywood. Building on the first talkie, 1927's *Jazz Singer,* American movies entered a golden age. The industry had for years drawn from a theater world moldering with minstrelsy, and "My Old Kentucky Home" slid easily into productions of all kinds. Movies and animated cartoons—including black-faced, white-gloved Mickey Mouse shorts—replayed that tradition and its racist stereotypes. Minstrel shows no longer commanded major stages or got film treatments, but they were still widely performed in smaller settings—clubs, college fraternities, and community fundraisers—well into and past the civil rights era. For many kids like me growing up in the 1970s, however, the cartoons' specific references—whitewashed in Americana and innocence like the Stephen Foster songs aimed at schoolchildren—grew ever more obscure.

Silent movies had given the old melody plenty of play. Organ or piano accompanists like Harry Campbell of the Foster Hall Quartet would supply music for the action on-screen. In 1926, Fleischer Studios released a silent animated short (a form commonly inserted in movie house programming) of the song lyrics with a karaoke-like bouncing ball to guide theater audiences in a sing-along. The score for Universal Pictures' 1927 Tom-show-based production, "$2,000,000 *Uncle Tom's Cabin*" ("You'll just roar at [the enslaved character] Topsy"), matched "My Old Kentucky Home" to slavery scenes. The Estonian-born immigrant Ernö Rapée's synchronized score had an opening overture with "My Old Kentucky Home" and other blackface minstrel songs from the 1840s and 1850s. Most movies did not come with scores, however. Rapée's 1924 book, *Motion Picture Moods,* offered musical selections to guide live accompanists. "My Old Kentucky Home" was listed as suitable for any scene relating to the "American Negro," "American Southern," or simply "American." Such was the song's mercurial power.

In the midst of economic disaster, 1930s Hollywood aimed to distract, thrill, and comfort viewers. Feel-good flicks were in particularly high demand. The dimpled and ringleted six-year-old Shirley Temple starred in *The Little Colonel* (1935) as a child who heals a family torn by lingering sectional animosities. Following well-established narrative tropes, the Oscar winner Lionel Barrymore played an embittered Kentucky colonel, a Confederate veteran who banishes his daughter for marrying a Yankee. The daughter returns years later with the irascible man's adorable grandchild, who, with emotional support from a Black man, works her magic.

The tap-dancing "heel-and-toe wizard" Bill "Bojangles" Robinson was cast as Walker, the colonel's butler and Shirley's protector. A duo like that would "raise the gooseflesh on the back of a [white] audience," the veteran director D. W. Griffith predicted. But what might have otherwise seemed risqué—the first interracial dance sequence in American movies—was charming. The dancing, deferential, smiling Walker mixed virtuosity with age to tame, as far as white audiences were concerned, Black masculinity by dancing with a white child in the "big house" where doing so served white people. In that context, it should have come as no surprise that the couple tapped across the color line to the tune of "My Old Kentucky Home."

Neither *The Little Colonel's* script nor the children's book by Annie Fellows Johnston that inspired the film included a duet for diminutive Shirley and the "King of Tap." Born in Richmond, Virginia, in 1878, the orphaned Robinson lived with his laundress grandmother, who had been enslaved for most of her life. According to her strict Baptist principles, dancing was devilry and even the word was forbidden. Beginning when he was eight, Bill delivered newspapers and blacked boots, tapping for pennies between customers. He eventually ran away to Washington, D.C., and landed a role as a "pickaninny" in Billy McClain's 1890s touring extravaganza, *The South Before the War.* Robinson toured the eastern states with the company for a year, singing "My Old Kentucky Home" for Uncle Eph, the aged runaway, upon his return to the plantation to die. Later, he moved to New York and perfected a unique tap style that involved holding his upper body erect like an Irishman dancing a jig. It demanded extreme physical control. Robinson's feet created a one-man rhythm section that dazzled 1920s Manhattan; his most famous act was a stair-step routine that left audiences breathless with wonder.

When he began working with Shirley Temple, Robinson was fifty-eight, earned $3,000 a week, wore a ten-carat diamond ring, and carried a pistol for self-defense. Temple was the top-paid Hollywood name of the year, petted and praised, and the same age Robinson had been when his parents died. One contemporary called her "less an actress than a world-wide emotion." The pair connected as performing children across a chasm of circumstances and years. Temple adored "Uncle Billy." Working with him was "the opposite of drudgery," she said, and she made her parents host Robinson and his wife, Fannie, for meals so she could see more of him.

The stair-step act had been planned as a solo. The "Little Colonel" (Shirley Temple as little Lloyd Sherman) is stuck spending the night in the big house with the colonel, her mean old grandfather. Crying for her mother, she refuses to go up to bed and threatens to run away from home. Robinson asks the pouting child if she would do as she was told "if I show you a brand-new way to go upstairs." He begins tapping his way upward in time to "My Old Kentucky Home," humming like a kazoo. Watching the shoot, Temple was mesmerized, and someone suggested they could finish the scene by dancing up together. "I want to do that too!" was added to the script as the Little Colonel, forgetting her homesickness, reaches for the butler's hand. The sequence required days of rehearsal—and a simplified choreography—but Temple was determined and responded to Robinson's smiles and chuckles of encouragement. "I was not acting," the star later wrote. "I was ecstatic." Shirley's taps weren't sharp enough, and the scene was ultimately dubbed, but the effect was perfect. A moment of discipline (fighting bedtime) became an occasion for joy until they nearly reach the top and her grandfather appears, demanding, "What's going on around here!" As for the dance, something difficult looked so easy that a little girl and a childlike old "darky" could do it—a cheery message amid hard times.

But a white girl was holding a Black man's hand in the movies! The duet had all the elements of a seduction: the refusal, the weakening, the joy of synchronicity climaxing in ascent and disapproval from the parent figure/superego. Instead, a boogeyman was defanged. The sexual threat white supremacy pressed onto Robinson's brown skin fell away, and the little "leading lady" wept no more. He was domesticated, a servant in a white-pillared mansion with a Confederate flag leaning in a corner. Costumers powdered Robinson's hair to age him, just as stage versions of *Uncle Tom's Cabin* had rendered Harriet Beecher Stowe's virile character a gray-headed old man. As the butler, Robinson endures the colonel's casual insults, which echoed the ones heaped on him as

In *The Little Colonel* (1935), Bill Robinson hummed "My Old Kentucky Home" as he began the stair-step dance sequence, which persuaded Shirley Temple's character to go upstairs to bed.

a Black man in real life. But no abuse would wipe away Uncle Billy's smile, his rhythm, or his gentleness toward white people. His rings and revolver were left well offstage, for Robinson's Walker was a devoted, threatless playmate. In lifting her spirits, the Black servant cleared the way for the Little Colonel to heal a white family's sectional rift, and in the process lift the troubled nation's collective spirit.

Bill Robinson brought polish and sophistication to a hackneyed story with a leading lady so sweet she almost made your teeth hurt. *The Little Colonel* won Bojangles a national audience—millions more than his sensational contemporary Josephine Baker could command from her perch at Paris's Folies Bergère. For this he traded his name in Broadway's bright lights for a servant's part. He danced and hummed to Stephen Foster and "Dixie." Some called Robinson an "Uncle Tom" for accommodating a racist system, but he remained pragmatic. "I like white folks to like me," he told *The New Yorker* in the Richmond accent he never lost. Shirley Temple loved him, and the stars remained close into her adulthood. During filming in Palm Springs, she thought it was wrong that Robinson was staying above a drugstore with the chauffeurs rather than in the bungalows other cast members were given. "Now, darlin', don't you fret," Robinson soothed. "I've got a secret. I may be staying at the chauffeur quarters, but *my* chauffeur is staying there too." Wealth took some of the sting out of racial injustices—at least he wanted Shirley to think so. Robinson held "no illusions about a black man's privileges" and "knew that *only* as her . . . trusted servant could he take the hand of a little golden-haired child" and dance to "My Old Kentucky Home." Decades later, Toni Morrison's young Black narrator in the 1970 novel *The Bluest Eye* explained one of the many ways this illusion caused harm. She "hated Shirley. Not because she was cute, but because she danced with Bojangles, who was *my* friend, *my* uncle, *my* daddy, and ought to have been soft-shoeing it and chuckling with me."

Robinson and Temple stole the show, yet the studio segregated them in the publicity rollout for *The Little Colonel.* Shirley climbed into the laps of older white male co-stars in promotional appearances, but never Robinson's. The two were never shown together in the media— not even in the same room. Her small white hand is all that touches "Uncle Billy," but censors in some southern states nixed the scene. Black papers sometimes spliced photographs together to assert the Robinson-Temple co-stardom. White America went on, unperturbed. Except for the places where it was literally verboten, and with "My Old Kentucky Home" as a sonic backdrop, the effect of studio and film was to supply an "immaculate amalgamation." It contained all of the thrill and none of the threat that actual racial mixing posed in the white American mind.

Hollywood in the 1930s repeatedly dipped into the southern punch bowl, but it never drank more deeply than with the adaptation of Margaret Mitchell's 1936 novel, *Gone with the Wind.* Writing to the producer David O. Selznick as filming began in early 1939, F. Scott Fitzgerald (then trying his hand at screenwriting) suggested an opening "montage of the most beautiful pre-war shots imaginable and played over it I'd like to hear the Stephen Foster songs right off the bat. I'd like to see young men riding, Negros [*sic*] singing, long shots of a barbecue, shots of Tara and Twelve Oaks and carriages and gardens and happiness and gaiety." Fitzgerald's vision was largely fulfilled. Because Foster seemed synonymous with the romance of a mythical South, the composer Max Steiner incorporated *eleven* Stephen Foster melodies into the soundtrack.

Gone with the Wind did more than anything else in the history of American culture to package a chattel-based "civilization" as charming and noble, aristocratic and picturesque. Generations of Americans watched and re-watched the movie and introduced it to their children. Schools used it to teach U.S. history. But as has always been true of Hollywood, the minds behind the blockbuster movie served up what paying audiences—which in the 1930s and 1940s meant white audiences— sought, and did so with polished pathos. Tourists streamed into Georgia and other former slave states seeking Tara while *Gone with the Wind* reinscribed minstrel stereotypes and ignored the Black experience of slavery, freedom, or Reconstruction. Following the 2020 murders of Ahmaud Arbery in Georgia and George Floyd in Minneapolis, HBO Max suspended streaming of the movie, then restored it with a warning. That same year Georgia's official tourist website promoted its "Gone with the Wind Tour," showing a Black family boarding a bus for a "nostalgic" ride "through the rich and romantic antebellum era that inspired Mitchell's novel."

Gone with the Wind, rated as one of the greatest films of all time, is concerned with the love triangle that binds its leading white characters, not the enslaved people who prop up their lifestyle. The resolution of that love story also echoed a version of history that ignored slavery as a cause of the war and focused on reunification in its wake. A passionate and rebellious belle (Scarlett O'Hara), deluded by love for the wrong man (the planter Ashley Wilkes), marries and enjoys great wealth with the shrewd smuggler (Rhett Butler) who truly loves her. The couple get rich forging a New South that values capitalism over plantation "civilization" and builds alliances over business deals with its former enemy. The implication was that mere nostalgia for an outdated economic system had caused the conflict. This wasn't even the film's worst abuse of history. As far as *Gone with the Wind* is concerned, emancipation changes nothing for its Black characters, who, whether haplessly or affectionately, cling to their former enslavers. After 1865, actual freed people by the thousands fled the people who had held title to their bodies.

· · ·

"I can't do it! She's hurting me!" cried Butterfly McQueen on the set of the director George Cukor's production. "I'm no stunt man. I'm an actress." A moment earlier during filming, Vivien Leigh as Scarlett had struck McQueen, playing an enslaved girl named Prissy, in the face. Her physical pain seemed not to register with the people on set. The segment led to a turn in the plot. Union troops are advancing on Atlanta, and Scarlett resolves to get the household to safety at Tara, her family's plantation, when a wail bursts from an upstairs bedroom. Melanie (Olivia de Havilland), the wife of Scarlett's beloved Ashley, has gone into labor. Prissy is sent for the doctor. "Run!" Scarlett hisses, or "I'll sell you south, I will." As she waits for the girl to return, Melanie's pains worsen, and Scarlett vows to beat Prissy for taking so long.

Prissy walks slowly toward the door; her quiet singing rises from the street: "Jes a few more days for to tote de weary load / No matter 'twill never be light." No doctor is with her. Threatening to "rip the hide off" the girl, Scarlett sets off for help, but she too fails. Prissy, whose mother was a midwife and who earlier boasted about her experience in the birthing room, becomes Scarlett's last recourse. In the celebrated line, Prissy confesses, "I don' know nuthin' 'bout birthin' babies!" Her mother never let her watch. Scarlett slaps the girl, knocking her to the ground in an assault interrupted only by Melanie's moans. Prissy is threatened with being sold. She experiences physical violence. But in the movie her suffering is nothing to Scarlett's troubles and Melanie's pain. In Technicolor inauthenticity, the fact that enslaved Black women commonly suffered rape, separation from their children, and assault was doubly effaced by a film that inflicted and simultaneously dismissed white brutality against Prissy *and* Butterfly McQueen. Southern whites were the burdened ones in *Gone with the Wind.* The same transformation had propelled Foster's song to worldwide popularity, so much so that Mitchell considered using the line "tote the weary load" from "My Old Kentucky Home" as the title for her novel.

Butterfly McQueen finished high school in New York City and danced professionally before landing a role in a Broadway play that brought her to Selznick's attention. He loved her distinctive squeaky, high-pitched voice. McQueen took the comic role, knowing it was riddled with blackface stereotyping, but it was a big chance for the daughter of a housekeeper and a stevedore to break into the movie business. The humiliations she endured in making *Gone with the Wind* stunned her, nonetheless. The director Cukor reportedly had "gone Southern" and wanted the "stupid little slave" to eat watermelon on camera, which McQueen refused. He liked to tease McQueen by asking "a prop man to get the Simon Legree whip" and warning that he would sell her downriver if her performance fell short. "Prissy enjoys the joke as much as any of us," a production adviser and friend of Margaret Mitchell's brightly assured *The Macon Telegraph*. As a fictional character, Prissy had no way to respond. As an actress, McQueen withdrew from the rest of the cast and crew. During the beating scene, she walked off the set, later offering Cukor a deal: "If she did slap me I would not scream, but if she did not slap me I would scream."

It was a small but costly bit of defiance. Hattie McDaniel, who played Mammy and became the first Black actor to win an Academy Award, warned McQueen that this lack of cooperation put her future in Hollywood at risk. (Indeed, in the following years film roles were few and many were uncredited, though she later found work in TV

Butterfly McQueen, as Prissy (a girl enslaved to Scarlett O'Hara), sang "My Old Kentucky Home" in *Gone with the Wind* (1939). McQueen's resistance to racist treatment in the production dimmed her future in Hollywood.

and received an Emmy for an after-school special.) Interviewed for the fiftieth anniversary of *Gone with the Wind* in 1989, Butterfly observed, "I didn't know they were going to make it so authentic." Prissy's beating, which follows her singing of "My Old Kentucky Home," is arguably the film's lone realistic moment.

Cukor was replaced by Victor Fleming as *Gone with the Wind*'s director. Fleming managed to insert a flash of cinematic resistance to Cukor's sadism. When Scarlett rushes to find the doctor, Prissy watches her leave and, under her breath, resumes the melody: "Jes' a few mo' days fo' to tote de wee-ry load." Scarlett cannot hear her, but McQueen's expression perhaps suggests that in Sherman's Union approach Prissy senses her own release.

If possible, Stephen Foster became even more ubiquitous. By the time David O. Selznick's Technicolor epic smashed box-office records and won ten Academy Awards, J. K. Lilly had given his ten-thousand-item collection to the University of Pittsburgh and spent more than half a million dollars—about $9.5 million in 2021. Lilly directed large annual subsidies to the new Foster Hall to help Fletcher Hodges continue canonizing the songwriter. School songbooks were only one part of a program to get Foster's music onto as many tongues as possible. In 1940, Hodges coordinated a national letter-writing campaign that persuaded the U.S. Postal Service to issue a penny Stephen Foster stamp. More than fifty-seven million green-and-white portraits of the songwriter literally touched millions of tongues. "My Old Kentucky Home" appeared in the National Education Association's *American Citizens Handbook* (1941) alongside the nation's founding documents. The civic-minded compilation aimed at new voters (twenty-one-year-olds at that time) extended nineteenth-century minstrelsy, encouraging Americans to sing about slavery, about "gay" human property.

World War II broke out in Europe six months after the release of *Gone with the Wind.* An hour-long NBC radio program broadcast the gathering hosted by the Honorable Order of Kentucky Colonels in Bardstown to celebrate Foster's and the nation's joint Fourth of July birthday and unveil a grand-scale allegorical oil painting of the bard by the renowned illustrator Howard Chandler Christy. A few days earlier Adolf Hitler toured Nazi-occupied Paris, and German submarines attacked merchant vessels in the Atlantic Ocean. Foster "reposes among the immortals as a symbol of our democracy," President Roosevelt intoned. Stephen Foster and a song about slavery now stood in for American liberty and democratic values.

By no accident did Mildred Lucille Watkins Chandler, the Virginia-born wife of Kentucky's Democratic senator A. B. "Happy" Chandler, appear as the "Angel of Inspiration" in Christy's work.

Chandler considered "My Old Kentucky Home" a "personal signature." Bob Hope declared of the politician's rendition, "It knocks 'em dead each time." Raised in a small town where "everybody was generally considered to be Confederate," Happy came closer to the presidency than any Kentuckian since Abraham Lincoln. As a Harvard law student in 1921, Chandler scouted the Crimson squad in advance of their game against the Praying Colonels of Kentucky's Centre College. After prepping Centre's players, the coach turned and said, "Happy, sing us a song." He sent them onto the gridiron with "My Old Kentucky Home." It "created a spell" that (combined with his research) fired the Colonels to victory over the Crimson in one of college football's great upsets.

The senator and former Kentucky governor A. B. "Happy" Chandler (*at microphones*), his wife, Mildred, and others sing "My Old Kentucky Home" for an early 1940s radio broadcast as Governor Keen Johnson looks on.

On the campaign trail for lieutenant governor at thirty-one and governor five years later, Chandler appeared hatless in white suits with Mildred at his side. When he finished a speech at a rally, he would call her to the stage, and together they sang "My Old Kentucky Home" or "The Old Rugged Cross." Crowds loved it. In 1937, Governor Chandler invited the illustrator Howard Chandler Christy to the Kentucky Derby. Because Chandler sang "My Old Kentucky Home" "at the drop of a hat," Christy got an earful of the melody.

The artist returned to paint portraits of the governor and first lady. Christy toured Federal Hill and began a large work with the raven-haired Mildred Chandler modeling as Stephen Foster's muse. A benevolent organization called the Kentucky Colonels purchased the painting for My Old Kentucky Home State Park. Seven favorite Foster melodies rise from the composer's gleaming head, and a grinning Black chorus hovers over his harpsichord. An L&N Railroad travel circular explained how the angel bestowed the "poetic flame, which has immortalized the spirit of the old South." Christy depicted "the faithful slave" handing "the gracious Colonel and his gentle wife . . . into their carriage drawn by Kentucky thoroughbreds."

Radio listeners on the Fourth of July 1940 couldn't see Christy's creation. But they and the thousands of locals who gathered on the lawn outside the Old Kentucky Home heard the American Legion Drum and Bugle Corps play "The Star-Spangled Banner" and the Plantation Singers sing a Foster medley. The recording artist Frank Luther contributed "Old Black Joe" from New York, and from Hollywood Bing Crosby gave a rendition of Foster's parlor tune "Beautiful Dreamer." Franklin Roosevelt sent a message of solidarity with allies in Europe battling totalitarianism. "As long as democracy endures," the president wrote, "we shall have that freedom of spirit under which alone songs like 'My Old Kentucky Home' . . . can find a voice." Happy, by then a U.S. senator, was detained in Washington but tuned in for the finale with Mildred Chandler performing the first two verses of Kentucky's state anthem. She ended with "The time has come when the darkies have to part, / Then my old Kentucky home, good night!"

On December 2, 1941, a veteran naval officer in charge of mine craft at the U.S. Navy's Pacific Fleet thanked Fletcher Hodges for twenty-five

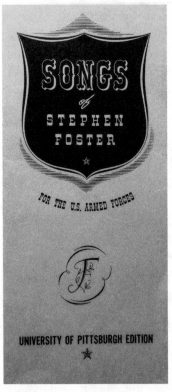

Hundreds of thousands of American World War II service members were given copies of *Songs of Stephen Foster for the U.S. Armed Forces* (1942). "My Old Kentucky Home" is the book's first melody.

copies of *The Stephen Foster Songbook*. His flagship was adding sing-alongs to movie nights. Admiral William R. Furlong grew up outside Pittsburgh and loved Foster, but he noticed that many of his sailors were "children of immigrants and unfamiliar with the 'fine old songs.'" Five days later Japanese warplanes bombarded Pearl Harbor, and twenty-five Stephen Foster songbooks went to the bottom of the Pacific with the USS *Oglala*. Furlong spent the rest of the war salvaging and repairing warships for military action, and Hodges made certain the admiral received a new set of the booklets.

Lilly's Foster program kept expanding through the war. Unable to pass the physical test to join the military, Fletcher Hodges contributed "to the national defense," as he said, by spreading the Foster gospel through the U.S. armed services. In 1942, a new, compact edition of

Songs of Stephen Foster for the U.S. Armed Forces reproduced the lyrics without musical notation. Once again, "My Old Kentucky Home" was the first tune in the book. More than 650,000 free copies ultimately went to posts throughout the globe. General Dwight D. Eisenhower believed the war would be won or lost on troop morale, and Foster's music was used for organized recreational activities. A War Department officer reported that the songbooks were "invaluable to the boys in the service," "more" than Hodges "will ever know." The Office of War Information played Foster on its radio network aimed at entertaining servicemen; a special lightweight Vinylite "V-disc" for "victory" containing an all-Foster program was distributed to U.S. bases. The songbook migrated into the communities that soldiers and sailors occupied after World War II, imprinting Foster on a new international generation. With ongoing support from the Lilly Endowment, Hodges and Foster Hall cemented the Pittsburgher as the "father of American folk music." A joint congressional resolution declared his music "a national expression of democracy," and his marble bust was installed in the Library of Congress's lobby.

Amid Foster Hall's promotional triumphs, and even as the United States and its allies were deep in a world war that had yet to turn their way, a Black member of Washington, D.C.'s board of education proposed eliminating "My Old Kentucky Home" and other minstrel songs from the music curriculum. Velma G. Williams was responding to teachers' complaints about their "offensive" phrases and their impact on students. The board's white majority seemed taken aback by the notion. One member pointed out that aside from the songs being a core part of the national folklore, "well-known colored singers" performed Foster's works. The proposal was tabled.

That day at a press conference, the nation's leading white liberal labeled the idea of banning "My Old Kentucky Home" "very foolish." First Lady Eleanor Roosevelt was embraced by many Black citizens and reviled by numerous whites for being "not just a friend—but the friend of racial equality." The proposal and Roosevelt's reaction made national news. Fletcher and Foster Hall stayed mum. Roosevelt, known for her enormous capacity for empathy, elaborated that "minorities" were "sometimes very sensitive because of a feeling of insecurity. They get over this as they gain security in themselves." With Eleanor Roosevelt on his side, Stephen Foster was in safe hands.

Both white and Black board members roundly scolded Velma Williams when the group reconvened two weeks later. One schooled her on the views of W. E. B. Du Bois and other intellectuals "as to the folklore value of the songs of Stephen Foster." Here was the old rift that since the 1890s divided Black leaders trying to uplift the race amid a nightmare world of Jim Crow degradation—how many steps back were necessary for each step forward? The superintendent "in charge of colored schools" testified in support of banning the songs. Pupils shunned them, and their language violated board policy about "derogatory" materials. Yes, Black performers sang them, but, he suggested, "it is entirely possible that these singers sacrifice, unknowingly, racial pride for commercial gain." The third Black voice in the debate, a U.S. Army colonel, simply said that this was no time to sow disunity. Perhaps if children were not taught by adults to see the slurs as "fighting words, they would not," a white member suggested. Velma Williams was gunning for a clean break from racial self-debasement as a strategy and defended her actions as being in "good faith" and in the interest of improving race relations. But, particularly in wartime, the perceived unifying power of the inauthentically authentic "My Old Kentucky Home" and "America's Troubadour" was too strong.

Visitors to the Old Kentucky Home often inquired about the scores of people the Rowans supposedly enslaved, and the invented cemetery, its "small stones" almost buried under leaves and dirt, was no longer sufficient. "We just had to make it authentic," explained Bardstown's mayor, J. F. Conway. A new split-rail fence around the cemetery would make it easier for tourists to find the final resting place of the people a new monument outside the home referred to as Judge Rowan's "Faithful Retainers." Some 1.2 million Black Americans served in the nation's armed forces, while the 1945 Fourth of July program at Federal Hill called out an "honor roll" of Foster characters and fictive creatures of the minstrel tradition—Old Black Joe; Uncles Ned, Mack, Ephraim, and Jake; and Aunts Sophia, Becky, Rachel, Maude, and May—as the Rowans' own slaves.

The organizers intuited rightly what was being asked. It was the same thing J. K. Lilly asked of "his" quartet of singers when he urged them to perform "some of that very funny stuff." It was the same thing

Bill "Bojangles" Robinson was asked when he agreed, with even a wink, to bunk with his chauffeur. And it was the same thing asked of Butterfly McQueen, who answered differently by refusing to eat watermelon and protesting racist abuse, and paid a price for it. Visitors to Federal Hill, which was always implicitly understood to mean white visitors, wanted to imagine minstrel figures invented for the comfort and enjoyment of white people as authentic enslaved humans. They had no use for authentic history, no use for facts about Black people sold south to die in sugarcane fields. Instead, they demanded that they be presented with inauthentic songs, inauthentic history. And because they were white, they got what they asked for.

By the end of World War II, the arsenal of democracy was victorious, and whereas Europe rapidly divided into icily warring spheres of Soviet and West, the molding of a future Japan fell entirely within the orbit of the United States of America, and U.S. leadership drew upon strains of history that predated the conflict.

When the Japanese government modernized education in the 1880s, Foster tunes were adapted for *shoka,* state-published songs with Japanese lyrics that were used in schools. "My Old Kentucky Home" became "Wakare" (Farewell). Officially banned while Japan and the United States were at war, the music flooded back with the American soldiers and sailors who occupied the country after surrender, bringing Lilly's *Songs of Stephen Foster* with them. Most Japanese people believed the songs belonged to them, but General Douglas MacArthur ordered Western composers be acknowledged as authors of the *shoka.* In 1947, Tokyo's Imperial Theatre mounted a biographical Foster musical, with the songs' original lyrics translated into Japanese. It was this echo chamber and fun house of misappropriated histories that my father stumbled into as a marine in 1950s Japan. Through the remainder of the twentieth century, children learned English via Foster songs. American jazz, folk, and rock and roll all found Japanese audiences during their own moments, but Foster was perpetually there, his portrait hung in music classrooms, the only American alongside classical European composers.

Foster's most popular melodies spread across the globe during his lifetime; travelers reported hearing them from India to Scotland, from Italy to Russia to Switzerland and France. Following World War I,

American jazz took the world by storm, and some white critics tried to dismiss Black artists and insist that Stephen Foster and white jazzmen were American music's true creative forces. But Lilly and his richly financed Foster Hall program truly canonized the songwriter as an essential American figure, and Lilly's project lifted Foster as a "folk" hero whose songs about slavery denoted freedom and democracy. That this belief by the hot war's end and the cold war's beginning was widely held without irony, but indeed with firm conviction, was not the work of Foster. Nor was it the work of the Black people whose lives his songs mawkishly memorialized. It was instead the work of generations of white Americans who sought not a past sanitized of racism but, worse, a patriotic, principled, democratic, and nonconfrontationally racist past that they could venerate without ironies.

Yet when Josiah Kirby Lilly died in 1948, Black Americans who had fought to end fascism abroad faced more, not less, racial segregation and repression at home. Lilly conceived of Foster as apolitical, but "My Old Kentucky Home" and its author were proposed as cultural staples of a freedom-loving America to be ingested domestically and exported abroad as cold war with the Soviet Union took hold. My father left the marines in 1958, never forgetting either hearing "My Old Kentucky Home" in Okinawa or the abysmal and unjust way Black enlistees were treated. And yet. And yet. Like generations down to the present, he had no qualms about singing a wistful song about slavery.

WHEREVER THE DARKY MAY GO

The D-Word as Destiny

In July 1950, American marines met Soviet-backed North Korean troops in combat, and Al Jolson stepped up to the microphone in Decca's Los Angeles studio to sing "My Old Kentucky Home." It was his last recording. Jolson is remembered today for starring in *The Jazz Singer* (1927), the first moving picture talkie. The movie is set during the vaudeville era, and Jolson played Jakie Rabinowitz, a Jewish immigrant in love with showbiz and in conflict with his disapproving cantor father. The film's title was a lie in plain sight. Jakie did not perform jazz music but, like Jolson, sang blackface songs about "mammy." Actually, *The Jazz Singer* conflated jazz, with its revolutionary syncopation, with Foster-style plantation nostalgia. It was a misrepresentation so generally accepted, however, that no one thought to complain. The perceived "blackness" of both genres was sufficient to equate them in the minds of the film-going public. Blackface had paved the road to assimilation for immigrants since at least the 1840s; Hollywood just picked up the old script.

Jolson's star had risen in a blackface sky. By 1950, he had been singing "My Old Kentucky Home" for half a century. Born Asa Yoelson in a Lithuanian village, he immigrated to Washington, D.C., at eight years old. His mother died a year after that, in 1895, and the boy endured a bleak period that included a stint in a reform school. Changing his name to Al, he started busking in front of the Raleigh Hotel within view of the U.S. Capitol and learning all the popular songs. The white politicians and lawyers flowing through the Raleigh's door tipped most generously for tunes like "My Old Kentucky Home" that "carried them dreaming back into the past." At eighteen, he was working in vaudeville and frequently "blacking up." Jolson's breakthrough came in 1911 when he was booked to open the brand-new Broadway Winter Garden Theatre as the minstrel character Erastus Sparkler—a "colored aristocrat," by definition a comedic phony who sings Stephen Foster tunes. Jolson later played E. P. Christy, portrayed as a greedy showman, in the Foster biopic *Swanee River* (1939), which included a Technicolor blackface minstrel show. In a swirl of appropriation and exuberantly inauthentic cross-racial and cross-ethnic influence, *Swanee River* cast a Jewish immigrant (Jolson) as an Irishman (Christy) who was posing as a Black man and exploiting an Anglo-Saxon northerner (Foster) via his song about an enslaved man from Kentucky—truly a layer cake of American social hierarchy. If some observers like to celebrate the melting-pot wonder of it all, it must be remembered that *Swanee River* credits only one Black actor, whereas the blackface minstrels got full billing. "Far from ignoring peoples of color, the white gaze renders them invisible," according to the film historian Michael Rogin. This happens "not by averting the eyes" but by fixing their gaze on imaginary tropes and maintaining whiteness as bedrock, "the unexamined given."

This tragic trick of white supremacy is one of Jolson's chief achievements. He came to it honestly enough. After all, no European immigrant to North America, dating back at least to 1619, had assimilated to the new continent without depending to some degree on the uses that darker-skinned people and representations of them could be put to. By Jolson's time it was more a cultural inheritance than an invention. Over the span of his life, however, it proved a protean inheritance.

Between the time Al Jolson sang about Kentucky outside the Raleigh Hotel in the 1890s and his final studio session in 1950, one aspect of "My Old Kentucky Home" had become a problem, and to sing of "darkies" became only more contentious during a decade marked by both a Black-led uprising against Jim Crow segregation and mounting anticommunist hysteria. The blackface minstrel figure's subordinate position, absurd airs, passive acceptance of white privileges, and affection for his oppressor pointed to a dark past and untenable present that Soviet propaganda regularly exploited. How could the United States talk of "freedom" while locking a whole race into legal peonage? There was no satisfying response. Someone—Jolson himself, his managers, or a Decca executive—put "My Old Kentucky Home" through a cleansing process. The sun still shone bright on the old Kentucky home, but now "everyone" was "gay." Not "the darkies" but "a friend" must part, casting "a shadow o'er the heart." On the other hand, Jolson retained certain cues. For example, he overrode Foster's published lyrics and inserted "Negro" dialect in the chorus that lamented "de ole Kentucky home far away." This iconic American anthem derived too much value from its origins in blackface dialect to easily leave the minstrelsy behind. Decca released Jolson's *Stephen Foster Songs* LP in 1951, months after the singer died, the same year Congress designated January 13 national Stephen Foster Memorial Day.

"My Old Kentucky Home" animated the land of Looney Tunes in Friz Freleng's 1953 short *Southern Fried Rabbit.* One scholar points to *Southern Fried Rabbit* as the last cartoon to treat the punishment of enslaved characters by their "masters" as a source of laughs. Mel Blanc, a vaudeville veteran and early Hollywood voice actor, toggled mirthfully between Bugs Bunny's nasal Brooklyn accent and Yosemite Sam's growly rasp in the Warner Bros. cartoon. "My Old Kentucky Home" is a keynote in a minstrel-laced send-up of a latter-day Confederate played by the hot-tempered Sam. The cartoon opens in a drought-wasted field where the carrot crop has failed. Bugs comes across a newspaper headline about Alabama's bumper harvest and sets off, with a reference to Al Jolson's hit "Alabamy Bound" and singing "Dixie." Reaching the Mason-Dixon Line (desert to the north, lush field to the south), Bugs dodges a bullet from a Confederate veteran still holding off the Union forces, though Bugs reminds him that the "War Between the States" ended decades ago. To get past the dug-in veteran, Bugs deploys a minstrel's bag of tricks. Changing his gray fur to brown and putting on tattered clothes, playing a banjo, and singing "My Old Kentucky Home," the wily rabbit convinces Sam he's "one of our boys." Believing Bugs is Black, Sam asks the rabbit to play "somethin' peppy out of that there skin box." "Yowza," Bugs replies, and picks up with "Yankee Doodle."

Sam explodes in fury, and Bugs stoops and grovels in an imitation of the Black actor Stepin Fetchit. The rabbit pushes a whip into the old Confederate's hand and casts himself to the ground, crying, "Don't beat me massa . . . don't whip this tired ol' body, no!"

One American icon (Looney Tunes) easily swallowed—and gained value from—another ("My Old Kentucky Home"), and Bugs and other animated characters kept the minstrel act alive for subsequent generations of twentieth-century cartoon-watching children. Enacting "My Old Kentucky Home" in blackface saves Bugs Bunny from a tail full of buckshot, but the trickster flourishes its godawful stereotypes ironically. The remainder of the cartoon deals Yosemite Sam and his anachronistic notions a series of humiliations. The retrograde Confederate is a fool. Though his land is lush, it is laughably outside reality. At the same time, the silliness of Yosemite Sam in *Southern Fried Rabbit* presents white violence as all bluster, victimless. Unlike real Black southerners before and after 1953, Bugs escapes unharmed.

Thousands of copies of the same paperback book were stacked around Waldemar E. Debnam's suburban Raleigh, North Carolina, home in the summer of 1955. The cover displayed the familiar Old Kentucky Home in pen and ink, dilapidated, deserted, overgrown, windows blown out, shutters hanging askew, ceiling ready to cave in. Debnam, a "neverist" on school desegregation, was engaged in a cottage industry, selling his manifesto, *Then My Old Kentucky Home, Good Night!* The plantation house stood for a region under assault. Debnam declared that the 1954 decision by "Apostle Warren and His Eight Disciples" in *Brown v. Board of Education* had placed the white South in "the worst ruptured condition we've been in since your folks and mine rose up and drove out the Carpetbagger and the Scalawag." No commercial house would publish the racist screed, but Debnam found a printer, and his wife, Stella (who loved Foster's song and supplied the book's title), fulfilled mail orders from across the country.

W. E. Debnam hosted a news commentary program that aired on nine radio stations over three states. He made his mostly rural white audience feel he was "standing close by you, putting one arm around your shoulder, and talking to you, as one brother to another." *Then My Old Kentucky Home, Good Night!* explained that the Bible, Thomas

The North Carolina radio personality Waldemar E. Debnam (in an undated photo) titled two successful segregationist books after Foster's hundred-year-old melody: *Weep No More, My Lady* (1950) and *Then My Old Kentucky Home, Good Night!* (1955).

Jefferson, and Abraham Lincoln all approved racial segregation. The National Association for the Advancement of Colored People had gone too far, not just with *Brown*, but also by advocating for Black voting rights and denouncing bans on interracial marriage. Debnam, operating under a conspiratorial cloud, believed that the NAACP was stoking a race war, if not colluding directly with the Soviet Union. In either case, the group undermined the global stature of the United States. That summer, white Mississippians gruesomely murdered fourteen-year-old Emmett Till for allegedly whistling at a white woman, a "crime" the "victim" later confessed she had fabricated.

Debnam made clear that interracial sex was a foundational fear and since the country's origins a prime method for inciting white people against—and for controlling—Black Americans. It was a fear that was always applied lopsidedly; white men's interracial sexual exploitation was policed, if at all, by mere rumors. When Thomas Jefferson's critics publicly damned him for sleeping with his human property and fathering their children, they had their facts right, and he was re-elected President. The horror that animated Debnam was the possibility of Black men having sex with white women. Debnam cited supposedly elevated rates of syphilis among Virginia's Black population and then offered an image of students in desegregated schools sitting "in each other's lap."

Debnam had a solution to the *Brown v. Board of Education* public school desegregation mandate. Parents willing to subject their children to Black teachers and classmates could enroll them in desegregated public schools. Other parents could maintain "racial integrity" by using a district voucher to cover tuition at another public school or private academy. *Then My Old Kentucky Home, Good Night!* sold eighty thousand copies, and a Charleston paper hailed it as "A Handbook for Southerners."

Foster's famous song also provided the title for an earlier successful white supremacist work by W. E. Debnam. In 1950, Eleanor Roosevelt, then chair of the United Nations' Human Rights Commission, stopped in Chapel Hill, North Carolina, on a speaking tour. The former first lady met with students at a coffee shop known to serve "any neat and orderly" customer, regardless of race. In her nationally syndicated column, "My Day," Roosevelt acknowledged the South's "grace of living" but expressed "sadness" about the region's underlying "poverty and unhappiness," and encouraged those in the "younger generation" pressing for change. W. E. Debnam took Roosevelt's lightly veiled swipes at Jim Crow as an insult to every right-thinking white man and woman of the region and aired a series of radio retorts. These he collected and published as *Weep No More, My Lady: A Southerner Answers Mrs. Roosevelt's Report on the "Poor and Unhappy South."*

A cartoon of bucktoothed Eleanor Roosevelt (one reviewer called her "the greatest busybody of our time") with tears springing from her eyes filled the cover of *Weep No More, My Lady.* A later deluxe edition had a Confederate gray cloth cover embossed with a rebel flag. The book was Debnam's extended lesson in Lost Cause history. The journalist sarcastically (and sometimes successfully) skewered Roosevelt's liberal pretensions and painted her as a Yankee bent on subjecting the region to its Black populace. Neither Roosevelt nor her female forebears, Debnam wrote, suffered the threat of violation by Black men that "settled like an unclean fog all over the South during those years of Reconstruction." She seemed to forget that outsiders "passing judgment on things they know little or nothing about" only damaged race relations. Debnam questioned whether poverty was the exclusive province of the former slaveholding states. He reminded her that every northern city had its "Negro ghetto" afflicted with destitution, crime, and moral decay. Debnam's defense of the South's racial system sold more than a quarter million copies.

Embedded in *Weep No More, My Lady* was a patriarchal edict that in promoting racial equality—or even human rights for Black citizens— Eleanor Roosevelt risked her credentials as a "lady." Debnam and men like him had things under control; there was no cause to cry for the South or its people, Black or white. The misguided so-called lady should pull herself together. That was certainly the view of the man who owned Monte Cristo Court motor lodge. The Grenada, Mississippi, motel kept a stack of *Weeps* on hand for more than a decade. Eleanor Roosevelt was dead when the repeat customer ordered another fifty copies to sell alongside color postcards showing off the swimming pool and slide.

Debnam's predictions of massive white resistance proved true. In 1957, the school year began with President Eisenhower ordering National Guard troops to protect nine Black students integrating Little Rock, Arkansas' Central High School. Congress weighed civil rights legislation aimed at voting rights. Amid these weighty concerns, Congressman Frank L. Chelf took to the House floor to defend the song he had learned when he was a child housed in a Louisville orphanage. After decades of pressure from the NAACP, broadcasters were sometimes substituting less offending terms for " 'darkies,' 'mammy,' 'massa,' " in certain songs. In a floor speech, Chelf told his colleagues that "network people" were trampling hallowed ground. On Derby Day, "the air is filled with the scent of sweet honeysuckle; your spine tingles, your muscles tighten, your throat goes dry, your eyes get misty . . . while you desperately try to swallow that redhot lump that seems to be everlastingly bouncing around in your throat, the soft, melodious strains of 'My Old Kentucky Home' float through the air."

The Kentucky congressman Frank Chelf posed with his harmonica outside the
U.S. Capitol on August 1, 1957, after pleading with the House Rules Committee
to stop national networks from "tampering" with controversial lyrics in "My Old
Kentucky Home." Chelf blamed the civil rights organization the NAACP for
pressuring networks and said he couldn't understand the motivation because Foster
"meant to honor our colored people."

He rose to defend no mere sectional preference. To alter any part
of Foster's melody would, he intoned, desecrate a sublime and "integral
part of America."

Newspapers across the country picked up Chelf's fight over Foster's
lyrics. The six-term lawmaker known for broad smiles and impromptu
rebel yells played the song for the House Rules Committee, hoping to
move them to tears and force the Federal Communications Commission to intervene. The committee members remained dry-eyed. One
congressman noted that Rotary International had lately eliminated the
d-word from its songbook. Chelf's resolution was tabled, but he moved
forward with a bill to slap broadcasters with a $25,000 fine and prison
time if they edited Foster's lyrics. No "fundamentally pro-American
group," he said, fingering Rotarians and civil rights advocates as unpatriotic and allied with communists, would modify these national treasures. Still, his bill sat dead in the water.

The following year, Frank Chelf faced off against Dinah Shore, a
singer and television personality with a weekly hour-long variety show
and an audience of forty million. *Time* magazine praised Shore's cheer-

leader persona and knack for lending "emotional urgency to the tritest lyric." Born to Jewish parents in 1916 in a small Tennessee town, Shore came off as the girl next door who used her "breezy Southern charm" and "homey" singing voice to score dozens of hits. But a dismayed constituent informed Chelf that on *The Dinah Shore Chevy Show* she performed "My Old Kentucky Home" minus the crucial word from the second line. "I like that gal's voice," the congressman told a reporter for the Associated Press by way of reopening debate on his stalled bill. But she had "to sing 'My Old Kentucky Home' the way Stephen Foster wrote it or not at all."

What legislation could not accomplish, cold war domestic politics could. By tarring the networks as un-American (and possibly communist), Chelf managed to bring them to heel. The House Interstate and Foreign Commerce Committee extracted pledges to make no substitutions in state anthems and to air Foster songs "just as they were written by the Southern bard." Southern bard from Pittsburgh! Any earlier understandings between the broadcasters and the NAACP were void. Chelf claimed victory for his district (which included Bardstown's My Old Kentucky Home State Park), for America, and even for what he called "the happy, friendly, carefree, God-fearing, God-loving, industrious colored folks" of the United States.

Over the course of Chelf's long political career, the Old Kentucky Home brand kept expanding in Bardstown. "'Tis summer, the darkies are gay" filled the air on a sweltering June afternoon in 1959, when nearly the whole town turned out for a parade. The cast of *The Stephen Foster Story* went singing down the main thoroughfare, like the traveling minstrel troupes of the last century. Some glided by on floral floats, and others rode in old-fashioned fringed surreys, all promoting the premiere of a new show, part musical, part historical tableau. The people behind *The Stephen Foster Story* celebrated over mint juleps. The playwright Paul Green mingled with Governor Happy Chandler and his wife, Mildred. Fletcher Hodges was there from the University of Pittsburgh's Lilly-funded Foster Hall. As they had in the 1920s "Let's Buy It" campaign, Kentucky's taxpayers completed what began as a private effort. A large state appropriation made possible the fifteen-hundred-seat open-air state-of-the-art amphitheater next to My Old Kentucky Home State Park's golf course. The logic went that warm-season visitors could tour Federal Hill and play eighteen holes or take in another local attraction before dinner and the show and would spend more dollars, even stay overnight.

The North Carolina–born Paul Green had earned a Pulitzer Prize in drama for *In Abraham's Bosom* (1927), a tragedy of Jim Crow injustice. Much of his later work focused on outdoor historical plays he called "symphonic dramas." North Carolina commissioned *The Lost Colony* in 1937 to draw seasonal tourists to coastal Roanoke Island, the first English settlement in North America. For his Bardstown patrons Green collapsed Foster's life into a single fictional year. Stephen and Jane McDowell fall in love. Stephen scores hits for Christy's Minstrels; onstage white actors in blackface re-created the minstrel show. The couple falters, then comes together in a hopeful ending. In between, the songwriter battles the temptations of the bottle, frets about his inability to provide for his wife, and visits the Rowans at Federal Hill on a business errand for a fictional Pittsburgh employer. (At a ball the Rowans throw in Foster's honor, a local belle tests his love for Jane.) Audiences also witnessed the enslaved Tom pleading with John Rowan not to sell him off for "loafing around and deadbeating." In Pittsburgh, Jane pledges to marry Stephen despite the "hard times" they might face, and her tears recall for the songwriter the image of Tom's wife, moaning and, according to stage directions, "slobbering" over her loss. Then the "great plantation song" about Kentucky comes to him all at once.

In a twist, Green tied the separation of a Black couple held in bondage to Foster reassuring his own "lady" and the triumph of young (white) love. And he scores a hit, commercially if not critically. *The Courier-Journal*'s drama critic found these "phony" scenes painful to watch, but *The Stephen Foster Story* was an instant success. Attendance at Federal Hill shot up by a third in 1959 alone.

And yet. Something was changing, if only what was allowed to go wholly unquestioned. Debnam wrote his screeds not from a position of confident security in white power but in response to perceived threats, and no reputable publisher would stamp its name on his words. Chelf waxed nostalgic on the Capitol floor about the "redhot lump" that rose in his throat each time he heard the song on Derby Day, not to punctuate a universally agreed-upon truism about the place of Black people, but to stem a slowly (oh, so very slowly) rising tide of uncertainty. His congressional colleagues shed no tears. Rotarians—by some measure the definition of mainstream America—had dropped the d-word in official materials. The pressures of the mid-twentieth century were introducing fracture lines in a history long comforting to whites but now showing too much of its underlying inauthenticity. Many who loved "My Old Kentucky Home" also unhesitatingly attested to their own (and often to Foster's) respect for Black people. When they grew misty-eyed singing along, they could see the harm but declared they intended none of it. A few, however, understood that the rejiggering of standards provoked a thought beyond intending no harm. What, if anything, did respect for Black people require them to do?

"Overlooked so far," observed the *Louisville Times* reporter David Hacker, "are the views of the people most affected by Foster's songs." Hacker, twenty-eight and hailing from Fort Wayne, Indiana, might have been the first white person to solicit such information. His informal poll of twelve Black Louisvillians revealed that two-thirds opposed the song as written. The other third considered it a relic and, like the physician C. Milton Young, had "other things more important to worry about." Eight Black citizens, including the local NAACP director, James Crumlin, musicians, and church leaders, expressed anger and frustration over whites' passionate defenses of Foster's lyrics. "They reflect the [earlier] times," the Louisville Urban League's Charles T. Steele told Hacker, "and there are still too many who want to perpetuate [those] times." If changes weren't made, this group argued, the song should be dropped altogether. A few weeks later Leon Davis, writing in the city's Black newspaper, suggested that

> those ardent defenders of the Foster songs who have those wonderful, pleasant, beautiful memories of "Mammys," "Aunties," and "darkies," [could] show some appreciation by allowing the many descendants of those lovable people the rights to freedom, dignity, peace, and happiness as human beings and American citizens.

The way whites simply spoke past Black people was a novel lesson to the young journalist. Hacker won an International Press Institute grant to study race relations in South Africa.

Racially targeted language—one Urban League official called it "the

obnoxious quadrivial 'darkies,' 'coon,' 'nigger,' and 'pickaninny'"—
became the fulcrum in a tug-of-war amid assertions that the terms were
degrading and should be dropped. Whites' beliefs in their kindly intentions toward Black people were no longer a sufficient defense.

Such a conflict was not easily settled, especially when it came to sentimental icons of whiteness like "My Old Kentucky Home." Requests
for basic respect met cries of censorship and, with no irony, accusa-
tions of rewriting history. Even right-thinking white liberals responded
as though something holy were being desecrated. While conceding that
this sort of language was best avoided in conversation—at least when
Black people were in earshot—they argued for preserving Foster's historical integrity, an idea that had the benefit of also allowing them to
avoid confronting their own racial complicity.

Reverence for Stephen Foster as an American genius was drummed
into the populace since the turn of the century by city fathers in
Pittsburgh, businessmen and governors, Confederate and Union veterans, Churchill Downs officials, a millionaire philanthropist, countless schoolteachers, the U.S. military, congressional resolutions, the
U.S. Postal Service, and even presidents. Any critique of Foster's songs
clashed with a claim that emerged in the 1870s in the North and was
repeated for decades. This creed held that Foster humanized enslaved
people and transmitted authentic blackness for those who had no
voice. In a conversation that had unfolded almost entirely among
whites, it was understood that his musical and empathetic gifts sanitized the ugliness of blackface minstrelsy and "taught us all to feel"
the "lowly joys and sorrows" of an uncomplaining people who sang,
danced, played the banjo, mourned the death of their enslavers, and
rolled joyfully "on the little cabin floor." Indeed, Foster's songs became
symbols of all-American values precisely because they refashioned their
meaning from disrespectful to slightly less disrespectful caricatures of
Black people.

At Bardstown's My Old Kentucky Home State Park during the
1950s, Lem Reed filled the vacancy left by the site's 1930s "Old Black
Joe" played by Bemis Allen. Reed, who sat under a tree with a cheery red
bandanna around his neck, authenticated Foster's mild portrayal of slavery. When tourists approached, Reed "touched a banjo and mumbled
softly as visitors threw him coins." A writer for the popular pictorial
magazine *Holiday* observed that Reed "wasn't actually playing or singing

"Uncle Lem Reed" contributed to a "plantation" atmosphere at My Old Kentucky Home State Park in the 1950s. An official tourism photo showed him with his banjo at the door to the mansion with costumed docents and guests. During the decade, the park attracted thirty-five to forty thousand annual visitors.

anything." He didn't have to. That wasn't what he was tossed coins for. "Uncle Lem lent something to the atmosphere." Grateful and unthreatening, he rounded out the plantation tour experience. Reed and Allen before him belonged to what Malcolm X remembered as "that world of Negroes who are both servants and psychologists, aware that white people are so obsessed with their own importance that they will pay . . . for the impression of being catered to and entertained." The historian Sam Dennison singled out Foster's songs for their remarkable ability to convince white people that their notion of blackness was "fact rather than fable."

. . .

The unsound assumption that Foster's music channeled the feeling and song of enslaved people survived the twentieth century, even as it sputtered out among Black Americans during the 1950s and early 1960s. Inhabiting a world that perpetually denigrated them, some descendants of the enslaved had used Stephen Foster's much-loved melodies to assert Black influence on the dominant culture and to thereby prove their essential Americanness. Conforming to white Americanness also, for very few, paid bills, including, for even fewer, their chauffeurs' salaries. Indeed, *ideas* of blackness as conceived and commodified and performed by Foster and countless other people with white skin *did* produce a young nation's first popular cultural invention. Blackface minstrelsy supplied a conceptual blueprint for commingling influences in American music, whether blues, gospel, jazz, soul, rock and roll, disco, hip-hop, or rap. The minstrel show and Foster's songs likewise presented a foundational model for white artists and companies to prosper from "Black" sounds. In its wake, a fraction of Black America also prospered.

But still Foster's profile among Black Americans plummeted. The concert soprano and Black choral evangelist Emma Azalia Hackley had defended "My Old Kentucky Home" around World War I as *American* because she believed his association with "blackness" could help the descendants of enslaved people claim recognition as full *Americans.* Rosa S. Gragg, a Detroit clubwoman, honored Foster in 1939 for tapping racially unifying "universal sentiment" that even offensive "dialect" could not "mar." This "dear and gentle heart" had transformed "the songs of a race" into "the folk songs of a nation," she argued. However, Hackley's pupil, the pathbreaking Black contralto Marian Anderson, ultimately rejected this position. During a session titled "The Negro in Music" at a 1952 NAACP conference, Anderson and other participants took issue with school curricula that used minstrel music. American youth imbibed destructive stereotypes packaged as harmless folk songs. In direct contrast to the efforts of J. K. Lilly and Foster Hall, the NAACP conference session called on schools to "reliev[e] the children of all races from Stephen Foster songs."

Foster was not (quite yet) universally rejected in Black circles. In 1954, some defended a New York City public housing development named after the Pittsburgh songwriter because it was thought that he "preserved the musical themes of the slaves." Such misconceptions help explain why Foster's elderly niece Evelyn Morneweck predicted that the

Black baritone and civil rights leader Paul Robeson would quit making linguistic substitutions and return to singing "My Old Kentucky Home" and other Foster works in their original form. Conflating Foster's plantation melodies with Black culture, Morneweck noted that Robeson took a strong interest "in Negro folk music." However, by the later 1950s, Black Americans wanted the slurs banished for good. Thomas A. Dorsey, "the father of gospel music" and president of the National Convention of Gospel Choirs and Choruses, suggested removing "racial references" from "My Old Kentucky Home" and other nineteenth-century songs. For authentic expressions of his race in American music, Dorsey endorsed spirituals, born of the same era and fashioned by people struggling to survive bondage. The verses of spirituals contained "nothing offensive . . . to anyone."

Dinah Shore, Paul Robeson, and even Al Jolson heard the call and made adjustments. Fletcher Hodges, director of Pittsburgh's Foster Hall, advised radio program directors to skip over the portion of "Oh! Susanna" about the steamboat explosion that "killed five hundred Nigga" so that Foster's music could appeal to the broadest audience. The blond baritone Nelson Eddy was in the vanguard for refusing to include racial slurs in his singing back in the late 1930s. Simon & Schuster made the switch in the fancifully illustrated family compendium *Fireside Book of Folk Songs* (1947). The NAACP scored what was seen as a notable achievement in 1939 when a popular radio commentator apologized for using the d-word to refer to Black racegoers at the Preakness Stakes in Baltimore. Louis Armstrong & His Orchestra recorded a Dixieland-style "My Old Kentucky Home" in 1960. Peanuts Hucko's clarinet lightened the summery mood, and Satchmo sang of Kentucky, where "the *folks* they are gay."

White people in general stood firm. Few could perceive the harm in the old lyrics. John Ed Pearce, a Virginia-born journalist and civil rights supporter, was frankly irritated; "racial justice is fine," he wrote in *The Courier-Journal,* but "this is getting ridiculous." Rather than asking for revisions that distorted "our musical history," he argued in 1957 that "songs about 'darkies' and 'mammy'" should inspire present-day "Negroes" by revealing "all the tremendous progress they have made." The *Wall Street Journal* editorial board judged the Dinah Shore–Frank Chelf debate "not inconsequential," because no law should keep Shore from singing as she pleased, whereas Chelf was also clearly within his rights to object. "Pressure group action" by the NAACP on networks should never, the editors argued, force conformity. But an untruth universally acknowledged was, of course, its own conformity. As the Civil Rights Act of 1964 was being debated, the niece of the Supreme Court justice Louis Brandeis (a transformative progressive thinker who lagged on racial equality) breezily pictured 1850s Federal Hill, where Foster "first observed the happy surroundings and considerate treatment of the slaves of that estate and so was inspired to write his master melodies."

The lump in Congressman Chelf's throat seemed to *depend* on voicing a single loaded word American Black people loathed. For fans of Waldemar Debnam's *My Old Kentucky Home, Good Night!*, Foster's tune stood in for the sacred home of white racial purity under attack from federal courts and the NAACP. Efforts to dismantle Jim Crow in education, public accommodations, and voting were met with church bombings, police dogs, and the murder of activists. By the 1960s, with the mask of civility removed from white resistance, mainstream white culture recognized the need for progress while also recognizing the need to distinguish itself from overt racists. Congress passed the Civil and Voting Rights Acts, and the demeaning d-word became de facto taboo.

The writing was on the wall. Hollywood and the recording industry and everyone in white America, down to many small children, was on notice that the word was hateful to Black people. A second grader at Louisville's Greathouse Elementary during Derby Week in 1958 sang "My Old Kentucky Home" as instructed, *without* the offending word. Keith L. Runyon knew from his music teacher that Stephen Foster was a great man who died after falling on a "tin can" and cutting his throat. The children noticed their teachers' careful emphasis on singing the state song "right," and he recalled a good deal of nervous "giggling." It "shamed us too."

A few in Louisville's Black community took issue with Foster's song for more than its single ugly word. Lyman T. Johnson taught history at the city's nearly all-Black Central High School and was hauled before the district's board of education for criticizing the state anthem to his students. "Whenever . . . they strike up 'My Old Kentucky Home,' and everybody stands," Johnson told his pupils, "you sit down." Some objected that they were "supposed to" stand for the official song. Johnson asked if they really believed they ought to "stand up" to be insulted? "That doesn't make sense." The anthem was another example of rac-

ist "tripe" served up in American classrooms in the guise of "history."
Eleven-year-old Marie Porter, who helped desegregate the all-white Stephen Foster Elementary School, learned in 1956 what it felt like to be
"barely tolerated." Her father taught her a lesson she never forgot about
the songwriter and her state's anthem: She must never sing "My Old
Kentucky Home," not in any form. It was "not our song."

White Kentuckians dismissed the protests from Lyman Johnson
and Marie's father, Woodford Porter Sr., as thoroughly as they had
Joseph Cotter's song revision three decades earlier following his visit
to the Kentucky home where his mother had been indentured to the
Rowans. At the height of the civil rights movement, white progressives
and reactionaries clashed over *how* to sing a song.

Few if any white people questioned whether to sing it. Entertainers who performed "My Old Kentucky Home" in the 1950s and 1960s
underwent a litmus test that exposed the extraordinary limits of liberal-
ism. Progressive white Americans might signal their commitments by
dropping an offensive term, a conscious (and relatively painless) way to
demonstrate support for racial progress. Some did so, while supporting,
to varying degrees, Black Americans' civil rights, both in social practice and in legislation. A few dove actively into efforts at racial redress,
but only a few. Correspondingly, white traditionalists cast themselves
as patriotic champions of freedom, preserving history from desecration
and shielding the nation from Soviet-style "political correctness." Clinging to the original "My Old Kentucky Home" gave license to speak or
think about blackness in ways all white people knew were demeaning.
This supplied a small comfort for those uneasy with the end of strict
racial segregation in schools, neighborhoods, and public accommodations.

The terrain white progressives and white conservatives struggled to
control could be captured in a word. If the racial slur contained in
"My Old Kentucky Home" denoted the mythical happy plantation
and whites' affection for docile "blackness," another protean word, the
"lady" enshrined in Foster's stirring chorus connoted lily-whiteness.
Lady was a status Americans still routinely denied to Black women.
The nineteenth-century minstrel show promulgated depictions of
Black femininity as sexually unconstrained, whereas in the Jim Crow

era "mammy," represented as rotund, servile, and safely asexual, gained favor. Real women who were not white continued to suffer under a racial system that denied them respectability. Acutely conscious of the way racism attacked Black womanhood, Emma Azalia Hackley wrote *The Colored Girl Beautiful* (1916) to promote self-respect and the cultivation of "real beauty," an internal quality tied directly to "real ladyship." Decades later, white Americans continued to exclude Black women from achieving "ladyship," whereas for white women violating the color line or being what was known as a "race traitor" denied them the status and respect their whiteness otherwise conferred. Foster used the term "lady" in his 1849 minstrel song "Nelly Was a Lady," which some white scholars have offered as evidence of respect for Black women, even as an antiracist breakthrough in the history of music. I am unconvinced.

The Richmond, Virginia, artist Willoughby Ions produced a popular series of hand-painted plates illustrating Foster melodies. For "My Old Kentucky Home" (1941), a white woman in antebellum dress weeps as a Black man kneels at her feet, pleading with her to stop crying. Ions found inspiration in Foster, a figure so central to American identity that he would "never go out of favor."

Regardless of Foster's intent, his audiences' perception of the lady of "My Old Kentucky Home" as white speaks to the starkness of the color line. Throughout the Jim Crow era and far beyond, the plantation mystique was inseparable from white womanhood, and Black females were not ladies. Not in Foster's songs, and not in the minds of the mass of white people.

The lady designation was carefully policed, by conservative and liberal alike. Anne Braden's parents were well-off, well-educated Kentuckians going back generations. Raised in the white upper-middle-class section of Anniston, Alabama, in the 1930s. Braden was schooled in a code of racial etiquette that included barely verbalized but explicit cues about the human beings around her. In genteel southern society it could be agreed that "slavery had certainly been wrong," but New Englanders had foisted the institution on the South. "Negroes" did "have their uses" as domestic servants and manual laborers. It was both morally right and wise for employers to treat the Black people who worked for them decently. But decency had clear, racially defined limits. Anne recalled that as a girl she "happened to say something to my mother about a 'colored lady.'" The response was immediate. "You never call colored people ladies, Anne," snapped her mother. "You say colored woman and white lady—never a colored lady."

Growing up in World War II Washington, D.C., my mother admired Clara, her family's live-in cook, housekeeper, and babysitter. This gracious, light-skinned Black woman supported a disabled child in an institution (the details were left unclear) while also studying at night via a correspondence course for her practical nursing degree. When my mother said something about Clara being a "lady," her father issued a sharp correction. "Colored women are not ladies." His tone surprised her. But the lesson sank in. Well into the early 1970s, the domestic workers who helped raise me and cooked and kept house for us addressed my mother as Mrs. Bingham, and in return were called Hattie, Iva, Louise, Mildred. My memory reflects this bluntly racist asymmetry; I cannot summon surnames we never used.

Anne Braden, on the other hand, rebelled. In the late 1940s, she moved to Louisville, Kentucky, where she met her husband, Carl. In 1954, they bought a home in an all-white suburb and transferred it to Andrew and Charlotte Wade, a Black couple with two children. The house was firebombed, and the Wades had to flee. Police deliberately

bungled the criminal investigation of the attack, and an opportunis-
tic district attorney targeted the Bradens as its perpetrators. They were
charged with conspiracy in seeking the violent overthrow of the civil
order.

Carl Braden was a reporter for my family's newspaper, *The Courier-
Journal* (Anne Braden had been a reporter there as well). Whereas the
paper defended Braden's right to hold leftist political beliefs others
found unsavory or wrong, its editors denounced the couple for transfer-
ring the home to the Wades. Such provocations, *The Courier-Journal*
believed, were inflammatory and immature; they would retard rather
than assist reform. In an atmosphere of white supremacist and anticommunist hysteria, a jury sentenced Carl to fifteen years in prison.
He was fired. Anne Braden forfeited the privileges of white ladyhood.
Though she continued attending her Episcopal church, liberals shunned
her, and I was wholly ignorant of her courageous stands, which continued through the decades. Neither Black women nor Braden qualified as
ladies in the progressive white family I grew up in.

"Cleansing" the only verse of "My Old Kentucky Home" most
people heard begat yet another problem. Stripped of its racial/racist sig-
nifier, the song's subject was thrown into shadow, both willfully and
innocently forgotten. An imaginary lady wept as a system of slavery,
already whitewashed by Stephen Foster, effectively vanished from view.
The "darky" discourse purported to resolve the song's racist burden,
while the larger truth that a minstrel song about the slave trade had
become a celebratory anthem continued unchallenged. The amputated
association lay just beyond the scrim of politeness, a phantom limb that,
like the unapologized-for institution of bondage, continued its throb-
bing ache.

THEY SING NO MORE

Black Power and Back to Bardstown

On the eve of the 1968 Kentucky Derby, the Louisville police detective Major Priest Fry warned racegoers to beware of con men and especially pickpockets who were likely to "strike" when "fans hear them play 'My Old Kentucky Home.'" Fry knew from experience that as "the horns blow" Foster's melody, people "forget about everything else." An ever-growing crowd was attracted by an internationally celebrated event that enjoyed exhaustive media coverage. The race attracted more than thieves. The 1968 Derby's most famous attendee was the former vice president Richard Nixon. As a candidate in that year's Republican primary, Nixon deployed an old tune about slavery to present a human face to the voting public. He arrived at Churchill Downs wearing a plaid sport coat and gray trousers as the guest of Kentucky's GOP governor. To a nation bogged down in a war in Southeast Asia and smoldering from unrest following Martin Luther King's assassination only four weeks earlier, the Kentucky Derby offered a festive respite anchored in tradition.

Nixon, who served as Dwight Eisenhower's vice president, lost his first presidential bid to John F. Kennedy in 1960. Eight years later he was hoping for a comeback. Nixon claimed to be in Louisville to see the "kind of race both Democrats and Republicans can win," but spent most of his visit with his back to the track shaking hands and signing programs in the grandstand's most trafficked section. After all the glad-handing, his wife, Pat, remarked, "Poor Dick, I don't think he's seen a horse." Nixon had enjoyed previous Derbies on television (by the mid-1960s the broadcast was a major network sports event), and he knew that millions of eyeballs tuning in from home would see him. It was for the audiences back at home that the conservative Californian told journalists that the "best part of the whole program" was not the race (he placed a bet or two and blithely tore up his losing tickets) but the mass sing-along that preceded the Run for the Roses. "I wanted to be here," Nixon told the press, "when the band played 'My Old Kentucky Home.'" Richard Nixon's endorsement of Stephen Foster's melody was aimed directly at the ears of voters whom he called the "silent majority," men and women reeling from rapid social change—feminism, racial integration, and youth rebellion. And the song seemed ready-made for a campaign that relied on a "southern strategy" of appealing to the region's white electorate, many of them registered Democrats.

The Derby's heavy media coverage made it a natural target for poli-ticians and for protest. In 1967, advocates for ending housing discrimi-nation threatened to upset the celebration, with the Reverend Martin Luther King Jr. preparing to join a Derby Week demonstration. Several days before the big race, five Black youths were arrested for "bolting" onto the racecourse as horses galloped into the final stretch. Rumors flew that activists planned to block access to the track or dangerously blow whistles to terrorize the Derby contenders. Robed Ku Klux Klan members materialized at the track and offered their services to defend the racecourse. Violence seemed likely, and to preserve the peace, King held the march miles away in Louisville's business district. Under pres-sure from the statewide Human Rights Commission, charged with pro-tecting citizens from discrimination, the lyrics of "My Old Kentucky Home" printed in an official tourist brochure exchanged the d-word for "old folks." The following year, just before Nixon's arrival, a Black mem-ber of Louisville's Human Relations Commission reminded the group what they surely already knew: "My Old Kentucky Home" contained "certain lines" that were "objectionable to many Negroes."

It was an irony lost on nearly everyone. The state that had been by a large majority pro-Union in the lead-up to the Civil War, had main-tained its neutrality until invaded by Confederate forces, and had suffered bloody campaigns to remain under Union control was now, by its own efforts, an icon for the side of the conflict it hadn't joined. In the upheaval of the late 1960s and early 1970s, the familiar business of the Derby clashed with broader social norms.

Churchill Downs, meanwhile, doubled down on plantation mythology and its coded references even as it made modern improvements and embraced television. The track's leadership hewed to the Old South theme that Matt Winn had established half a century earlier. Bill Corum, the sportswriter and broadcaster who succeeded Winn, hailed the track's "gables, spires and balustraded porticoes." They recalled "the time of forebears, who hewed a new civilization out of the 'dark and bloody ground.'" While celebrating "the thoroughbred," Derby goers could hear "the rustle of taffeta, the sense of a world apart, the gentle laughter, the Rebel-scarlet silk of the Lost Cause." An Iowa man seeking tickets assured the management of Churchill Downs that he had always harbored a fondness for the land of slavery and cotton. "I hate Lincoln," he wrote, wagering that the sentiment would win him favorable consideration. "He was a heel." A reporter in 1965 touted the way the Derby brought "the Old South's heritage . . . to life, softly and elegantly." It was commonly thought that "My Old Kentucky Home" had been played and sung at the storied race since the Derby began in 1875, though it was a 1930s addition. Familiar as the melody was to Americans, not all 100,000-plus racegoers knew the lyrics. In the midst of the civil rights movement and on the centennial of the Civil War, the track in 1961 added Foster's original lyrics to its Kentucky Derby program. That way, everyone could easily sing along. There they remained when Nixon attended the race, when white Americans accepted that it was impolite, impolitic, or both to utter words that generations of their Black fellow citizens called out as demeaning.

Nixon's infamous "southern strategy" worked. Defeating the Democrat Hubert Humphrey and the racist firebrand George Wallace (who ran as an independent), Nixon was able to keep campaign promises. That included the one he made to Kentucky governor Louie Nunn that if victorious in November, Nixon would return to the track the following year. In May 1969, he became the first sitting president to pass through the gates of Churchill Downs and sing the song about slavery before the nation.

As the Secret Service whisked him into the racecourse grounds, the

President Richard Nixon at the 1969 Kentucky Derby. He told the press that the singing of "My Old Kentucky Home" was his favorite part of the event. *Left to right:* Mary Lou Whitney, Richard Nixon, First Lady Pat Nixon, Nancy and Ronald Reagan, and C. V. Whitney. The Whitneys were socially prominent Republican Party supporters and thoroughbred breeders.

president passed the nineteen-year-old Blaine Hudson and a dozen fellow Black Student Union (BSU) members from the University of Louisville picketing at the track gates. One of their signs referred to the president's "law and order" rhetoric and hard-line policing: "No. 1 pig Nixon set stage for pigs to brutalize black people." The protesters used the blunt language of the Black Power movement—a confrontational revision of the Reverend Martin Luther King Jr.'s tactics in the face of injustice. The youths expressed outrage that people came from all over "to witness animals galloping around a track" but would never "journey across town to find living proof that Black People" were human beings, not "figments" of whites' terrified and "insane imagination."

J. Blaine Hudson III entered high school as President Lyndon B. Johnson signed the Civil Rights Act of 1964 and Voting Rights Act of 1965. He graduated from the city's premier public school and won a coveted scholarship to the University of Louisville. Hudson later reflected that up to 1968 his conscious years spanned "a time when this nation, however grudgingly, was making progress in the area of race." Even as Robert Kennedy and Martin Luther King fell to assassins and riots broke out in American cities, Hudson believed the movement could get "back on track" if civil rights groups maintained pressure. Like thousands of Black college students in the late 1960s, he joined the BSU and embraced language and behavior that white administrators considered both ill-mannered and unreasonable. They held those opinions even as the college campuses they administered had scarcely changed beyond tolerating a handful of Black students (often athletes). The "demands" of the University of Louisville's BSU included the appointment of Black members to the school's board of trustees, hiring Black professors, targeting scholarship money and other outreach to underrepresented Black communities, establishing a Pan-African studies program, and acquiring library books on Black history and culture. Though their requests may today seem mild, when placed against a status quo of every trustee being white, every professor being white, every outreach and scholarship dollar having for decades gone exclusively to whites, and library holdings that uniformly reflected the ideas, words, and books of whites, their language was not. It was time, according to the BSU, to "unlearn the white mind."

Black Power sounded (and sometimes looked) militant. At Cornell in early 1969 students armed with rifles faced off with university leaders and police. In California, the Black Panther Party established parallel social services to liberate people from governmental institutions infused with white supremacy. Racial pride—battered by slavery, Jim Crow, and poverty—must be restored, and not in the image of whiteness. So many generations, the BSU's circular pointed out, had been "trained to feel inferior." Desegregation was not an end in itself but merely a first step toward an inclusive society. *Brown v. Board of Education* and new civil rights laws had already provoked white backlash—including mass flight to suburbs. Talk of revolution from people with black or brown skin and bloody clashes between law enforcement and Columbia and Harvard students filled the news and were roundly condemned by white leaders of both parties.

A reckoning of some sort seemed to be in the offing. Hudson declared in the group's Derby Week 1969 circular that "all whites are either consciously or unconsciously racist"—a concept so wholly undigestible to white Americans that it required rebranding in order to reemerge half a century later as "unconscious bias."

The university failed to move forward on the BSU reforms after months of negotiations, and on Derby Eve the students were arrested for taking over an administrative building at the university. As the president's jet approached Louisville on the morning of the 1969 Kentucky

After spending a night in jail for occupying a University of Louisville building on May 1, 1969, Black Student Union protesters picketed the Kentucky Derby to draw attention to demands for more representation and resources on campus. "The darkies," their statement read, "are not gay any longer."

Derby, Hudson and eight fellow demonstrators posted bail. Facing expulsion, Blaine and his compatriots paced the pavement in front of Churchill Downs, holding signs and chanting slogans, while inside at the racecourse Nixon and a record-breaking crowd lifted their voices. The BSU's Derby Day statement, in contrast, identified Stephen Foster's tune depicting plantation life in Kentucky as another example of a system riddled with racism that white people could or would not see. Let it be known, the statement read, "The darkies are not gay any longer."

With that brief, ironic line, Hudson hoped to explode the central image that Foster's song had embedded in American thought: that even Black Americans missed the days of slavery. The melody had brought genuine pleasure to generations of Americans. It had been marketed and sold and held up as a crowning example of the nation's music, so much so that as the thoroughbreds came onto the track at Churchill Downs,

an almost exclusively white crowd could rise as one and woozily, patriot-
ically, wistfully, reverently honor it as they honored "The Star-Spangled
Banner." Hudson and his fellow demonstrators wished Churchill Downs
to acknowledge that it had been sacralizing a song about slavery for
decades in sound and (now) print. They raised their complaints against
a near monolith of white certainty about the century-old song's history
and meanings. They were almost entirely ignored. Fletcher Hodges, still
guiding the Lilly collection at the University of Pittsburgh, was asked
about the anthem's antiquated lyrics. Hodges mockingly suggested that
"in these days of soul" Churchill Downs might substitute "brothers" for
the offending d-word. "That seems to be acceptable."

It probably comes as no surprise that the gonzo journalist Hunter S.
Thompson's encounter with the Derby during this contentious era
would inflame traditionalists. In his celebrated 1970 essay, "The Kentucky Derby Is Decadent and Depraved," Thompson (a Louisville
native) related the moment when his companion, the illustrator Ralph
Steadman, tried to sketch clubhouse spectators from below as they sang
"My Old Kentucky Home." Offended by the artist's lack of respect for
the hallowed ritual, a well-dressed racegoer screeched, "Turn around,
you hairy freak!"

For the most part, from 1930 onward the press had seen "My Old
Kentucky Home" as Churchill Downs wanted, as a beloved institution.
The veteran local sportswriter Billy Reed described the general consensus: for those few minutes, "everyone can be a Kentuckian." By the
early 1970s, some journalists began to note division, not unity, in the
song. Clarence Matthews had covered two decades of Derby festivities
when he hit a wall. In a 1971 column addressed directly to the white
readers of *The Louisville Times,* Matthews described Black Louisvillians'
exasperation with the Kentucky Derby's " 'Old South' ways." What
whites perceived as "sentimental, traditional, innocuous" left Blacks
resentful. Singing "My Old Kentucky Home" and having bandanna-
headed "Aunt Jemimas" serve burgoo breakfasts arose from a segregated
American memory house. The tenor of many Derby rituals sentimentalized and even celebrated what Matthews called "an unpleasant era
in Kentucky." Black people wanted none of it. But those in charge,
eyes perhaps blurred with their own tears, seemed not to notice or care.
They extended the same disinterest to the *Louisville Times* journalist's
complaints.

Matthews had had enough of the Derby by 1971. That year I was just getting started. At six, I could read the offensive words to "My Old Kentucky Home," right there in the race day program my parents brought home from the track. But by 1972, the d-word was gone. Churchill Downs replaced Foster's original second line with "'Tis summer, the *people* are gay." CBS had partnered with the track since the first national broadcast in 1952 and for years parried NAACP complaints about the signature song. By the early 1970s, CBS was hearing from a more influential constituency, the white management of major advertisers. The slur, they said, had to go. Corporations didn't want their products associated with a patently racist display, or any controversy it might cause, no matter how embedded Foster's song was in Derby ritual. Exactly what was said and when and by whom remains unclear. That the point wasn't a matter of principle was reflected in the fact that the track's business decision came and went without any statement. On Derby Day 1972 only one sportswriter seems to have taken note. When the band "busted out" with "My Old Kentucky Home" and fans joined their voices "as tradition dictates," the journalist Melvin Durslag, who had traveled from California to Kentucky in expectation of an authenticating experience, claimed to have turned to a Black man nearby, who reassured the disappointed visitor that "Negroes" had "no objection to darkies." Tellingly, the source for Durslag's quotation goes unnamed.

Churchill Downs' cleansing of "My Old Kentucky Home" came after more than fifty years of Black objections to the song. Lonnie Ali, a Louisville native who married the heavyweight champion Muhammad Ali, observed that Churchill Downs "couldn't have been thinking about Black people" when they made the switch. Black grooms and waiters formed a large portion of the racecourse's employees, but "the aristocracy that enjoyed the horse race" was almost entirely white, and *they* were not calling for reform. In 1914 and again in the civil rights era the NAACP pushed to remove Foster's music from school songbooks; instead, various artists and Churchill Downs tinkered around the margins. Many people, Black and white, undoubtedly felt relieved that the d-word was gone. Others bemoaned the change and clung to the old way in spite of the revision. In 1975, Rick Cushing reminded readers of *Louisville* magazine that Foster's tune was "the lament of the slave." But not just the slave. Cushing suggested that in banishing that reference, Kentucky was dismissing a "double tragedy." Slave auctions, he said, left "many a slave-owner" nursing "his own pangs of anguish." He repeated the exculpatory myth that being enslaved in Kentucky was "better" than being enslaved in other states. Having factually abused history, he went on to declare it unfortunate that the country was losing these historical touchstones. Cushing's focus on white myths and victimhood accentuated the point that a song about Black people as victims had almost never been a song about Black people as victims to the white people who sang, played, or heard it.

Fifty years earlier, the Mississippi-born Thomas D. Clark came to the University of Kentucky and published the first twentieth-century scholarly history of the commonwealth. It puzzled Clark that a song he interpreted as "*Uncle Tom's Cabin* set to music" was so widely cherished. Antebellum Kentuckians, especially in the slaveholding areas of the Bluegrass and cities, had strengthened laws around human bondage before the Civil War, and Harriet Beecher Stowe was a hated figure. This clear-eyed outsider focused on the cognitive dissonance of Kentucky's enslaving past and the fetishizing of "My Old Kentucky Home," publishing controversial articles in the 1930s and 1940s about the contradiction. He noted that the lyrics moved from utopia ("The sun shines bright") to crisis ("The time has come when the darkies have to part") to resolution in death ("the trouble all will end"). Something beyond the words or music made the song work in schoolrooms, in football stadiums, and at the Derby, Clark thought. He would ask his (all white) history students whether "My Old Kentucky Home" told "a story of gladness or of sorrow." "Gladness," was the invariable answer. Clark concluded that these young mid-century men and women were "captivated by a dream" of a happy past, a time before the disruptions of Civil War and Reconstruction.

Clark's students witnessed the gradual liberation of "My Old Kentucky Home" from the taboo d-word. The cleansing ironically converted a "happy" past with slavery to a happy present where slavery never happened at all. In capitulating to advertisers, Churchill Downs simultaneously removed a stain on the Derby, helped Americans forget that they were singing about slavery, and effaced any shame or need of apology. The track's communications director during the 1980s felt certain that slavery scarcely "entered people's minds" when the ritual singing began just before the race. "My Old Kentucky Home" "represented something totally different," explained Karl Schmitt Jr., a Louisville native and sports marketer. It recalled "your birthplace, home, another time when you were younger." With the exception of foreign journalists who sometimes questioned the song's racial references, "the whole slavery thing was lost" on the crowd. Schmitt's challenge was to get Derby visitors who didn't know, or barely knew, the lyrics, to sing along. The track began hiring professionals to perform (always just the first verse and chorus) so the network broadcast of "My Old Kentucky Home" would be intelligible for millions watching from home. Spectators followed the lyrics as they flashed on the track's tote board, saving the trouble of hunting them down in their programs. The response was always positive when the track announcer asked them to "please rise and sing along." Schmitt expressed the consensus that the song about slavery had transitioned from something racially unsuitable to a melody that simply connected people to tradition.

The consensus more or less got it exactly wrong. Written, and for generations sung, when racism was transparently unproblematic, the song had transitioned into a version that late twentieth-century whites could continue to sing as transparent racism became impolite.

Black veterans of the 1960s understood this. As one observer explained, when the song came on "people just grimaced." "We ignored it," Muhammad Ali's childhood neighbor Bob Coleman told me about his Derby experiences, which unfolded mostly at private homes where a TV would be tuned to the race about to happen a few miles away. Not very many Black Louisvillians were in the stands for Derby Day, but Woodford and Harriett Porter, owners of a successful chain of funeral homes, had box seats every year. Porter served on the board of education while Louisville schools desegregated, and his children were veterans of sit-ins that broke Jim Crow in the city's businesses. When the band struck up "My Old Kentucky Home" and everybody rose, the Porters remained seated. Their daughter Marie still cannot comprehend how a demeaning song could be treated so worshipfully. "Why do white people like it so much?" she asked in 2018, shaking her head. Neither Porter nor Coleman had examined the full three verses that paint a man's appalling death in the cane fields. The old line from the first verse, "'Tis summer, the darkies are gay," said enough. "It's a white song," Coleman said to me. "It's your song."

"There is no nostalgia in slavery," the Louisville journalist Clarence Matthews declared in 1971, writing of the recoil Black citizens felt toward "My Old Kentucky Home" and Derby Week. For white institutions and white Americans this had been patently not true, though in certain realms it was fading. Foster's combination of parlor sentiment with blackface minstrelsy saturated "My Old Kentucky Home" with nostalgia. From the Daughters of the Confederacy to the American Automobile Association's Glidden Tour to *Gone with the Wind*, a mist of reverence coiled around the brutality of human bondage, and the romance of the "Old South" flourished under the fabled twin spires. In 1976, the track's president, Lynn Stone, touted the "emotional experience" the Derby offered. "It's the South. It's the horses, the gambling, the tobacco, the whiskey. It's the river town, the farms, the mint juleps," he continued. "It creates an antebellum image. The whole mystique."

The singer-songwriter Randy Newman's "Old Kentucky Home" (1970) took the opposite approach. Snatching a reverential pebble from the father of American music's repertoire, Newman fashioned something new and full of ironic uneasiness. This artful dodger of American pop composers was born in Los Angeles to Jewish parents. His mother was nicknamed Dixie, and Randy spent childhood summers with relatives in New Orleans, where he connected with the southern musical vernacular and its racial contradictions. The music and lyrics were Newman's, but in "Old Kentucky Home" he repurposed Foster's recognizable opener, "The sun shines bright on my old Kentucky home," as his refrain. A hillbilly character drunk on "turpentine, dandelion wine" aims "this gun of mine" at birds on a telephone wire. He's "doin' fine" amid misogyny, incest, addiction, and domestic abuse. In Newman's rendition, the "young folks roll on the floor" evokes sexual liberties rather than quaint "pickaninnies"; the songwriter seemed to be piquing listeners likely to think of Appalachian cabin dwellers as inbred and dissolute while countenancing early 1970s sexual liberation. This Kentucky home was clearly nothing to idealize, yet the song's speaker sounds unfazed, just hoping to "keep them hard times away from my door." "It's about mountain people's ignorance," Newman said, "or making fun of people who think that's funny"—like his own college-educated self and audience.

"Old Kentucky Home" appeared on side two of Newman's critically acclaimed *12 Songs*. The singer's laconic warble nearly slips into an alcoholic slur, backed by a loopy country arrangement featuring the Byrds' guitarist Clarence White and Ry Cooder on slide. The melody is foot-tappingly infectious, but the lyrics turn the charming country groove dark. The music critic Greil Marcus called this "white trash" ballad a "timeless tribute to nothingness." Newman, who eventually turned to scoring Hollywood films, favored his listeners with deceptively simple yet disturbing tunes capable of revealing the collective complicity in social ills from racism to rape. This time, the acceptance of domestic brutality and poverty was hung on Foster's winning compositional "hook."

Newman's satirical paean to Stephen Foster was not a hit. By the time of its release, nearly half a million had paid to hear the original tune performed onstage as part of *The Stephen Foster Story,* Bardstown's summer outdoor musical. Bardstown was tied more tightly than ever to "My Old Kentucky Home," and as the preservationist William Barrow Floyd discovered, holding it to historical account provoked impassioned resistance.

Floyd was a gay man, and beginning in the 1970s "My Old Kentucky Home" provoked titters for another word in the song's well-known original second line, "'Tis summer, the darkies are gay," sung as "the people are gay" since the 1972 Derby. Jim Gray, a politician who came out publicly in 2005, served as a delegate from Kentucky to the Democratic National Convention while a college student in 1972 and as Lexington's mayor in 2011. In the decades before he came out, Gray attended countless civic occasions at which people singing or hearing the state anthem winked or snickered uncomfortably about an identity he felt compelled to hide. Chris Hartman, executive director of Kentucky's Fairness Campaign, an LGBTQ advocacy organization, recalled the year the group planned to hum the state song on kazoos in the annual pride parade. It would be a nice bit of humor—embracing the little word that carried such weight. Hundreds of the plastic instruments were being handed out when someone took Hartman aside and explained the tune's racist undertones. The kazoos were quickly collected, and the state anthem has apparently never been put to official use in Kentucky's LGBTQ rights movement.

As a queer man in the 1970s, William Barrow Floyd saw the raised eyebrows when "the people are gay" was sung. Perhaps he laughed inwardly. His zeal for old places, old paintings, old furniture, and early American history emerged decades earlier, when he was growing up during World War II in a Tara-like house on a Kentucky farm. During a visit to the nation's capital, the precocious ten-year-old toured Mount Vernon and consulted with a Smithsonian Institution curator about the patriotic paintings of Jean Leon Gerome Ferris. Floyd became an authority in early American art, architecture, and decorative arts. In 1977, while serving as Kentucky's curator of historic properties, he supervised an interior restoration at Federal Hill that would reveal how the Rowan family lived when the mansion was completed about 1820. His passion for decorative originalism had the effect of dangerously detaching Federal Hill from its mythic visitor.

The site closed for six months. Applying values of historical accuracy (at least when it came to dates and the provenance of physical objects), Bill Floyd would restore Federal Hill to its "original" glory. Conscious of his reputation in the world of professional antiquarians, he might also have had in mind recent embarrassing reports published in the national media. One *New York Times* journalist in the early 1970s followed a hoop-skirted hostess through the house "cracked up" to be the inspiration for Foster's enduring melody. Even though the barest fact-checking cast the Pittsburgher's presence into doubt, the guide pointed to the mint julep goblets "Cousin Stephen" liked to drink from. Prior to Floyd's 1977 renovation, tourists were told that the house was "much the same as it was" when Foster visited "at least three times." Here was the piano (procured to decorate the Kentucky Building at the 1904 World's Fair) the genius touched, and, more prosaically, here was the silver-plated chamber pot next to the "bed he slept in." The "most valuable piece of furniture in the house," the desk where the song itself was composed, merited special attention. The guides sounded silly, and to a connoisseur like Floyd the shrine was a mess of gee-whiz gimcrackery.

Floyd researched the Rowans and Federal Hill's contents and consulted national experts on period interiors. Then he purged the site of a "hodgepodge" that "had no association with the house, Kentucky, or Foster." The "Stephen Foster bedroom" became Judge Rowan's bedchamber. Floyd banished the chamber pot, a reliable source of comic relief during sometimes lugubrious guided tours. Colonel LaBree's old yarn about the bricks for Federal Hill having been imported from England and "carted over land from the Atlantic" was verboten, along with the wild claim that Rowan owned 150 human beings. Floyd made clear that the Duncan Phyfe chairs Madge Rowan Frost told everyone were

Tourists at My Old Kentucky Home, Nelson County, Kentucky, 1977.
Photograph by Ted Wathen.

a gift to Judge Rowan from the Marquis de Lafayette had actually belonged to the Frost family of St. Louis. The French general never set foot in Bardstown.

Marian Conliffe, the Old Kentucky Home site manager, panicked. The department of parks ordered her tour scripts scrapped. When pausing before the famed "secretaire," docents could say only that "local tradition has it" that Foster wrote the song "at this desk." Pressed, the guide would have to confess: there was "no solid evidence that Foster visited here." How to square this new tour with fifty years of "tradition," or even the vivid *Stephen Foster Story* visitors might have seen the night before? Conliffe hoped "to be factual," but this was not going to work. Floyd's deputy tried to reassure her. "It is not your fault that you have been handed a burden, one of lies, stretched myths, and erroneous folklore, concerning Foster and Federal Hill." Floyd was adamant. He refused to have his restoration, now thoroughly "based on facts," tied to

Woman wearing a hoopskirt, My Old Kentucky Home, Nelson County, Kentucky, 1977. Photograph by Ted Wathen.

"a presentation based on romanticism and fantasy." Conliffe must trust that "honesty and authenticity will pay off in the long run." This bracing admonition about the house museum's interpretation had, however, a limit. No steely-nerved white person subjected Foster's song "My Old Kentucky Home," which the site enshrined, to such an appraisal.

Four months after the reopening, Conliffe filed a desperate report. Visitors were unhappy about the way " 'myths' had been disputed." Many simply would not believe they were untrue. Hearing complaints, some locals grew concerned. Erleen Johnson, a local historian and sometime cast member in *The Stephen Foster Story,* defiantly deployed the "Foster slept here" approach when the local chamber of commerce asked her to escort a Tokyo journalist around Bardstown. Mitsuyo Miyamoto was on an assignment to profile the most American of American places, leading him naturally to My Old Kentucky Home State Park. Johnson also rose to protest when, during the 1977 Kentucky Derby broadcast, a host announced that "My Old Kentucky Home" had come from the pen of "a man who never set foot in the state." (He was, in fact, incorrect: Foster traveled to Kentucky with his mother as a child, though Johnson did not know this.) Johnson went to the media. "Let it be declared," Johnson said, "that Stephen's visits to Kentucky are fact and are verified by the written word of those who were in a position to know." She offered the same limp proofs Foster biographers had examined and dismissed for decades.

The Stephen Foster Story and My Old Kentucky Home were big business for the town and the state. Pride in "heritage" soared with the 1976 bicentennial year. Bardstown could not afford to forgo Stephen Foster's presence, so the town found ways to ignore Bill Floyd's decrees. In advance of a 1979 visit from President Jimmy Carter, Osso Stanley Jr. (whose father helped lead the 1921 "Let's Buy It" campaign) ridiculed the expensive redo at Federal Hill. Focusing on the Rowans of the 1820s sidelined the melody written in 1853. Tourists weren't coming to hear about Judge Rowan's contributions as a jurist or to imbibe obscurities about Kentucky's early nineteenth-century decorative arts. They came to see *the* place that had inspired Foster's "deathless" song. The union between song and site, no matter how fictional, was necessary to the site's existence; to undermine it, Stanley warned, was madness.

Visitors to My Old Kentucky Home exited through the back. They could guide themselves to the one-story log wing or ell (the Rowan family's original dwelling) that held a kitchen and smokehouse. These cruder spaces featured no fine furniture and were apt to bring slavery to mind—if only as an afterthought, absent any commentary or elaboration. No tuneful Black minstrel replaced Lem Reed after he died in 1955; still Federal Hill and nearly every white American institution either romanticized or evaded slavery and what it meant to be enslaved. Yet, as Federal Hill closed for renovations, at least one out of every three Americans watched ABC's ten-hour television miniseries *Roots* (1977), based on Alex Haley's best-selling book tracing his family history from African capture, through slavery, to freedom.

I was among the millions who viewed *Roots* that January. The network feared that viewers would reject a program focused on slavery as too brutal or negative, and casting recognizable white actors was one way producers hoped to reassure the audience. I recognized Ed Asner of *The Mary Tyler Moore Show*, playing a slave ship captain suffering from moral qualms. Nonetheless, *Roots* shocked me. "To see that all these horrible things were really happening made me sick," I wrote in a sixth-grade essay. "I really wouldn't think the law would permit such a horrible thing to be done. And to think some of *our* ancestors were doing it!"

There it was on the ruled page of my composition book—dismay, doubt, and the "horrible" feeling that I was implicated. Night after night, *Roots* seemed to be saying, I continued, "that never were any of the white men good. They were all cruel." Did *Roots*'s creators exaggerate so viewers would "feel sorrier for the slaves," I wondered, "*or* were they [slaveholders] all bad?" I noticed that *Roots* placed southern white women somewhere between evil free white men and victimized Black people, but this was of little comfort. (This myth of shared subjection has been roundly critiqued.) Faced with a crime beyond measure, I took it personally. People were either bad or good, and my logic was simple and simplistic, and desperate. I yearned for "good" white people within the slavery system. If they were there, then maybe "*our* ancestors" and whiteness itself could be redeemed.

The Stephen Foster Story and "My Old Kentucky Home" as both a song and a place succeeded because so many white Americans yearned, as I did, for exoneration. *Roots* probed some of slavery's physical and psychic wounds and celebrated the fortitude required to survive it in ways few people with my skin color had seriously considered. And it damned the people of my skin color for having perpetrated, by commission and omission, those wounds. Most preferred to look away. A year after *Roots* aired, Erleen Johnson, Bardstown's local historian, urged the site manager at Federal Hill and the director of *The Stephen Foster Story* to explain that "servants stayed on" after emancipation "because it was their home." Looking into a much less varnished past, Johnson and I instinctively reverted to tales white history books and songs had been telling for generations.

It is not clear if Johnson got her wish, but blatant reminders of white cruelty quietly disappeared. During the 1980s the director of *The Stephen Foster Story* modified the ugly scene of John Rowan selling Tom, and the city of Bardstown removed the auction block that had remained in front of the courthouse since antebellum times. As for me, the profound shock of *Roots* eventually wore off. It had shown me and its immense television audience eight episodes of cruelty and injustice. We talked about our shock, and perhaps debated the program's realism, but after being entertained, we weren't asked to do anything differently. With respect to the present, the thing to do was try not to be a "bad" white person—in the language of the time, not "be prejudiced." I hated the KKK and applauded affirmative action and, it's clear now, more or less waited for the problem to resolve itself. The legacy of slavery and Jim Crow coursing through the present remained obscure if not invisible. When Derby Day came around, I was glad to hear once more the sweet strains of "My Old Kentucky Home."

10

WEEP NO MORE

A Sonic Monument

The 1970s and the Carter presidency closed in a mist of "malaise." Alarming declines in domestic manufacturing, skyrocketing trade deficits, and spiking unemployment (over 10 percent in late 1982) created a sense of crisis in Kentucky, where poverty and education lagged behind the national average. Louisville was stamped as "strike city" for its rocky labor relations. A dashing new governor, John Y. Brown Jr. (born 1933), led the effort to rebrand and diversify the commonwealth's economy. His father served in Congress and as Speaker of Kentucky's House of Representatives, but "Johnny" was drawn to business. In 1964, Brown and a partner purchased Colonel Harland Sanders's Kentucky Fried Chicken and transformed the sit-down chain into a fast-food powerhouse. The company went public in 1970 with three thousand stores operating in forty-eight countries. Brown's $284 million interest in the company would equal more than $1 billion today. Adding to his cachet, just before running for office, the chicken magnate married Phyllis George, a former Miss America and network television newscaster. The glamorous couple shined a celebrity spotlight on the Bluegrass State.

Brown's business experience led him to seek economic relief from afar. KFC had expanded in Japan more quickly than it had in any other foreign market. "My Old Kentucky Home" featured in KFC Japan's

Harland Sanders opened a roadside restaurant in Corbin, Kentucky, in 1930. By 1963, the "Colonel" had franchised more than eight hundred Kentucky Fried Chicken outlets. A 1954 box for single servings of chicken featured the 1853 Foster song and the Bardstown tourist attraction.

promotionals, piggybacking on the melody that millions of Japanese people had learned in school. A 1974 KFC campaign persuaded Japanese families to buy a bucket of fried chicken as a Christmas meal. Only 1 percent of Japan's population is Christian, but "My Old Kentucky Home" morphed into a secular holiday "carol," and diners consumed "Kentucky for Christmas" in a tradition that continues to this day, when almost 10 percent of KFC sales in Japan occur over the holiday. An early 1980s television spot for the restaurant chain featured "My Old Kentucky Home," with its original d-word lyrics. A lush choral arrangement backed a long shot of a mother and daughter in prairie dresses striding through a meadow. Brown's Asian success inspired his hunt for international investors to sell on Kentucky's commercial opportunities. With the Japanese economy booming, Kentucky opened a Far East trade office in Tokyo.

John Y. Brown did not run for reelection in 1983, but his Democratic successor expanded his Tokyo outpost and landed a whale. Martha Layne Collins targeted automotive manufacturing at a time when Japanese imports were crushing American carmakers like Ford, GM, and Chevrolet. Collins was a seasoned political figure, a former home economics teacher with rural roots. In real Kentucky homes, people were struggling. Coal mining, tobacco, and the horse industry were weakening or in deep decline. "I had to get [Kentucky people] jobs," Collins recalled. Rumored as a potential pick as Walter Mondale's running mate, Governor Collins was passed over for Geraldine Ferraro, but she chaired 1984's Democratic National Convention. In her first year in office Collins visited Japan twice in hopes of luring businesses. Her peers were doing the same dance, but as the lone female governor Collins had an edge: "They didn't forget me!"

"My Old Kentucky Home" was the theme in 1984 when KFC celebrated fifteen years in Japan. Five thousand fourth, fifth, and sixth graders took part in a sponsored essay contest about what Kentucky and its fried chicken meant to them. "When I think of the state of Kentucky," one student explained, "I think of Mr. Abraham Lincoln first, then Mr. Stephen Foster then Kentucky Fried Chicken." Thirty-six winners were treated to a weeklong international trip: first stop, My Old Kentucky Home in Bardstown. The fourth grader Chiho Maejima said his mother knew "My Old Kentucky Home" and told him a great deal about the songwriter. "Foster wrote sad black people's songs and happy 'Camptown Races' songs and calm songs about American farms."

The KFC celebration continued in Japan with a multiweek tour by *The Stephen Foster Story*'s full cast and crew. The tenor David Brown, who taught voice and music at Louisville's performing arts high school, started with *The Stephen Foster Story* in 1969. He had risen to assistant musical director, and his wife, a professor of music, played John Rowan's wife, Rebecca. When the head musical director could not lead the fall tour, Brown got a leave of absence and the trip of a lifetime. A half-hour television special on Kentucky, Foster, the play, and "My Old Kentucky Home" warmed up the Japanese public for the KFC-sponsored tour. At the request of KFC Japan, Brown added a twenty-minute finale, an audience sing-along. Brown arranged subtitles, but they were scrapped when shouts erupted in the sold-out houses: "No Japanese. Want English!" They already knew and loved Foster's lyrics. The show moved from Tokyo to Osaka to Nara and back to Tokyo, and half the players remained for a third week of media appearances at schools and KFC restaurants. Brown remembered fans mobbing the players in parking lots, chasing their buses, and hanging over the overpasses to watch the troupe go by. Stephen Foster was as famous in Japan as the Rolling Stones. Brown floated through the grueling, ovation-filled weeks. "We were rock stars."

Kentucky's Far East trade representative, Jiro Hashimoto, escorted Toyota Motors executives to *Stephen Foster Story* performances. Hashimoto's targets often brought up "My Old Kentucky Home"; its familiarity lubricated otherwise formal exchanges. The *Stephen Foster* players were barely back in the United States before Collins called on Toyota's top man, Shoichiro Toyoda. The state was a front-runner for an $800 million assembly plant with more than three thousand jobs. Eleven U.S. states were vying for the plant, and when Toyota announced a site visit to Kentucky and other finalists, the forty-eight-year-old Collins laid plans for the most important dinner party of her life. She was determined to leave Toyota officials with an indelible impression.

The governor and her team whisked the automakers from the tarmac in Lexington via scenic roads to Frankfort and the white-pillared executive mansion where the Toyota group dined with business and university leaders. For dessert, alongside baked Alaska, a surprise detachment of singers from *The Stephen Foster Story* in full costume performed a Foster medley ending with "My Old Kentucky Home." The visitors tapped their feet and applauded. Collins called the music a piece of "our fiber," authentic and appealing.

No truer words were spoken. By the end of the twentieth century the song was entwined in the braided cord that for so many, but whites especially, bound state, region, and nation. It was a nursed legacy Kentucky could leverage. Ever since the 1904 world's fair, Kentucky leaders had internalized a faith that "My Old Kentucky Home" advanced the cause of capitalism in the commonwealth. The "lady" governor opened the state's economic door with the same bounteous hospitality the mythical plantation mistress showered on strangers. A shared appreciation for Foster's airs took the edge off grubby negotiations, including Collins's $125 million tax incentive package. One month later, Shoichiro Toyoda sank a spade into a rainy field in Scott County designated for the largest Japanese investment ever made in the United States. He called the site "our new 'old Kentucky home.'" Kentucky had a secret weapon in the race, Collins later told *Forbes* magazine. His name was Stephen Foster.

Three months after the groundbreaking, in March 1986, two dozen college students sporting jeans and windbreakers circled the bronze

At the 1986 groundbreaking for a Toyota automobile factory in Georgetown, Kentucky, Governor Martha Layne Collins presented a framed print of My Old Kentucky Home to the company's president, Shoichiro Toyoda.

feet of Abraham Lincoln's statue in Kentucky's soaring capitol dome. A Christian missionary program in Japan's university town of Sendai offered a several-week "homestay" in Ohio to learn English and study "everything American." The field trip to the Bluegrass State provided a break from regular classes and Ohio's industrial and agricultural flatlands. The itinerary followed the same tourist trail forged at the dawn of auto travel: Lincoln's birthplace at Sinking Spring; a black-fenced Claiborne Farm, home to the Triple Crown winner Secretariat; a replica pioneer fort in Harrodsburg; and My Old Kentucky Home State Park. The group posed for a picture on Federal Hill's wide staircase, which Foster himself, they were told, climbed after setting down the song they knew from school and KFC commercials.

In Frankfort, officials from Collins's office ushered the young visitors to a gallery where they could watch lawmakers in action. The assembly passed a resolution formally welcoming the Sendai students. The visitors rose from their seats as one. The foreign students had prepared their own gesture of thanks. They would serenade the legislators with Kentucky's internationally famous state anthem. The lawmakers stood.

But when Representative Carl Hines of Louisville's Forty-Third District heard the second line, "'Tis summer, the darkies are gay," he froze. Then he sat down. The four-term Democrat and lone Black member of Kentucky's House of Representatives felt responsible for representing the state's entire Black population. Hines was known for his mild manner, but he could not "stand there and listen to foreigners denigrate Black people." It was, he said, "an insult" to every Black Kentuckian.

The students' chaperone, a retired Ohio school principal who volunteered on church-sponsored people-to-people initiatives, was caught off guard. From his "musical mission" tours of Japan, Joseph Seamon knew that Foster songs were loved even in remote areas where Westerners hardly went. Of course the students should sing "My Old Kentucky Home" in Kentucky! Seamon assured Hines that no offense was intended. Hines excused the kids, but warned the big new Kentucky employer, Toyota Motors, about following appropriate norms with respect to Black people. More troubling was his colleagues' tolerance of a racial slur in the house of state; Hines was the only one to protest.

The Sendai student incident came during a discouraging period for Carl Hines, a veteran of the Korean War: his service on Louisville's board of education coincided with white flight (and the resulting tax shortfall), which forced city schools to merge with the county system; his work to integrate housing was being choked off by the Reagan administration; his real estate business was an uphill battle in a part of the city warped by urban renewal and redlining. The General Assembly's Black Caucus had just two members in 1986, Hines and Senator Georgia Powers. Severely marginalized within their respective legislative bodies, members of the caucus strained to bring attention to education, housing, and health policies that were failing Black citizens. "They rarely had a chance to do anything significant," recalled the veteran political reporter Bob Johnson.

The singing Japanese youths presented Hines with a wrong that his colleagues were in a position to immediately right. Although fourteen years had passed since Churchill Downs amended "My Old Kentucky Home" at the Derby, Hines discovered that Kentucky's official anthem remained as Stephen Foster wrote it. Statutorily, the Japanese singers were correct; the Sendai students *had* performed the authorized state song. Back in 1967, William E. Peters of the Scott County Improvement Association joined a long line of Black people urging removal of lyrics that alienated "the Negro tourist and the Negro citizen." The governor at the time, the Democrat Ned Breathitt, responded that any such change rested with the legislature.

While the students' white Ohioan host, Joseph Seamon, was seemingly unaware of the cleansing "My Old Kentucky Home" had undergone over the previous two or three decades, Kentucky's elected officials knew you didn't use the d-word in public. In the steady silence that surrounded the song's racially demeaning history, no proposal was ever advanced in Frankfort to correct the slur. Eight days after the Japanese-accented "Weep no more, my lady" lofted over the members of the Kentucky House of Representatives, Hines introduced a resolution to rid "My Old Kentucky Home" of phrases that "convey connotations of racial discrimination that are not acceptable in our present society." "People" would henceforth replace the d-word in each verse. Thus, "The head must bow and the back will have to bend, / Wherever the people may go; / A few more days, and the trouble all will end, / In the field where the sugar-canes grow." Georgia Powers introduced the resolution in the senate. Both bodies passed it in voice votes. Years later, Hines lamented that Kentucky trailed other states "in so many areas" and how ineffective he had felt against a conservative white majority. But at least in this "very quiet negative action," he had left a mark.

Thirty years after Congressman Frank Chelf played "My Old Kentucky Home" on his harmonica in Washington, D.C., to demand that the original lyrics be forever protected, lawmakers in his own state rejected Foster's 1853 words. No objections were made; no comments registered; no reporters seem to have asked lawmakers or the public their opinion. Hines's action merited 150 words in *The Courier-Journal*'s statehouse news roundup. A brief editorial in Owensboro's *Messenger-Inquirer* was headlined " 'People' Preferable." Governor Collins had no recollection of the 1986 "My Old Kentucky Home" incident when asked about it thirty years later. In fact, the "simple resolution" was the same action the representatives had used to welcome their Japanese visitors the week before and lacked the force of law. It required no gubernatorial signature. House Resolution 159 amending the state song's lyrics is cited in the state's statute books, but it is a legally empty gesture.

The state dusted its hands of a fleeting embarrassment. This was preferable to confronting the embarrassment. Even Hines admitted "it didn't make a big splash." The Black-owned *Louisville Defender* elected not to confront it at all, declining to print anything about the change

that had "people" dying mysteriously in faraway sugarcane fields. Tellingly, few whites noticed, and those who did were apologetic toward
their own ancestors. The Owensboro editorialist argued that the barriers
to racial equality fell with emancipation, that "darkies" became "people"
in 1865.

But dust, as we all know, tends to resettle on old surfaces. The 1986
resolution did not change the meaning of the song itself. Nor did it
stop full-throated traditionalists—including leading Democrats, supposedly more progressive on racial issues—from singing it the old way
into the twenty-first century. In Chicago, at the 1996 convention that
nominated Bill Clinton for a second term, Kentucky's governor led his
delegation in a sing-along of "My Old Kentucky Home" complete with
the old slur. People cringed, but no one made a fuss. In 2002, the Derby
entries filed onto the racecourse, and the announcer instructed over the
loudspeaker, "We will now sing 'My Old Kentucky Home.'" The writer
John Jeremiah Sullivan watched groups of young men in "bespoke poplin suits" join in the anthem, their arms round one another's shoulders.
At the second line, in unison, they belted out the taboo term. Churchill
Downs had its own "charged" racial history; after winning fifteen of
the first twenty-eight Derbies, Black jockeys were gradually but completely excluded from the sport, and the Old South atmosphere dominated the track's twentieth-century brand. It was not so out of place for
privileged young revelers to claim the space, recharging racial tensions
and commitments. Sullivan saw that something communal motivated
them. "Each looks to his friends' faces as they sing and sway, as if for
confirmation of the feeling they are feeling." Disproving legislators and
wishful editorialists, white attendees unabashedly demonstrated their
full awareness of the song's overtones—for their own and others' ears.
In the early years of this century, a newly transplanted New Englander
attended his first Derby Day party. He joined a friend's annual family
Derby gathering, and when the university marching band began to play,
the partygoers overrode the broadcast and restored the original lyric.
The "brazen, outright, and above all proud hollering of really vile racist
language" by his educated, socially respected hosts left the newcomer
speechless. His friend apologized, embarrassed: it was, she said, "tradition." Calling out racist language or ideas in white settings is disruptive.
Given the alcohol-infused anticipation surrounding the playing of "My
Old Kentucky Home," debating the d-word might provoke a brawl.

· · ·

The d-word discussion was only one iteration of this song's usefulness, extending over the course of a century and a half, in whitewashing and ultimately ghosting chattel slavery from American consciousness. Ghost, but not repair. As "My Old Kentucky Home" was edited in the 1950s, 1960s, 1970s, 1980s, and beyond, the broader nation dodged deep discussions of slavery, Reconstruction, Jim Crow, and ongoing policies and systems that preserved and sometimes deepened racial inequities. Neoconservatives gutted antipoverty programs and assaulted affirmative action, while neoliberals advanced the myth of meritocracy. Both engaged in "tough on crime" rhetoric and approved law enforcement budgets that disproportionately damaged the lives of poor people of color. A misguided "lift all boats" concept of economic growth stranded millions below the official poverty line despite working full-time at the minimum wage.

It damns only whites to acknowledge the small metrics of racial success over these same years. In a 2000 interview, Blaine Hudson remembered waking one day in the 1970s to the realization that progress had stalled in 1968 or 1969 and the "different kind of world" he thought the country was headed for never came about. In 2010, almost eighty years old, Carl Hines felt glad that two or three generations of Black people had been spared lyrics that represented them as happy singing slaves. Throughout his formative years, the NAACP had fought the d-word, assuming that if white people accorded Black Americans respect in public spaces, in schools, and over airwaves, something like tolerance would follow, a world where the content of one's character would trump the color of one's skin. Hines was proud to have dealt the slur what appeared to be its official deathblow in Kentucky. But, as a real estate agent in the wake of the 2008 financial crisis over mortgage-backed securities, he fully understood that the work to root out inequity was far from done. To him, the revised "My Old Kentucky Home" seemed all right. "I think," he said, reflecting, "it's a pretty song."

No doubt, this is true. The song's pleasing, memorable melody, played year over year, explains much of its longevity. But so has its institutionalization. Beyond Churchill Downs, Foster's 1853 ballad about slavery has echoed loudly in basketball arenas and football stadiums, generating pride and unity for Kentucky fans and their teams. At University of Kentucky's men's basketball final home game of the 1987–1988 season, the former governor A. B. "Happy" Chandler rose from his wheelchair in the middle of Rupp Arena. "And now, for one of the most emotional moments in sport," NBC's Tom Hammond announced on the national broadcast. The octogenarian legend closed his blue eyes and crooned. Cheerleaders locked arms and swayed. Graduating players towered over parents who joined them on the floor. Happy, known for his tendency to use racist language, moved smoothly over "'Tis summer, the people are gay." Indeed, Chandler's poignant rendering of the onetime blackface minstrel tune on Senior Nights in the 1970s and 1980s might have helped reconcile UK's overwhelmingly white fan base to changing standards of racial etiquette and the changing racial makeup of college sports.

As far back as 1913, the UK band had sounded "My Old Kentucky Home" across the gridiron at Wildcats games. A student called it "as sacred as a hymn," inspiring "men to do things they are otherwise not capable of doing." The school's 1917 songbook, bound in royal blue and white, contained "The Star-Spangled Banner," "Dixie," and other "Southern favorites." Over the twentieth century, Stephen Foster's 1850s hit became a cherished feature of UK sports and student culture. Happy Chandler's grandson, the former congressman Ben Chandler, said of Senior Night, "My Old Kentucky Home" was "the signature song at the signature event at the state's signature university."

The school's marching band leader, Harry Clarke, whose musicians backed Chandler's nostalgic Senior Night performances, came to the University of Kentucky in 1968. That year of political unrest (Martin Luther King was assassinated in the spring) prompted Clarke to scratch "Dixie" from the playlist, infuriating some students and alumni. But "My Old Kentucky Home" was sacrosanct. Clarke used it sparingly during football season, but not due to any awareness of it being controversial. He feared overuse would dull its impact, and he wanted the band to "milk it for all it's worth." Foster's melody was, after all, more hymn than fight song. The men's basketball coach Joe B. Hall took a white freshman to task in the early 1970s for goofing off at a game during "My Old Kentucky Home." "It was important to all Kentuckians," he explained, and insulting the team's fan base was not to be tolerated.

At the next practice, player Kevin Grevey stood up and delivered the anthem.

Clarke went from band leader to director of UK's School of Music, but since he stepped down from that role "My Old Kentucky Home" has been played at just about every football and basketball competition. When it didn't launch the kickoff at a 2002 football game, fans were so upset that a state senator drew up legislation to mandate Foster's rightful place in Big Blue athletic contests. On nights when the men's team comes out on top, the song becomes transparently triumphalist. Fans roar along with the nostalgic melody about slavery, their arms raised with their index fingers pointed to the ceiling, embodying the glory of, for that moment at least, being No. 1. UK has an official school hymn, but in Clarke's view Foster's song is the school's true alma mater.

Everett McCorvey began directing opera and vocal music programs at UK in 1991, five years after the state song was officially repaired. The tenor has performed "My Old Kentucky Home" at athletic events, community gatherings, weddings, funerals, and, repeatedly, before the state legislature on the opening day of sessions. Voice students are required to learn the song (though those arriving from Japan often already have it down, he noted). McCorvey judged Foster's 1853 work strong enough to "get by" on its melody alone, rare for a state anthem. Growing up Black in segregated Montgomery, Alabama, he knew the way music can rally hatred. That's not what "My Old Kentucky Home" does. McCorvey viewed the song as Foster's effort to express "the life and difficulty of a slave." While most people "don't go that deeply into it," it is always worthwhile to know the historical and social context of a piece of music. Echoing the viewpoint of W. C. Handy decades earlier, McCorvey suggested that Black spirituals more effectively convey the experience of bondage. Still, "My Old Kentucky Home" is part of the nation's musical heritage.

Younger opinions differed.

It was the way he learned to sing "My Old Kentucky Home" in elementary school "with a smile on my face" that so disturbed the UK baseball captain Dorian Hairston when he found out around 2014 that the state song was about slavery. "How do you take a child," he asked, "and teach them this tragedy and sell it to them as something beautiful?" In an effort to boost fan turnout, the athletic department added a playlist to home baseball matchups. Steve Winwood's "I'm Winning" blared through a public address system, followed by "My Old Kentucky Home." Having felt the eyes of white fans on Black players like him and having heard Black basketball athletes called "boys," Hairston assembled information about the origins of "My Old Kentucky Home" and met with the marketing director. "We didn't hear the song again," but it upset Hairston that nobody mentioned it to him or to the team. Hairston is a poet, high school teacher, and coach, and "My Old Kentucky Home" still makes him cringe. He doesn't want to hear people sing about a Black man sold downriver, and he can't help "imagining what [white fans] are thinking"—or not appreciating—about "our history with slavery."

The changes Hairston prompted in UK's baseball program had no impact at the football and basketball games that draw huge audiences. Hairston is not the only Black person to dash out of Rupp Arena as the final buzzer sounds. What if, he mused in 2018, "the state song reflected my belonging as a human being and not someone who was owned"?

In his 1855 lecture to the Rochester Ladies' Anti-slavery Society, Frederick Douglass blessed "the poets" for dramatizing the wrongs of chattel slavery in their work. Perhaps it is their profession's need to worry words and confront their meanings and contexts, but more than a century and a half later poets continue to do some of the same work. Two native Kentucky authors, one white, one Black, care deeply about words but hear this song about slavery quite differently.

The farmer, novelist, essayist, activist, and poet Wendell Berry has known "My Old Kentucky Home" as long as he can remember. His life and labor center on the Henry County, Kentucky, landscape where he was born. Berry has stood by a rural culture that the twentieth century demeaned and abandoned. He has excoriated an industrial economy that regards nature and human beings principally as exploitable resources. In that same county, his great-grandfather, "the bearded tall man whose voice / and blood are mine," owned other people, a legacy Berry probed in his 1970 memoir, *The Hidden Wound.* Asked what "My Old Kentucky Home" evokes, Berry pictured Stephen Foster visiting a Kentucky farm. A white family and a handful of Black people labored together. They knew one another as individuals—even as they occupied a brutal system that placed one group over the other. Because they truly knew one another, he observed, there was "great danger that you [a member of the white family] would love them [Black people]." As the song progresses, "Hard Times" come; someone knocks with a note of a debt owed and is paid with human chattel. The lady? She would be "the mistress," he surmised. She sorrowed. After all, Berry said, "people had compassion."

But the focus on *her* tears, I am convinced, requires us to forget the greater wrong, the enormity of it. Foster's song centered white sorrow, perhaps evoking white compassion, and there any obligation ended.

Kentucky's first Black poet laureate, the University of Kentucky professor Frank X Walker, sits down at football games and ducks out of basketball matchups when he hears the marching band start up "My Old Kentucky Home." Other fans have heckled him for disrespect. His poem "Oh, Weep No More Today" expresses the pained confusion the anthem arouses, the fear "of what it is white folks / hear in that white sheet   music / that gets them so full of tears / when they sing those songs." In the early 1980s, while an undergraduate at the University of Kentucky, Walker first encountered Foster's original "My Old Kentucky Home" printed in full on the back flap of the free Student Government Association's calendar/datebook. It stuck in Walker's throat for more than two decades, and in 2002 he called for a reconsideration of a song that almost nobody questioned. His generation of Black youth, he explained, many the first from their families to access higher education, was busy trying to make it and feared speaking out. They were told (and tried to believe) that if they brushed off discrimination and worked hard, racism would "go away." Much patience was required from those, like Walker, who were knocking at the door.

Kentucky's official commitment to the song continued into the twenty-first century with the U.S. Mint's Fifty States Quarter Program.

Walker objected to "My Old Kentucky Home" for painting a picture of Kentucky as "a great place to be a slave." Whites have taken pains over centuries to explain (to themselves, to the world, to their fellow Black Americans) how comfortably enslaved people lived, how kindly they were treated, how few were their cares. But the people of the United States must accept and teach their children that there was "no good place" to be in bondage. Some geographies were more immediately threatening to Black life, including the sugar and cotton plantations where laborers perished at extraordinary rates, and Kentucky did not have sugar or vast tracts of cotton. But, Walker noted, Kentucky's tantalizing proximity to free states across the Ohio River could have made slavery all the more psychologically torturous. An accident of miles, like an accident of skin, damned generations.

The claim currently circulating that "My Old Kentucky Home" is an antislavery song is another wishful distortion, according to Frank X Walker. If that was Foster's intent, he did a poor job of it, since the soul being sold downriver longs not for freedom but to return to the site of slavery. Walker also takes exception to the emasculating stereotypes Foster's sentimental plantation melodies promoted. Whites felt so threatened by Black men that they categorized and denigrated them as asexual—immature "boys" or bent-backed uncles—thus denying Black manhood even linguistic space. To Walker, "My Old Kentucky Home" has been a "dog whistle" that calls up white supremacist Old South myths but is ritually played and sung and enjoyed "out of context and without its historical baggage."

Frederick Douglass's forgotten line about "My Old Kentucky Home" awakening sympathy "for the slave" appeared in Ken Emerson's *Doo-Dah! Stephen Foster and the Rise of American Popular Culture* (1997) and has been seized upon by institutions invested in preserving "My Old Kentucky Home." For years, the first sentence of Wikipedia's "My Old Kentucky Home" entry called the song an "anti-slavery ballad." Praise from a heroic abolitionist supplied an "amulet" against critics.

But it's a dodge. Frederick Douglass set his life against the cruelties and wrongs of racism. "My Old Kentucky Home" interested him momentarily as a possible means by which his white countrymen would feel compassion, would redress the sins of slavery and white supremacy, would make amends. He would never approve his words being twisted to protect a song—one that for generations accompanied a whole lot of

Frederick Douglass once hoped that "My Old Kentucky Home" would spur those who heard it to think and act in sympathy with slavery's victims. After Reconstruction, he railed against a reunified white culture that romanticized slavery and a white political system that robbed millions of Black citizens of civil rights and suffrage. In 2020 and 2021, Churchill Downs cited Douglass to defend the traditional singing of Foster's melody as the horses make their way to the starting gate for the longest continuously held American sporting event.

racist "business as usual"—to celebrate a national sporting event. Notwithstanding pious latter-day tributes to abolitionism, defending a profitable business by shackling "My Old Kentucky Home" to Douglass's plea is historically indefensible. Even a cursory knowledge of factual slavery makes it reprehensible.

In 1996, the year the first Grammy Award was given for Best Rap Album, Kevin Drane graduated from high school in Louisville and joined a group called the Thorobreds. At Morris Brown College in Atlanta, Drane could not afford a meal outside the dining hall and was constantly aware of his single mother's financial needs back home. Selling drugs was the only way he knew at the time to meet what he felt were his responsibilities. All along, Drane, known as KD, made music.

One evening in 2004 in Atlanta's Mudnoc Studios, KD, the rapper

Goodfella, and Fish Scales of the chart-topping group Nappy Roots listened to a buoyant beat by a German producer. When the trio decided to try using it for a collaboration, nobody gave a thought to Stephen Foster. But over the next forty-eight hours, they created a single titled "My Kentucky Home." Drane had in mind the contrast between Atlanta's booming Black world, with its money, sports stars, businesspeople, and artists, and Kentucky, which still operated on a (white) "good old boy method." He wanted to "bridge the gap" musically and commercially, melding the edgy "gangster" identity he and Goodfella adopted with Nappy Roots' mainstream appeal. Drane aimed to capture an audience that included "white, Black, and middle," even the "racist Kentucky guy," and especially middle-aged white women, who, he was told, purchased more CDs than any other demographic. To do that, he needed another voice. Drane called Demi Demaree, a singer for the Villebillies, a Louisville band that blended country, rock, and rap. The project would be "kinda street" but not too much, with a touch of "gangsta hardcore" all wrapped around Kentucky.

Drane drove all night to Demaree's house in Louisville to present the concept. Together, they headed back to the Atlanta studio. The four artists wrote the lyrics together, and by evening were laying down tracks. Each vocalist performed a section. The subjects were Kentucky and partying, themes that worked across racial audiences. Fish Scales launched

The Louisville-born gangsta rapper KD (Kevin Drane, *left*) co-wrote "My Kentucky Home" in 2004 and recruited Demi Demaree (*right*) to record it with him.

with "High times, sittin by the river." "Nothin gonna stop me," Drane began, and ended as a "bluegrass CEO cat" helping his "homies" out of poverty and crime. Demaree sang rather than rapped the chorus:

Come on down where the bluegrass rolls, and the country cold wind blows
where the city lights still glow
to my Kentucky home.

Demaree remembered the others were satisfied, but to him the hook didn't work. He rerecorded his part, this time ending the choral "come on down" with a trailing repetition "to my *ol'* Kentucky home, my *ol'* Kentucky home." Just as it had for Randy Newman decades earlier, Foster's hook made the song click. A harmonica riff lifted from a Crosby, Stills, Nash & Young song closed the chorus, and the effect was infectious. Cruising home on I-75 to Louisville, Drane, Demaree, and the Villebillies' manager Will Walk played the track over and over. "We knew it was a hit."

Major record labels signed both KD and the Villebillies based on the potential they saw in "My Kentucky Home." The demo swept Kentucky pop radio, though the DJs at the Black station where Drane took it handed it back, saying it was too "white" for their listeners. He didn't mind much. The song's popularity soared, and Drane recalled feeling seen and heard as more than "a nigger." He headlined at the Kentucky State Fair. And when Lexington, Kentucky, police arrested him for smoking a joint outside a club where he was scheduled to perform, the song proved useful. "Lexington was considered a racist place, no Black officers," Drane remembered. As he waited to be booked, a precinct staff member recognized his name from the song. Instead of charging him, the police escorted Drane back to the venue, where the rapper gave them autographed CDs and posters. He went onstage wearing his jail bracelet, feeling on top of the world.

Drane knew of the state song, knew it was somehow tainted, and he experienced Kentucky as a racist place. He also wanted his song to project love for his current home, which is why he drew the line at including "ol'" in the title, even though it was there in the lyrics. Demaree grew up in a working-class family and learned "My Old Kentucky Home" at his Catholic school in second grade. He wasn't intentionally quoting Foster and had no idea the iconic song was about slavery. "You are a mix of your experience and sounds," Demaree explained. If anyone would have known, he said, he would have imagined it would have been his three Black collaborators, but the subject never came up.

It did come up, though, on Derby Day 2002, when the Pulitzer Prize–winning jazz trumpeter and composer Wynton Marsalis prepared to join the University of Louisville Cardinal Marching Band in their pre-race performance. Marsalis's manager, Andre Guess, a Louisvillian, arranged the appearance. Jazz at Lincoln Center was planning a $130 million home for the program Marsalis directed, and they needed to bring the campaign to the finish line. The national prominence of Wynton playing at the Derby was part of that effort.

Ten minutes ahead of post time, before the band marched into position, an official handed Marsalis a small card with the music to "My Old Kentucky Home," the kind of card horn players clip to the end of their instruments.

"Man, what the fuck is this?" is what Guess remembered his client and close friend saying. "What is this bullshit? What is this lyric right here—'the darkies.' No! I'm not playing this shit. I'm not going out on television playing this shit." The card held Foster's 1853 lyrics.

Andre envisioned millions of viewers anticipating the trumpet great—a household name. If he didn't show up, that would be the headline. "Wynton, you got to go out there. We agreed to this."

"You agreed to it! I didn't agree! Aren't you from here? This is your fault—don't you know your state song?"

Guess isn't sure if he did know the background of "My Old Kentucky Home." If he did, he'd forgotten. "We had a moment." The star was furious. As Guess saw it, the show had to go on. "You're getting your ass out there, and I don't care if you just put the horn to your mouth and act like you're playing, but you have to get out there."

The sun shone bright that afternoon. NBC's footage cut between close-ups of a somber-seeming Marsalis and joyous fans singing along to what the announcer called "the most sentimental moment in sports, when one imagines even the horses get misty-eyed."

Marsalis played "My Old Kentucky Home." But, Guess recalled, "the only reason he did it was because of our relationship." Guess, who is Black, could not see it then but understands now that his friend was thinking about the world watching him play an old minstrel song and seeing him as "complicit."

. . .

Foster's song about slavery materializes from time to time in twenty-first-century pop culture. The hit cable television series *Mad Men,* set amid a booming 1960s Madison Avenue advertising agency, was in its third season in 2009 when the episode "My Old Kentucky Home" aired. During a Derby-themed garden party, the adman Roger Sterling appears in blackface onstage with a Dixieland band. "I did this at home with a little shoe polish," he explains to the guests, and then drops to his knees in the "mammy" posture made famous by blackface Al Jolson. Sterling's wife beams down at him as he performs the classic Derby tune. Sterling doesn't say "darkies"; he doesn't need to. The transgressive scene pairing "My Old Kentucky Home" with blackface minstrelsy was shocking enough.

The queer performance artist Taylor Mac's *24-Decade History of Popular Music* (2016)—an ecstatic twenty-four-hour one-man show—wove an alternate American history by pegging each decade since the U.S. founding to a popular song. In the immersive spectacle, audience members played multiple roles onstage, voted, and cheered on Mac's command. Mac dismantled American shibboleths while robing himself in a succession of cuckoo costumes that were half junkyard, half drag queen—all while affirming the unifying and inclusive possibilities of song. The 1850s segment used "My Old Kentucky Home" in a *lucha libre* smackdown to determine the true "father of American song." An audience member stood in for Stephen Foster, the canonized progenitor, facing off in a mock wrestling ring against the queer hero Walt Whitman, played by Mac. Whitman is the radical idealist and patriotic hedonist. Foster is the straight man, who wore "his politics lightly," as most Americans historically have. As performed by Mac, "My Old Kentucky Home" had no chance against "Song of Myself."

In the fall of 2016, the Louisville-based Black a cappella quartet Linkin' Bridge reached the final stage of NBC's hit musical competition show *America's Got Talent* (*AGT*). Linkin' Bridge had wowed the judges with "Over the Rainbow" and, in a surprise, the 1973 power ballad "Free Bird" by the southern rockers Lynyrd Skynyrd. Linkin' Bridge members had backstories that aligned with "street" stereotypes, but their image was soothingly "soul." The baritone Montre Davis had survived an impoverished and abusive childhood and served multiple prison sentences for drug dealing and other felonies, and the group's stated aim has been "to bring people of all races and creeds together through their music." Twelve-year-old Grace VanderWaal went home the winner of that season's *AGT*, but the men have been hometown celebrities ever since.

With the recognition accrued from *AGT*, Linkin' Bridge wanted to increase their national audience. The Derby was a natural venue. "We never thought about going to the horse races," Davis recalled of his youth. That was "for white people with money." Montre Davis had learned "My Old Kentucky Home" as a middle schooler, and its melody remained with him. When the grandmother who raised him for much of his early life heard Davis humming Foster's tune, she scolded him: "You don't need to be singing that song." He didn't question, and she didn't offer an explanation. Years later, in 2017, Linkin' Bridge released a music video of "My Old Kentucky Home" with their distinctive a cappella arrangement and sent it to Churchill Downs. Their harmonies unfold over backdrops including Muhammad Ali's modest pink-painted childhood home, the Louisville Slugger Museum, a black tobacco barn and green fields on a country road, and Churchill Downs itself—pride-invoking urban and rural, gritty and pastoral spaces that alternately read "Black" and "white."

It was a controversial move for a Black singing group, and national events turned up the heat. Months after the video release, white supremacists massed in Charlottesville for a "Unite the Right" rally to protect a Robert E. Lee monument. The vilest expressions of racial superiority boomed into cable news cameras, and before the weekend was over, a white supremacist had killed a counterprotester. Confederate monuments became a national preoccupation as people learned that Black citizens had been offended by them all along. After a months-long process, Pittsburgh officials removed the city's 1900 monument to Stephen Foster that showed a grinning Black man playing the banjo at the songwriter's feet.

Linkin' Bridge was accused of selling out. Fencing off music into permissible and impermissible buckets violates the group's creed; they had already crossed a boundary with a "Free Bird" cover, since Lynyrd Skynyrd was known for deploying Confederate flags at concerts and on merchandise. Montre Davis felt certain theirs was the "best version" of

Following public hearings, Pittsburgh officials in 2018 removed a 1900 sculpture honoring the city's famous son. The position of the white songwriter above the stereotyped Black minstrel figure had long been a source of complaints.

"My Old Kentucky Home" ever recorded. The song could do useful work, he felt, including bridging racial divides.

Because of the criticism the "My Old Kentucky Home" video attracted, Davis later checked on the song's background. He read that Foster's famous melody was an "anti-slavery ballad" and watched a public television documentary about Kentucky's Underground Railroad that linked the song to Harriet Beecher Stowe's antislavery novel. When he googled "Stephen Foster" and "Underground Railroad," Davis learned that Foster and his wife were radical abolitionists who used their New Hampshire farm to speed runaways to liberty. If people had a problem with the song, he felt solid telling them it was originally written to combat the chattel system.

But so much American culture built atop the history of slavery is anything but solid.

Linkin' Bridge continued performing "My Old Kentucky Home," and white audiences, at least, responded warmly. How many others who bothered to check have, like Davis, assumed that the abolitionist named Stephen Symonds Foster was the author of Kentucky's anthem? The group confidently returned to "My Old Kentucky Home" in 2019, filming a second music video that incorporated the Old Kentucky Home in Bardstown. During filming, the group toured Federal Hill's cellar, where they were told the lie that here the white Rowans hid Black fugitives. In fact it was where the people the Rowans enslaved were forced to live.

I have long wondered how Louisville's most celebrated native son felt about the song I had been thinking about for years.

"I never heard Muhammad sing that song, ever," his widow told me. For a brief period in the mid-1970s when Ali was in his thirties and managing a comeback after being banned from boxing for his conscientious objection to the Vietnam War, I dreamed of "the Champ" becoming my neighbor. After school one day I spotted slowly rolling up the street a van emblazoned with Ali's motto, "Float like a butterfly, sting like a bee." It turned in to a gated driveway that led to a mansion then for sale; that house and my own were fraternal twins, built for a pair of turn-of-the-century flour baron brothers in different styles but the same grand scale. That evening at family dinner I excitedly relayed the news that Muhammad Ali might move within shouting distance. It met a cool reception. As the editor and publisher of the city's dailies, my father (and his father before him) had endorsed civil rights measures up through court-ordered school busing to integrate public schools. There were death threats for that. My dad had instituted a model affirmative action program in the newsrooms. These actions did not affect my daily life, except for the red panic buttons a security specialist installed around our house and property. I attended a private school in a rural setting. All my neighbors were white.

Ali would have shattered the residential color line, and for reasons they did not explain, my parents had no wish to welcome the world champion. I have filled in explanations ever since: Perhaps they were averse to the tourists he would draw? The parties he might throw? Perhaps. No matter, I felt confused. Because also perhaps doing the right thing extended only so far.

I met the retired heavyweight champ in 2003 during the planning for a center to honor his life as an athlete and global humanitarian. Parkinson's disease made it difficult for him to speak, but Ali's charisma was still intoxicating. I didn't tell him that I wished he had made his Kentucky home next to mine all those years before, nor did we speak of the song about slavery. In 1981 and again in 2006 he served as grand marshal of the Kentucky Derby Festival parade and joined celebrations filled with renditions of "My Old Kentucky Home." Muhammad Ali didn't sing the Foster tune, but neither did he get hung up on it. "My Old Kentucky Home," profitably embedded in state and corporate branding, went unquestioned in a town and nation where racism remained unresolved. It was that lack of resolution that preoccupied Muhammad in 2003. Many locals had denounced Ali as a draft dodger and radical follower of Islam, so I said how hopeful I was that the city was finally lifting up his life story and his message of peace and justice. He listened, then looked straight at me and said something I asked him to repeat twice before I understood: "I'm still just a nigger." Ali might have meant a number of things, but it seared my liberal soul to hear Louisville's own Black superhero say that.

I wanted to "do right." At the time, I had young children and made sure they knew what their state song was really about. I mixed it into the bedtime repertory—all three verses with the d-word sprinkled through—we were *not* going to hide from the way horror was wrapped in such a pretty tune. Around that time, the essayist John Jeremiah Sullivan, whose father was a Louisville sportswriter, was thinking along the same lines and wrote that "the Derby commissioners should make the crowd sing the whole thing, rather than bowdlerizing one line."

If we lingered over all of Foster's words, perhaps we would come to some understandings. If we read them as sentences, not verse. "The head must bow and the back will have to bend, wherever the darky may go." And, after bowed head and bent back, the reward was that in a few more days the trouble all will end, for death haunts the field where the sugarcanes grow. The trouble never ended for the families left behind, and with that sentence hanging over it still these many years later, it has not ended for my country.

CODA

My Old Kentucky HOME

In 2020, "My Old Kentucky Home" once again became a matter of public debate.

A pandemic gripped the world. Americans were terrified. The beloved country and folk musician John Prine was among the early victims of the coronavirus. During his daily pandemic press conference, Kentucky's governor played the singer's rendition of "My Old Kentucky Home" against a montage of Bluegrass State houses lit green for compassion and solidarity. An Owensboro DJ followed up with an online sing-along aimed at boosting community spirit: at an appointed hour listeners posted themselves on social media performing (or lip-syncing) the state anthem in unison. A few weeks later, Churchill Downs mounted a "virtual" Kentucky Derby celebration on the first Saturday in May—the race's customary date—and the governor said, "One of my favorite traditions of the Kentucky Derby is singing 'My Old Kentucky Home.'" During these hard times, elected officials and the media certified the song as a healing balm.

COVID-19 lockdowns were in full force in late May when an appalled world watched a Minneapolis police officer kneel for more than nine minutes on the neck of a Black man suspected of passing a counterfeit $20 bill. The killing of George Floyd turned klieg lights on policing and racism in the United States. In the heat of global outrage and protests, the spotlight fell on the overlooked police killing two months earlier of a twenty-six-year-old medical worker in a midnight drug raid. The apartment door Louisville police broke down that night was decorated with brightly colored letters that spelled out "HOME."

The unifying "My Old Kentucky Home" sing-alongs came to a halt, drowned out by chants of "Breonna Taylor—say her name."

Amid a summer of racial reckoning and protest, Churchill Downs planned for the rescheduled Kentucky Derby in September. That date— when the nation, indeed the world, would be watching Louisville— became a leverage point for those demanding "Justice for Breonna." Some protesters talked of targeting the Derby itself.

Foster's old, old song found itself in the news. *BloodHorse* magazine, the racing industry mainstay, reported that Churchill Downs Inc.'s higher-ups might scrap the ritual singing. The question of what to do divided people. Some threatened to boycott the Derby permanently if the track abandoned the icon. Others pleaded with Churchill Downs to suspend the onetime blackface tune out of respect for Breonna Taylor, who was "gunned down in her 'Kentucky Home.'" The Kentucky senator and Republican majority leader, Mitch McConnell, advised Churchill Downs' president "absolutely" to stand by a song that was "very much a part of our culture and tradition." Defenders nodded to the song's long history and tradition but didn't specify or want to linger on what history and which traditions. Foster's tune, McConnell told a reporter, "used to have some language that I think could have been viewed as racially insensitive," before confirming that such insensitivities had been dealt with "thirty or forty years ago."

For a small but growing number of people, however, the old remedy was inadequate.

Two days before the race, Churchill Downs announced, "This will be a Derby unlike any other," and pledged "concrete action" to achieve "the changes America so desperately needs." Suspense ran high when the jockeys guided their mounts onto the track in front of an empty grandstand. The announcer asked the television audience to "pause to recognize the inequities that many in our nation still face and reflect with renewed hope for a more just country to truly take root, grow, and flourish." A red-jacketed bugler then played the melody, slow and clear, like taps. Due to the pandemic, almost no one was there to sing the lyrics.

. . .

What should we do with this song, this legacy?

The choice Churchill Downs made points, perhaps unintentionally, in one direction. Listen to the language used. "Take root, grow, and flourish" comes directly from Frederick Douglass, who spent a lifetime seizing on any help in the fight against slavery and then racial oppression post-emancipation. Douglass's 1855 proposition that "My Old Kentucky Home" might assist his cause hints at an answer to the question of what is to be done with Foster's song in this twenty-first century. For generations, white Americans have formulated the answers. The time has come to let Black voices be heard and for white people to be guided by them.

For Black Americans, the question has always been not whether "My Old Kentucky Home" is redeemable but whether it might be useful. This began in earnest with Frederick Douglass and has continued ever since. Henrietta Vinton Davis tried to turn the song to Black liberation through theater; the New York City "darky team" playing for a private party spurned it as hateful; Black parents in Boston and Washington, D.C., tried to ban it. In response white people and the organizations they controlled steadfastly upheld "My Old Kentucky Home." Some have gone so far as to believe that its sweet strains enabled all to "forget social and racial differences." Generation after generation of whites have cashed in on a song that helped sanitize the American past. And each generation of white Americans has implicitly expected Black people to be quiet, take note, or, even better, sing along with them. For white people, the song supplies emotional release, an escape from reality. Not for Black people.

In 1922, a poet and school principal whose mother had been indentured to the Rowans in Bardstown foresaw a day "when the head will never bow / Wherever the Negro may go. / A few more years and he'll show the nation how / He will thrive where the sugar canes grow." Besides being ignored, Joseph Cotter's rewriting of Foster's narrative proved overly optimistic. His people had by that time been emancipated for half a century, yet they were forced to bow their heads and bend their backs, bear injustice and swallow righteous grievances. The swallowing continued for close to a century after Cotter's call for change, for respect. That reality resides within the lyrics of "My Old Kentucky Home," but not in how it has been expressed and felt by white audiences for almost 170 years. What slavery built and stole is beyond calculation but not beyond admitting.

James Baldwin excoriated *Uncle Tom's Cabin* as proof of the feebleness of sentimentalism as a strategy against oppression. Millions of Americans embraced "everybody's protest novel," as Baldwin called the book, yet a hundred years after its publication America disenfranchised, denied rights to, and systematically humiliated millions of Black citizens. History showed that in matters of racial justice white *feeling* had failed to resolve the problems it fed upon. People could read or watch or hear of horrors committed against Baldwin's race and still say this "has nothing to do with us." "Whatever unsettling questions are roused" in whites, he damned as "evanescent, titillating, remote." The pleasures of such "spurious emotion" masked an "inability to feel." Or at the least to translate that feeling into a new reality.

Foster, "the master of the quivering lip," took Stowe a step further and converted the sentimentalized agony of slavery into solace and nostalgia for whites. His song of a Kentucky home became a feature of proud heritage, public celebration, and collective revelry. It has undammed rivers of white tears since 1853, many of them from people who never knew they were singing a song about slavery, about a Black man torn from his family and sold down the river to his death. Still, its public performances have a tribal quality. Stephen Foster's appalling accomplishment was to embed the bleeding sore at the center of American society, economics, politics, and law in music so supple, sentimental, and joy-making that race-based slavery, its subject, slipped out of the minds of generations of Americans. The singing is a nation's song to its white self.

I submit that the half measures taken to redeem and preserve Foster's melody have been inadequate. Deleting the d-word, as was done between the 1950s and the 1980s, split white people between those who "got it" and those who refused to give up a song with its offensive slur. Progressives felt satisfied and traditionalists felt resentful. It purported to "fix" a song without questioning its celebrated place in the culture. Washing out the "darkies" was quite literally the least white people could do. Against the backdrop of their actual history, and the inauthentic history they told themselves, this minimum was meaningful. But insufficient. It was not the last time that white progressives managed to acknowledge racism, only to allow wishfulness to wash out acknowledgment and obfuscate the past. It's a useful play in the long book of white America's progressive dodges. Just as the passage of civil rights laws did not usher in an equal playing field, purging one word to resolve the racist burden of "My Old Kentucky Home" was not enough. The truth is that to this day a minstrel song about a man exchanged for cash and sent away from his family to die serves as a celebratory anthem. The larger truth is that persistent systems of racial injustice are challenged only faintly—when challenged at all—by white America.

Whatever Black people choose to do with "My Old Kentucky Home" does not change what I know now: its public performance in spaces led and controlled by white Americans is by definition an act of white supremacy, whether done consciously or unthinkingly. For me, singing and celebrating Stephen Foster's song is no longer possible. For me, "My Old Kentucky Home" is unredeemable.

Alexander Woollcott's prediction that there would never "be an America without" Stephen Foster's plantation melodies is true in that there is no America without chattel slavery and the investments in racism that shaped and followed it. Young Allison, the early twentieth-century journalist who labored to enshrine "My Old Kentucky Home," wanted to redeem its author from obscurity and establish him as a unique American. But Foster's gift was a capacious talent for appealing to conventional America. His gift was to take what was culturally pervasive and render it entertaining, infectious, memorable, undeniably beautiful. White ingenuity softened the edges of whites' cruelties to Black human beings in the pursuit of profit; this is the work of a system that at some level knows it is doing wrong. Allison felt sure that a single song could help his state and help rehabilitate the songwriter, make him respectable. But he was attempting the impossible, because the compromises of "My Old Kentucky Home" are the nation's. They are not respectable.

White allies of a century ago like Young Allison opposed lynching, just as earlier in this century they were disturbed by the killings of Trayvon Martin, Michael Brown, and Tamir Rice. Allison did not like blackface minstrelsy. But he embraced the inauthenticity of both the song and the monument he helped build to it. And that monument was not to an authentic Kentucky home where a man who had escaped enslavement had been held and abused but to the plantation house of a family that was complicit in that abuse. Nowhere did Allison say, "I'm sorry." Nowhere have progressives like him said, "Please forgive us."

I write as another progressive white American, a wearer of Derby hats, and, yes, a shedder of sentimental tears. I write as a Kentuckian and as a historian, and I recognize that relinquishing "My Old Kentucky Home," leaving its future fate to Black Americans, will not erase racial inequity. Letting go of a song I have loved, jettisoning it in public and private, cannot ameliorate the past. But giving up something we love can be a sign of love. Relinquishing "My Old Kentucky Home" signals regret for wrongs this single melody encapsulates. It is a gesture that seeks forgiveness and chooses compassion over tribal satisfaction, no matter how innocuous that satisfaction has felt. Neat and tidy history cleansed of the cruel and incriminating cannot convey the right moral lessons. History is not a safe place, nor should we expect it to be. As this long look at an old, old song comes to a close, it points to the greater work that is ongoing—and patient. Reckoning is an act of hope.

I don't believe it can be wrong to love a song, but I do believe we commit wrongs when we do not understand what we claim to love. Refusing to look closely at uncomfortable aspects of history has hurt this nation and may be its undoing. Eleanor Roosevelt used to tell college students, "Study history realistically. You'll love your country just as much." In that sense, reckoning is also an act of patriotism.

Nearly 170 years ago, Foster copyrighted Black loss for white pleasure, comfort, and distraction. Over time, American society erected "My Old Kentucky Home" as a sonic monument—impressive, opaque, and also contested—to white feeling and white forgetting, to a nation's own segregated memory. "My Old Kentucky Home" has been handed down and held up as a thing to cherish, a hallowed ritual, a delight to me and countless others who have infused it with emotional warmth. But that legacy is not reason to ask, why *would* anyone question it? The failure to question "My Old Kentucky Home" and history—and the evidence of racial hierarchy visible with and without the klieg lights—favors nostalgia over hope, forgetting over repair.

One little song reproduced slavery's brutality for the sentimental and material benefit of white people. Listening in to that history through a single melody is a small but possibly potent act. Foster's song may or may not be celebrated much further into this century, but comprehending how it has lived in and with us for so long is a step in a new direction. Reckoning is an act of love.

ACKNOWLEDGMENTS

Everyone knows what it's like to have a song stuck in their head. You push it out of your ears for a time, but then it takes up residence once more, note by note, word by word. "My Old Kentucky Home" has been ringing in my ears since sometime in the latter 1990s when I recognized what its lyrics were really about. Scores of people have given precious time and counsel as I pieced together this seductive song's life story and loaded meanings.

Archivists and local historians illuminated my way. My greatest debt goes to the Center for American Music at the University of Pittsburgh for an early travel to research grant and years of unfailing professional aid from Kathryn Miller Haines, Christopher Lynch, and Deane Root. The archives at My Old Kentucky Home State Park were critical to developing the story of the song—site director Matthew Colin Bailey facilitated a sweltering summer of research in a storage room behind the gift shop. The Filson Historical Society in Louisville sponsored an early public lecture, and its staff—including Jennie Cole, Abby Glowgower, Jim Holmberg, Jana Meyer, and Heather Potter—answered queries and opened collections. Special thanks to Carrie Daniels and Tom Owen for assistance at University of Louisville's Archives and Special Collections; Jessica Whitehead at the Kentucky Derby Museum; Terry L. Birdwhistell at University of Kentucky Libraries; Kelly Dunnagan and Paul Burns at the Louisville Free Public Library; Kelly Spring at the Joyner Library Special Collections at East Carolina University; and Michelle Jarrell, archivist at Eli Lilly and Company. Archivists at the Schomburg Center for Research in Black Culture, the New York Public Library for the Performing Arts, and the Library of Congress for extended special assistance. Expert genealogical assistance came from Cynthia Maharrey. Pen Bogert shared his research on the early history of the Rowan family and the people they held in slavery. The ship landing and departure data he tracked down put to rest the appealing myth that Foster composed "My Old Kentucky Home" at the Rowan mansion in 1852 during his steamboat journey from Pittsburgh to New Orleans. Terry Borton kindly lit up the world of lantern slides. Dan Gediman helped focus my thinking as he worked on his podcast, *The Reckoning*. James Nicolson, historian of the Kentucky Derby, laid crucial groundwork and helped me untangle numerous confusions. Ted Wathen contributed photographs. The book benefited directly from conversations with Ken Emerson, Stephen Foster's most recent biographer, and from exchanges with musicologists Douglas Shadle and James Davis.

Countless people shared memories and insights of the song, immeasurably enriching the story told here. I am particularly indebted to interviewees Lonnie Ali, Jecorey Arthur, Matthew Colin Bailey, Wendell and Tanya Berry, Edie Bingham, Charles Booker, David Brown, John Y. Brown Jr., John Y. Brown III, Ben Chandler, Harry Clarke, Bob Coleman, Martha Layne Collins, Montre Davis, Demi Demaree, Debbie and Les Dornan, Kevin Drane, Jim Gray, Andre Guess, Dorian Hairston, C. Ray Hall, Jiro Hashimoto, Carl R. Hines Sr., Jim Host, Joni Jenkins, Bob Johnson, Jeanie Kahnke, Everett McCorvey, Morgan McGarvey, Gregory McMahon, J. Evan McMahon, Marie Porter, Billy Reed, Sadiqa Reynolds, Keith Runyon, Karl Schmitt, Greg Seamon, Frank X Walker, and James Calleroz White. Kentucky scholars and journalists were enormously helpful along the way. I am especially thankful to Dick Clay, Tom Eblen, Bani Hines Hudson, Michael Jones, Patrick Lewis, Estill C. Pennington, Aaron Rosenblum, Dan Vivian, George Wright, and John and Catherine Smith.

From the earliest, feeble stabs at drafting chapters I have relied on the fresh ears of friends and associates who read all or part of what I produced. Jeffrey Skinner brought incisiveness and joy in creation to our exchanges, and I got to read his poetry in progress. Leah Hagedorn's brilliant comments improved many of my ideas and even more of my sentences. Megan Pillow Davis deployed her sharp critical lens and pushed me to include ways my and my family's involvements with the song echoed pleasures and stereotypes that reinforced oppressive systems. Clara Bingham read, mentored, and believed in this project. She fed and housed and cheered me whenever work brought me to New York City.

Thanks to the Helium Club crew, and especially Marie Porter and

David Jones Jr. for blunt comments offered more than a decade ago following an informal presentation on Foster's old song. Without their demonstrated interest and early encouragement, this book might not exist today.

Debby Hurst and Debbie Coleman have been a dream team. Thank you for being the best life helpers anyone could imagine.

Martha Sherrill has been my book whisperer, dispensing wisdom and advice when the mysteries of moving from idea to page to published book seemed overwhelming. Support and valuable suggestions from Joan Bingham, Catherine Clinton, Joe Drape, David Michaelis, Dan Okrent, Bill Powers, and Ted Widmer kept me rolling forward. Thomas LeBien brought the music back to the project at a decisive moment; our exchanges were meaty and meaningful and I truly cannot thank him enough.

When I went looking for an agent, a tip led to Lynn Nesbit. She brightened the minute I mentioned "My Old Kentucky Home" (she could hum the melody and picture the sheet music, having learned it on the piano as a child). Lynn has been an unfailingly positive force since our first meeting. Thanks also to her highly effective assistant, Mina Hamedi.

I am deeply grateful to Vicky Wilson at Knopf. She immediately understood the iconic nature of this single American song and saw the tale through multiple drafts. Thanks also to her assistant Marc Jaffee and Soonyoung Kwon in design, for making such a beautiful book.

This became a family journey. My family has been patient and supportive as I dug back generations to forebears who sang along to "My Old Kentucky Home" and forward into my children's early years. More than anyone else, Stephen Reily steadied and inspired the Kentuckian he chose to spend a life with so many years ago. He read every chapter and made important suggestions and distilled core concepts into clear language. My futile struggle to find the "right" way to sing Foster's old song to our three children paved my entryway into this topic. My hopes rest on them and their generation to sing about and bring about a home for all, one that need not be so far away.

ABBREVIATIONS

ARCHIVES

CAM   Center for American Music, University of Pittsburgh

ELCA   Eli Lilly and Company Archive, Indianapolis

FHS   Filson Historical Society

KHS   Kentucky Historical Society

MOKHSP My Old Kentucky Home State Park

NYPLPA New York Public Library for the Performing Arts, Dorothy and Lewis B. Cullman Center

MANUSCRIPT COLLECTIONS

AMS   American Minstrel Show Collection, Harvard Theatre Collection, Houghton Library, Harvard University

BLBP   Benjamin L. LaBree Papers, Filson Historical Society

BSU   Black Student Union Collection, University of Louisville Archives and Special Collections

FHC   Foster Hall Collection, Center for American Music, University of Pittsburgh

HCCP   Howard Chandler Christy Papers, Lafayette College Special Collections

JKLC   Josiah Kirby Lilly Correspondence, Center for American Music, University of Pittsburgh

KOHC   Kentucky Oral History Commission Collection, Civil Rights Movement in Kentucky Oral History Project

NSP   Nate Salsbury Papers, Beinecke Rare Book and Manuscript Library, Yale University

OWSP   Osso Willis Stanley Papers, Filson Historical Society

RFP   Rowan Family Papers, Western Kentucky University Manuscript and Folk Life Archives

ROTHERT-YEA Otto A. Rothert Collection on Young Ewing Allison, Filson Historical Society

SBTW   South Before the War Company Papers, Irving S. Gilmore Music Library, Yale University

SCFP   Stephen Collins Foster Papers, University of Kentucky Special Collections

WEDP   Waldemar E. Debnam Papers, East Carolina Manuscript Collection, East Carolina University

YEAP   Young E. Allison Papers, Filson Historical Society

INDIVIDUALS

BLB   Benjamin L. LaBree
FH   Fletcher Hodges
GR   George Robinson
JKL   Josiah Kirby Lilly Sr.
JSC   Joseph Seamon Cotter
JTH   John Tasker Howard
JWT   John W. Townsend
MC   Marian Conliffe
MF   Morrison Foster
MRF   Madge Rowan Frost
OWS   Osso Willis Stanley
RWB   Robert Worth Bingham
SF   Stephen Foster
TDC   Thomas D. Clark
WBF   William B. Floyd
WED   Waldemar E. Debnam
YEA   Young E. Allison

PUBLICATIONS

CJ   *The Courier-Journal* (Louisville, Ky.)
NYT   *The New York Times*

NOTES

PREFACE: THE FORGETTING

xiii The novel reproduced: Margaret Mitchell, *Gone with the Wind* (1936; New York: Macmillan, 1965), 273.

xiii "tear-compelling": "Stephen Collins Foster," *Etude* 34 (Sept. 1916): 623.

xiv "unbelievable experiences": Barry Bingham Jr., oral history by author and Keith L. Runyon, Feb. 10, 2004.

xiv Shared laughter across cultures: Brian Rouleau, *With Sails Whitening Every Sea: Mariners and the Making of an American Maritime Empire* (Ithaca, N.Y.: Cornell University Press, 2014), 43–73.

xv "Any good man": Frank Deford, "The Sun Shines Bright," *Sports Illustrated,* April 29, 1974, 82, vault.si.com.

xv "Fantasies cost lives": Claudia Rankine, *Just Us* (Minneapolis: Graywolf Press, 2020), 329.

xvi "nigger hell": Harry Smith, *Fifty Years of Slavery in the United States of America* (Grand Rapids: West Michigan Printing, 1891), 15.

xvi "national heritage": J. Heywood Alexander, ed., *To Stretch Our Ears: A Documentary History of America's Music* (New York: W. W. Norton, 2002), 135.

xvi "genuine folk": JTH, *Stephen Foster, America's Troubadour* (New York: Thomas Y. Crowell, 1934), 2.

xvi "to sale one of us": Sophia Word, interview by Pearl House, Federal Writers' Project, *Kentucky Slave Narratives: A Folk History of Slavery in Kentucky from Interviews with Former Slaves* (Bedford, Mass.: Applewood Press, 2006), 66.

xvii On an appointed day: Maxwell S. Barber, "Love of Liberty and Freedom," Maude Ward Lafferty Papers, box 2, folder 1, University of Kentucky Special Collections.

xvii "An honest assessment": Ta-Nehisi Coates, "The Case for Reparations," *Atlantic,* June 2014, www.theatlantic.com.

xvii "father of American music": "Stephen Foster," Songwriters Hall of Fame, www.songhall.org.

xvii "minstrel with wool": William Makepeace Thackeray, quoted in George P. Upton, "The Romance of Stephen Foster," *Etude* 32 (Nov. 1914): 734.

xvii "the filthy scum": Frederick Douglass, *North Star,* Oct. 27, 1848.

xviii "awaken antislavery principles": Frederick Douglass, *The Anti-slavery Movement: A Lecture by Frederick Douglass Before the Rochester Ladies' Anti-slavery Society* (Rochester, N.Y.: Press of Lee, Mann, 1855), 40.

xviii "a living symbol": TDC, "My Old Kentucky Home in Retrospect," *Filson Club History Quarterly* 22 (April 1948): 115.

CHAPTER 1: 'TIS SUMMER, THE DARKIES ARE GAY

3 But not much more: The *James Millinger,* piloted by Dunning Foster, docked in Louisville on February 24, 1852, and departed the same day for New Orleans. On the way back to Pittsburgh, the same boat arrived and departed on March 17, 1852. It is "highly improbable" that Foster could have made the eighty-mile round-trip to Bardstown in that brief period. Pen Bogert, email to author, Nov. 18, 2020.

4 In its first six weeks: Ken Emerson, *Doo-Dah! Stephen Foster and the Rise of American Popular Culture* (New York: Da Capo Press, 1997), 192.

6 outrageously long tailcoat/phallus: Brian Roberts, *Blackface Nation: Race, Reform, and Identity in American Popular Music, 1812–1925* (Chicago: University of Chicago Press, 2017), 164–66.

6 "true to nature": MF, *My Brother Stephen* (1896; Indianapolis: Foster Hall, 1932), 25–26.

7 "the very lowest puddles": "Obituary, Not Eulogistic," *Dwight's Journal of Music,* July 10, 1858.

7 "because it was popular": Emerson, *Doo-Dah!,* 106.

8 "blackness [that] aroused": Saidiya V. Hartman, *Scenes of Subjection: Terror, Slavery, and Self-Making in Nineteenth-Century America* (New York: Oxford University Press, 1997), 27.

10 "present": William Foster Sr. to William Foster Jr., July 14, 1834, FHC, quoted in Christopher Lynch, "Stephen Foster and the Slavery Question," in *American Music* 40, no. 1 (forthcoming, Spring 2022).

10 "All my gone by": Eliza C. Foster to William Foster Jr., May 14, 1832, quoted in Emerson, *Doo-Dah!,* 40.

10 One of Stephen's brothers: In 1842, Eliza took her son Henry to visit the mistress of Wood Lawn, which he deemed "one of the most delightful places" he had ever seen. Henry Foster to William Foster Jr., March 25, 1842, quoted in Lynch, "Stephen Foster and the Slavery Question."

10 "Stephen was not": MF, *My Brother Stephen,* 31.

10 "commic [sic] songster": SF to William Foster Sr., Jan. 13, 1837, in *Ste-*

phen Collins Foster: A Guide to Research, ed. Calvin Elliker (New York: Garland, 1988), 89.

10 "Brother William": SF to William Foster Jr., ca. 1840, in Elliker, *Stephen Collins Foster,* 90.

11 "to musick, for which": William Foster Sr. to William Foster Jr., Sept. 3, 1841, quoted in JTH, *Stephen Foster,* 106.

11 "practical business men": MF, *My Brother Stephen,* 37.

11 Indeed, cotton was: Margaret Elder, "Pittsburgh Industries That Used to Be," *Western Pennsylvania History* 12 (Oct. 1929): 216–17, cited in Lynch, "Stephen Foster and the Slavery Question."

11 get Stephen a job: Evelyn Morneweck, *Chronicles of Stephen Foster's Family* (Pittsburgh: University of Pittsburgh Press, 1944), 1:282, quoted in Lynch, "Stephen Foster and the Slavery Question."

11 "a young man addicted": YEA, "My Old Kentucky Home," Aug. 22, 1917, folder 98, YEAP. Such, apparently, was the "West India Frenchman" who left a mixed-race child, Olivia Pise, a servant in the Foster home when Stephen was small. MF, *Biography, Songs, and Musical Compositions of Stephen C. Foster, Author of "The Old Folks at Home"* (Pittsburgh: Percy F. Smith, 1896), 10–11.

11 "derived directly or indirectly": Edward E. Baptist, *The Half Has Never Been Told: Slavery and the Making of American Capitalism* (New York: Basic Books, 2014), 321–22.

11 "golden egg": George McHenry, *The Cotton Trade: Its Bearing upon the Prosperity of Great Britain and Commerce of the American Republics, Considered in Connection with the System of Negro Slavery in the Confederate States* (London: Saunders, Otley, 1863), 110, quoted in Sven Beckert and Seth Rockman, eds., *Slavery's Capitalism: A New History of American Economic Development* (Philadelphia: University of Pennsylvania Press, 2016), 3.

11 "blur of commodities": Beckert and Rockman, *Slavery's Capitalism,* 27.

12 Peters and various pirate: Emerson, *Doo-Dah!,* 115, 138.

12 Arguably, on that warm fall night: Ibid., 127.

13 reportedly paid $100: JTH, *Stephen Foster,* 138, 140.

13 likely one-third: Brian P. Luskey, "Jumping Counters in White Collars: Manliness, Respectability, and Work in the Antebellum City," *Journal of the Early Republic* 26 (Summer 2006): 182.

13 "would have meant": Henry Russell, quoted in Emerson, *Doo-Dah!,* 132. Before this time, a handful of American music and musical instrument sellers published notated songs and rewarded composers with an agreed-upon number of copies of the sheet music and perhaps a modest sum. See JTH, *Stephen Foster,* 152.

13   "songbirds": "Mr. Herbert Renton Knows His Minstrels," *Foster Hall Bulletin*, Aug. 1932, CAM.

13   "was always encouraging": Bayard Taylor, quoted in William W. Austin, *"Susanna," "Jeanie," and "The Old Folks at Home": The Songs of Stephen C. Foster from His Time to Ours* (New York: Macmillan, 1975), 29.

13   "Any line of music": George F. Root, *Story of a Musical Life: An Autobiography* (Cincinnati: John Church, 1891), 3–4.

13   For every copy: SF to Firth & Pond, Sept. 12, 1849, quoted in Austin, *"Susanna,"* 25.

13   Six months later: Emerson, *Doo-Dah!*, 152.

14   Had American copyright law: Joseph Figliulo, "'Dear Friends and Gentle Hearts': The Ironic Relationship Between American Copyright Law and the Artist," *University of Pittsburgh Law Review* (Winter 1999): 641–60.

14   "species of National Amusement": Undated clipping, Christy, E. P., 1815–1862, MS Thr 556 (33), digital sequence 11, AMS, iiif.lib.harvard.edu.

14   Some scholars have posited: Eric Lott advanced this class-oriented thesis in his influential work *Love and Theft: Blackface Minstrelsy and the American Working Class* (New York: Oxford University Press, 1993). The study of blackface minstrelsy has its own history. Significant works include Robert C. Toll, *Blacking Up: The Minstrel Show in Nineteenth-Century America* (New York: Oxford University Press, 1974), which presents blackface as an expression of American racism; Eileen Southern, *The Music of Black Americans: A History* (New York: Norton, 1983), which sees authentic Black sound in blackface; David R. Roediger, *The Wages of Whiteness: Race and the Making of the American Working Class* (New York: Oxford University Press, 1993), which underscores the way power and whiteness interacted; and Dale Cockrell's *Demons of Disorder: Blackface Minstrels and Their World* (New York: Cambridge University Press, 1997), which examines the social milieu of the creators of the genre. Minstrelsy, especially as it merged with melodramas such as *Uncle Tom's Cabin,* is a generative element in Saidiya Hartman's *Scenes of Subjection.* The significance of blackface in a nation struggling to address its original sin of slavery is considered in Roberts, *Blackface Nation.* Yuval Taylor and Jake Austen, in *Darkest America: Black Minstrelsy from Slavery to Hip-Hop* (New York: W. W. Norton, 2012), bring the "tradition" to present-day performance in popular culture and address the Black audience for minstrelsy. The way blackface evolved within and shaped the understanding of American music and the music business

and blackness is reconsidered by Matthew D. Morrison in "Race, Black-sound, and the (Re)Making of Musicological Discourse," *Journal of the American Musicological Society* 72 (Fall 2019): 781–823.

15 No wonder music: The American actor John Howard Payne wrote the lyrics to "Home! Sweet Home!" using music by the English composer Sir Henry Bishop. It was popular for nearly a century.

15 "I would ten thousand": Harriet Jacobs, *Incidents in the Life of a Slave Girl: Written by Herself* (1861; New York: Penguin Books, 2000), 34.

15 "A minstrel show came": Quoted in Toll, *Blacking Up*, 33.

15 "Especial Amusement of the President": Quoted in ibid., 31.

15 "millionaire negro singer": "The Millionaire Negro Singer," *NYT,* Feb. 9, 1857.

15 Christy first assembled: "Obituary, Not Eulogistic."

15 "highly respectable": "Authentic Memoir of E. P. Christy," undated clipping, *Age,* Christy, E. P. 1815–1862, MS Thr 556 (33), digital sequence 5, AMS, iiif.lib.harvard.edu.

16 The chorus so central: Morrison, "Race, Blacksound, and the (Re)Making of Musicological Discourse," 814–16.

17 "ladies and gentlemen": Christy's Minstrels playbill, Ordway Hall, Boston, April 9, 1855, and undated 1853 playbill, AMS, iiif.lib.harvard.edu. The performance had three parts. A series of songs and jokes by a "line" of corked-up singing musicians playing banjo, fiddle, tambourine, and bones opened the evening. A pompous "interlocutor" at the center and crude end men—Brudder Tambo (tambourine) and Brudder Bones (playing the jawbone)—carried on a dialogue jammed with puns and wisecracks. The "olio" (meaning "stew"), or second part, offered variety acts—acrobats, dancers, contortionists, comb players, plus a comical blackface political "stump speech" about a current issue (sometimes women's suffrage, temperance, or abolition) filled with grammatical errors and malapropisms—a precursor to vaudeville. A one-act play, typically set on a plantation, formed the third part of the classic minstrel show and concluded with a spirited "walkaround" in which the ensemble paraded, singing, dancing, and playing.

17 His minstrels always: Toll, *Blacking Up*, 52–57.

17 Christy merged sentimental: Christy found that in addition to the usual "uncouth" acts, minstrel show audiences enjoyed songs that touched their tender emotions. The impresario might have found a template for his sentimental harmonies in the New Hampshire antislavery family that toured widely as the Hutchinson Singers.

17 "genuine negro fun": Quoted in Lott, *Love and Theft*, 145.

17   "the Ethiopian business": In this letter from 1852, Foster referred to the 1850–1851 period of courtship and early marriage. See SF to E. P. Christy, May 25, 1852, in Elliker, *Stephen Collins Foster,* 97.

17   "beautiful and expressive ballad": On sheet music cover of "Mother Thou'rt Faithful to Me" (Baltimore: F. D. Benteen, 1851).

18   He owed his brother: Morrison Foster Ledger/diary 1849–1854, FHC, cited in Lynch, "Stephen Foster and the Slavery Question."

18   Did Jane press him: During their New York honeymoon, the couple could have met Christy himself and witnessed the minstrel bring down the house with Stephen's own "Camptown Races." They hadn't, indicating that at least one or both wanted nothing to do with the blackface scene. Steven Saunders examines Foster's alienation from the world of blackface in "The Social Agenda of Stephen Foster's Plantation Melodies," *American Music* 30 (Fall 2012): 282.

18   But respectable melodies: JTH, *Stephen Foster,* 165.

18   Stephen bent over: Pregnancies generally last 40 weeks, or 280 days, give or take. The calculation appeared in Foster's sketchbook, where he drafted his songs and kept his accounts. Emerson, *Doo-Dah!,* 153.

18   "before any other band": SF to Christy, June 12, 1851, in Elliker, *Stephen Collins Foster,* 95–96. The songwriter flattered the minstrel—he had composed the work with Christy "expressly" in mind—and promised him exclusive rights to premiere "all the new [Foster] songs."

19   "trashy and offensive words": SF to Christy, May 25, 1852, in Elliker, *Stephen Collins Foster,* 97. Christy noted "skunk" on letter's reverse.

21   demeaned people, including children: Stacey Patton, "In America Black Children Don't Get to Be Children," *Washington Post,* Nov. 26, 2014. The sexualization of Black children for white consumption with products like the alligator is treated in Patton's " 'With All My Love': The Circulation of Black Child Pornography Through the Mails During Jim Crow," paper presented at the Tenth Southern Conference on Women's History, Charleston, S.C., June 13, 2015.

21   The movement to end chattel slavery: Cheryl C. Boots, *Singing for Equality: Hymns in the Anti-slavery Movements, 1640–1855* (Jefferson, N.C.: McFarland, 2013); Scott Gac, *Singing for Freedom: The Hutchinson Family Singers* (New Haven, Conn.: Yale University Press, 2007).

22   far-fetched female solidarity: Harriet Beecher Stowe, *Uncle Tom's Cabin; or, Life Among the Lowly* (Boston: John P. Jewett, 1852), chap. 10.

CHAPTER 2: THE CORN TOP'S RIPE

24   "trashy" material: SF to Christy, May 25, 1852, in Elliker, *Stephen Collins Foster,* 97.

24   Christy's Minstrels slotted: Christy's Minstrels Playbills, Aug. 11, Sept. 12, Sept. 15, Nov. 2, 1853, playbills from Mechanics' Hall, AMS.

24   minstrelsy and the parlor: Nicholas E. Tawa, *Sweet Songs for Gentle Americans: The Parlor Song in America, 1790–1860* (Madison: University of Wisconsin Press, 1980), 98–99.

24   "higher form of music": *New York Musical World,* Jan. 1853, quoted in Austin, *"Susanna,"* 204.

24   He came on business: Austin, *"Susanna,"* 25.

25   "turn his attention": *New York Musical World,* Jan. 1853, quoted in Austin, *"Susanna,"* 204.

25   earned him a few: SF predictions of future earnings to Firth & Pond, digital.library.pitt.edu. Based on Foster's royalties, "My Old Kentucky Home" is estimated to have sold sixty-eight thousand copies. My thanks to Ian Stapp for making these calculations available through the Center for American Music in the University of Pittsburgh Library System.

25   On tour in Europe: S. Frederick Starr, *Bamboula! The Life and Times of Louis Moreau Gottschalk* (New York: Oxford University Press, 1995), 139–40.

25   "boisterous romp": Ibid., 283.

25   "coruscating runs on the treble": Jeremy Nicholas, "Piano Music by Louis Moreau Gottschalk," liner notes from Philip Martin, *Gottschalk Piano Music* (London: Hyperion, 1990), 6.

26   Bound and protected: Candace Bailey, "Binder's Volumes as Musical Commonplace Books: The Transmission of Cultural Codes in the Antebellum South," *Journal of the Society for American Music* 10 (Nov. 2016): 446–69.

26   McKissick carefully penciled: Mark Slobin et al., eds., *Emily's Songbook: Music in 1850s Albany* (Middletown, Wis.: A-R Editions, 2011), 25, 7–9.

26   Later in her long life: Ibid., 8.

26   "A long, sad": Ibid., 26.

26   "Father Abraham": Mabel Osgood Wright, *My New York* (New York: Macmillan, 1930), 62.

26   "thin-voiced, bleating singers": Ibid., 192.

26   "Father was resting": Ibid., 193.

27   "virtuous suffering and familial": Lott, *Love and Theft,* 188.

27   " 'blackness' as a fundamental": Ibid., 195; Jennie Lightweiss-Goff,

"'Long Time I Trabble on de Way': Stephen Foster's Conversion Narrative," *Journal of Popular Music Studies* 20 (June 2008): 157–58.

28 "black feeling": Sarah Sillin, "Seduction's Offspring: Resisting Sentimental Violence from Wilson to Wells," *African American Review* 52 (Fall 2019): 278.

28 "tempestuous outbursts": Morneweck, *Chronicles of Stephen Foster's Family*, 2:426.

28 But few details about: Deane L. Root, "The 'Mythstory' of Stephen C. Foster or Why His True Story Remains Untold," *American Music Research Center Journal* 15 (2005): 26.

28 he drank even more: Emerson, *Doo-Dah!*, 203–4.

28 decamping to Manhattan: Ibid., 201. For the family's reaction, see Dunning Foster to MF, March 3, 1854, in JTH, *Stephen Foster*, 389.

28 He was trying to complete: *The Social Orchestra* was published in 1854.

28 were not enough: SF to MF, July 8, 1853, in Elliker, *Stephen Collins Foster*, 99.

28 "flutter[ed] down on every": Henry James, *A Small Boy and Others* (New York: Scribner's, 1913), 160.

28 if millions read: Thomas E. Gossett, *"Uncle Tom's Cabin" and American Culture* (Dallas: Southern Methodist University Press, 2005), 260; Austin, *"Susanna,"* 235.

28 "overlapped and nearly coalesced": Lott, *Love and Theft*, 225. Hartman, *Scenes of Subjection*, 17–32, analyzes commonalities between minstrelsy and antislavery melodrama.

29 "rated as one of the best": Edward Le Roi Rice, *Monarchs of Minstrelsy: From "Daddy" Rice to Date* (New York: Kenny, 1911), 34.

29 his own *Uncle Tom's Cabin!*: *Uncle Tom's Cabin! or Real Life in Old Kentuck! Portraying the Happiness of the Negroes of the South—Introducing the Harmony That Prevails upon Plantations, Their Holiday Festivals, Marriages, Congo Dances*, Barrett Broadside S68Z991853, Albert and Shirley Small Special Collections Library, University of Virginia.

29 "the merriment and pastimes": Sanford, quoted in Toll, *Blacking Up*, 94.

29 "happy . . . with plenty": Toll, *Blacking Up*, 94–95.

29 "Den hand de Banjo": Playbill for Sanford's Opera House, Philadelphia, Oct. 11, 1853, Clifton Waller Barrett Collection, University of Virginia, utc.iath.virginia.edu.

30 satisfied southern youths: Jimmy Dalton Raines, "Samuel S. Sanford and Negro Minstrelsy" (PhD diss., Tulane University, 1967), 1–4, 109–11.

30 "ladies and children": Ibid., 125.

30 "Happy Uncle Tom": Toll, *Blacking Up*, 95.

30 "deep down on the East side": James, *Small Boy and Others*, 161.

30 "Abolitionist part[y]": Sarah Meer, *Uncle Tom Mania: Slavery, Minstrelsy, and Transatlantic Culture in the 1850s* (Athens: University of Georgia Press), 108.

30 "facile intimacy": Hartman, *Scenes of Subjection*, 19.

30 "the point exactly": James, *Small Boy and Others*, 163.

31 "plied the backroads": Emerson, *Doo-Dah!*, 200.

32 "summons to insurrection": Ibid., 108.

32 "no more tramp": Martin Delany, *Blake; or, The Huts of America* (N.p., 1861–1862), 105, web.archive.org.

33 He feared that: Douglass, *Anti-slavery Movement*, 3, 30.

33 Garrison circulated scandalous: David Blight, *Frederick Douglass: Prophet of Freedom* (New York: Simon & Schuster, 2018), 223–24.

33 "the poets": Douglass, *Anti-slavery Movement*, 40.

33 "unite with anybody": Ibid., 33.

33 "ugly stereotypes": Ibid., 40. Considered as a whole, Douglass's writings about music and the cause of equality and freedom centered abolition's hymns and sacred music. See Roberts, *Blackface Nation*, 110–19.

33 "kill the degrading": Joshua McCarter Simpson, quoted in Vicki Lynn Eaklor, *American Antislavery Songs: A Collection and Analysis* (Westport, Conn.: Greenwood, 1988), 20.

33 "the first thing I know": "The Fugitive's Dream," in Eaklor, *American Antislavery Songs*, 384–85.

34 White people in the 1850s: Eric Foner, *Gateway to Freedom: The Hidden History of the Underground Railroad* (New York: W. W. Norton, 2015), 23.

34 "return to the 'old Kentucky home'": "A Nut for Abolitionists," *Louisville Daily Courier*, May 23, 1855.

35 "perfectly satisfied that Canada": *Louisville Daily Courier*, Oct. 15, 1855.

35 "very much exasperated": *Louisville Daily Courier*, May 2, 1860.

35 "the darkies don't know": Chauncey Cooke, *Soldier Boy's Letters to His Father and Mother, 1861–1865* (Independence, Wis.: News-Office, 1915), 36.

36 "a Northern man": Blight, *Frederick Douglass*, 276.

36 local Buchanan Glee Club: Lynch, "Stephen Foster and the Slavery Question."

36 "tolerating if not toadying": Emerson, *Doo-Dah!*, 108.

36 "wine flowed freely": Jane Foster as recounted to her granddaughter, quoted in JTH, *Stephen Foster*, 310.

36 packets of decent clothes: JTH, *Stephen Foster*, 309.

36 "from sheer want": John Mahon, "The Last Years of Stephen C. Foster,"

New York Clipper, March 1877, reprinted in *Foster Hall Bulletin* 10 (May 1934): 2–6.

36 One night at his lodging: Emerson, *Doo-Dah!,* 298.

36 "He suffered much": Jane Foster as recounted to her granddaughter, quoted in JTH, *Stephen Foster,* 310.

37 For all his hits: Austin, *"Susanna,"* xv.

37 from its "vulgar" origins: Robert Nevin, "Stephen C. Foster and Negro Minstrelsy," *Atlantic Monthly,* Nov. 1867, 616.

38 "the most popular emotion": Charles Hamm, *Yesterdays: Popular Song in America* (New York: W. W. Norton, 1978), 217.

38 "father of American music": Songwriters Hall of Fame, www.songhall.org.

40 held fourteen people: 1850 Federal Census, Slave Schedule, Orange County, North Carolina, Ancestry.com.

40 "My earliest memory": RWB to Margaret Mitchell, Feb. 16, 1937, Robert Worth Bingham Papers, Library of Congress. My great-grandfather was born in 1871, so Robert Hall Bingham seemingly continued his night riding beyond the first years of Reconstruction, well into the 1870s.

40 Year in, year out: Bennett L. Steelman, "Robert Bingham," in *Dictionary of North Carolina Biography,* ed. William S. Powell (Chapel Hill: University of North Carolina Press, 1979), 1:157.

41 "That's the beauty": Paul Beatty, *The Sellout* (New York: Farrar, Straus and Giroux, 2016), 189.

CHAPTER 3: THE LITTLE CABIN FLOOR

43 Hays also managed a troupe: Bill C. Malone, "William S. Hays: The Bard of Kentucky," *Register of the Kentucky Historical Society* 93 (Summer 1995): 291.

43 "ill-equipped for freedom": Ibid., 299. Also see Martha Carol Chrisman, "Popular Songs of the Genteel Tradition: Their Influence on Education in Public Schools of Louisville, Kentucky, 1850–1880" (PhD diss., University of Michigan, 1985), 44–46.

43 "nothing to put a blush": Hays to MF, Oct. 25, 1875, FHC.

44 The Bromo-Seltzer company: "My Old Kentucky Home," 1882 Bromo-Seltzer Collection, Sheet Music Collection, FHS.

44 "this sweet, simple ballad": "My Old Kentucky Home," *American Art Journal,* June 20, 1896, 165.

44 "docile subservience": Willa Cather, *My Ántonia* (1918), bk. 2, chap. 7, www.gutenberg.org. Cather might have modeled d'Arnault on Blind Tom Wiggins, a savant pianist and touring performer born into slavery.

44 an old "negro" song: *Book Buyer: A Summary of American and Foreign Literature,* n.s., 4 (Feb. 1887–Jan. 1888): 410.

45 Virginia's Hampton Normal and Agricultural: Jamaica Plain, Mass., "Concert by the Hampton Colored Students!," undated (ca. 1873) broadside, Readex American Broadsides and Ephemera, series 21709.

45 "genuine soul music": The Reverend Theodore L. Cuyler, quoted in Lawrence Schenbeck, *Racial Uplift and American Music, 1878–1943* (Jackson: University Press of Mississippi, 2012), 68.

46 "minstrel mask": Annemarie Bean, James V. Hatch, and Brooks McNamara, eds., *Inside the Minstrel Mask: Readings in Nineteenth-Century Blackface Minstrelsy* (Middletown, Conn.: Wesleyan University Press, 1996).

46 "mature and perfect": *St. Joseph (Mo.) Daily Herald,* quoted in Jocelyn L. Buckner, "Spectacular Opacities: The Hyers Sisters' Performances of Respectability and Resistance," *African American Review* 45 (Fall 2012): 312.

47 "young ladies": John Tullidge in the *Deseret News,* quoted in Henry T. Sampson, *The Ghost Walks: A Chronological History of Blacks in Show Business, 1865–1900* (Metuchen, N.J.: Scarecrow Press, 1988), 10.

47 Hyers Sisters' manager: Buckner, "Spectacular Opacities," 315.

47 Born outside Nashville: "Bradford, Joseph (1843–1886)," in *Tennessee Biographical Dictionary* (New York: Somerset Publishers, 1994), 48.

47 In 1875, in Clinton: Melissa Janczewski Jones, "The Clinton Riot of 1875: From Riot to Massacre," *Mississippi History Now,* www.mshistory now.mdah.ms.gov. On South Carolina, see Stephen Budiansky, *The Bloody Shirt: Terror After the Civil War* (New York: Penguin, 2008), and Mark M. Smith, "'All Is Not Quiet in Our Hellish County': Facts, Fiction, Politics, and Race in the Ellenton Riot of 1876," *South Carolina Historical Magazine* 95 (April 1994): 142–55.

48 The play's "slight" plot: *Newport (R.I.) Daily News,* Nov. 20, 1876.

49 "it's too late": Joseph Bradford, *Out of Bondage: A Dramatization Written for the Hyers Sisters* (1876), Manuscript Plays Collection, Library of Congress Copyright Office, drama deposits, 1863–1973, box 37.

49 "de shout of freedom": "Good-By Dear Cabin Home" (1877), music and lyrics by C. A. White, levysheetmusic.mse.jhu.edu.

49 live in "elegant" surroundings: Bradford, *Out of Bondage.*

49 The concert included: Errol Hill, "The Hyers Sisters: Pioneers in Black Musical Comedy," in *The American Stage,* ed. Ron Engle and Tice Miller (Cambridge, U.K.: Cambridge University Press, 1993), 120–22.

49 "a mile and a half": Mark Twain, quoted in Buckner, "Spectacular Opacities," 315.

49 "refinement, culture, and attractiveness": *New York Evening Telegram,* quoted in James M. Trotter, *Music and Some Highly Musical People* (Boston: Lee and Shepard, 1878), 173.

49 "Yankees is a heap": Bradford, *Out of Bondage.*

49 "retired negro trader": Tarleton Arterburn, 1880 Census; Pen Bogert, email to author, March 25, 2020.

49 "iron-barred coops": Kentucky Historical Marker 1989, "Site of Arterburn Brothers Slave Pens," www.hmdb.org.

49 "bill of sale": "Uncle Tom's Cabin," *CJ,* May 3, 1876.

51 "touching to eyes and ears": *The Book Buyer* (New York: Charles Scribner's Sons, 1887), 586.

51 Fine horses stand tied: Stephen Collins Foster, *My Old Kentucky Home,* illustrated by Charles Copeland and Mary Hallock Foote (Boston: Ticknor and Fields, 1887).

53 "America's first great screen": Terry Borton and Deborah Borton, *Before the Movies* (New Barnet, U.K.: John Libbey, 2014), 8.

53 attended the pro-slavery: Sanford's Opera House broadside, Aug. 16, 1861, from the Theatre Division, NYPLPA, utc.iath.virginia.edu.

53 He also cheered: "Education of an Artist: The Diary of Joseph Boggs Beale," ed. Nicholas B. Wainwright, *Pennsylvania Magazine of History and Biography* 97 (Oct. 1973): 497–98.

54 Sales were weak: Advertisement, "Economic Series," from McIntosh Stereopticon Co. catalog, 37th ed. (Chicago, 1910?), 179. I am grateful to Terry Borton, the expert on American magic lantern history, for his help estimating sales based on the kinds of packages "My Old Kentucky Home" was included in. Terry Borton, email to author, May 30, 2019.

55 do-it-yourself minstrel shows: Rhae Lynn Barnes, "Darkology: The Hidden History of Amateur Blackface Minstrelsy and the Making of Modern America, 1860–1970" (PhD diss., Harvard University, 2016).

55 "Blacks in blackface": Henry T. Sampson, *Blacks in Blackface: A Sourcebook on Early Black Musical Shows* (Metuchen, N.J.: Scarecrow Press, 1980).

55 "a showman": Tom Fletcher, *100 Years of the Negro in Show Business* (1954; repr., New York: Da Capo Press, 1984), 7.

55 "very tough on us": Ibid., 57.

56 range of artistic expression: Ibid., 10–12.

56 "fertile brain and boundless": Ibid., 226.

56 "for having too much": Sampson, *Ghost Walks,* 399.

56 Black theater royalty: Ibid., 245.

56 McClain pitched an idea: Errol Hill and James V. Hatch, *A History of African American Theater* (New York: Cambridge University Press,

2003), 135. The historian Chris Dingwall details the Whallen and Martell productions in "The Sale of Slavery: Memory, Culture, and the Renewal of America, 1877–1920" (PhD diss., University of Chicago, 2015).

56   "picturesque spectacle": *The South Before the War* program, Dec. 17, 1895, NYPLPA.

56   The Whallen machine: Karen R. Gray and Sarah R. Yates, "Boss John Whallen: The Early Louisville Years (1876–1883)," *Journal of Kentucky Studies* 1 (July 1984): 171–86.

56   "old plantation life": SBTW souvenir booklet, quoted in Barbara L. Webb, "Authentic Possibilities: Plantation Performance in the 1890s," *Theater Journal* 56 (March 2004): 66.

56   1888 parade of industry: For the parade float, see *CJ,* Sept. 6, 1888, 10.

56   Those who knew Reverend Drake: *CJ,* March 11, 1886, 8.

57   Billy hired almost: Webb, "Authentic Possibilities," 66.

57   "Clever Colored Talent": *New York Clipper,* April 16, 1892, quoted in Lynn Abbott and Doug Seroff, *Out of Sight: The Rise of African American Popular Music, 1889–1895* (Jackson: University Press of Mississippi, 2009), 361.

57   The ad did not mention: Cotton Picking, promotional pamphlet, SBTW.

58   "Can you smell": *South Before the War* script, box 1, folder 2, SBTW.

58   "pickaninny chorus": *Plantation Return of Uncle Eph,* SBTW. (The *New York Clipper* referred to this skit as "Under a Southern Sky.")

58   The star roles: Abbott and Seroff, *Out of Sight,* 361.

58   "genuine colored men": *New York Clipper,* Jan. 21, 1893, 3. Artists like Katie Carter, whose proto-tap-dancing buck-and-wing solos so impressed one critic as to "beggar description," was one performer whose career took off after *The South Before the War.* See Jacqui Malone, *Steppin' on the Blues: The Visible Rhythms of African American Dance* (Urbana: University of Illinois Press, 1996), 60.

58   "2 Pickaninny Bands": Ad for *The South Before the War, Chicago Tribune,* Oct. 14, 1894, 39, quoted in Webb, "Authentic Possibilities," 66.

58   "equally divided between": Webb, "Authentic Possibilities," 66.

58   "antics of niggerdom": Unidentified review from Dec. 17, 1895, *South Before the War* file, NYPLPA.

58   Black theatergoers came: Recent theater historians have acknowledged the artistry achieved within (and despite) the racist strictures of "Negro minstrelsy." Noting that turn-of-the-century Black audiences flocked to see Black minstrel stars, a more nuanced reading of race in the theater has emerged. See Webb, "Authentic Possibilities," 63–82, and Taylor and Austen, *Darkest America.*

58 "for successful stage management": Indianapolis *Freeman,* Feb. 18, 1893.

58 It went on tour: Hill and Hatch, *History of African American Theater,* 143.

59 He selected his wife: *Black America* program, June 1895 Scrapbook, NSP.

59 "Black disappearance hypothesis": William Darity, "Many Roads Lead to Extinction: Early AEA Economists and the Black Disappearance Hypothesis," *History of Economics* 21 (Jan. 1994): 47–64. See also Khalil Gibran Muhammad, *The Condemnation of Blackness: Race, Crime, and the Making of Modern Urban America* (Cambridge, Mass.: Harvard University Press, 2010).

60 "phenomenal melody of his voice": *Black America* program, June 1895, NSP.

60 Prior to curtain time: Roger Allen Hall, "'Black America': Nate Salsbury's Afro-American Exhibition," *Educational Theatre Journal* 29 (1977): 51.

60 "These are not actors": Unidentified newspaper clipping from Boston, Aug. 1895, Scrapbook of Clippings, Billy Rose Theatre Division, NYPLPA, MWEZ + n.c. 4650.

60 "open carriage": Webb, "Authentic Possibilities," 78.

60 "Monster Chorus": *Black America* program, NSP.

61 "mad scramble": Hall, "'Black America,'" 53; "In the Gloaming," *Illustrated American,* June 29, 1895, 826–28; Dorothy Berry, "Black America, 1895," *Public Domain Review,* Feb. 24, 2021, publicdomainreview.org.

61 "colored talent": Fletcher, *100 Years,* 94.

61 forced to live: Toll, *Blacking Up,* 162.

61 "all these negroes": *Boston Transcript,* July 1895, undated clipping, *Black America* Scrapbook, Theater Collection, NYPLPA.

62 "the most stupid person": McClain, quoted in Indianapolis *Freeman,* Jan. 10, 1899.

62 Lynching reached gruesome: Equal Justice Initiative, *Lynching in America: Confronting the Legacy of Racial Terror,* 3rd ed. (Montgomery, Ala.: Equal Justice Initiative, 2017), 87n282, citing Manfred Berg, *Popular Justice: A History of Lynching in America* (Lanham, Md.: Ivan R. Dee, 2011), 159–60.

62 They lived and performed: "America Has All of the Champions," *Buffalo Enquirer,* Aug. 28, 1899.

62 "Negro must wake up": McClain, quoted in Bill Reed, *Hot from Harlem: Profiles in Classic African American Entertainment* (Los Angeles: Cellar Door Books, 1998), 51.

63 The first generation: Fletcher, *100 Years,* xx.

64 A movement has begun: The Slave Dwelling Project, slavedwellingproj ect.org; Stephen Small, "Still Back of the Big House: Slave Cabins and Slavery in Southern Heritage Tourism," *Tourism Geographies* 15 (2013): 405–23.

CHAPTER 4: THE SUN SHINES BRIGHT

65 a song that felt: My thanks to Jim Davis of Fredonia University for making this point. Jim Davis, email to author, Sept. 7, 2018.

66 "We have long thought": *Wichita Searchlight,* June 16, 1900, 4.

66 "a badge of servitude": "Harlan's Great Dissent," louisville.edu.

66 "can be as separate": Booker T. Washington, Atlanta Compromise Speech, 1895, historymatters.gmu.edu.

66 "so long as people": "Foster Memorial Unveiling Exercises," *Pittsburgh Press,* Sept. 13, 1900, 1, 10.

67 "permanently cast in a military": Nina Silber, *Romance of Reunion: Northerners and the South, 1865–1900* (Chapel Hill: University of North Carolina Press, 1997), 173.

68 When the United States: Ibid., 178–79.

68 "the permanent obliteration": Commander John B. Gordon, quoted in David Blight, *Race and Reunion: The Civil War in American Memory* (Cambridge, Mass.: Harvard University Press, 2002), 353.

68 "soldierly-looking man": "My Old Kentucky Home," *American Art Journal,* June 20, 1896, 165.

68 Five years later: Finding Aid for United Confederate Veterans Collection, FHS, filsonhistorical.org.

69 "Confederate women who": "The Social Side of the Reunion," *CJ,* May 27, 1900, 15.

69 "Make yourself at home": *CJ,* May 30, 1900, 28.

69 one of two songs: "Today's Reunion Program," *CJ,* May 30, 1900, 1.

69 "typical Southern darkies": *CJ,* June 3, 1900, 4.

69 "wicked falsehoods": Karen L. Cox, *Dixie's Daughters: The United Daughters of the Confederacy and the Preservation of Confederate Culture* (Gainesville: University Press of Florida, 2003), 95.

69 "How were the slaves": Ibid., 97.

70 "At last he sleeps": Mrs. A. L. Mitchell, *Songs of the Confederacy and Plantation Melodies* (Cincinnati: George B. Jennings, 1901), 31–33.

70 Mitchell packaged and mailed: *Confederate Veteran,* Jan. 1906, 44.

70 "Colonel Calhoun Is My": William Cressy, *My Old Kentucky Home,* 1906, Harvard Theatre Collection, Houghton Library, Harvard University.

71 Stephen Foster "was visiting": "Announcements," *CJ,* Oct. 13, 1895.

71 "Bourbon capital of the world": "Bourbon Comes from Bardstown," Visit Bardstown, www.visitbardstown.com.

71 Even the pink silk: "Handsome Nuptials at Bardstown," *CJ,* Oct. 16, 1895.

72 "settling polite questions": Mrs. Thaddeus Horton, "Romances of Some Southern Homes," *Ladies' Home Journal,* Sept. 1900, 9–10.

73 "they claim me": Charlotte Foster to William Foster, Sept. 26, 1828, quoted in Emerson, *Doo-Dah!,* 36–37.

73 "very clever and generally": Charlotte Foster to Eliza Foster, Oct. 12, 1828, quoted in Emerson, *Doo-Dah!,* 37.

73 Her former suitor: Atkinson Hill Rowan to Eliza Foster, Nov. 19, 1829, quoted in Emerson, *Doo-Dah!,* 39.

73 Madge's father, John junior: There is evidence that John Rowan Jr. supported a proposed new state constitution that would have gradually eliminated slavery. His wife opposed him on this point. John Rowan Jr. to Rebecca Rowan, Feb. 9, 1847, box 1, folder 2, RFP.

73 A trained lawyer: Randall Capps, *The Rowan Story: From Federal Hill to My Old Kentucky Home* (Cincinnati: Creative Company, 1976), 49–50.

73 recruited for political: John Rowan to John Rowan Jr., April 19, 1841, RFP.

73 He should take: John Rowan to John Rowan Jr., April 22, 1842, RFP.

74 explain his unmarked grave: BLB to JKL, Oct. 13, 1933, folder 199, JKLC.

74 elderly enslaved couple: Capps, *Rowan Story,* 62.

74 Rebecca eventually leased: *Francis A. Coomes v. William L. Rowan, Rebecca K. Rowan, and Felix G. Murphy,* Nelson County Circuit Court (Equity), filed May 11, 1857; Rebecca Rowan to Col. William P. Boone, Aug. 31, 1856, box 1, folder 1, Rebecca Carnes Rowan Collection, Western Kentucky University Manuscript and Folk Life Archives.

74 "scion of a wealthy": "My Old Kentucky Home," *Boston Herald,* Jan. 22, 1899, 13.

74 "House Still Standing": "My Old Kentucky Home," *Union County Courier* (Elk Point, S.D.), Sept. 23, 1897. More notices followed in 1898 (Missouri, Indiana, Charleston).

74 Turn-of-the-century: R. E. Hughes, *That Kentucky Campaign; or, The Law, the Ballot, and the People in the Goebel-Taylor Contest* (Cincinnati: R. Clarke, 1900). On Kentucky's image, see Maryjean Wall, *How Kentucky Became Southern: A Tale of Outlaws, Horse Thieves, Gamblers, and Breeders* (Lexington: University Press of Kentucky, 2012), 93–97; James C. Klotter, *Kentucky: Portrait in Paradox, 1900–1950* (Frankfort:

Kentucky Historical Society, 1996), 51–72; Tommy R. Thompson, "The Image of Appalachian Kentucky in American Popular Magazines," *Register of the Kentucky Historical Society* 91 (Spring 1993): 176–202; Stoddard Johnson, "Romance and Tragedy of Kentucky Feuds," *Cosmopolitan,* Sept. 1899, 551; and George C. Wright, *Racial Violence in Kentucky, 1865–1940: Lynchings, Mob Rule, and "Legal Lynchings"* (Baton Rouge: Louisiana State University Press, 1990).

74   "Main Street Man": "Mr. R. E. Hughes Secretary Exhibit Organization," *CJ,* Nov. 6, 1902.

75   "the shotgun makes music": "My Old Kentucky Home," *Central Record* (Lancaster, Ky.), March 14, 1901.

75   Hughes took charge: "Mr. R. E. Hughes Secretary Exhibit Association."

75   A specially commissioned piano player: *Kentucky at the World's Fair, St. Louis 1904, Being a Report of the Commission Authorized by an Act of the General Assembly to the Governor* (1904), 16, 57.

76   8,275 times: see Associated Press, Nov. 12, 1904, cited in 1906 Foster Day Program, Rothert-YEA.

76   "Southern Airs Arouse": "Legion; Still the Object of Honors and Compliments," *CJ,* Sept. 27, 1904, 1.

76   "surprising interpretation": "Louisville Day Tuesday," *CJ,* Sept. 26, 1904, 5.

76   Some twelve hundred: Robert Rydell, *All the World's a Fair: Visions of Empire at American International Expositions, 1876–1916* (Chicago: University of Chicago Press, 1984), 154–84; Virgilio R. Pilapil, "Dogtown USA: An Igorot Legacy in the United States," *Journal of the Filipino American National Historical Society* 2 (1992), faculty.webster.edu.

76   "quartet of brown savages": *Kentucky at the World's Fair,* 57.

76   Filipino "boys": "The Latest," *CJ,* Nov. 17, 1904, 1.

76   "commercial self": "Success Crowned Louisville Day at the World's Fair," *CJ,* Sept. 28, 1904.

77   "We earnestly desired": Frederick Douglass, introduction to *The Reason Why the Colored American Is Not in the World's Columbian Exposition* (Chicago: Ida B. Wells, 1893).

77   "a small nation": W. E. B. Du Bois, "The American Negro at Paris," *American Monthly Review of Reviews,* Nov. 1900, 577; W. E. B. Du Bois, *Black Lives 1900: W. E. B. Du Bois and the Paris Exposition* (London: Redstone Press, 2019).

77   The National Association: Paul Friswold, "The Forgotten History of Racism at the 1904 World's Fair in St. Louis," *Riverfront Times* (St. Louis), May 2, 2018.

77   "old furniture": *Kentucky at the World's Fair,* 52.

77   Beckham ordered a fair: Memorandum by John W. Muir, March 13, 1960, MOKHSP.

79   The Louisville insurance agent: Biscoe Hindman became commander in chief of the Sons of Confederate Veterans for 1900–1901. Walter Lee Hopkins, ed., *Year Book and Minutes of the Annual Convention of the Sons of Confederate Veterans* (Richmond, Va.: Dudley Printing, 1926), III–12. The vote was thirteen for RWB, seventy-six for Hindman.

79   "Lost Cause Ball": "Louisville Men Do Homage to Pretty Visitors," *CJ*, June 1, 1900, 4.

79   A winning concept: "In Park: Commercial Club Will Hold Open Meeting Plan Homecoming Week," *CJ*, Aug. 3, 1905, 2.

79   "exiles": "Embraces Her Returning Children," *CJ*, June 14, 1906, 1. Such reunions spread as mobility, dislocation, and nostalgia overlapped with modern transportation and business development efforts. See Susan J. Matt, *Homesickness: An American History* (New York: Oxford University Press, 2011), 135–40.

79   "Song Will Bring": Alfred Whitehouse, "My Old Kentucky Home, Sons and Daughters of the Bluegrass to Hold a Big Reunion," *American Citizen* (Kansas City, Mo.), May 18, 1906, 4.

79   "would live as long": R. E. Hughes, *Kentucky the Beautiful* (Chicago: Corbitt Railway Printing, 1901), 12.

80   Enid Yandell: "To Erect Statue," *CJ*, Dec. 14, 1905, 5.

80   "floral" parade: "Streets Abloom with Fair Women and Bright Flowers," *CJ*, June 16, 1906, 3. Hardin was not always warmly embraced; in Colorado her view that women need not marry prompted comparisons to "every short-haired-tiger-mouthed female lecturer." Women who lived apart from "home or family," according to the *Western Empire*, were drifting "nearer to hell." "Marriage Not an Incident and Surely Not a Failure," *Plaindealer* (Ouray, Colo.), June 22, 1906, 1, reprinted from *Western Empire* (Montrose, Colo.).

80   Governors of at least: "Every Train Adds to Crowd," *CJ*, June 12, 1906, 1.

80   "'The HOMESTEAD' that inspired": Foster Day program, Rothert-YEA, quoting Nevin, "Stephen C. Foster and Negro Minstrelsy," 16.

81   "colored man": 1906 Foster Day Program, Rothert-YEA. Perhaps in hopes of underscoring the song's continued relevance, "The Home Coming planners exchanged the words 'colored man' for Nevin's 'slaves.'"

81   "heads bowed and eyes": "Kentuckians Pay Hearty Tribute to Stephen Collins Foster," *CJ*, June 15, 1906, 1, 3.

81   Instead, a local artist: "Accept Statue," *CJ*, April 26, 1906, 8.

81   The money to cast: Unsigned carbon from Louisville Public Library reference librarian to Clarence Roland, Sept. 8, 1917, in Foster scrapbook,

First Unitarian Church Records Collection, FHS. The seated Foster was given to the library in 1910, where it remained until the 1960s as part of the library's museum. Paul Burns (Louisville Free Public Library), email to author, July 3, 2018.

81 "just as it had been": Jessie Welch Rose, "Stephen Collins Foster and My Old Kentucky Home," n.d., FHC.

81 "chains of slavery": Jessie Welch Rose, "Grandmother Was Jeanie with the Light Brown Hair," *Courier-Journal Magazine,* Aug. 5, 1962, 113.

82 "Cousin Stephen": Deposition of Josie Montgomery by John Muir, Bardstown, Jan. 20, 1964, MOKHSP.

83 No separate slave housing: An archaeology report ca. 2015 commissioned for My Old Kentucky Home State Park suggests "early cabin foundations" not too distant from the Rowan house may exist, but the cellar is the only confirmed living space used by enslaved people. Matthew Colin Bailey (former site manager of the park), email to author, Sept. 17, 2020.

83 The whole package: Rebecca McIntyre, *Souvenirs of the Old South: Northern Tourism and Southern Mythology* (Gainesville: University Press of Florida, 2011); Julian Ralph, *Dixie; or, Southern Scenes and Sketches* (New York: Harper & Brothers, 1895).

83 No wonder Madison Avenue: Karen Cox, *Dreaming of Dixie: How the South Was Created in American Popular Culture* (Chapel Hill: University of North Carolina Press, 2013); Maurice Manring, *Slave in a Box: The Strange Career of Aunt Jemima* (Charlottesville: University Press of Virginia, 1998); David Pilgrim, *Understanding Jim Crow: Using Racist Memorabilia to Teach Tolerance and Promote Social Justice* (Oakland: PM Press, 2015).

83 "white-haired old negro": "Historic Kentucky for Glidden Tourists," *Brooklyn Daily Eagle,* March 20, 1910, 11; reprinted in *Piqua (Ohio) Daily Call,* April 2, 1910. Also see "Glidden Tour; Some Great Attractions to Be Seen," *Lowell (Mass.) Sun,* April 22, 1910, 7.

84 "at Appomattox, and came home": RWB to Mitchell, Feb. 18, 1937, box 18, RWB Papers, Library of Congress, Washington, D.C.

CHAPTER 5: TO TOTE THE WEARY LOAD

86 "Darkey Team": "Darkey Teams Do Not Know Southern Songs," from *New York Mail,* in *Daily People,* Dec. 25, 1911, 3.

87 leading social scientists: Muhammad, *Condemnation of Blackness.*

88 left Foster behind: Fletcher, *100 Years,* 171, 132.

88 "Coon" songs poured forth: James H. Dormon, "Shaping the Popular

Image of Post-Reconstruction American Blacks: The 'Coon Song' Phenomenon of the Gilded Age," *American Quarterly* 40 (Dec. 1988): 450–71. Sam Lucas, the Hyers Sisters' co-star, pursued a songwriting career that included "coon" music.

89 For advocates of Black respectability: Schenbeck, *Racial Uplift.*

89 "darky gibberish": "Composers of Songs," *Plaindealer* (Topeka, Kans.), Jan. 13, 1899, 5; "Crappy Dan, de Spo'tin Man" (1896), memory.loc.gov, and "Syncopated Sandy" (1897), repository.library.brown.edu.

89 "look foolish": "Why Not?," *Iowa State Bystander* (Des Moines), Nov. 10, 1899.

89 "The future of music": Dvořák, interview, *New York Herald,* May 2, 1893; also Schenbeck, *Racial Uplift,* 112–13.

90 "bitter pill for prejudiced": Harry Smith, editor of *The Cleveland Gazette,* quoted in Douglas W. Shadle, "Did Dvorak's 'New World' Symphony Transform American Music?," *NYT,* Dec. 14, 2018. For an extended treatment of this debate, see Shadle, *Antonín Dvořák's "New World Symphony"* (New York: Oxford University Press, 2021).

90 "What matters it to": "Dr. Dvorak's Year in America," *New York Evening Post,* Sept. 30, 1893, quoted in Shadle, *Antonín Dvořák's "New World Symphony,"* 109.

90 "as art songs": Schenbeck, *Racial Uplift,* 112–13.

90 "in his Old Kentucky": "Honored at His Home," Indianapolis *Freeman,* March 22, 1902.

90 "Frederick Douglass Day": "Douglass Day in South Indiana," Indianapolis *Freeman,* March 10, 1906.

90 Louisville's Black Knights: "The K. of P. Parade a Monster Demonstration," Indianapolis *Freeman,* Sept. 2, 1911, 6.

91 After the meal: "Annapolis Notes," *Washington (D.C.) Bee,* July 25, 1914, 5. For the picnic's social context, see Elizabeth Taylor Dowling, *The Original Black Elite: Daniel Murray and the Story of a Forgotten Era* (New York: Amistad, 2017).

91 "well of sorrow": Handy, quoted in Austin, *"Susanna,"* 313.

91 Was the Black baritone: Indianapolis *Freeman,* July 1, 1905, in Sampson, *Blacks in Blackface,* 1137.

91 send-off concert: Indianapolis *Freeman,* Oct. 28, 1905; on Hackley, see Juanita Karpf, "The Vocal Teacher of Ten Thousand: Emma Azalia Hackley as Community Music Educator, 1910–1922," *Journal of Research on Musical Education* 47 (Winter 1999): 322.

91 The manager pressed: Lynn Abbott and Doug Seroff, *Ragged but Right: Black Traveling Shows, "Coon Songs," and the Dark Pathway to Blues and Jazz* (Jackson: University Press of Mississippi, 2012), 38–39.

91 "would not have believed": "Music and Drama," *CJ*, April 13, 1908.

92 Rossini, not Foster, was her usual: On the other hand, Dvořák selected Jones as soloist in his choral arrangement of "Old Folks at Home" in New York City in 1894. See Shadle, *Antonín Dvořák's "New World Symphony,"* 91–93; and Edmund Rubin, "Jeannette Meyer Thurber (1850–1946): Music for a Democracy," in *Cultivating Music in America: Women Patrons and Activists Since 1860,* ed. Ralph P. Locke and Cyrilla Barr (Berkeley: University of California Press, 1997), 153.

92 And more so during: John Graziano, "The Early Life and Career of the 'Black Patti': The Odyssey of an African American Singer in the Late Nineteenth Century," *Journal of the American Musicological Society* 53 (Oct. 2000): 585–89.

93 "rebel tradition": Mamie Garvin Fields, *Lemon Swamp and Other Places: A Carolina Memoir* (New York: Free Press, 1985), 43–45; Francis Miles Finch, "The Blue and the Gray," *Atlantic,* Sept. 1867, 369.

93 came home "heartbroken": "School Board Heeds Protest," *Boston Globe,* Nov. 13, 1914, 5. See also for the NAACP, "The Boston Songs," *Crisis* 9 (Jan. 1915): 128. Also see Mark Schneider, *Boston Confronts Jim Crow* (Lebanon, N.H.: University Press of New England, 1977), 145.

94 countless blackface tunes: Katya Ermolaeva, "Dinah, Put Down Your Horn: Blackface Minstrel Songs Don't Belong in Music Class," *GEN,* Oct. 13, 2019, gen.medium.com. See, for instance, the illustrated and annotated *Fireside Book of Folk Songs,* selected and edited by Margaret Bradford Boni and arranged for the piano by Norman Lloyd (New York: Simon & Schuster, 1947).

94 "Negro's . . . true friend": *Washington (D.C.) Bee,* Nov. 21, 1914, 4.

94 "part of the most": "Those Negro Melodies," *Rochester (N.Y.) Democrat and Chronicle,* Dec. 1, 1914, 8.

94 "absurd": *Indianapolis News,* Nov. 14, 1914, 6.

94 "the black man": *Decatur (Ga.) Daily,* Nov. 24, 1914, 2.

94 "that the descendants": *Winston-Salem (N.C.) Journal,* Nov. 25, 1914, 4.

95 "Pass the beans": "The Old Darkey Songs," *Owensboro (Ky.) Messenger,* Nov. 25, 1914, 4.

95 "somebody valuation": Karpf, "Vocal Teacher of Ten Thousand," 325.

95 "Negro composers": Grace Lucas Thompson, "What Our Women Are Doing," Indianapolis *Freeman,* Dec. 25, 1914.

95 "soul of a toiling": Karpf, "Vocal Teacher of Ten Thousand," 325; "Folk Song Festival," *Boston Globe,* Nov. 29, 1914.

96 Davis's play: *Our Old Kentucky Home* is sometimes attributed to Davis's friend John Edward Bruce (1856–1924), a journalist who contributed to Black papers around the country under the pen name Bruce Grit. Other

scholars view the work as a collaboration between Bruce and Davis. I hold that she wrote it and Bruce's name offered protection and possibly legitimacy in a patriarchal culture. Bruce, an underappreciated voice in the pre–Harlem Renaissance years, challenged Douglass's and Du Bois's and later the NAACP's integrationist approach. He eventually approved the use of violence to beat back white attacks on property and civil liberties. He was not noted for his feminism, and Black women's abilities and courage and raw power are so central to the play that it is difficult to imagine Davis not being directly engaged in creating the heroine she played in the play she produced (Bruce said they co-wrote the drama, and Davis's papers have not been found). Never published, an incomplete manuscript copy is held in the John E. Bruce Papers at the New York Public Library's Schomburg Center for Research in Black Culture. Thomas Robson, "A More Aggressive Plantation Play: Henrietta Vinton Davis and John Edward Bruce Collaborate on *Our Old Kentucky Home*," *Theatre History Studies* 32 (2012): 123–24; Errol Hill, *Shakespeare in Sable: A History of Black Shakespearean Actors* (Amherst: University of Massachusetts Press, 1984), 72; William Seraile, ed., *Bruce Grit: The Black Nationalist Writings of John Edward Bruce* (Knoxville: University of Tennessee Press, 2003), 126.

96   By contrast, reciting: Hill and Hatch, *History of African American Theater,* 87–89; Hill, *Shakespeare in Sable,* 64–65; on gender and the profession, see Marian Wilson Kimber, *The Elocutionists: Women, Music, and the Spoken Word* (Urbana: University of Illinois Press, 2017).

96   "beautiful quadroon": *Washington (D.C.) Evening Star,* July 20, 1883.

96   "our first American lady reader": *Washington (D.C.) Bee,* July 21, 1883, quoted in Hill, *Shakespeare in Sable,* 65.

96   prominent Black agent: The agent was James Monroe Trotter. See Hill, *Shakespeare in Sable,* 65.

96   Harriet Beecher Stowe's husband: *Hartford Courant,* Nov. 27, 1883, 3.

96   "The color line": *National Convention of Colored Men* program, Louisville, Ky., Sept. 24, 1883.

96   "merely preaching the gospel": "The Negro and His Leader," *CJ,* Sept. 27, 1883, 4.

97   "striving to uplift": "Miss Henrietta V. Davis," *St. Paul Appeal,* April 15, 1899, 3.

97   She married and left: Hill, *Shakespeare in Sable,* 72.

97   "rich, flexible and expressive": *Sunday Truth* (Buffalo), quoted in Hill, *Shakespeare in Sable,* 71.

97   "no darker than": Ibid.

97   Then the scene shifts: Davis, *Our Old Kentucky Home,* Bruce Papers.

100   "comely, light-colored": *Washington Star,* Nov. 12, 1898, 8.

100   Such a "startling" plot: "Henrietta Vinton Davis's 'My Old Kentucky Home' Play," *Colored American* (Washington, D.C.), Feb. 14, 1903, 6.

101   "taken from real life": *Waterloo (Ind.) Press,* March 9, 1899, 1.

101   gave an elocution performance: *St. Paul Globe,* April 18, 1899, 8.

101   threw a reception: *St. Paul Appeal,* April 22, 1899, 3.

101   The Black laborer: Donald G. Matthews, *At the Altar of Lynching: Burning Sam Hose in the American South* (New York: Cambridge University Press, 2017).

101   "musical farce": Hill, *Shakespeare in Sable,* 83.

101   renounced the theater and entered: William Seraile, "Henrietta Vinton Davis and the Garvey Movement," *Afro Americans in New York Life and History* 7 (July 1983): 7–24.

101   Touching ground as Garvey's emissary: Colin Grant, *Negro in a Hat: The Rise and Fall of Marcus Garvey* (New York: Oxford University Press, 2010), 384–85.

101   "Breathes there the man": Sir Walter Scott, *The Lay of the Last Minstrel* (1805; Austell, Ga.: Palala Press, 2016), canto 6.

102   "tell a plantation story": "What Every American Traveler Should Know," *New York Times Magazine,* Feb. 2, 1913, 3.

102   Native American children forcibly: Charles W. Johnson, *Songs of the Nation: Patriotic and National,* Indian School, ed. (Boston: Silver, Burdette, 1912).

102   Daughters of the Confederacy wept: 1909 Lexington meeting minutes, United Daughters of the Confederacy Collection, box 2, folder 5, KHS.

102   White southern troops: James W. Evans, *Entertaining the American Army: The American Stage and Lyceum in the World War* (New York: Association Press, 1921), 207.

CHAPTER 6: WHERE ALL WAS DELIGHT

104   "the whole story": YEA to Otto Rothert, Aug. 16, 1917, folder 5, Rothert-YEA. On the condition of the roads, see Old Kentucky Home Commission minutes, Dec. 8, 1921, MOKHSP.

105   "shrine": John Eschrich, "My Old Kentucky Home Is Dedicated at Bardstown as Shrine for State, Nation," *CJ,* July 5, 1923, 3.

105   "central spot": Otto Rothert, "Young E. Allison Memorial Meeting, Henderson, 1933," *Filson Club History Quarterly* 7 (1933): 186–87.

105   "Kentucky's most famous": My Old Kentucky Home State Park website, parks.ky.gov. For a fuller account of the campaign Allison led, see Emily Bingham, "'Let's Buy It!': Tourism and the My Old Kentucky

Home Campaign in Jim Crow Kentucky," *Ohio Valley History* 19 (Fall 2019): 27–56.

105   Tourism in Kentucky: Edward King, *The Great South* (Hartford: American Publishing, 1875), 693–725.

105   351-foot obelisk: Anne E. Marshall, *Creating a Confederate Kentucky: The Lost Cause and Civil War Memory in a Border State* (Chapel Hill: University of North Carolina Press, 2010), 175–82.

106   "pipsqueak Dixie picnic": *Time,* May 10, 1937, quoted in James C. Nicholson, *The Kentucky Derby: How the Run for the Roses Became America's Premier Sporting Event* (Lexington: University Press of Kentucky, 2012), 135.

106   "starry pen": YEA, "The Old Piano," in *Select Works of Young E. Allison* (Louisville, Ky.: John P. Morton, 1935).

106   "little Yank": YEA, "An Incident of War," *Southern Magazine,* Oct. 1894, reprinted in *Select Works of Young E. Allison,* 218.

107   an acclaimed poem inspired: His 1891 *Treasure Island* poem, "Derelict," was adapted for a 1901 Broadway musical production of the story. See biostat.wustl.edu/~erich/music/songs/derelict.html.

107   "lapsed into intangible": Wallace T. Hughes, letter to the editor, *CJ,* July 15, 1923, 36.

107   A friend scoured: YEA to E. J. Wohlgemuth, Oct. 8, 1918, folder 5, Rothert-YEA.

107   "cared nothing for": YEA to Wohlgemuth, Aug. 6, 1918, folder 5, Rothert-YEA.

107   "negro character": YEA, undated notes on blackface minstrelsy, folder 32, Rothert-YEA.

107   "those faraway beautiful": MRF to YEA, Oct. 15, 1917, YEAP.

107   "inefficient darkies": MRF to YEA, Oct. 31, 1917, YEAP.

107   "the hospitality of": MRF to YEA, Sept. 18, 1917, YEAP.

108   "in spite of the uncertainty": MRF to YEA, Sept. 18, 1917, folder 62, YEAP.

108   at his "chateau": YEA, "The Story of 'My Old Kentucky Home,'" MS, Aug. 22, 1917, Rothert-YEA.

108   "yarn" about Stephen Foster: YEA to Otto Rothert, Nov. 28, 1918, folder 5, Rothert-YEA.

108   "dear old Kentucky home": MRF to YEA, Aug. 15, 1919, YEAP.

108   "a dilapidated pile": OWS, in Allan Trout, "Writer-Judge Engineered Federal Hill's Comeback," *CJ,* Sept. 3, 1961.

108   "good for nothing": MRF to YEA, July 1, 1919, folder 62, YEAP.

108   "get out of their power": MRF to YEA, Aug. 19, 1919, folder 62, YEAP.

108   "historic places": MRF to YEA, March 26, 1919, folder 62, YEAP.

108 "ne'er do well": Henry Watterson, "Looking Backward: Men, Women, and Events During Eight Decades of American History," *CJ*, May 11, 1919, 31, excerpted from *Marse Henry: An Autobiography* (New York: George H. Doran, 1919). Watterson claimed to have heard about the plagiarism from the Louisville songwriter Will S. Hays: Watterson, "Looking Backward," 66.

109 "When the darkey could": Poem, Unveiling of Stephen Foster Bust program, KHS, June 17, 1919, folder 32, Rothert-YEA.

109 "genius" of "universal" appeal: YEA, *Stephen C. Foster and American Songs* (Louisville, Ky.: Insurance Field, 1920).

109 "weak and fatal love": YEA, quoted in Watterson, "Looking Backward," 66.

109 "emotional history": YEA, *Stephen C. Foster and American Songs.*

109 Only one American: American Automobile Association, "History of the AAA Glidden Tour," exchange.aaa.com. The establishment of the Bureau of Public Roads and passage of the Federal Aid Road Act of 1916 inaugurated the first national system for funding state road construction. Rising auto production and the Good Roads movement made a new "tourist landscape" possible: Marguerite Shaffer, *See America First: Tourism and National Identity, 1880–1940* (Washington, D.C.: Smithsonian Institution Press, 2001), 137. National pride and interest in heritage marked U.S. tourism in the automobile age, while unique landscapes distinct from "old Europe" had dominated earlier eras: John F. Sears, *Sacred Places: American Tourist Attractions in the Nineteenth Century* (Amherst: University of Massachusetts Press, 1999); Anne Farrer Hyde, *An American Vision: Far Western Landscape and National Culture* (New York: New York University Press, 1990). See also James J. Flink, *The Automobile Age* (Cambridge, Mass.: MIT Press, 1990); and Peter J. Hugill, "Good Roads and the Automobile in the United States, 1880–1929," *Geographical Review* 72 (July 1982): 327–49.

109 One project, the Dixie Highway: Tammy Ingram, *Dixie Highway: Road Building and the Making of the Modern South, 1900–1930* (Chapel Hill: University of North Carolina Press, 2014), 55–58; Charles C. Swearingen, "Boone Way Historical Highway from Louisville to Lexington, North Carolina," *CJ*, Oct. 7, 1917, D3.

109 The state was poised: "Investment in and Mileage of Good Roads Before 1916," in Hugill, "Good Roads and the Automobile in the United States," 338–39.

110 "mystical" effects: Charles B. Hosmer, *Presence of the Past: A History of the Preservation Movement in the United States Before Williamsburg* (New York: G. P. Putnam and Sons, 1965), 266.

110 Kentucky had no "house museum": The houses of Henry Clay, Cassius Clay, Mary Todd Lincoln, John Hunt Morgan, the Speed family, and the sister of the explorer William Clark opened decades after Federal Hill became My Old Kentucky Home. Women-led voluntary organizations museumized George Washington's Mount Vernon (1860), Andrew Jackson's Hermitage (1889), and the house of Joel Chandler Harris of Uncle Remus fame (1913). Tours of the Paul Revere house in Boston began in 1908. Colonial Williamsburg was not yet a twinkle in John D. Rockefeller's eye. Linda Young, *Historic House Museums in the United States and the United Kingdom: A History* (Lanham, Md.: Rowman & Littlefield, 2016), 71–73. Young connects preindustrial religious sites of pilgrimage and house museums of heroes. See also Patricia West, *Domesticating History: The Political Origins of America's House Museums* (Washington, D.C.: Smithsonian Institution Press, 1999).

110 "Visitors Will Not Come": Richard P. Hebel to YEA, May 6, 1921, folder 89, Rothert-YEA.

110 Allison felt reasonably: YEA, "Views of Historic 'Old Kentucky Home,' Meager Records Leave Doubt of Stephen Foster's Residence There," *Louisville Herald,* April 10, 1921, folder 61, YEAP.

110 "a hard, selfish, and pretentious": YEA to Virginia Lockett, April 9, 1925, YEAP.

110 "dilettante of art": YEA, "Story of 'My Old Kentucky Home.' "

110 "more publicity than": Allen Reager to YEA, April 14, 1921, YEAP.

110 "the immortal song": House Resolution No. 42, *Acts of the General Assembly of the Commonwealth of Kentucky* (Frankfort, Ky., 1920), 729, passed March 20, 1920. Delays in making the appointments alarmed Stanley, who feared Frost would make a private sale. OWS to Edwin P. Morrow, Aug. 24, 1920, OWSP.

110 entire farm was valued: James S. Ray to H. V. Loving, Sept. 20, 1911, OWSP.

110 "shattered windows and shutters": Catherine Conner, *From My Old Kentucky Home to the White House: The Political Journey of Catherine Conner* (1999; Lexington: University Press of Kentucky, 2015), 34. Prohibition was slated to slash tax revenues: Klotter, *Kentucky,* 243–44; Lowell H. Harrison and James C. Klotter, *A New History of Kentucky* (Lexington: University Press of Kentucky, 1997), 304–5.

111 Morrow appointed three millionaires: Morrow to Arch H. Pulliam, Aug. 27, 1920, folder 1, OWS Papers, FHS. Members included RWB, publisher of *The Courier-Journal;* C. Lee Cook, an inventor and manufacturer; A. T. Hert, president of American Creosoting; Mrs. Clement French, a close friend of the Morrow family's from Maysville; Harry

Giovannoli, editor of *The Lexington Herald;* and Arch H. Pulliam, a Louisville insurance man. Stanley did not accept an appointment due to his other role as Madge Frost's attorney.

111 "general newspaper propaganda": Old Kentucky Home Commission Minutes, March 16, 1921, YEAP.

111 "silver-tongued": OWS, quoted in Trout, "Writer-Judge Engineered Federal Hill's Comeback."

111 "has made us all": Edwin P. Morrow, 1921 proclamation, folder 44, BLBP.

111 Some questioned the high: Marvin H. Lewis, Report of Old Kentucky Home Commission, July 13, 1921, MOKHSP.

111 would attract hundreds: Clipping [1921], BLBP.

111 on par with Philadelphia's Independence Hall: "Another View of the 'Home,'" unidentified (Kentucky) clipping [1921], folder 44, BLBP.

111 "shared memory of Kentuckians": "Old Kentucky Home Is Saved," *Louisville Herald,* July 23, 1921, folder 44, BLBP.

112 "Meager Records Leave Doubt": YEA, "Views of Historic 'Old Kentucky Home.'" This article had YEA's byline, but it seems unlikely he would pick the headline. While lamenting the slimness of the historical record, the writer piled on circumstantial accounts and wishful "memories" to build his case for the purchase.

112 Tales placed Stephen: Had he somehow reached Federal Hill, Foster would have found the land leased out and the house without furniture. The Rowans, just back from their diplomatic stint, were living at the local tavern. Deposition of A. G. Townsend, Bardstown, Aug. 24, 1853, *J. R. Buchanan & Co. v. Rowan's Executors &c.,* Louisville Chancery Court, Case 8154, filed Feb. 26, 1852. Also see BLB to JKL, Oct. 13, 1933, folder 199, JKLC, referring to letters from early 1853 from Rebecca Rowan to John Rowan Jr. referencing debt, alcoholism, and the empty house. For leasing, see *Francis A. Coomes v. William L. Rowan, Rebecca K. Rowan, and Felix G. Murphy,* Nelson County Circuit Court (Equity), filed May 11, 1857. Thanks to Pen Bogert for sharing his public records research on the Rowan family and the people they held in bondage.

112 A favorite myth: YEA, "Views of Historic 'Old Kentucky Home.'"

112 destroyed in a blaze: Capps, *Rowan Story,* 51.

112 "long since lost": YEA, "'My Old Kentucky Home': The Song and the Story," *Courier-Journal Sunday Magazine,* April 10, 1921, 1–9.

112 A recent biography: Harold Vincent Milligan, *Stephen Collins Foster: A Biography of America's Folk-Song Composer* (New York: G. Schirmer, 1920), 68.

112 "flimsy": [YEA], "Foster and Kentucky," *Louisville Times,* Oct. 1, 1921,

folder 32, Rothert-YEA. (YEA left his name off this particularly embarrassing piece of propaganda.) His son later claimed that his father never argued that Foster wrote the song at Federal Hill, only that he had visited the place. Young E. Allison Jr. to JWT, Sept. 6, 1932, folder 124, YEAP.

113 "hopeless, tragic": YEA, " 'My Old Kentucky Home': The Song and the Story."

113 "yearning of no race": Instructional pamphlet, "Old Kentucky Home Celebrations in the Schools," 1921, prepared by the Old Kentucky Home Commission, black file drawer 2, MOKHSP.

113 The climax came in May: "Many Towns Throughout State Join in Movement to Raise Funds for 'Kentucky Home,' " newspaper clipping, April 21, 1921, folder 44, BLBP.

114 "expatriates . . . endowed with": "Old Kentucky Home Celebrations in the Schools," MOKHSP.

114 volunteers in 171 towns: "Many Towns Throughout State Join in Movement to Raise Funds for 'Kentucky Home.' "

114 placards in windows: OWS to Marvin Lewis, April 29, 1921, and OWS to president of Quaker Made Stores, May 24, 1921, folder 1, OWSP.

114 Young women literally buttonholed: Fundraising Tag, "Every Son and Daughter of Kentucky a Contributor to the Old Kentucky Home Fund," [May 1921], YEAP.

114 "as mammies and pickaninnies": Saturday, "Special Celebration—Old Kentucky Home Day Spectacle," unidentified Louisville newspaper clipping, [May 1921], BLBP.

114 "kindly, childlike obedience": Willard Rouse Jillson, *The Old Kentucky Home: An Historical Sketch of the Old Bardstown Country Homestead of John Rowan* (Frankfort, Ky., 1921).

114 "inspired a powerful sympathy": Lucien V. Rule, *The Light Bearers: Home Mission Heroes of Presbyterian History: Centennial Story of an Old Country Church and Neighborhood in the Presbytery of Louisville* (Louisville, Ky.: Brandt, Connors and Fowler, 1926), 162.

115 "costly garments": JSC, memoir, typescript, 9, MOKHSP.

115 "half house of bondage": Ibid., 6; Rule, *Light Bearers,* 165.

115 "free papers": JSC, memoir, typescript, 12, MOKHSP.

115 During Joseph's childhood: Ibid., preface.

115 "little brown guide": JSC, "A Visit to Federal Hill, Bardstown, Ky.," *Louisville Leader,* Feb. 4, 1922, 1, 8.

118 "black bodies swinging": Abel Meeropol, "Strange Fruit," 1937. Billie Holiday made the protest song against lynching a signature.

118 "legal lynchings": Wright, *Racial Violence,* 201–3, 215–305.

118 "Jim crowed, lynched": "Thursday Night at Schubert's," editorial, *Louisville Leader,* Feb. 4, 1922, 8.

118 "general apathy": Marvin H. Lewis, Report to Old Kentucky Home Commission, July 13, 1921, MOKHSP.

118 failed to get local: OWS to YEA, April 7, 1921, YEAP; Marvin Lewis to OWS, April 8, 1921, and OWS to Marvin Lewis, June 7, 1921, OWSP.

118 Kentuckians had not loosened: An Act Accepting . . . Title to Federal Hill, *Journal of the Kentucky Senate Regular 1922 Session,* vol. 2 (Frankfort, Ky.), 1730–1735, March 6, 1922. The amount raised was $60,800, per "Old Kentucky Home Is Saved."

119 had arrived in Kentucky: LaBree wedding announcement, *CJ,* June 2, 1911.

119 "born and destined": MRF to BLB, July 25, 1922, folder 12, BLBP.

119 He built a strong: See folder 12, BLBP. LaBree also produced volumes on the "Notable Men" of Kentucky and Cincinnati.

119 Kentucky locate its central: Undated memorandum, "MY OLD KENTUCKY HOME," folder 44, BLBP.

119 a cyclone tore: Minutes of Old Kentucky Home Commission, April 21, 1923, MOKHSP.

119 shrine as hokum: J. Rowan Boone, conversation with MOKHSP staff member, see notes Oct. 5, 1976, MOKHSP cabin files.

119 which furniture the sale: MRF to YEA, July 31, 1922, folder 62, YEAP.

119 taxes ate into: MRF to YEA, July 8, 1922, folder 62, YEAP.

119 refused to vacate: MRF to YEA, July 28, 1922, folder 62, YEAP.

119 "Those who would commune": John Eschrich, "My Old Kentucky Home Is Dedicated at Bardstown as Shrine for State, Nation," *CJ,* July 5, 1923. Federal Hill was ahead of Charleston, Natchez, and Colonial Williamsburg in costuming at tourist attractions.

120 "home—'the holy of holies'": Ibid. Morrow often returned to the Old Kentucky Home trope. See his Address to the Joint Session of the Kentucky Legislature, Jan. 16, 1922, *Journal of the Regular Session of the Commonwealth of Kentucky* (Frankfort, Ky., 1922), 208.

120 LaBree's ledgers count: LaBree logbooks, BLBP, show visitors coming largely from Illinois, Indiana, Ohio, Michigan, and New York.

120 "taste of the hospitality": "Nation's Second Shrine in Today's Rotogravure," *Louisville Herald-Post,* May 2, 1926, folder 1, BLBP.

120 "fall in the spirit": "New Hotel for Bardstown," *Kentucky Standard* (Bardstown, Ky.), Nov. 21, 1922, folder 48, BLBP.

121 "commercialization of the southern": W. Fitzhugh Brundage, *The Southern Past: A Clash of Race and Memory* (Cambridge, Mass.: Harvard University Press, 2005), 184.

121 "immortalized Kentucky throughout": *Acts of the General Assembly of the Commonwealth of Kentucky* (Frankfort, Ky.: State Journal Company, 1928), 851–52. Nine states preceded Kentucky in choosing state songs.

121 The number of white: Frank Hobbs and Nicole Stoops, *Demographic Trends in the 20th Century: Census 2000 Special Reports,* Series CENSR-4 (Washington, D.C.: U.S. Government Printing Office, 2002).

122 "greatest and shrewdest showman": Arthur Daley, "An Optimistic Young Fellow," *NYT,* May 6, 1948, 35.

122 "fresh flavor of legend": "The Man Who Brought Legend to Louisville," *CJ,* Oct. 7, 1949, 12.

122 "Tell 'em about it": Winn, quoted in L. A. Tarpley, "Downs Dresses Up More for Derby Fans' Comfort," *CJ,* April 30, 1941.

122 "long line of": Matt Winn, *Down the Stretch: The Story of Colonel Matt J. Winn as Told to Frank G. Menke* (New York: Smith and Durrell, 1944), quoted in Nicholson, *Kentucky Derby,* 67.

123 "colonial style": "Derby Teems with Sentiment," *CJ,* May 5, 1912.

123 "ladies and gentlemen": Winn, quoted in Deford, "Sun Shines Bright."

123 "reminiscent of an Old South": Samuel Thomas, *Churchill Downs: A Documentary History of America's Most Legendary Racetrack* (Louisville, Ky.: Kentucky Derby Museum, 1995), 194, quoting *CJ,* April 30, 1941.

123 "gave vent to their delight": Sam H. McMeekin, "Bradley's Behave Yourself Wins the Kentucky Derby," *CJ,* May 8, 1921, 1.

123 In 1927, Chicago's WGN: "Matt Winn," National Museum of Racing and Hall of Fame, www.racingmuseum.org.

123 "crooning 'My Old'": "Kentucky Derby Booked for WGN," *NYT,* May 8, 1927.

123 "exuded 'My Old'": Damon Runyon, clipping, May 19, 1929, paper unknown, "My Old Kentucky Home" file, Jim Bolus Collection, Kentucky Derby Museum Permanent Collection.

124 "moment of moments": "Derby Crowd Gets Soaked," *CJ,* May 5, 1935, 55.

124 "muted and slow": Bryan Field, "Gallant Fox Takes Derby as Lord Derby and 60,000 Look On," *NYT,* May 18, 1930, 28.

124 In the early 1930s: Tom Owen, email to author, Nov. 20, 2020.

124 "loud band": "At Churchill Downs," *Time,* May 16, 1932.

124 "along toward sunset": Nicholson, *Kentucky Derby,* 64.

125 "antebellum mansion": Tom R. Underwood, "'They're Off' and All Kentucky Roars," *Kentucky Progress Magazine* 7 (Spring 1936): 104.

125 "nonsense," said Allison: "A Voter," [YEA], *CJ,* Aug. 10, 1928, folder 195, YEAP.

125 "sledges in winter": Postcard, file cabinet drawer 2, MOKHSP.

125 "tawdry myth and legend": "A Voter," [YEA], *CJ*, Aug. 10, 1928.

125 "Old Joe": Richard Gilbert, "'My Old Kentucky Home' Netted Foster $1,372," *Kentucky Progress Magazine* 4 (Sept. 1931): 18–19, 42.

125 "an old servant": See letter from Annie (Mrs. Ben) Johnson, file cabinet drawer 2, MOKHSP, in response to Gilbert, "'My Old Kentucky Home' Netted Foster $1,372."

125 "slave cemetery": Matthew C. Bailey (director of MOKHSP), interview by author, Aug. 24, 2016. An archaeological investigation discovered no human remains and, eighteen inches under the surface, solid bedrock. For more, see Eric King, "My Old Kentucky Home's Secret Slave History," WLKY News, Feb. 24, 2011, www.youtube.com.

126 "atmosphere of tradition": Jillson, *Old Kentucky Home.*

126 "publicity work": BLB to Ludie Kinkead, Aug. 13, 1931, Miscellaneous Collection, FHS.

126 "factotum": Lorena Callahan to JKL, Dec. 18, 1933, JKLC.

126 "the pug nose of truth": Callahan to JKL, May 23, 1931, JKLC.

127 "like waving": JWT to Harold Vincent Milligan, Oct. 15, 1931, box 1, SCFP.

127 "Stephie, old boy": JWT to JKL, Dec. 12, 1931, folder 47, JKLC.

127 "ran around that": JWT to YEA, Feb. 2, 1932, folder 124, YEAP.

127 "Mrs. Frost remembered": YEA to JWT, Feb. 7, 1932, box 1, SCFP.

128 "Have it your way": YEA to JWT, Feb. 4, 1932, box 1, SCFP.

128 An estimated one in six: Out of a population of 210,000 enslaved people in Kentucky in 1850, an estimated 3,400 a year were sold. Marion B. Lucas, *A History of Blacks in Kentucky: From Slavery to Segregation, 1760–1891* (1992; Lexington: University Press of Kentucky, 2003), xvi, 99. The continuing exodus of Black Kentuckians is documented in Hobbs and Stoops, *Demographic Trends in the 20th Century.*

129 "restored slave quarters": Clipping from *In Kentucky* 2 (1938), 29, file cabinet drawer 2, MOKHSP.

129 an imagined geography: Colin L. Anderson, "Segregation, Popular Culture, and the Southern Pastoral: The Spatial and Racial Politics of American Sheet Music, 1870–1900," *Journal of Southern History* 85 (Aug. 2019): 577–610; Manring, *Slave in a Box.*

129 "ultra-cultured Negro": Rule, *Light Bearers.*

130 Allison's 1881 account: Picador, "Cradle of Uncle Tom's Cabin," *CJ*, Sept. 2, 1928, 36.

130 Allison also quietly: RWB to YEA, July 8, 1929, folder 30, YEAP.

130 "happy home": YEA, "'My Old Kentucky Home': The Song and the Story," 6.

130 "on faith": "The 'Old Kentucky Home' Tradition," *CJ,* March 4, 1934, 24.

131 oblivious that some: Marie Porter, interview by author, Jan. 30, 2019.

132 "the romance and the charm": "Man Who Brought Legend to Louisville."

132 "As a place of pilgrimage": "Another View of the 'Home,'" unidentified (Kentucky) clipping [1921], folder 44, BLBP.

132 "the happy home": YEA, "'My Old Kentucky Home': The Song and the Story," 6.

CHAPTER 7: WE WILL SING ONE SONG

133 "flood of memories": JKL, quoted in Mariana Whitmer, "Josiah Kirby Lilly and the Foster Hall Collection," *American Music* (Fall 2012): 326.

133 "little hut among the bushes": John G. Bowman, *Unofficial Notes* (Pittsburgh: privately printed, 1963), 143.

133 Others had beaten: JTH, draft memoir typescript, B25, CAM.

134 "Foster revival": Fletcher Hodges, review of "Swanee River," *Foster Hall Bulletin,* July 4, 1940, 5.

134 "There will never": Alexander Woollcott, "WABC Cream of Wheat Broadcast," Feb. 17, 1935, Radio Programs boxes, CAM.

134 two biopics: *Harmony Lane,* dir. Joseph Santley (1935), starring Douglass Montgomery, and *Swanee River,* dir. Sidney Lanfield (1939), starring Don Ameche. More than eleven hundred movies, television shows, commercials, and cartoons used his songs; over a hundred used "My Old Kentucky Home." Kathryn Haines (CAM), interview by author, 2016.

135 "just and holy": From Eli Lilly's recruiting poster for the Eighteenth Indiana Light Artillery Battery, in James H. Madison, *Eli Lilly: A Life, 1885–1977* (Indianapolis: Indiana Historical Society, 1989), 1.

135 almost no one else: Michelle C. Jarrell, "Colonel Eli Lilly: The Right Man for the Job," *Traces: Magazine of the Indiana Historical Society* 29 (Winter 2017): 51.

135 He leased a house: Harold S. Wilson, *Confederate Industry: Manufacturers and Quartermasters in the Civil War* (Oxford: University Press of Mississippi, 2005), 190–92; though federal troops burned the McGehee home, its soaring columns still stand.

135 Though he had fought: "The Name Lilly," reprinted from the April–July 1942 issue of the *Lilly Review,* 4.

135 "mountains of something white": JKL, memoir, MS, 1, 3, ELCA.

135 Mississippi venture yielded: "Colonel Eli Lilly (1838–1898)," *Lilly Archives,* Jan. 2008; Jarrell, "Colonel Eli Lilly," 45, 51.

136 "yellow as gold": JKL, memoir, MS, 3, ELCA.

136 "softly from loneliness": Ibid.

136 "Heavenly music": Ibid., 4.

136 "Oh, the comfort": Bowman, *Unofficial Notes,* 142.

136 "fusillade of Ethiopian": *Foster Hall Bulletin* 6 (Aug. 1932).

136 "traditions unbased on facts": Fletcher Hodges, "A Pittsburgh Composer and His Memorial," *Western Pennsylvania Historical Magazine* 21 (1938): 3–32.

136 "Even a group of educated": John Chamberlain, review of *Stephen Foster,* by JTH, *NYT,* Jan. 12, 1934.

136 "affairs right": Bowman, *Unofficial Notes,* 142.

136 "America's first composer": JKL, *Fosteriana at Foster Hall* (Indianapolis, ca. 1934).

136 set the record straight: JTH, draft memoir typescript, B26, CAM.

136 "fascinating sport": JTH, *Stephen Foster,* 363.

136 American flag paperweight: Bowman, *Unofficial Notes,* 143.

137 They reportedly paid: Accounts of the "sketchbook" price vary. JTH's memoir, MS, B27, CAM, says $25,000. Geraldine Bair, "Beautiful Dreamers: The Founding of the Stephen Foster Memorial in Pittsburgh, Pennsylvania, 1927–1937," MS, March 1997, CAM, put the price at $15,000.

138 "Nothing to Sell": JTH, draft memoir, CAM. On radio programming, see Whitmer, "Josiah Kirby Lilly and the Foster Hall Collection," 330–32.

138 Lilly then commissioned: *Songs of Stephen Foster: Prepared for Schools and General Use,* ed. Will Earhart and Edward B. Birge (1934; Pittsburgh: University of Pittsburgh Press, 1938). The editors were the head of Pittsburgh's School of Music and an Indiana University music professor.

138 "lovable, child-like character": Bair, "Beautiful Dreamers," 93.

138 "which of course I cannot": Irene Crislak to JKL, Oct. 21, 1936, JKLC.

138 "little Mexican children": Margaret E. Mack to JKL, Nov. 30, 1936, JKLC.

138 "so well the American": Sklar to JKL, May 24, 1934, JKLC.

138 Lilly Ridgely Lilly: JTH, memoir, B34; Madison, *Eli Lilly,* 83.

138 "emissaries": JKL to John W. Muir, July 20, 1933, black file drawer 8, MOKHSP.

138 "$100 REWARD": *Bardstown Standard,* Aug. 24, 1933, black file drawer 12, MOKHSP.

138		The prize went: BLB to JKL, Sept. 12, 1933, folder 199, JKLC.

138		"one of the greatest": JTH, *Our American Music* (New York: Thomas Y. Crowell, 1929), 188–89.

139		"drew from his pocket": JTH, memoir, B20–22, B30, CAM.

139		"roamed" door to door: "Foster Hall Quartet Sings Christmas Carols 17 Hours," *Indianapolis Star,* Dec. 26, 1934.

139		When he snored: JKL to GR, Dec. 29, 1934, JKLC.

139		Lilly offered the men: JKL to GR, Aug. 31, 1932, folder 132, JKLC.

139		"You fellows have": JKL to GR, Jan. 3, 1935, JKLC.

140		Had they worked: The Black population of Indianapolis was 11.2 percent; 3.7 percent of the Lilly workforce was from that group and was strictly segregated—as at many companies. Michelle Jarrell (Eli Lilly and Company archivist), conversation with author, Oct. 28, 2019.

141		occasionally performed: "Dr. and Mrs. W. E. Brown Celebrate," Indianapolis *Freeman,* April 10, 1915.

141		Campbell spent his twenties: David Leander Williams, *Indianapolis Jazz: The Masters, Legends, and Legacy of Indiana Avenue* (Charleston, S.C.: History Press, 2014), 40–41.

142		"last hired": Cheryl Lynn Greenberg, *To Ask for an Equal Chance: African Americans in the Great Depression* (New York: Rowman & Littlefield, 2010), 27–28.

142		"on the bricks": GR to JKL, Sept. 12, 1933, JKLC.

142		Women's Art Association: *Tipton (Ind.) Daily Tribune,* March 20, 1934, 3.

142		On a recording: Foster Hall Quartet, "My Brudder Gum" (Gennett Records, 1934, privately released), CAM. Robinson and the other members of the group took pride in the studio session and made the eighty-mile trip to Gennett a second time to get a copy "for our own personal use, and as a memento so that we may be able to show our race what we have done of record." They were "thrilled by our own voices," which they had never heard played through a phonograph. The quartet left the studio empty-handed. Gennett refused to give the artists a copy until Lilly sent permission. GR to JKL, Feb. 1, 1935, and JKL to GR, Feb. 15, 1935, JKLC.

142		"some of that very funny": JKL to GR, June 25, 1934, JKLC. See reference to the group's "monkey-shines," "Past International Head of Kiwanis Cites Need of Moral Courage Now," *Princeton (Ind.) Daily Clarion,* May 5, 1939.

142		"interpretive genius native": Lorena Callahan to Evelyn Morneweck, Nov. 19, 1933, FHC, CAM.

142		"SOUP LINE": GR to JKL, Sept. 24, 1934, JKLC.

142 Invoices from 1933 averaged: 1933 correspondence from CAM contains total invoices of $1,766.

142 "agreed you had been": GR to JKL, Sept. 12, 1933, JKLC.

143 daughter's college graduation: GR to FH, April 14 and 20, 1937, JKLC.

143 "We certainly had": GR to FH, July 12, 1939, JKLC.

143 On Christmas morning: "Quartet Carries Christmas Spirit to 40 Homes with Carol Singing," *Indianapolis Star,* Dec. 26, 1943, 8.

143 "colored organizations": "Foster Hall Four on Radio Program," *Indianapolis Recorder,* March 10, 1945.

144 more than half of households: Stephen Smith, "Radio: The Internet of the 1930s," APM Reports, Nov. 10, 2014, www.apmreports.org.

145 "unverified": *Songs of Stephen Foster,* 12; Donald Wayne, "Stephen Foster Tour," *Holiday,* Oct. 1953, 92.

145 "a shrine known": WNYC, Sept. 13, 1935, Radio Programs 1932–1948, FHC.

145 "on the terrace": WBNS, Jan. 14, 1935, Radio Programs 1932–1948, FHC.

145 "the work of one man": Alexander Woollcott, 1939 RCA Key radio variety show, Jan. 8, 1939, Radio Programs 1932–1948, FHC.

145 "be an America": Woollcott, "WABC Cream of Wheat Broadcast," Feb. 17, 1935, Radio Programs 1932–1948, FHC.

145 "legacy beyond price": Woollcott, 1939 RCA Key radio variety show, Jan. 8, 1939.

146 "you had to be with": Mary Bingham, interview by author, 1994, tape 3, side 1. Also see Alexander Woollcott, *Long, Long Ago* (New York: World Book, 1943), 184; and Sam Thomas, ed., *Barry Bingham: A Man of His Word* (Lexington: University Press of Kentucky, 1993), 217.

146 "lovely old house": Woollcott, "WABC Cream of Wheat Broadcast," Feb. 17, 1935, Radio Programs 1932–1948, FHC.

146 "Old Kentucky Home chimes": Terry L. Birdwhistell, "WHAS Radio and the Development of Broadcasting in Kentucky, 1922–1942," *Register of the Kentucky Historical Society* 79 (Autumn 1981): 340–41; Credo Fitch Harris, *Microphone Memoirs of the Horse and Buggy Days of Radio* (New York: Bobbs-Merrill, 1937), 79.

146 The receding waters left: Rick Bell, *The Great Flood of 1937* (Louisville, Ky.: Butler Books, 2007).

146 "gloom-chasing": "City to Bid 1937 Flood Farewell," *CJ,* Feb. 16, 1937, 1.

146 "In a full-throated": "Mass Meeting Cheers Show City Has Plenty of Morale to Rebuild," *CJ,* Feb. 17, 1937, 1.

146 hope and a prayer: William A. Cummings, "Groping in the Dark: An Early History of WHAS Radio" (master's thesis, University of Louisville, 2012), 129–53.

146   placed full-page ads: Susan E. Tifft and Alex S. Jones, *The Patriarch: The Rise and Fall of the Bingham Dynasty* (New York: Summit Books, 1991), 148.

147   well into and past: Barnes, "Darkology." For a selection of stereotyped depictions of blackness in cartoons, see the Jim Crow Museum of Racist Memorabilia online: www.ferris.edu.

147   Fleischer Studios released: Fleischer's Car-Tunes, in Nicholas Sammond, *Birth of an Industry: Blackface Minstrelsy and the Rise of American Animation* (Durham, N.C.: Duke University Press, 2015), 150–52.

147   "You'll just roar": Promotional poster for *Uncle Tom's Cabin* (1927), dir. Harry A. Pollard. See Joanna R. Smolko, "Southern Fried Foster: Representing Race and Place Through Music in Looney Tunes Cartoons," *American Music* 30 (Fall 2012): 346. The makers of the film tamed sections showing slavery to pass muster with Daughters of the Confederacy officials, who patrolled Hollywood's presentation of history. Even with cuts, some cinemas in former slave states barred the film for being too sympathetic to the plight of enslaved Black people. See Thomas Cripps, *Slow Fade to Black: The Negro in American Film, 1900–1942* (New York: Oxford University Press, 1977), 159.

147   Estonian-born immigrant: Uncle Tom's Cabin and American Culture website, University of Virginia, utc.iath.virginia.edu.

147   "American Negro": Ernö Rapée, *Motion Picture Moods for Pianists and Organists* (New York: G. Schirmer, 1924), 282–83, 375.

148   "heel-and-toe wizard": "Shirley Temple and Lionel Barrymore in 'The Little Colonel,'" *NYT,* March 22, 1935, 26.

148   "raise the gooseflesh": D. W. Griffith quoted in Shirley Temple Black, *Child Star: An Autobiography* (New York: McGraw-Hill, 1988), 90.

148   Born in Richmond: Jim Haskins and N. R. Mitgang, *Mr. Bojangles: The Biography of Bill Robinson* (New York: William Morrow, 1988), 28–29.

148   Beginning when he was eight: Ibid., 34–35.

148   earned $3,000 a week: Carole Marks and Diane Edkins, *The Power of Pride: Stylemakers and Rulebreakers of the Harlem Renaissance* (New York: Crown, 1999), 189.

148   wore a ten-carat: John F. Kasson, *The Little Girl Who Fought the Great Depression: Shirley Temple and 1930s America* (New York: W. W. Norton, 2014), 96.

148   carried a pistol: Fletcher, *100 Years,* 301.

148   "less an actress": Unidentified article (ca. 1938) from Shirley Temple's scrapbook, quoted in Karen Orr Vered, "White and Black in Black and White: Management of Race and Sexuality in the Coupling of Child-

Star Shirley Temple and Bill Robinson," *Velvet Light Trap: A Critical Journal of Film* 39 (Spring 1997): 56.

148 "Uncle Billy": Black, *Child Star,* 92.

149 someone suggested they: Haskins and Mitgang, *Mr. Bojangles,* 225.

149 "I was ecstatic": Black, *Child Star,* 92.

150 Bill Robinson brought: Kristen Hatch, *Shirley Temple and the Performance of Girlhood* (New Brunswick, N.J.: Rutgers University Press, 2015), 80.

150 "I like white folks": St. Clair McKelway, "Profiles: Bojangles—1," *New Yorker,* Oct. 6, 1934, 26–28.

150 into her adulthood: Haskins and Mitgang, *Mr. Bojangles,* 230–31.

150 "Now, darlin'": Donald Bogle, *Bright Boulevards, Bold Dreams: The Story of Black Hollywood* (New York: Ballantine Books, 2005), 162.

151 "no illusions about": Hazel Scott, quoted in Kasson, *Little Girl Who Fought the Great Depression,* 102. (Scott's husband, Adam Clayton Powell Sr., officiated at Robinson's Harlem funeral.)

151 "hated Shirley": Toni Morrison, *The Bluest Eye* (1970; New York: Vintage, 2007), 19.

151 censors in some southern states: Black, *Child Star,* 98.

151 Black papers sometimes: Vered, "White and Black in Black and White," 52–65.

151 "immaculate amalgamation": Hatch, *Shirley Temple and the Performance of Girlhood,* 80.

151 "montage of the most": Fitzgerald to Selznick, Jan. 10, 1939, in *Dear Los Angeles: The City in Diaries and Letters, 1542 to 2018,* ed. David Kipen (New York: Modern Library, 2018), 117. Fitzgerald worked briefly for Selznick; see Arthur Krystal, "Slow Fade: F. Scott Fitzgerald in Hollywood," *New Yorker,* Nov. 16, 2009.

152 rated as one: The 1939 work ranks sixth on the American Film Institute's list of greatest films. www.afi.com.

152 "I can't do it": Stephen Bourne, *Butterfly McQueen Remembered* (Lanham, Md.: Scarecrow Press, 2008), 12.

153 Mitchell considered using: André Bernard, *Now All We Need Is a Title: Famous Book Titles and How They Got That Way* (New York: W. W. Norton, 1997), 81–82.

153 knowing it was riddled: The Prissy character owes much to Harriet Beecher Stowe's comically ignorant Topsy in *Uncle Tom's Cabin,* a character who became a minstrel staple in theatrical interpretations of the novel.

153 "a prop man": Susan Myrick, quoted in Bourne, *Butterfly McQueen Remembered,* 12.

153 "stupid little slave": McQueen, quoted in Stephen Bourne, "Obituary: Butterfly McQueen," *Independent,* Oct. 23, 2011.

153 "a prop man": Susan Myrick, quoted in Bourne, *Butterfly McQueen Remembered,* 12.

154 McQueen withdrew: Cripps, *Slow Fade to Black,* 360–61.

154 "If she did slap me": McQueen, quoted in Max Alexander, "Once More, the Old South in All Its Glory," *NYT,* Jan. 29, 1989.

154 "I didn't know": Interview with Butterfly McQueen, *The Making of a Legend: Gone with the Wind* (dir. David Hinton, 1988), clip at www .youtube.com.

155 senses her own release: One reviewer noted the irony of pairing the song with the approach of Union forces. "Gone with the Wind," *Time,* Dec. 25, 1939, 30–32, in Cripps, *Slow Fade to Black,* 361.

155 spent more than: The estimate includes the value of the collection, Lilly's endowment of it, and his gifts toward constructing the Gothic-style shrine at the university. He and his family continued to underwrite its work for decades. Bowman, *Unofficial Notes,* 147.

155 penny Stephen Foster stamp: Adam Bernstein, "Devoted Curator Fletcher Hodges," *Washington Post,* March 17, 2006; Foster appeared on stamp No. 879, issued May 3, 1940, www.mysticstamp.com.

155 The civic-minded compilation: Joy Elmer Morgan, *The American Citizens Handbook* (Washington, D.C.: National Education Association, 1941). The NAACP took issue with the inclusion of racially demeaning material.

155 "reposes among": "Painting Pays Honor to Stephen Foster," *NYT,* July 5, 1940, 15.

156 "personal signature": A. B. Chandler, *Heroes, Plain Folks, and Skunks: The Life and Times of Happy Chandler,* with Vance H. Trimble (Chicago: Bonus Books, 1989), viii.

156 "everybody was generally": Ibid., 115.

156 "Happy, sing us": Ibid., 41.

156 "created a spell": Ben Chandler, interview by author, June 21, 2017.

156 Crowds loved it: Ibid.

156 invited the illustrator: A. B. Chandler to Christy (telegram), April 26, 1937, box 1, folder 123, HCCP.

156 "at the drop": Ben Chandler, interview by author, June 21, 2017.

157 The artist returned: Chandler to Christy, Nov. 20, 1937, box 1, folder 123, HCCP; "Howard Chandler Christy Completes Portrait of Mrs. Chandler," *CJ,* Nov. 20, 1937, 14.

157 Christy toured: "The Kentucky Colonels, the Christy Painting, and Foster," *L&N Magazine,* March 1942, 8.

157 "poetic flame": "The Stephen Collins Foster Portrait," 1942 Kentucky Sesquicentennial Menu, Louisville and Nashville Railroad, and unidentified item [bookmark?], HCCP.

157 "As long as democracy": "Program of Stephen Collins Foster Portrait Presentation by the Honorable Order of Kentucky Colonels at the Old Kentucky Home, Bardstown, KY, July Fourth, 1940," HCCP. See Bing Crosby, *Stephen Foster Songs* (four-disc set) (Decca Records, 1946).

157 "children of immigrants": Furlong to FH, Dec. 2, 1941, FHC.

157 Furlong spent the rest of the war: William Rea Furlong Papers, Naval Historical Foundation Collection, Manuscript Division, Library of Congress, Washington, D.C.; FH to William Furlong, Sept. 30, 1942, FHC.

158 Unable to pass: Deane Root (CAM curator), interview by author, Dec. 19, 2017.

158 "to the national defense": FH to commanding officer, U.S. Marines, Sept. 3, 1941, folder 30, FHC.

158 Once again: *Songs of Stephen Foster for the U.S. Armed Forces* (Pittsburgh: University of Pittsburgh Press, 1942).

158 More than 650,000: Compiled from annual reports, budgets, and correspondence, FHC. See *University of Pittsburgh Newsletter,* June 1943, 4, folder 30, FHC. For the book's global reach, see Major Howard Bronson to FH, June 14, 1943, folder 30, FHC.

158 "invaluable to the boys": Major Howard Bronson to FH, Feb. 23, 1943, FHC.

159 The Office of War: Great Moments in Music Radio Program, Sept. 19, 1945, Jan Peerce Collection of Sound Recordings, Rodgers and Hammerstein Archives of Recorded Sound, NYPLPA.

159 "V-disc" for "victory": Sound disc "SF Program: Armed Forces Radio Service," in L (Special) 95-03, Jan Peerce Collection of Sound Recordings.

159 The songbook migrated: Dennis G. Sprang, *America Ascendant: The Rise of American Exceptionalism* (Lincoln: University of Nebraska Press, 2019), 190–92.

159 ongoing support: Foster Hall Annual Reports (1948–1949) and (1950–1951) and update Jan. 12, 1953, CAM.

159 "a national expression": JTH, *Stephen Foster,* 371.

159 "well-known colored": "Bland's Songs Found 'Offensive' to Pupils," *Pittsburgh Courier,* March 14, 1942, 4.

159 "very foolish": Ibid.

159 "not just a friend": David Michaelis, *Eleanor* (New York: Simon & Schuster, 2020), 339.

159   "minorities" were "sometimes": Eleanor Roosevelt paraphrased in *Grand Junction (Colo.) Daily Sentinel*, March 8, 1942, 3.

159   "as to the folklore": "Pittsburgh School Board Refuses to Ban 'Offensive' Songs," *Pittsburgh Courier*, March 28, 1942, 18.

160   "We just had": Marion Porter, "Slaves' Graves at Old Kentucky Home Presented to the State in Observance of Independence," *CJ*, July 5, 1945.

160   "honor roll": Program, "Dedication of Old Slave Burial Ground," July 4, 1945, MOKHSP.

162   When the Japanese government: Kazuko Miyashita, "Foster's Songs in Japan," *American Music* 30 (Fall 2012): 313; Erleen Johnson, "Stephen Foster's Music in Japan," *Music Clubs Magazine* (Winter 2000): 21–22.

162   In 1947, Tokyo's: Miyashita, "Foster's Songs in Japan," 315.

162   his portrait hung: Jiro Hashimoto, email to author, Oct. 6, 2018.

162   some white critics: In *So This Is Jazz* (New York: Little, Brown, 1926), Henry O. Osgood rejected the significance of Black musicians to "legitimate" jazz. See Nicholas M. Evans, " 'Racial Cross-Dressing' in the Jazz Age: Cultural Therapy and Its Discontents in Cabaret Nightlife," in *Hop of Pop: The Politics and Pleasures of Popular Culture*, ed. Henry Jenkins, Tara McPherson, and Jane Shattuc (Durham, N.C.: Duke University Press, 2002), 400–403.

CHAPTER 8: WHEREVER THE DARKY MAY GO

163   It was his last: Larry F. Kiner and Philip R. Evans, eds., *Al Jolson: A Bio Discography* (Metuchen, N.J.: Scarecrow Press, 1992), 649.

164   "carried them dreaming": Michael Alexander, *Jazz Age Jews* (Princeton, N.J.: Princeton University Press, 2001), 142–43.

164   "colored aristocrat": "Al Jolson (1886–1950)," in *Encyclopedia of American Jewish History*, vol. 1, ed. Stephen Harlan Norwood and Eunice G. Pollack (Santa Barbara, Calif.: ABC-CLIO, 2008), 501.

164   "Far from ignoring": Michael Rogin, *Blackface, White Noise: Jewish Immigrants in the Hollywood Melting Pot* (Berkeley: University of California Press, 1998), 27.

165   the last cartoon: Christopher P. Lehman, *The Colored Cartoon: Black Representation in American Animated Short Films, 1907–1954* (Amherst: University of Massachusetts Press, 2007), 110–11.

165   "one of our boys": *Southern Fried Rabbit* might have screened as a short in movie houses showing John Ford's *The Sun Shines Bright*, which co-starred Fetchit (born Lincoln Theodore Monroe Andrew Perry). Both were released the same week.

166   kept the minstrel act: Smolko, "Southern Fried Foster," 344–72; Kathryn Miller Haines, "Stephen Foster's Music in Motion Pictures and Television," *American Music* 30 (Fall 2012): 373–88.

166   Thousands of copies: "Debnam Says Book Orders Coming Fast," *Raleigh (N.C.) Times,* July 21, 1955.

166   "neverist": Unidentified clipping, box 3, folder 6, WEDP.

166   "Apostle Warren": WED, *Then My Old Kentucky Home, Good Night!* (Raleigh, N.C.: Graphic Press, 1955), 1, 4.

166   "standing close by": Carl Coerch, "Debnam Views the News," *State* (Raleigh, N.C.), Oct. 28, 1950, 3–4. See James F. Harper, "Waldemar Eros Debnam," *North Carolina Dictionary of Biography,* 2:47–48.

168   "in each other's lap": WED, *Then My Old Kentucky Home, Good Night!,* 2. On the Till case, see Timothy B. Tyson, *The Blood of Emmett Till* (New York: Simon & Schuster, 2017).

168   "racial integrity": WED, *Then My Old Kentucky Home, Good Night!,* 118. North Carolina and six other southern states diverted taxpayer funding to support students attending "segregation academies." See Matt Barnum, "Critics of Vouchers Say They Are Marred by Racism and Exacerbate Segregation. Are They Right?," *Chalkbeat,* July 23, 2017, www.chalkbeat.org.

168   sold eighty thousand copies: WED to Walton M. Byars, Sept. 26, 1963, WEDP.

168   "A Handbook for Southerners": Editorial, *Charleston (S.C.) News and Courier,* July 6, 1955.

168   "any neat and orderly": Eleanor Roosevelt, "My Day," Feb. 6, 1950, erpapers.columbian.gwu.edu; "Edward and Theodore Danziger," Chapel Hill–Carrboro Business Hall of Fame, businesshalloffame.weebly.com.

168   "grace of living": Eleanor Roosevelt, "My Day."

168   "the greatest busybody": Caskif Norvell, "I'll Take My Stand," review of *Weep No More, My Lady,* by WED, *Jefferson Republican* (Charleston, W.V.), n.d., box 4, folder 1, WEDP.

168   A later deluxe: Libby Davis to WED, May 10, 1958, box 1, folder 5, WEDP.

169   "settled like an unclean": WED, *Weep No More, My Lady* (Raleigh, N.C.: Graphic Press, 1950), 42.

169   "passing judgment on things": Ibid., 57.

169   "Negro ghetto": Ibid., 9.

169   more than a quarter million: WED to Walton M. Byars, Sept. 26, 1963, WEDP. The cover price was fifty cents.

169   "lady": WED, *Weep No More,* 57.

169   The Grenada, Mississippi: O. E. Zoder to WED, [Aug. 1963], box 1, folder 3, WEDP.

169   disrespecting Kentucky's state anthem: "Radio-TV Networks Ban Racial Terms," *Plaindealer* (Kansas City, Kans.), July 26, 1957.

169   "network people": Robert L. Riggs, "'Tis Summer, Chelf Not Gay," *CJ*, July 31, 1957.

170   impromptu rebel yells: "Democrat Frank Chelf, a Member of Congress for 11 Terms, Is Dead," *CJ*, Sept. 3, 1982.

170   One congressman noted: William F. Abbogast, "Chelf Plea for Foster Songs Brings Elvis into the Issue," *Louisville (Ky.) Times*, Aug. 2, 1957.

171   "fundamentally pro-American": Chelf quoted in Nick Tochka, "The Battle over 'America's Troubadour,'" *Van*, June 7, 2018, van-us.atavist .com.

171   "emotional urgency": "Is There Anyone Finah?," *Time*, Dec. 16, 1957, 64.

171   "breezy Southern charm": "Dinah Shore, Homey Singer and Star of TV, Dies at 76," *NYT*, Feb. 25, 1994.

171   "I like that": "Dinah Shore Was Warned by Rep. Frank Chelf," *Pittsburgh Courier*, July 12, 1958.

171   "just as they": Robert L. Riggs, "Chelf Not Just Whistling Dixie," *CJ*, Jan. 8, 1957.

171   Any earlier understandings: "State Songs by Foster No Longer Will Be Censored," *Lexington (Ky.) Herald-Leader*, Oct. 3, 1958.

171   "the happy, friendly, carefree": Chelf quoted in Tochka, "Battle over 'America's Troubadour.'"

171   The people behind: Charles Whaley, "Bardstown Goes Gala for 'Foster' Premiere," *CJ*, June 27, 1959. Catherine Conner, a Democratic Party fixture who had helped the 1921 campaign to buy Federal Hill, was central to the *Stephen Foster Story* project. Conner, *From My Old Kentucky Home to the White House*, 167–69.

172   For his Bardstown patrons: Paul Green, *The Stephen Foster Story: A Symphonic Drama Based on the Life and Music of the Composer* (New York: Samuel French, 1960), 60, 61, 99.

172   "phony": William Mootz, "Enthusiastic Audience of 1,158 Welcomes 'Stephen Foster Story,'" *CJ*, June 27, 1959.

172   Attendance at Federal Hill: 1958 (38,637) and 1959 (51,605), untitled memo, 1960, file cabinet drawer 2, MOKHSP.

173   "Overlooked so far": David Hacker, "Should Foster Be Censored? Views Here Vary," *Louisville Times*, July 31, 1957.

173   "those ardent defenders": Leon Davis, "There Are More Important Things Than Foster's Songs," *Louisville Defender*, Aug. 15, 1957.

174 Hacker won an International Press: "On the Scene Report," *CJ*, May 1, 1960, 133.

174 "the obnoxious quadrivial": "Radio Singer Refuses to Use 'Nigger' in Song," *Indianapolis Recorder*, April 10, 1937, 13.

174 "taught us all to feel": Nevin, "Stephen C. Foster and Negro Minstrelsy," 608–16.

175 "touched a banjo": Wayne, "Stephen Foster Tour," 97.

175 "that world of Negroes": Malcolm X, *The Autobiography of Malcolm X*, with Alex Haley (1965; New York: Ballantine Books, 1992), 78.

176 "fact rather than fable": Sam Dennison, *Scandalize My Name: Black Imagery in American Popular Music* (New York: Garland, 1982), 101.

176 "universal sentiment": Rosa S. Gragg, "The Influence of the Negro on the Life and Works of Stephen Collins Foster" (speech delivered Jan. 12, 1939, Ebenezer AME Church, Detroit), Foster and the Negro folder, FHC.

176 "reliev[e] the children": Cora M. Patton to Marian Anderson, Aug. 6, 1952, quoted in *The Textbook as Discourse: Sociocultural Dimensions of American Schoolbooks,* ed. Eugene Povenzo Jr., Annis Shaver, and Manuel Bello (New York: Routledge, 2011), 221. Minstrel tunes survive as children's songs (see Ermolaeva, "Dinah Put Down Your Horn") or Christmas carols: see Kyna Hamill, "'The Story I Must Tell': 'Jingle Bells' in the Minstrel Repertoire," *Theatre Survey* 58 (2017): 375–403.

177 "preserved the musical": "Note on Racial Harmony," *Courier: America's Best Weekly* (New York edition of *Pittsburgh Courier*), July 17, 1954, 1.

177 "in Negro folk music": Carol Sutton, "Niece Wants Foster Songs Sung as They're Written: Says Change Takes Away Part of History," *CJ*, July 4, 1958.

177 "nothing offensive . . . to anyone": "Song Writer Says Revision Would Help Foster's Tunes," *CJ*, Aug. 5, 1957.

177 to the broadest audience: FH to Elmer Sulzer, Feb. 8, 1934, folder 297, JKLC.

177 The blond baritone Nelson Eddy: "Radio Singer Refuses to Use 'Nigger' in Song," 13.

177 Simon & Schuster: Margaret Bradford Boni, *Fireside Book of Folk Songs* (New York: Simon & Schuster, 1947).

177 The NAACP scored: "Edwin C. Hill Sorry He Said 'Darky': Noted Radio Commentator Apologizes to Negroes," *Plaindealer* (Kansas City, Kans.), May 26, 1939, 1.

177 "the *folks* they are gay": Louis Armstrong and His Orchestra, "Old Kentucky Home," *Satchmo Plays King Oliver* (Audio Fidelity Records, 1960).

177   "racial justice is fine": John Ed Pearce, "Let's Leave the Songs of Our Racial Past Alone," *CJ*, July 30, 1957.

178   "not inconsequential": "Art and Individuals," *Wall Street Journal*, July 3, 1958, 8.

178   "first observed the happy": Adele Brandeis, "A Pennsylvanian Who Hymned Kentucky," *CJ*, Jan. 13, 1964.

178   "tin can": Runyon, interview by author, June 5, 2018.

179   "Whenever . . . they strike up": Lyman T. Johnson, oral history by Dwayne Cox, May 6, 1976, 18, ohc.library.louisville.edu.

179   "barely tolerated": Marie Porter, interview by author, Jan. 8, 2018.

180   "real ladyship": E. Azalia Hackley, *The Colored Girl Beautiful* (Kansas City, Mo.: Burton, 1916), www.gutenberg.org.

181   evidence of respect: Root, "'Mythstory' of Stephen C. Foster," 31.

181   "slavery had certainly been wrong": Anne Braden, *The Wall Between* (1958; Knoxville: University of Tennessee Press, 1999), 21.

181   "happened to say something": Ibid., 21.

181   "Colored women are": Edith S. Bingham, interview by author, May 5, 2020.

CHAPTER 9: THEY SING NO MORE

183   "strike" when "fans": Bill Peterson, "'Jack Tout' and His Friends Want to Meet You," *CJ*, May 3, 1968.

183   "kind of race": "'Another Kind of Race': Nixon Remarks at Derby," *Cincinnati Enquirer*, May 5, 1968.

184   "Poor Dick, I don't": Paul Bulleit, "Nixon Picks 'My Old Kentucky Home' over Race," *CJ*, May 5, 1968.

184   "bolting": Shirley Povich, "Cloud of Uncertainty Hovers over Derby," *CJ*, May 5, 1967. See Samuel Abramson, "Disorder at the Derby: Race, Reputation, and Louisville's 1967 Open Housing Crisis," *Ohio Valley History* 15, no. 2 (Summer 2015): 28–48; and Tracy E. K'Meyer, *Civil Rights in the Gateway to the South: Louisville, Kentucky, 1945–1980* (Lexington: University Press of Kentucky, 2009), 134–37.

184   Under pressure from: "'The Sun Shines' on State Song but Clouds Form," *CJ*, Jan. 25, 1967.

184   d-word for "old folks": Jean Howerton, "A Melody That's 'More Than a Song,'" *CJ*, April 29, 1969.

184   "certain lines": Louisville Human Relations Commission Meeting Minutes, May 2, 1968, 6, folder 2, Martin Perley Papers, FHS.

185   "gables, spires": Bill Corum, *Off and Running* (New York: Henry Holt, 1959), 281–82.

185 "I hate Lincoln": Quoted in Nicholson, *Kentucky Derby,* 169–70.

185 "the Old South's heritage": Ibid., 170.

185 if victorious in November: Dean Eagle, "Sports Fan Nixon Might Attend Kentucky Derby," *CJ,* Nov. 10, 1968.

186 "No. 1 pig": Don Ridings, "U of L Blacks Picket Downs," *CJ,* May 4, 1969.

186 "a time when": James Blaine Hudson, oral history by Betsy Brinson, Aug. 23, 2000, KOHC, kyoralhistory.com.

186 Like thousands of Black: Ibram H. Rogers, *The Black Campus Movement: Black Students and the Racial Reconstruction of Higher Education, 1965–1972* (New York: Palgrave Macmillan, 2012).

187 "demands": Hudson, oral history by Brinson.

187 "unlearn the white mind": BSU Circular, Oct. 1968, BSU.

187 "trained to feel": "The Goal of the Black Revolution," BSU Circular, Sept. (?) 1968, BSU.

187 "all whites are": BSU Circular, April 29, 1969, BSU.

187 students were arrested: Bill Peterson, "Blacks Take Over Building at U of L; Police Arrest 22," *CJ,* May 2, 1969.

188 "The darkies are": Ridings, "U of L Blacks Picket Downs."

189 "in these days of soul": Howerton, "Melody That's 'More Than a Song.'"

189 "Turn around, you hairy freak": Hunter S. Thompson, "The Kentucky Derby Is Decadent and Depraved," in *The Great Shark Hunt* (New York: Summit Books, 1979), 23.

189 "everyone can be": Billy Reed, interview by author, March 27, 2018. In 2021, Reed called for Kentucky to drop the song. Billy Reed, "It's Time to Update Kentucky's State Song and Send 'My Old Kentucky Home' to the Dustbin," *Northern Kentucky Tribune,* Aug. 1, 2021.

189 "'Old South' ways": Clarence Matthews, "Few Blacks Join in Derby Festivities," *Louisville Times,* May 3, 1971.

190 "busted out": Melvin Durslag, "Riva Ridge Puts Form Back in Derby," *San Antonio Light,* May 7, 1972.

190 "couldn't have been": Lonnie Ali, interview by author, April 28, 2020.

190 "the lament of": Rick Cushing, "Out of Tragedy, a Kind of Anthem," *Louisville,* April 1975, 96–97, 99.

191 "*Uncle Tom's Cabin* set": TDC, "My Old Kentucky Home in Retrospect," 106.

191 moved from utopia: TDC, "The Slavery Background of Foster's My Old Kentucky Home," *Filson Club History Quarterly* 10 (Jan. 1936): 12.

191 "captivated by a dream": TDC, "My Old Kentucky Home in Retrospect," 105.

191   "entered people's minds": Karl Schmitt Jr., interview by author, Dec. 4, 2018.

192   "people just grimaced": Betty Bayé, interview by author, March 3, 2020.

192   "We ignored it": Coleman, interview by author, Dec. 12, 2019.

192   "Why do white people": Marie Porter, interview by author, Jan. 8, 2018.

192   "It's your song": Bob Coleman, interview by author, Dec. 12, 2019.

192   "There is no nostalgia": Matthews, "Few Blacks Join in Derby Festivities."

193   "emotional experience": Steve Cady, "Derby Week: When the South Rises," *NYT,* April 25, 1976.

193   "It's about mountain": Randy Newman, in Kevin Courrier, *Randy Newman's American Dreams* (Toronto: ECW Press, 2005), 111.

194   "white trash" ballad: Greil Marcus, *Mystery Train: Images of America in Rock and Roll Music,* 6th rev. ed. (1975; New York: Plume, 2015), 107.

194   "hook": Courrier, *Randy Newman's American Dreams,* 111.

194   nearly half a million: Roy Bongartz, "Kentucky's Out-of-State Native Son," *NYT,* May 14, 1972.

194   compelled to hide: Gray, interview by author, July 27, 2021.

194   annual pride parade: Hartman, interview by author, July 27, 2021.

195   interior restoration at Federal Hill: WBF, oral history by Estill Curtis Pennington, July 28, 1981, Archives of American Art, Smithsonian Institution, www.aaa.si.edu.

195   "cracked up": Bongartz, "Kentucky's Out-of-State Native Son."

195   "much the same": "Call of Kentucky," Kentucky State Department of Public Instruction booklet, quoted in Robert Tolf, "South's Foster Child: Stephen Foster, the Yankee Who Turned into the South's Heart," *NYT,* Oct. 3, 1976.

195   "bed he slept in": Tolf, "South's Foster Child."

195   "hodgepodge": WBF to MC, April 5, 1977, file cabinet drawer 2, MOKHSP.

195   Floyd banished: WBF, directions to guides, 1977, office files, MOKHSP.

196   "local tradition has it": MC to WBF, March 24, 1977, file cabinet drawer 2, MOKHSP.

196   "It is not your fault": Gordon Moffett to MC, March 23, 1977, file cabinet drawer 2, MOKHSP.

197   "based on facts": WBF to MC, April 5, 1977, file cabinet drawer 2, MOKHSP.

197   "'myths' had been": MC to Louis Hempel, Nov. 28, 1978, file cabinet drawer 2, MOKHSP.

197   locals grew concerned: Erleen Johnson to FH, Feb. 2, 1979, banker's box, MOKHSP.

197 escort a Tokyo journalist: Johnson, "Stephen Foster's Music in Japan," 21.

198 "a man who never": Thomas Watson, "Inspiration for Our State Song Defended," Associated Press, *Danville (Ky.) Advocate-Messenger,* May 2, 1978.

198 They came to see: OWS, Speech, July 1979, folder 5, OWSP.

198 They could guide themselves: 1977 tour guide script, MOKHSP.

199 "To see that all": Emily Bingham, "From Slavery to Freedom," Jan. 1977. The deep involvement of white women in slaveholding and the slave trade is treated in Stephanie E. Jones Rogers, *They Were Her Property: White Women as Slave Owners in the American South* (New Haven, Conn.: Yale University Press, 2019).

199 "servants stayed on": Johnson to Bert Ballard, Jan. 28, 1978, banker's box, MOKHSP.

199 During the 1980s: Beverly Bartlett, "Bardstown," *CJ,* July 8, 1991.

CHAPTER 10: WEEP NO MORE

201 mist of "malaise": Jimmy Carter's July 15, 1979, speech about the state of the nation became known as the "malaise" speech, though he never used that word.

201 "strike city": Jay Lawrence, "Louisville's Labor Climate Is Chilly," *CJ,* June 6, 1982. *The Wall Street Journal* picked up on the designation.

201 KFC had expanded: "The Colonel Comes to Japan" was one of thirteen installments for *Enterprise,* a 1981 WGBH series of TV documentaries on business case studies hosted by the former CBS newsman Eric Sevareid.

202 A 1974 KFC campaign: John Y. Brown Jr., interview by author, Dec. 12, 2018; K. Annabelle Smith, "Why Japan Is Obsessed with Kentucky Fried Chicken for Christmas," *Smithsonian,* Dec. 14, 2012, www.smithsonianmag.com; "How KFC Became a Christmas Tradition in Japan—Cheddar Examines," www.youtube.com.

202 through a meadow: 1983 KFC Japan television commercial, www.youtube.com/watch?v=nnxHzIfkoMM.

202 Kentucky opened a Far East: "Collins Honors 2 Men for Helping Foster Kentucky-Japan Trade Ties," *CJ,* March 14, 1985.

203 "I had to get": Martha Layne Collins, interview by author, May 22, 2018.

203 "When I think": David Goetz, "Young 'Ambassadors' from Japan Embark on Tour of Kentucky," *CJ,* Aug. 20, 1984.

203 "No Japanese. Want English!": David Brown, interview by author,

Sept. 14, 2018. For more details, see Judy Bryant, "Japan's Love for Foster's Music Makes 'Story' Cast's Trip a Natural," *CJ*, May 4, 1985; Associated Press, "Outdoor Drama Moves to Japan Next Month," *Kokomo (Ind.) Tribune*, Aug. 16, 1985.

204   as the Rolling Stones: Dale E. Hall, "The Unknown Stephen Foster," *American Music Teacher* 26 (Feb.–March 1977): 25.

204   "We were rock stars": David Brown, interview by author, Sept. 14, 2018.

204   Hashimoto's targets often: Jiro Hashimoto, email to author, Oct. 8, 2018.

204   The state was a front-runner: "Collins Says State Is Among Finalists for Japanese Firms," *CJ*, Oct. 25, 1985.

204   "our fiber": Collins, interview by author, May 22, 2018.

204   "our new 'old'": Cheryl Truman and Art Jester, "Company Executives Formally Announce $800 Million Plant," *Lexington Herald-Leader*, Dec. 12, 1985.

204   Kentucky had a secret: "Bless Stephen Foster," *Forbes*, June 16, 1986, 163.

205   study "everything American": Greg Seamon, interview by author, Oct. 12, 2018.

205   The field trip: Email and photographs from Bokuro Urabe to Les and Debbie Dornan, Oct. 22, 2018. Unable to find a student from the 1986 cohort, I relied on Urabe, who participated in the 1985 homestay in Ohio and took the same tour of Kentucky.

206   "stand there and listen": Carl Hines, interview by author, Nov. 30, 2010.

206   "an insult": "Japanese Students' Use of Old Lyrics Angers Black House Member," *CJ*, March 12, 1986.

206   "musical mission" tours: Les Dornan, interview by author, Oct. 17, 2018. The people-to-people mission program was known as P.R.O.M.I.S.E.S. (People Relating Our Mission in Service Extension and Study). In Japan, the Ohioans performed music and dance shows across the country.

206   "They rarely had": Johnson, interview by author, 2018; Carl Hines, oral history by Catherine Herdman, June 28, 2006, Kentucky Legislature Oral History Project, Louie B. Nunn Center for Oral History, University of Kentucky. nunncenter.net.

207   "the Negro tourist": "Revising My Old Ky Home Is Assembly's Job, Breathitt Says," *Louisville Times*, Jan. 25, 1967.

207   "convey connotations of racial": HR 159 (BR 2587)—C. Hines, Adopt the Modern Version of "My Old Kentucky Home," 1986 Legislative Record Final Action (April 16, 1986); "House Adopts Revised Lyrics for State Song," *CJ*, March 20, 1986.

207   "in so many areas": Hines, oral history by Herdman.

207 "'People' Preferable": "'People' Preferable in Foster's Lyrics," *Owensboro (Ky.) Messenger-Inquirer,* March 29, 1986.

207 House Resolution 159: Kentucky Revised Statutes 2.100, apps.legisla ture.ky.gov, contains an annotation indicating that resolutions were passed in 1986 substituting a "modern" version of "My Old Kentucky Home," but this in no way changed the original designation of Foster's 1853 melody, adopted in 1928.

208 "it didn't make": Hines, oral history by Herdman.

208 "darkies" became "people": "'People' Preferable in Foster's Lyrics."

208 Kentucky's governor led: John Y. Brown III, interview by author, March 22, 2018.

208 "bespoke poplin suits": John Jeremiah Sullivan, *Blood Horses: Notes of a Sportswriter's Son* (New York: Picador, 2004), 157–58. In Virginia, where the state anthem, "Carry Me Back to Old Virginia," a slight update of James Bland's "Carry Me Back to Old Virginny" (1878), was dropped in 1997, it remains a cherished relic among neo-Confederate groups. One leader wept in describing the tune and defended the minstrel melody as the work of this "Negro Stephen Foster," who knew what life on the plantation was like, who "lived it" and "loved it." Nicole Maurantonio, *Confederate Exceptionalism: Civil War Myth and Memory in the Twenty-First Century* (Lawrence: University Press of Kansas, 2019), 23, 25.

208 "brazen, outright, and above all": Aaron Rosenblum, "Kentucky Derby Stories: When 'My Old Kentucky Home' Was New to Me," Medium, May 1, 2019, medium.com.

209 "different kind of world": Hudson, interview by Betsy Brinson, KOHC, kyoralhistory.com.

209 "I think": Hines, interview by author, Nov. 3, 2010.

210 "And now, for one": A. B. "Happy" Chandler's "My Old Kentucky Home," March 2, 1988, Kentucky Sports Video, www.youtube.com.

210 known for his tendency: Todd Murphy, "Chandler Denies Slur amid Demands He Quit UK Board," *CJ,* March 1, 1989.

210 "as sacred as a hymn": John W. Cowan, "Tribute to the Composer of 'My Old Kentucky Home,'" *Idea,* Jan. 22, 1914. The first use of the song in UK sports I have located dates from a 1913 UK student publication: "Louisville Cardinals Mourn to the Music of 20 to 0," *Idea,* Nov. 27, 1913.

210 "men to do things": "Wildcat Band Receives Praise from Southern Newspapers, Citizens," *Kentucky Kernel,* Nov. 23, 1923.

210 "Southern favorites": "'Wild Cats' Adapted to Victorious Moods," *Kentucky Kernel,* Nov. 1, 1917.

210 "the signature song": Ben Chandler, interview by author, June 21, 2017.

210 "milk it for all": Harry Clarke, interview by author, Jan. 23, 2020.

211 "It was important": Joe B. Hall, *Coach Hall: My Life on and off the Court* (Lexington: University Press of Kentucky, 2019), 1–2.

211 state senator drew up: Mark Story, "Ohio St. 'Dots the i.' Georgia Has 'Uga.' What Is UK Football's Defining Symbol?," *Lexington Herald-Leader,* Aug. 13, 2018.

211 school's true alma mater: Clarke, interview by author, Jan. 23, 2020.

211 "get by": McCorvey, interview by author, May 22, 2018.

211 "with a smile": Dorian Hairston, interview by author, Dec. 13, 2018.

212 "the state song reflected": Ibid.

212 "the bearded tall man": Wendell Berry, "My Great-Grandfather's Slaves," in *Collected Poems, 1957–1982* (San Francisco: North Point Press, 1985), 56.

212 a legacy Berry probed: Wendell Berry, *The Hidden Wound* (1970; Berkeley, Calif.: Counterpoint Press, 1989). The moral wound of slavery scarred both races, Berry wrote, and he lamented the Great Migration of rural Black people along with the subsequent industrialization of agriculture.

213 "great danger that": Wendell Berry, interview by author, April 25, 2017.

213 "of what it is": Frank X Walker, "Oh, Weep No More Today," in *Isaac Murphy: I Dedicate This Ride* (Lexington, Ky.: Old Cove Press, 2010), 41.

213 in 2002 he called: Frank X Walker, "The Song Doesn't Remain the Same: Reflections on My Old Kentucky Home," *Ace Weekly,* Nov. 21, 2002, www.aceweekly.com.

214 racism would "go away": Frank X Walker, interview by author, April 26, 2018.

214 If that was Foster's intent: Walker in "Churchill Downer: The Forgotten Racial History of Kentucky's State Song," *Morning Edition,* May 6, 2016, www.npr.org.

214 "dog whistle": Walker, interview by author, April 26, 2018.

214 Frederick Douglass's forgotten line: Emerson, *Doo-Dah!,* 107.

214 has been seized upon: History Overview, My Old Kentucky Home website, www.visitmyoldkyhome.com, claimed the song was "abolitionist inspired" (this was altered in 2020, as was the Wikipedia page calling "My Old Kentucky Home" an "antislavery ballad"); Kevin Flanery (president of Churchill Downs Racetrack), interview by author, Jan. 24, 2020.

214 "amulet" against critics: Ken Emerson, interview by author, March 11, 2020.

215 "business as usual": Lott, *Love and Theft,* 195.

216 "bridge the gap": Kevin Drane, interview by author, May 8, 2019.

217   "to my *old* Kentucky": Demaree, interview by author, Dec. 16, 2019.

217   "We knew it was a hit": Angie Fenton, "The Buzz," *CJ,* Aug. 24, 2005.

217   it was too "white": Drane, interview by author, May 8, 2019.

218   "You are a mix": Demaree, interview by author, Dec. 16, 2019.

218   "Man, what the fuck": Andre Guess, interview by author, July 1, 2021.

218   "the most sentimental moment": "2002 Kentucky Derby—War Emblem: Broadcast," NBC, www.youtube.com.

218   "the only reason": Guess, interview by author, July 1, 2021.

219   "I did this at home": "My Old Kentucky Home," *Mad Men,* dir. Jennifer Getzinger, aired Aug. 30, 2009.

219   "his politics lightly": TDC, "Slavery Background of Foster's My Old Kentucky Home," 12.

220   "to bring people": Linkin' Bridge website, www.wearelinkinbridge.com.

220   "We never thought about": Jim Davis, interview by author, July 7, 2020.

220   sent it to Churchill Downs: Linkin' Bridge, "My Old Kentucky Home," April 30, 2017, www.youtube.com.

220   After a months-long: Dan Majors, "City's Art Commission Unanimous: Statue of Stephen Foster Needs to Go," *Pittsburgh Post-Gazette,* Oct. 25, 2017.

221   "best version": Jim Davis, interview by author, July 7, 2020.

221   he felt solid telling: Ibid.; the documentary was *Kentucky's Underground Railroad—Passage to Freedom,* dir. Guy Mendes, 2000; for the Foster who was an abolitionist, see "Stephen Symonds Foster," Wikipedia, en.wikipedia.org.

222   "I never heard Muhammad": Lonnie Ali, interview by author, April 28, 2020.

223   "I'm still just": Muhammad Ali, conversation with author, June 31, 2003; Sheldon S. Shafer, "Ali Center Will Feature Public Plaza," *CJ,* July 1, 2003.

223   "the Derby commissioners": Sullivan, *Blood Horses,* 159.

CODA: MY OLD KENTUCKY HOME

224   During his daily pandemic: "Governor Beshear Ends News Conference with Touching Tribute to John Prine," WLKY, April 9, 2020, www.wlky.com.

224   An Owensboro DJ: Keith Lawrence, "Roos Promoting a Mass Sing-along Saturday," *Owensboro (Ky.) Messenger-Inquirer,* April 8, 2020.

224   "One of my favorite": Governor Andy Beshear, Facebook, May 2, 2020, www.facebook.com/watch/?v=1331988690522823.

225 The apartment door: Rukmini Callimachi, "Breonna Taylor's Life Was Changing. Then the Police Came to Her Door," *NYT,* Aug. 30, 2020.

225 might scrap the ritual: Gregory A. Hall, "Churchill Downs Mulls Presentation of 'My Old Kentucky Home,'" *BloodHorse,* Sept. 2, 2020, www.bloodhorse.com.

225 "gunned down": Keith L. Runyon and Eleanor Bingham Miller, "Kentucky Derby: Drop 'My Old Kentucky Home' and Weep for Breonna Taylor," *CJ,* Sept. 2, 2020.

225 "absolutely" to stand by: Mitch McConnell, in Nicole Acevedo, "Kentucky Derby Will Play 'My Old Kentucky Home' Despite Criticism," NBC News, Sept. 5, 2020, www.nbcnews.com.

225 For a small but growing: Joe Gerth, "Kentucky's State Song 'My Old Kentucky Home' Celebrates Slavery and It Needs to Go," *CJ,* May 3, 2019; Hannah Drake, quoted in "Churchill Big on Words, Not Deeds," *LEO Weekly,* Sept. 9, 2020.

225 "This will be a Derby": Churchill Downs Communications, "A Statement to Our Community from Churchill Downs," Sept. 3, 2020, www.kentuckyderby.com.

225 "pause to recognize": Ben Tobin, "Here's What Abolitionist Frederick Douglass Said About 'My Old Kentucky Home' Song," *CJ,* Sept. 5, 2020.

226 "forget social and racial": Robert MacGowan, *The Significance of Stephen Collins Foster* (Indianapolis, 1932), 14.

226 "when the head will": JSC, "A Visit to Federal Hill, Bardstown, Ky.," *Louisville Leader,* Feb. 4, 1922, 8.

227 "everybody's protest novel": James Baldwin, "Everybody's Protest Novel," in *Notes of a Native Son* (Boston: Beacon Press, 1955), 12–15.

227 "the master of the quivering": Hall, "Unknown Stephen Foster," 26.

228 "be an America without": Woollcott, "WABC Cream of Wheat Broadcast," Feb. 17, 1935, Radio Programs boxes, CAM.

229 "Study history realistically": "The League and Gas," *Montgomery (Ala.) Advertiser,* April 21, 1936, quoted in Michaelis, *Eleanor,* 337.

229 segregated memory: Blight, *Race and Reunion,* 2.

BIBLIOGRAPHY

MANUSCRIPT COLLECTIONS

Allison, Young E. Papers. Filson Historical Society, Louisville, Ky.

American Minstrel Show Collection. Harvard Theatre Collection. Houghton Library, Harvard University.

Billy Rose Theatre Division. New York Public Library for the Performing Arts, Dorothy and Lewis B. Cullman Center.

Bingham, Robert Worth. Papers. Filson Historical Society, Louisville, Ky.

———. Papers. Manuscript Division, Library of Congress, Washington, D.C.

Black Student Union Collection. University of Louisville Archives and Special Collections.

Bruce, John E. Papers. New York Public Library Schomburg Center for Research in Black Culture, New York.

Christy, Howard Chandler. Papers. Lafayette College Special Collections.

Clifton Waller Barrett Collection. University of Virginia Library.

Debnam, Waldemar E. Papers. East Carolina Manuscript Collection. East Carolina University.

Eleanor Roosevelt Papers Project. Department of History. Columbian College of Arts and Sciences, Washington, D.C.

Eli Lilly and Company Archive, Indianapolis.

First Unitarian Church Records Collection. Filson Historical Society, Louisville, Ky.

Foster, Stephen Collins. Papers. University of Kentucky Special Collections.

Foster Hall Collection. Center for American Music, University of Pittsburgh.

Furlong, William Rea. Papers. Naval Historical Foundation Collection. Manuscript Division, Library of Congress, Washington, D.C.

Jan Peerce Collection of Sound Recordings. Rodgers and Hammerstein Archives of Recorded Sound. New York Public Library for the Performing Arts, Dorothy and Lewis B. Cullman Center.

Kentucky Derby Museum Permanent Collection. Kentucky Derby Museum, Louisville, Ky.

Kentucky Oral History Commission Collection. Civil Rights Movement in Kentucky Oral History Project. Kentucky Historical Society, Frankfort, Ky.

LaBree, Benjamin L. Papers. Filson Historical Society, Louisville, Ky.

Lafferty, Maude Ward. Papers. University of Kentucky Special Collections.

Lilly, Josiah Kirby. Correspondence. Center for American Music, University of Pittsburgh.

My Old Kentucky Home State Park Archives, Bardstown, Ky.

New York Public Library for the Performing Arts, Dorothy and Lewis B. Cullman Center.

Otto A. Rothert Collection on Young Ewing Allison. Filson Historical Society, Louisville, Ky.

Perley, Martin. Papers. Filson Historical Society, Louisville, Ky.

Radio Programs. Center for American Music, University of Pittsburgh.

Rebecca Carnes Rowan Collection. Western Kentucky University Manuscript and Folk Life Archives.

Rowan Family Papers. Western Kentucky University Manuscript and Folk Life Archives.

Salsbury, Nate. Papers. Beinecke Rare Book and Manuscript Library, Yale University.

South Before the War Company. Papers. Irving S. Gilmore Music Library, Yale University.

Stanley, Osso Willis. Papers. Filson Historical Society, Louisville, Ky.

United Daughters of the Confederacy Collection. Kentucky Historical Society, Frankfort, Ky.

PLAYS AND FILMS

Black America, 1895.

Bradford, Joseph. *Out of Bondage*. Manuscript Plays Collection. Library of Congress Copyright Office, 1876.

Butler, David, dir. *The Little Colonel*. Fox Film, 1935.

Cressy, William. *My Old Kentucky Home*. Harvard Theatre Collection. Houghton Library, Harvard University, 1906.

Fleming, Victor, dir. *Gone with the Wind*. Metro-Goldwyn-Mayer, 1939.

Ford, John. *The Sun Shines Bright*. Argosy Pictures, 1953.

Freleng, Friz. *Southern Fried Rabbit*. Warner Bros., 1953.

Getzinger, Jennifer, dir. "My Old Kentucky Home." *Mad Men*, Aug. 30, 2009.

Green, Paul. *The Stephen Foster Story: A Symphonic Drama Based on the Life and Music of the Composer*. New York: Samuel French, 1960.

Lanfield, Sidney, dir. *Swanee River*. 20th Century Fox, 1939.

Mendez, Guy, dir. *Kentucky's Underground Railroad—Passage to Freedom.* Kentucky Educational TV, 2000.

Nathan, John, dir. "The Colonel Comes to Japan." *Enterprise,* 1981.

Pollard, Harry A., dir. *Uncle Tom's Cabin.* Universal Studios, 1927.

Santley, Joseph, dir. *Harmony Lane.* Mascot Pictures, 1935.

The South Before the War, 1892.

BOOKS, ARTICLES, THESES, AND DISSERTATIONS

Abbott, Lynn, and Doug Seroff. *Out of Sight: The Rise of African American Popular Music, 1889–1895.* Jackson: University Press of Mississippi, 2009.

———. *Ragged but Right: Black Traveling Shows, "Coon Songs," and the Dark Pathway to Blues and Jazz.* Jackson: University Press of Mississippi, 2012.

Abramson, Samuel. "Disorder at the Derby: Race, Reputation, and Louisville's 1967 Open Housing Crisis." *Ohio Valley History* 15, no. 2 (Summer 2015): 28–48.

Alexander, J. Heywood, ed. *To Stretch Our Ears: A Documentary History of America's Music.* New York: W. W. Norton, 2002.

Alexander, Michael. *Jazz Age Jews.* Princeton, N.J.: Princeton University Press, 2001.

Allison, Young E. "'My Old Kentucky Home': The Song and the Story." *Courier-Journal Sunday Magazine,* April 10, 1921.

———. *Select Works of Young E. Allison.* Louisville, Ky.: John P. Morton, 1935.

———. *Stephen C. Foster and American Songs.* Louisville, Ky.: Insurance Field, 1920.

Allison, Young E., and Robert Louis Stevenson. "Derelict." Erich's Songbook. www.americanradioworks.org.

Anderson, Colin L. "Segregation, Popular Culture, and the Southern Pastoral: The Spatial and Racial Politics of American Sheet Music, 1870–1900." *Journal of Southern History* 85 (Aug. 2019): 577–610.

Ashe, Samuel A., ed. *Biographical History of North Carolina, from Colonial Times to the Present.* Greensboro, N.C.: C. L. Van Noppen, 1905.

"At Churchill Downs." *Time,* May 16, 1932.

Austin, William W. *"Susanna," "Jeanie," and "The Old Folks at Home": The Songs of Stephen C. Foster from His Time to Ours.* New York: Macmillan, 1975.

Bailey, Candace. "Binder's Volumes as Musical Commonplace Books: The Transmission of Cultural Codes in the Antebellum South." *Journal of the Society for American Music* 10 (Nov. 2016): 446–69.

Baldwin, James. *Notes of a Native Son.* Boston: Beacon Press, 1955.

Baptist, Edward E. *The Half Has Never Been Told: Slavery and the Making of American Capitalism.* New York: Basic Books, 2014.

Barnes, Rhae Lynn. "Darkology: The Hidden History of Amateur Blackface Minstrelsy and the Making of Modern America, 1860–1970." PhD diss., Harvard University, 2016.

Barnum, Matt. "Critics of Vouchers Say They Are Marred by Racism and Exacerbate Segregation. Are They Right?" *Chalkbeat,* July 23, 2017. www .chalkbeat.org.

Bean, Annemarie, et al., eds. *Inside the Minstrel Mask: Readings in Nineteenth-Century Blackface Minstrelsy.* Middletown, Conn.: Wesleyan University Press, 1996.

Beatty, Paul. *The Sellout.* New York: Farrar, Straus and Giroux, 2016.

Beckert, Sven, and Seth Rockman, eds. *Slavery's Capitalism: A New History of American Economic Development.* Philadelphia: University of Pennsylvania Press, 2016.

Bell, Rick. *The Great Flood of 1937.* Louisville, Ky.: Butler Books, 2007.

Berg, Manfred. *Popular Justice: A History of Lynching in America.* Lanham, Md.: Ivan R. Dee, 2011.

Bernard, André. *Now All We Need Is a Title: Famous Book Titles and How They Got That Way.* New York: W. W. Norton, 1997.

Berry, Dorothy. "Black America, 1895." *Public Domain Review,* Feb. 24, 2021. publicdomainreview.org.

Berry, Wendell. *Collected Poems, 1957–1982.* San Francisco: North Point Press, 1985.

———. *The Hidden Wound.* 1970. Berkeley, Calif.: Counterpoint Press, 1989.

Bingham, Emily. "'Let's Buy It!': Tourism and the My Old Kentucky Home Campaign in Jim Crow Kentucky." *Ohio Valley History* 19 (Fall 2019): 27–56.

Birdwhistell, Terry L. "WHAS Radio and the Development of Broadcasting in Kentucky, 1922–1942." *Register of the Kentucky Historical Society* 79 (Autumn 1981): 333–53.

Black, Shirley Temple. *Child Star: An Autobiography.* New York: McGraw-Hill, 1988.

"Bless Stephen Foster." *Forbes,* June 16, 1986, 163.

Blight, David. *Frederick Douglass: Prophet of Freedom.* New York: Simon & Schuster, 2018.

———. *Race and Reunion: The Civil War in American Memory.* Cambridge, Mass.: Harvard University Press, 2002.

Bogle, Donald. *Bright Boulevards, Bold Dreams: The Story of Black Hollywood.* New York: Ballantine Books, 2005.

Boni, Margaret Bradford. *Fireside Book of Folk Songs.* New York: Simon & Schuster, 1947.

Boots, Cheryl C. *Singing for Equality: Hymns in the Anti-slavery Movements, 1640–1855.* Jefferson, N.C.: McFarland, 2013.

Borton, Terry, and Deborah Borton. *Before the Movies.* New Barnet, U.K.: John Libbey, 2014.

"The Boston Songs." *Crisis* 9 (Jan. 1915): 128.

Bourne, Stephen. *Butterfly McQueen Remembered.* Lanham, Md.: Scarecrow Press, 2008.

Bowman, John G. *Unofficial Notes.* Pittsburgh: privately printed, 1963.

Braden, Anne. *The Wall Between.* 1958. Knoxville: University of Tennessee Press, 1999.

Brundage, W. Fitzhugh. *The Southern Past: A Clash of Race and Memory.* Cambridge, Mass.: Harvard University Press, 2005.

Buckner, Jocelyn L. "Spectacular Opacities: The Hyers Sisters' Performances of Respectability and Resistance." *African American Review* 45 (Fall 2012): 309–23.

Budiansky, Stephen. *The Bloody Shirt: Terror After the Civil War.* New York: Penguin, 2008.

Capps, Randall. *The Rowan Story: From Federal Hill to My Old Kentucky Home.* Cincinnati: Creative Company, 1976.

Cather, Willa. *My Ántonia.* Boston: Houghton Mifflin, 1918.

Chandler, A. B. *Heroes, Plain Folks, and Skunks: The Life and Times of Happy Chandler.* With Vance H. Trimble. Chicago: Bonus Books, 1989.

Chrisman, Martha Carol. "Popular Songs of the Genteel Tradition: Their Influence on Education in Public Schools of Louisville, Kentucky, 1850–1880." PhD diss., University of Michigan, 1985.

Clark, Thomas D. "My Old Kentucky Home in Retrospect." *Filson Club History Quarterly* 22 (April 1948): 104–16.

———. "The Slavery Background of Foster's My Old Kentucky Home." *Filson Club History Quarterly* 10 (Jan. 1936): 1–17.

Coates, Ta-Nehisi. "The Case for Reparations." *Atlantic,* June 2014, 54–71.

Cockrell, Dale. *Demons of Disorder: Blackface Minstrels and Their World.* New York: Cambridge University Press, 1997.

"Colonel Eli Lilly (1838–1898)." *Lilly Archives* (Jan. 2008): 1–6.

Conner, Catherine. *From My Old Kentucky Home to the White House: The Political Journey of Catherine Conner.* 1999. Lexington: University Press of Kentucky, 2015.

Cooke, Chauncey. *Soldier Boy's Letters to His Father and Mother, 1861–1865.* Independence, Wis.: News-Office, 1915.

Corum, Bill. *Off and Running.* New York: Henry Holt, 1959.

Courrier, Kevin. *Randy Newman's American Dreams.* Toronto: ECW Press, 2005.

Cox, Karen L. *Dixie's Daughters: The United Daughters of the Confederacy and the Preservation of Confederate Culture.* Gainesville: University Press of Florida, 2003.

———. *Dreaming of Dixie: How the South Was Created in American Popular Culture.* Chapel Hill: University of North Carolina Press, 2013.

Cripps, Thomas. *Slow Fade to Black: The Negro in American Film, 1900–1942.* New York: Oxford University Press, 1977.

Cummings, William A. "Groping in the Dark: An Early History of WHAS Radio." Master's thesis, University of Louisville, 2012.

Cushing, Rick. "Out of Tragedy, a Kind of Anthem." *Louisville,* April 1975, 96–97, 99.

Darity, William. "Many Roads Lead to Extinction: Early AEA Economists and the Black Disappearance Hypothesis." *History of Economics* 21 (Jan. 1994): 47–64.

Debnam, Waldemar E. *Then My Old Kentucky Home, Good Night!* Raleigh, N.C.: Graphic Press, 1955.

———. *Weep No More, My Lady.* Raleigh, N.C.: Graphic Press, 1950.

Deford, Frank. "The Sun Shines Bright." *Sports Illustrated,* April 1974, 80–92.

Delany, Martin. *Blake; or, The Huts of America.* N.p., 1861–1862.

Dennison, Sam. *Scandalize My Name: Black Imagery in American Popular Music.* New York: Garland, 1982.

Dingwall, Chris. "The Sale of Slavery: Memory, Culture, and the Renewal of America, 1877–1920." PhD diss., University of Chicago, 2015.

Dormon, James H. "Shaping the Popular Image of Post-Reconstruction American Blacks: The 'Coon Song' Phenomenon of the Gilded Age." *American Quarterly* 40 (Dec. 1988): 450–71.

Douglass, Frederick. *The Anti-slavery Movement: A Lecture by Frederick Douglass Before the Rochester Ladies' Anti-slavery Society.* Rochester, N.Y.: Press of Lee, Mann, 1855.

———. Introduction to *The Reason Why the Colored American Is Not in the World's Columbian Exposition.* Chicago: Ida B. Wells, 1893.

Dowling, Elizabeth Taylor. *The Original Black Elite: Daniel Murray and the Story of a Forgotten Era.* New York: Amistad, 2017.

Du Bois, W. E. B. "The American Negro at Paris." *American Monthly Review of Reviews,* Nov. 1900, 575–77.

———. *Black Lives 1900: W. E. B. Du Bois and the Paris Exposition.* London: Redstone Press, 2019.

Eaklor, Vicki Lynn. *American Antislavery Songs: A Collection and Analysis.* Westport, Conn.: Greenwood, 1988.

Elliker, Calvin. *Stephen Collins Foster: A Guide to Research.* New York: Garland, 1988.

Emerson, Ken. *Doo-Dah! Stephen Foster and the Rise of American Popular Culture.* New York: Da Capo Press, 1998.

Equal Justice Initiative. *Lynching in America: Confronting the Legacy of Racial Terror.* 3rd ed. Montgomery, Ala.: Equal Justice Initiative, 2017.

Ermolaeva, Katya. "Dinah, Put Down Your Horn: Blackface Minstrel Songs Don't Belong in Music Class." *GEN,* Oct. 13, 2019. gen.medium.com.

Evans, James W. *Entertaining the American Army: The American Stage and Lyceum in the World War.* New York: Association Press, 1921.

Evans, Nicholas M. "'Racial Cross-Dressing' in the Jazz Age: Cultural Therapy and Its Discontents in Cabaret Nightlife." In *Hop of Pop: The Politics and Pleasures of Popular Culture,* edited by Henry Jenkins, Tara McPherson, and Jane Shattuc, 388–414. Durham, N.C.: Duke University Press, 2002.

Fields, Mamie Garvin. *Lemon Swamp and Other Places: A Carolina Memoir.* New York: Free Press, 1985.

Figliulo, Joseph. "'Dear Friends and Gentle Hearts': The Ironic Relationship Between American Copyright Law and the Artist." *University of Pittsburgh Law Review* (Winter 1999): 641–60.

Finch, Francis Miles. "The Blue and the Gray." *Atlantic,* Sept. 1867, 369.

Fletcher, Tom. *100 Years of the Negro in Show Business.* 1954. New York: Da Capo Press, 1984.

Flink, James J. *The Automobile Age.* Cambridge, Mass.: MIT Press, 1990.

Foner, Eric. *Gateway to Freedom: The Hidden History of the Underground Railroad.* New York: W. W. Norton, 2015.

Foster, Morrison. *Biography, Songs, and Musical Compositions of Stephen C. Foster, Author of "The Old Folks at Home."* Pittsburgh: Percy F. Smith, 1896.

———. *My Brother Stephen.* Indianapolis: Foster Hall, 1932.

Foster, Stephen Collins. *My Old Kentucky Home.* Illustrated by Charles Copeland and Mary Hallock Foote. Boston: Ticknor and Fields, 1887.

———. *Songs of Stephen Foster for the U.S. Armed Forces.* Pittsburgh: University of Pittsburgh Press, 1942.

———. *Songs of Stephen Foster: Prepared for Schools and General Use.* Edited by Will Earhart and Edward B. Birge. 1934. Pittsburgh: University of Pittsburgh Press, 1938.

Frick, John W. *"Uncle Tom's Cabin" on the American Stage and Screen.* New York: Palgrave Macmillan, 2012.

Gac, Scott. *Singing for Freedom: The Hutchinson Family Singers.* New Haven, Conn.: Yale University Press, 2007.

Gilbert, Richard. "'My Old Kentucky Home' Netted Foster $1,372." *Kentucky Progress Magazine* 4 (Sept. 1931): 18–19, 42.

Gossett, Thomas E. *"Uncle Tom's Cabin" and American Culture.* Dallas: Southern Methodist University Press, 2005.

Grant, Colin. *Negro in a Hat: The Rise and Fall of Marcus Garvey.* New York: Oxford University Press, 2010.

Gray, Karen R., and Sarah R. Yates. "Boss John Whallen: The Early Louisville Years (1876–1883)." *Journal of Kentucky Studies* 1 (July 1984): 171–86.

Graziano, John. "The Early Life and Career of the 'Black Patti': The Odyssey of an African American Singer in the Late Nineteenth Century." *Journal of the American Musicological Society* 53 (Oct. 2000): 543–96.

Greenberg, Cheryl Lynn. *To Ask for an Equal Chance: African Americans in the Great Depression.* New York: Rowman & Littlefield, 2010.

Hackley, E. Azalia. *The Colored Girl Beautiful.* Kansas City, Mo.: Burton, 1916.

Haines, Kathryn Miller. "Stephen Foster's Music in Motion Pictures and Television." *American Music* 30 (Fall 2012): 373–88.

Hall, Dale E. "The Unknown Stephen Foster." *American Music Teacher* 26 (Feb.–March 1977): 25–27.

Hall, Gregory A. "Churchill Downs Mulls Presentation of 'My Old Kentucky Home.'" *BloodHorse,* Sept. 2020. www.bloodhorse.com.

Hall, Joe B. *Coach Hall: My Life on and off the Court.* Lexington: University Press of Kentucky, 2019.

Hall, Roger Allen. "'Black America': Nate Salsbury's Afro-American Exhibition." *Educational Theatre Journal* 29 (1977): 49–60.

Hall, Wade. *The Rest of the Dream: The Black Odyssey of Lyman T. Johnson.* Lexington: University Press of Kentucky, 1988.

Hamill, Kyna. "'The Story I Must Tell': 'Jingle Bells' in the Minstrel Repertoire." *Theatre Survey* 58 (2017): 375–403.

Hamm, Charles. *Yesterdays: Popular Song in America.* New York: W. W. Norton, 1978.

Harris, Credo Fitch. *Microphone Memoirs of the Horse and Buggy Days of Radio.* New York: Bobbs-Merrill, 1937.

Harrison, Lowell H., and James C. Klotter. *A New History of Kentucky.* Lexington: University Press of Kentucky, 1997.

Hartman, Saidiya V. *Scenes of Subjection: Terror, Slavery, and Self-Making in Nineteenth-Century America.* New York: Oxford University Press, 1997.

Haskins, Jim, and N. R. Mitgang. *Mr. Bojangles: The Biography of Bill Robinson.* New York: William Morrow, 1988.

Hatch, Kristen. *Shirley Temple and the Performance of Girlhood.* New Brunswick, N.J.: Rutgers University Press, 2015.

Hill, Errol. "The Hyers Sisters: Pioneers in Black Musical Comedy." In *The American Stage,* edited by Ron Engle and Tice Miller, 115–30. Cambridge, U.K.: Cambridge University Press, 1993.

———. *Shakespeare in Sable: A History of Black Shakespearean Actors.* Amherst: University of Massachusetts Press, 1984.

Hill, Errol, and James V. Hatch. *A History of African American Theater.* New York: Cambridge University Press, 2003.

Hoagland, Alison K. *The Log Cabin: An American Icon.* Charlottesville: University of Virginia Press, 2019.

Hodges, Fletcher. "A Pittsburgh Composer and His Memorial." *Western Pennsylvania Historical Magazine* 21 (1938): 3–32.

———. Review of "Swanee River." *Foster Hall Bulletin,* July 4, 1940, 5.

Hopkins, Walter Lee, ed. *Year Book and Minutes of the Annual Convention of the Sons of Confederate Veterans.* Richmond, Va.: Dudley Printing, 1926.

Horton, Mrs. Thaddeus. "Romances of Some Southern Homes." *Ladies' Home Journal,* Sept. 1900, 9–10.

Hosmer, Charles B. *Presence of the Past: A History of the Preservation Movement in the United States Before Williamsburg.* New York: G. P. Putnam and Sons, 1965.

Howard, John Tasker. *Our American Music.* New York: Thomas Y. Crowell, 1929.

———. *Stephen Foster, America's Troubadour.* New York: Thomas Y. Crowell, 1934.

Hughes, R. E. *Kentucky the Beautiful.* Chicago: Corbitt Railway Printing, 1901.

———. *That Kentucky Campaign; or, The Law, the Ballot, and the People in the Goebel-Taylor Contest.* Cincinnati: R. Clarke, 1900.

Hugill, Peter J. "Good Roads and the Automobile in the United States, 1880–1929." *Geographical Review* 72 (July 1982): 327–49.

Ingram, Tammy. *Dixie Highway: Road Building and the Making of the Modern South, 1900–1930.* Chapel Hill: University of North Carolina Press, 2014.

"In the Gloaming." *Illustrated American,* June 29, 1895, 826–28.

"Is There Anyone Finah?" *Time,* Dec. 16, 1957. content.time.com.

Jacobs, Harriet. *Incidents in the Life of a Slave Girl: Written by Herself.* 1861. New York: Penguin Books, 2000.

James, Henry. *A Small Boy and Others.* New York: Scribner's, 1913.

Jarrell, Michelle C. "Colonel Eli Lilly: The Right Man for the Job." *Traces: Magazine of the Indiana Historical Society* 29 (Winter 2017): 44–55.

Jillson, Willard Rouse. *The Old Kentucky Home: An Historical Sketch of the Old Bardstown Country Homestead of John Rowan.* Frankfort, Ky., 1921.

Johnson, Charles W. *Songs of the Nation: Patriotic and National.* Boston: Silver, Burdette, 1912.

Johnson, Erleen. "Stephen Foster's Music in Japan." *Music Clubs Magazine* (Winter 2000): 21–22.

Karpf, Juanita. "The Vocal Teacher of Ten Thousand: Emma Azalia Hackley as Community Music Educator, 1910–1922." *Journal of Research on Musical Education* 47 (Winter 1999): 319–30.

Kasson, John F. *The Little Girl Who Fought the Great Depression: Shirley Temple and 1930s America.* New York: W. W. Norton, 2014.

Kimber, Marian Wilson. *The Elocutionists: Women, Music, and the Spoken Word.* Urbana: University of Illinois Press, 2017.

Kiner, Larry F., and Philip R. Evans, eds. *Al Jolson: A Bio Discography.* Metuchen, N.J.: Scarecrow Press, 1992.

King, Edward. *The Great South.* Hartford: American Publishing, 1875.

Kipen, David, ed. *Dear Los Angeles: The City in Diaries and Letters, 1542 to 2018.* New York: Modern Library, 2018.

Klotter, James C. *Kentucky: Portrait in Paradox, 1900–1950.* Frankfort: Kentucky Historical Society, 1996.

Klotter, James C., and Craig Thompson Friend. *A New History of Kentucky.* 2nd ed. Lexington: University Press of Kentucky, 2018.

K'Meyer, Tracy E. *Civil Rights in the Gateway to the South: Louisville, Kentucky, 1945–1980.* Lexington: University Press of Kentucky, 2009.

Krystal, Arthur. "Slow Fade: F. Scott Fitzgerald in Hollywood." *New Yorker,* Nov. 16, 2009, 36–41.

Krythe, Maymie. *Sampler of American Songs.* New York: Harper & Row, 1972.

Lehman, Christopher P. *The Colored Cartoon: Black Representation in American Animated Short Films, 1907–1954.* Amherst: University of Massachusetts Press, 2007.

Lightweiss-Goff, Jennie. "'Long Time I Trabble on de Way': Stephen Foster's Conversion Narrative." *Journal of Popular Music Studies* 20 (June 2008): 150–65.

Lott, Eric. *Love and Theft: Blackface Minstrelsy and the American Working Class.* New York: Oxford University Press, 1993.

Lucas, Marion B. *A History of Blacks in Kentucky: From Slavery to Segregation, 1760–1891.* 1992. Lexington: University Press of Kentucky, 2003.

Luskey, Brian P. "Jumping Counters in White Collars: Manliness, Respectability, and Work in the Antebellum City." *Journal of the Early Republic* 26 (Summer 2006): 173–219.

Lynch, Christopher. "Stephen Foster and the Slavery Question." *American Music* 39, no. 4 (forthcoming, Winter 2021).

MacGowan, Robert. *The Significance of Stephen Collins Foster.* Indianapolis, 1932.

Madison, James H. *Eli Lilly: A Life, 1885–1977.* Indianapolis: Indiana Historical Society, 1989.

Malone, Bill C. "William S. Hays: The Bard of Kentucky." *Register of the Kentucky Historical Society* 93 (Summer 1995): 286–306.

Malone, Jacqui. *Steppin' on the Blues: The Visible Rhythms of African American Dance.* Urbana: University of Illinois Press, 1996.

Manring, Maurice. *Slave in a Box: The Strange Career of Aunt Jemima*. Charlottesville: University Press of Virginia, 1998.

Marcus, Greil. *Mystery Train: Images of America in Rock and Roll Music*. 1975. New York: Plume, 2015.

Margolick, David. *Strange Fruit: Billie Holiday and the Biography of a Song*. New York: Ecco, 2001.

Marks, Carole, and Diane Edkins. *The Power of Pride: Stylemakers and Rulebreakers of the Harlem Renaissance*. New York: Crown, 1999.

Marshall, Anne E. *Creating a Confederate Kentucky: The Lost Cause and Civil War Memory in a Border State*. Chapel Hill: University of North Carolina Press, 2010.

Matt, Susan J. *Homesickness: An American History*. New York: Oxford University Press, 2011.

Matthews, Donald G. *At the Altar of Lynching: Burning Sam Hose in the American South*. New York: Cambridge University Press, 2017.

Maurantonio, Nicole. *Confederate Exceptionalism: Civil War Myth and Memory in the Twenty-First Century*. Lawrence: University Press of Kansas, 2019.

McIntyre, Rebecca. *Souvenirs of the Old South: Northern Tourism and Southern Mythology*. Gainesville: University Press of Florida, 2011.

McKelway, St. Clair. "Profiles: Bojangles—1." *New Yorker*, Oct. 6, 1934, 26–28.

McWhirter, Christian. *Battle Hymns: The Power and Popularity of Music in the Civil War*. Chapel Hill: University of North Carolina Press, 2012.

Meer, Sarah. *Uncle Tom Mania: Slavery, Minstrelsy, and Transatlantic Culture in the 1850s*. Athens: University of Georgia Press, 2005.

Michaelis, David. *Eleanor*. New York: Simon & Schuster, 2020.

Milligan, Harold Vincent. *Stephen Collins Foster: A Biography of America's Folk-Song Composer*. New York: G. Schirmer, 1920.

Mitchell, Mrs. A. L. *Songs of the Confederacy and Plantation Melodies*. Cincinnati: George B. Jennings, 1901.

Mitchell, Margaret. *Gone with the Wind*. 1936. New York: Macmillan, 1965.

Miyashita, Kazuko. "Foster's Songs in Japan." *American Music* 30 (Fall 2012): 308–25.

Morgan, Joy Elmer. *The American Citizens Handbook*. Washington, D.C.: National Education Association, 1941.

Morneweck, Evelyn Foster. *Chronicles of Stephen Foster's Family*. 2 vols. Pittsburgh: University of Pittsburgh Press, 1944.

Morrison, Matthew D. "Race, Blacksound, and the (Re)Making of Musicological Discourse." *Journal of the American Musicological Society* 72 (Fall 2019): 781–823.

Morrison, Toni. *The Bluest Eye*. 1970. New York: Vintage, 2007.

Muhammad, Khalil Gibran. *The Condemnation of Blackness: Race, Crime, and the Making of Modern Urban America.* Cambridge, Mass.: Harvard University Press, 2010.

"My Old Kentucky Home." *American Art Journal,* June 20, 1896, 165.

Nevin, Robert. "Stephen C. Foster and Negro Minstrelsy." *Atlantic Monthly,* Nov. 1867, 608–16.

Nicholson, James C. *The Kentucky Derby: How the Run for the Roses Became America's Premier Sporting Event.* Lexington: University Press of Kentucky, 2012.

Oberfirst, Robert. *Al Jolson: You Ain't Heard Nothin' Yet.* London: Barnes, 1980.

"Obituary, Not Eulogistic." *Dwight's Journal of Music* 13 (July 1858): 118.

Onofrio, Jan. *Tennessee Biographical Dictionary.* New York: Somerset Publishers, 1999.

Osgood, Henry O. *So This Is Jazz.* New York: Little, Brown, 1926.

Patton, Stacey. "In America Black Children Don't Get to Be Children." *Washington Post,* Nov. 26, 2014. www.washingtonpost.com.

Perry, Imani. *May We Forever Stand: A History of the Black National Anthem.* Chapel Hill: University of North Carolina Press, 2018.

Pilapil, Virgilio R. "Dogtown USA: An Igorot Legacy in the United States." *Journal of the Filipino American National Historical Society* 2 (1992). faculty .webster.edu.

Pilgrim, David. *Understanding Jim Crow: Using Racist Memorabilia to Teach Tolerance and Promote Social Justice.* Oakland: PM Press, 2015.

Povenzo, Eugene, Jr., et al., eds. *The Textbook as Discourse: Sociocultural Dimensions of American Schoolbooks.* New York: Routledge, 2011.

Raines, Jimmy Dalton. "Samuel S. Sanford and Negro Minstrelsy." PhD diss., Tulane University, 1967.

Ralph, Julian. *Dixie; or, Southern Scenes and Sketches.* New York: Harper & Brothers, 1895.

Rankine, Claudia. *Just Us.* Minneapolis: Graywolf Press, 2020.

Rapée, Ernö. *Motion Picture Moods for Pianists and Organists.* New York: G. Schirmer, 1924.

Reed, Bill. *Hot from Harlem: Profiles in Classic African American Entertainment.* Los Angeles: Cellar Door Books, 1998.

Rice, Edward Le Roi. *Monarchs of Minstrelsy: From "Daddy" Rice to Date.* New York: Kenny, 1911.

Roberts, Brian. *Blackface Nation: Race, Reform, and Identity in American Popular Music, 1812–1925.* Chicago: University of Chicago Press, 2017.

Robson, Thomas. "A More Aggressive Plantation Play: Henrietta Vinton Davis and John Edward Bruce Collaborate on *Our Old Kentucky Home.*" *Theatre History Studies* 32 (2012): 120–40.

Roediger, David R. *The Wages of Whiteness: Race and the Making of the American Working Class.* New York: Oxford University Press, 1993.

Rogers, Ibram H. *The Black Campus Movement: Black Students and the Racial Reconstruction of Higher Education, 1965–1972.* New York: Palgrave Macmillan, 2012.

Rogers, Stephanie E. Jones. *They Were Her Property: White Women as Slave Owners in the American South.* New Haven, Conn.: Yale University Press, 2019.

Rogin, Michael. *Blackface, White Noise: Jewish Immigrants in the Hollywood Melting Pot.* Berkeley: University of California Press, 1998.

Roosevelt, Eleanor. "My Day." Feb. 6, 1950. erpapers.columbian.gwu.edu.

Root, Deane L. "The 'Mythstory' of Stephen C. Foster or Why His True Story Remains Untold." *American Music Research Center Journal* 15 (2005): 20–36.

Root, George F. *Story of a Musical Life: An Autobiography.* Cincinnati: John Church, 1891.

Rose, Jessie Welch. "Grandmother Was Jeanie with the Light Brown Hair." *Courier-Journal Magazine,* Aug. 5, 1962.

Rosenblum, Aaron. "Kentucky Derby Stories: When 'My Old Kentucky Home' Was New to Me." Medium, May 1, 2019. medium.com.

Rothert, Otto. "Young E. Allison Memorial Meeting, Henderson, 1933." *Filson Club History Quarterly* 7 (1933): 181–204.

Rouleau, Brian. *With Sails Whitening Every Sea: Mariners and the Making of an American Maritime Empire.* Ithaca, N.Y.: Cornell University Press, 2014.

Rule, Lucien V. *The Light Bearers: Home Mission Heroes of Presbyterian History: Centennial Story of an Old Country Church and Neighborhood in the Presbytery of Louisville.* Louisville, Ky.: Brandt, Connors and Fowler, 1926.

Rydell, Robert. *All the World's a Fair: Visions of Empire at American International Expositions, 1876–1916.* Chicago: University of Chicago Press, 1984.

Sammond, Nicholas. *Birth of an Industry: Blackface Minstrelsy and the Rise of American Animation.* Durham, N.C.: Duke University Press, 2015.

Sampson, Henry T. *Blacks in Blackface: A Sourcebook on Early Black Musical Shows.* Metuchen, N.J.: Scarecrow Press, 1980.

———. *The Ghost Walks: A Chronological History of Blacks in Show Business, 1865–1900.* Metuchen, N.J.: Scarecrow Press, 1988.

Saunders, Steven. "The Social Agenda of Stephen Foster's Plantation Melodies." *American Music* 30 (Fall 2012): 282.

Schenbeck, Lawrence. *Racial Uplift and American Music, 1878–1943.* Jackson: University Press of Mississippi, 2012.

Schneider, Mark. *Boston Confronts Jim Crow.* Lebanon, N.H.: University Press of New England, 1977.

Scott, Walter. *The Lay of the Last Minstrel.* 1805. Austell, Ga.: Palala Press, 2016.

Sears, John F. *Sacred Places: American Tourist Attractions in the Nineteenth Century.* Amherst: University of Massachusetts Press, 1999.

Seraile, William. "Henrietta Vinton Davis and the Garvey Movement." *Afro Americans in New York Life and History* 7 (July 1983): 7–24.

———, ed. *Bruce Grit: The Black Nationalist Writings of John Edward Bruce.* Knoxville: University of Tennessee Press, 2003.

Shadle, Douglas W. *Antonín Dvořák's "New World Symphony."* New York: Oxford University Press, 2021.

Shaffer, Marguerite. *See America First: Tourism and National Identity, 1880–1940.* Washington, D.C.: Smithsonian Institution Press, 2001.

Silber, Nina. *Romance of Reunion: Northerners and the South, 1865–1900.* Chapel Hill: University of North Carolina Press, 1997.

Sillin, Sarah. "Seduction's Offspring: Resisting Sentimental Violence from Wilson to Wells." *African American Review* 52 (Fall 2019): 277–92.

Slobin, Mark, et al., eds. *Emily's Songbook: Music in 1850s Albany.* Middletown, Wis.: A-R Editions, 2011.

Small, Stephen. "Still Back of the Big House: Slave Cabins and Slavery in Southern Heritage Tourism." *Tourism Geographies* 15 (2013): 405–23.

Smith, Harry. *Fifty Years of Slavery in the United States of America.* Grand Rapids: West Michigan Printing, 1891.

Smith, K. Annabelle. "Why Japan Is Obsessed with Kentucky Fried Chicken for Christmas." *Smithsonian,* Dec. 14, 2012. www.smithsonianmag.com.

Smith, Mark M. "'All Is Not Quiet in Our Hellish County': Facts, Fiction, Politics, and Race in the Ellenton Riot of 1876." *South Carolina Historical Magazine* 95 (April 1994): 142–55.

Smolko, Joanna R. "Southern Fried Foster: Representing Race and Place Through Music in Looney Tunes Cartoons." *American Music* 30 (Fall 2012): 344–72.

Southern, Eileen. *The Music of Black Americans: A History.* New York: W. W. Norton, 1983.

Sprang, Dennis G. *America Ascendant: The Rise of American Exceptionalism.* Lincoln: University of Nebraska Press, 2019.

Starr, S. Frederick. *Bamboula! The Life and Times of Louis Moreau Gottschalk.* New York: Oxford University Press, 1995.

Stowe, Harriet Beecher. *Uncle Tom's Cabin; or, Life Among the Lowly.* Boston: John P. Jewett, 1852.

Sullivan, John Jeremiah. *Blood Horses: Notes of a Sportswriter's Son.* New York: Picador, 2004.

Tawa, Nicholas E. *Sweet Songs for Gentle Americans: The Parlor Song in America, 1790–1860.* Madison: University of Wisconsin Press, 1980.

Taylor, Yuval, and Jake Austen. *Darkest America: Black Minstrelsy from Slavery to Hip-Hop.* New York: W. W. Norton, 2012.

Thomas, Samuel. *Churchill Downs: A Documentary History of America's Most Legendary Racetrack.* Louisville, Ky.: Kentucky Derby Museum, 1995.

———, ed. *Barry Bingham: A Man of His Word.* Lexington: University Press of Kentucky, 1993.

Thompson, Hunter S. "The Kentucky Derby Is Decadent and Depraved." In *The Great Shark Hunt.* New York: Summit Books, 1979.

Thompson, Tommy R. "The Image of Appalachian Kentucky in American Popular Magazines." *Register of the Kentucky Historical Society* 91 (Spring 1993): 176–202.

Tifft, Susan E., and Alex S. Jones. *The Patriarch: The Rise and Fall of the Bingham Dynasty.* New York: Summit Books, 1991.

Tochka, Nick. "The Battle over 'America's Troubadour.'" *Van,* June 7, 2018. van-us.atavist.com.

Toll, Robert C. *Blacking Up: The Minstrel Show in Nineteenth-Century America.* New York: Oxford University Press, 1974.

Trotter, James M. *Music and Some Highly Musical People.* Boston: Lee and Shepard, 1878.

Tyson, Timothy B. *The Blood of Emmett Till.* New York: Simon & Schuster, 2017.

Underwood, Tom R. "'They're Off' and All Kentucky Roars." *Kentucky Progress Magazine* 7 (Spring 1936): 104.

Upton, George P. "The Romance of Stephen Foster." *Etude* 32 (Nov. 1914): 783–84.

Vered, Karen Orr. "White and Black in Black and White: Management of Race and Sexuality in the Coupling of Child-Star Shirley Temple and Bill Robinson." *Velvet Light Trap: A Critical Journal of Film* 39 (Spring 1997): 52–65.

Wainwright, Nicholas B., ed. "Education of an Artist: The Diary of Joseph Boggs Beale." *Pennsylvania Magazine of History and Biography* 97 (Oct. 1973): 485–510.

Walker, Frank X. "Oh, Weep No More Today." In *Isaac Murphy: I Dedicate This Ride.* Lexington, Ky.: Old Cove Press, 2010.

———. "The Song Doesn't Remain the Same: Reflections on My Old Kentucky Home." *Ace Weekly,* Nov. 21, 2002. www.aceweekly.com.

Wall, Maryjean. *How Kentucky Became Southern: A Tale of Outlaws, Horse Thieves, Gamblers, and Breeders.* Lexington: University Press of Kentucky, 2012.

Watterson, Henry. *Marse Henry: An Autobiography.* New York: George H. Doran, 1919.

Webb, Barbara L. "Authentic Possibilities: Plantation Performance in the 1890s." *Theater Journal* 56 (March 2004): 63–82.

West, Patricia. *Domesticating History: The Political Origins of America's House Museums.* Washington, D.C.: Smithsonian Institution Press, 1999.

"What Every American Traveler Should Know." *New York Times Magazine,* Feb. 2, 1913.

Whitmer, Mariana. "Josiah Kirby Lilly and the Foster Hall Collection." *American Music* 30 (Fall 2012): 326–43.

Williams, David Leander. *Indianapolis Jazz: The Masters, Legends, and Legacy of Indiana Avenue.* Charleston, S.C.: History Press, 2014.

Wilson, Harold S. *Confederate Industry: Manufacturers and Quartermasters in the Civil War.* Oxford: University Press of Mississippi, 2005.

Winn, Matt. *Down the Stretch: The Story of Colonel Matt J. Winn as Told to Frank G. Menke.* New York: Smith and Durrell, 1944.

Woollcott, Alexander. *Long, Long Ago.* New York: World Book, 1943.

Wright, George C. *History of Blacks in Kentucky: In Pursuit of Equality, 1890–1980.* Lexington: University Press of Kentucky, 2008.

———. *Racial Violence in Kentucky, 1865–1940: Lynchings, Mob Rule, and "Legal Lynchings."* Baton Rouge: Louisiana State University Press, 1990.

Wright, Mabel Osgood. *My New York.* New York: Macmillan, 1930.

X, Malcolm. *The Autobiography of Malcolm X.* With Alex Haley. 1965. New York: Ballantine Books, 1992.

Young, Linda. *Historic House Museums in the United States and the United Kingdom: A History.* Lanham, Md.: Rowman & Littlefield, 2016.

INTERVIEWS AND ORAL HISTORIES

Conducted by author unless otherwise noted

Ali, Lonnie. April 28, 2020.

Bailey, Matthew C. Aug. 24, 2016.

Bayé, Betty. March 3, 2020.

Berry, Wendell. April 25, 2017.

Bingham, Barry, Jr. Oral history interview by Emily Bingham and Keith L. Runyan, Feb. 10, 2004.

Bingham, Edith S. May 5, 2020.

Bingham, Mary. Summer 1994.

Brown, David. Sept. 14, 2018.

Brown, John Y., Jr. Dec. 12, 2018.

Brown, John Y., III. March 22, 2018.

Chandler, Ben. June 21, 2017.

Clarke, Harry. Jan. 23, 2020.

Coleman, Bob. Dec. 12, 2019.

Collins, Martha Layne. May 22, 2018.

Davis, Montre. July 7, 2020.

Demaree, Demi. Dec. 16, 2019.

Dornan, Les, and Debbie Dornan. Oct. 17, 2018.

Drane, Kevin. May 8, 2019.

Emerson, Ken. March 11, 2020.

Flanery, Kevin. Jan. 24, 2020.

Floyd, William B. Oral history interview by Estill Curtis Pennington in Lexington, Ky., July 28, 1981. Archives of American Art, Smithsonian Institution. www.aaa.si.edu.

Gray, Jim. July 27, 2021.

Guess, Andre. July 1, 2021.

Hairston, Dorian. Dec. 13, 2018.

Hall, C. Ray. March 2, 2017.

Hartman, Chris. July 27, 2021.

Hines, Carl. Nov. 30, 2010.

Hines, Carl. Oral history conducted by Catherine Herdman in Louisville, Ky., June 28, 2006. Kentucky Legislature Oral History Project, Louie B. Nunn Center for Oral History, University of Kentucky. nunncenter.net.

Hudson, James Blaine. Oral history conducted by Betsy Brinson in Louisville, Ky., Aug. 23, 2000. Kentucky Oral History Commission Collection, Civil Rights Movement in Kentucky Oral History Project. kyoralhistory .com.

Jarrell, Michelle. Oct. 28, 2019.

Johnson, Bob. 2018.

Johnson, Lyman T. Oral history conducted by Dwayne Cox in Louisville, Ky., May 6, 1976. University of Louisville Oral History Center. ohc.library .louisville.edu.

McCorvey, Everett. May 22, 2018.

Porter, Marie. Jan. 8, 2018, and Jan. 30, 2019.

Reed, Billy. March 27, 2018.

Root, Deane. Dec. 19, 2017.

Runyon, Keith L. June 5, 2018.

Schmitt, Karl, Jr. Dec. 4, 2018.

Seamon, Greg. Oct. 12, 2018.

Walker, Frank X. April 26, 2018.

Word, Sophia. Interview by Pearl House. *Kentucky Slave Narratives: A Folk History of Slavery in Kentucky from Interviews with Former Slaves.* Bedford, Mass.: Applewood Press, 2006.

ONLINE RESOURCES

"A. B. 'Happy' Chandler's 'My Old Kentucky Home.'" YouTube. KySports-Video, March 31, 2010. www.youtube.com/watch?v=fsQj46swDvI.

Acevedo, Nicole. "Kentucky Derby Will Play 'My Old Kentucky Home' Despite Criticism." NBC News, Sept. 5, 2020. www.nbcnews.com/news/us-news/kentucky-derby-will-play-my-old-kentucky-home-despite-criticism-n1239415.

American Automobile Association. "History of the AAA Glidden Tour." exchange.aaa.com/wp-content/uploads/2012/10/AAA-Glidden-History.pdf.

"Bourbon Comes from Bardstown." Visit Bardstown. www.visitbardstown.com/bourbon.

"Butterfly McQueen." YouTube. Evemag13, March 4, 2009. www.youtube.com/watch?v=Qy90YiCon3M.

"Churchill Downer: The Forgotten Racial History of Kentucky's State Song." *Morning Edition,* NPR Code Switch, May 6, 2016. www.npr.org/sections/codeswitch/2016/05/06/476890004/churchill-downer-the-forgotten-racial-history-of-kentuckys-state-song.

Churchill Downs Communications. "A Statement to Our Community from Churchill Downs." Kentucky Derby, Sept. 3, 2020. www.kentuckyderby.com/horses/news/a-statement-to-our-community-from-churchill-downs.

"Edward and Theodore Danziger." Chapel Hill–Carrboro Business Hall of Fame. businesshalloffame.weebly.com/edward-and-theodore-danziger.html.

"Foster Chronology from 1800." Center for American Music, University of Pittsburgh. www.pitt.edu/~amerimus/FosterChronology1800.html.

"How KFC Became a Christmas Tradition in Japan—Cheddar Examines." YouTube. Cheddar, Dec. 18, 2018. www.youtube.com/watch?v=46JaN2NZoks.

ケンタッキーフライドチキン CM/Kentucky Fried Chicken "Kentucky Home" Commercial—Japan, 1983. YouTube. Colin Sanders, June 19, 2017. www.youtube.com/watch?v=nnxHzIfkoMM.

King, Eric. "My Old Kentucky Home's Secret Slave History." YouTube. WLKY News, Feb. 24, 2011. www.youtube.com/watch?v=yhMXOty9kko.

Linkin' Bridge. "My Old Kentucky Home." YouTube. Pamela Jankowski, April 30, 2017. www.youtube.com/watch?v=tAk5liX3Nco.

———. "New 'Old Kentucky Home' Video." YouTube. May 3, 2019. www.youtube.com/watch?v=Spx60RD-yE4.

"Matt Winn." National Museum of Racing and Hall of Fame. www.racingmuseum.org/hall-of-fame/matt-winn.

"My Old Kentucky Home Is One of the Most Iconic 19th Century Homes in

America." My Old Kentucky Home State Park. www.visitmyoldkyhome
.com/history-overview.

"My Old Kentucky Home State Park." Kentucky Department of Parks. parks
.ky.gov/parks/recreationparks/old-ky-home/history.aspx.

"Racist Cartoons." Jim Crow Museum of Racist Memorabilia, Ferris State University. www.ferris.edu/jimcrow/cartoons.

Railton, Stephen. "Uncle Tom's Cabin and American Culture." University of
Virginia. utc.iath.virginia.edu/index2f.html.

The Slave Dwelling Project. slavedwellingproject.org.

"Stephen Foster." Songwriters Hall of Fame. www.songhall.org/profile/Stephen
_Foster.

"Villebillies and Nappy Roots—My Old Kentucky Home." YouTube. Faded
Music Feed, April 13, 2016. www.youtube.com/watch?v=1mu1JhE_dOw.

WLKY Digital Team. "Governor Beshear Ends News Conference with Touching Tribute to John Prine." WLKY, April 9, 2020. www.wlky.com/article
/gov-beshear-pays-tribute-to-grammy-award-winner-john-prine-during
-wednesday-press-conference/32087340.

INDEX

Page numbers in italics *refer to illustrations and captions.*

Page

iii   Courtesy of the E. Azalia Hackley Collection of African
        Americans in the Performing Arts, Detroit Public Library

xv   Cobb, Irvin. *Kentucky*. New York: George H. Duncan Co., 1924.

4   Library of Congress

7   Library of Congress

8   Library of Congress

9   Center for American Music, University of Pittsburgh Library
        System

14   Center for American Music, University of Pittsburgh Library
        System

16   Special Collections, Musselman Library, Gettysburg College

21   Collection of the author

27   *Godey's Lady's Book* 66 (January 1863), 108.

31   National Theatre Broadside, June 10, 1855, American Minstrel
        Show Collection, Harvard Theatre Collection, Houghton Library,
        Harvard University.

34   Wikimedia Commons

37   *The Etude* 34 (September 1916), 626.

39   Center for American Music, University of Pittsburgh Library
        System

45   *Hampton Institute: A Pictorial Review of Its First Century, 1868–
        1968*. Hampton: Prestige Press, 1968.

48   Collection of the Boston Athenaeum

50   Kentucky Historical Society

52   *My Old Kentucky Home*. Boston: Ticknor and Fields, 1889.

53   *My Old Kentucky Home*. Boston: Ticknor and Fields, 1889.

54   Center for American Music, University of Pittsburgh Library
        System

57   *The Courier-Journal*, September 6, 1888.

59   Wisconsin Historical Society

167	Waldemar E. Debnam Papers, East Carolina Manuscript Collection, East Carolina University
170	AP Wirephoto
175	Filson Historical Society, Louisville, Kentucky
180	Center for American Music, University of Pittsburgh Library System
186	Photo by Jon Webb, *The Courier-Journal*, May 4, 1969.
188	Photo by Michael Coers, *The Courier-Journal*, May 2, 1969.
196	Ted Wathen / Kentucky Documentary Photographic Project
197	Ted Wathen / Kentucky Documentary Photographic Project
202	Collection of the author
205	Photo by David Perry, *Lexington Herald-Leader*, May 6, 1986. *Lexington Herald-Leader* photographs, University of Kentucky Libraries
213	U.S. Mint
215	Library of Congress
216	Courtesy of Kevin Drane
216	Courtesy of Demi Demaree
221	Center for American Music, University of Pittsburgh Library System

A NOTE ON THE TYPE

This book was set in Adobe Garamond. Designed for the Adobe Corpora-
tion by Robert Slimbach, the fonts are based on types first cut by Claude
Garamond (ca. 1480–1561). Garamond was a pupil of Geoffroy Tory and is
believed to have followed the Venetian models, although he introduced a
number of important differences, and it is to him that we owe the letter we
now know as "old style." He gave to his letters a certain elegance and feeling
of movement that won their creator an immediate reputation and the patron-
age of Francis I of France.

Composed by North Market Street Graphics,
Lancaster, Pennsylvania

Printed and bound by Berryville Graphics,
Berryville, Virginia